ALL THINGS POSSIBLE

ALL THINGS POSSIBLE

Setbacks and Success in Politics and Life

ANDREW M. CUOMO

HARPER

An Imprint of HarperCollins*Publishers*

HarperCollins books may be purchased for educational, business, or sales promotional use. For information, please e-mail the Special Markets Department at SPsales@harpercollins.com.

All illustrations that appear on the chapter-opener pages are courtesy of the author except for those of the following chapters, which are reprinted with permission: Chapter 2: Vic DeLucia/The New York Times/Redux. Chapter 4: AP Photo/Brian K. Diggs. Chapter 5: AP Photo/Beth A. Keiser. Chapter 7: AP Photo/Shiho Fukada. Chapter 11: AP Photo/Mike Groll, File.

FIRST EDITION

Library of Congress Cataloging-in-Publication Data has been applied for.

ISBN: 978-0-06-230008-9

14 15 16 17 18   OV/RRD   10 9 8 7 6 5 4 3 2 1

To my family, whose love saved me.

*To my friends, whose hard work and commitment
rebuilt the state . . . and me too.*

*And to New Yorkers, who are a loving, giving, courageous,
inviting community.*

Contents

Author's Note

This book traces my rapid rise from a political neophyte to a thirty-nine-year-old member of President Clinton's cabinet, my painful fall into political oblivion and personal turmoil, and the rebound that led me to become governor of New York. Rather than a traditional autobiography, this memoir is a series of stories that have defined my public and private lives. It ranges from my teenage years, when I watched my father battle for families in Queens, to the sudden unraveling of my world in my midforties to my memorable achievements as governor of New York, such as the historic passage, against long odds, of marriage equality and gun safety for all New Yorkers.

I have spent many years studying, practicing, failing, and succeeding, with profound highs and humiliating lows, with moments of joy in what I helped to accomplish, and others in which I paid a high price for my hubris. It is my aim that these candidly told stories—some of which were exhilarating to retell, others discomforting—may illuminate the hard-won insights I've accumulated: how failure is inextricably bound up with success, how our strengths can become our weaknesses, the necessity of being both relentless and un-yielding in pursuing our dreams.

Equally, I hope that this book will offer a renewed sense of possibility for our nation's politics, shedding some light on how we can break through the gridlock, dysfunction, and distrust. Americans are tired of good intentions, hardened positions, and lofty rhetoric; they want results. I've tried to pull back the curtain on what I think it takes to wage and win the good fight, to be both bold and pragmatic, using the most effective strategies I've relied on to turn paralysis into progress and to forge a politics of common purpose.

Finally, as you will discover in these pages, it is from these sometimes stirring successes and always searing setbacks that I have come to believe that all things are possible if we, each of us and together as a country, are willing to challenge and change the status quo, in our own lives, in our busi-nesses, and in our politics.

Prologue

September 3, 2002

During the nineteen months I'd been running for governor, I made hundreds of speeches at hundreds of venues. From Albany to Tonawanda, Alexandria Bay to Yonkers, every event began the same way. I walked in. Cameras flashed. I greeted the cheering crowd as I crossed the stage to a red-white-and-blue-draped rostrum with an ANDREW CUOMO FOR GOVERNOR poster covering the front. Supporters chanted, "Andrew! Andrew! Andrew! Andrew!" Someone—usually my running mate, Charlie King—introduced me. "Thank you," I said, smiling broadly. "Thank you, thank you."

Today, I walked across the stage in the New York Hilton Midtown ballroom. Bill Clinton and New York congressman Charles Rangel stood beside me. Greeting the audience felt as familiar as being home. But what comes now, I thought, is the literal beginning of the end. My family and friends were there, but not to celebrate with me. They were there to comfort me. It was a political wake. The media had come to record my public demise. The applause for a job half-completed sounded like the ersatz enthusiasm parents gin up for their child's last-ranked team as its players are awarded medals for participation. I was dropping out of the primary race a week before the votes would be cast. I had failed.

Until now, I'd been on the upswing. I ran my first political campaign at age twenty-four and founded the nation's largest nonprofit organization to help the homeless before I turned thirty. Then I became assistant secretary of the Department of Housing and Urban Development—an appointment that scaled up my model for addressing homelessness to the national level. At age thirty-nine, I was one of the youngest cabinet members in U.S. history, appointed by Bill Clinton.

Being secretary of the Department of Housing and Urban Development was a hands-on job—and highly visible. I traveled with the president on Air Force One as he led an effort, during a time of prosperity, to put poverty back on the front burner—to shine a light on "places left behind" in the new economy. I also set out to help save an agency Republicans had written off, and, at times, had tried to abolish. As a cabinet secretary, I represented the United States on trips to South Africa, China, and Mexico. I met with Israeli prime minister Ehud Barak and Palestinian leader Yasser Arafat to talk about creating economic and community development programs to advance the peace process.

My wife, Kerry, and I joined the first family for movie nights in the White House theater and occasionally spent a weekend with the president and first lady at Camp David. On the much more formal side of life in Washington, D.C., we were the Clintons' invited guests at a number of private and state dinners.

I was also close to Vice President Al Gore. I shared his vision of making government leaner and more efficient. I was mentioned as one of the possible running mates for the 2000 presidential election.

My career ascended like a dot-com stock in the early years of the Internet bubble.

It crashed just as hard. Now, at forty-four, I was standing before fifty friends, family members, and supporters—and the media—defeated and exhausted.

I knew going into the gubernatorial race that politics was a tough game. I'd learned that basic truth not during bad times but during one of the best—in 1982 when my father was sworn in as the fifty-second governor of the State of New York.

We arrived at the Executive Mansion in Albany, thrilled and a little overwhelmed. The four-story mansion, then 125 years old, whose architectural style *The New Yorker* once described as "Hudson River Helter-Skelter," was considerably grander than our family home in Queens. The staff lined up to welcome us. I stood in the wide front hall. Looking up, I saw the outgoing governor, Hugh Carey, coming down the stairs. He was carrying two awkwardly large cardboard boxes. His steps were uncertain. He was leaning to the side, trying to see around the boxes so he wouldn't trip. I didn't know what to do. Two state workers were walking up the staircase. Oh, good, I thought. They're going to help him.

They walked right past him.

I thought to myself, *Boy, when it's over, it's over*, and never allowed myself to forget that lesson.

That's how I felt now, standing behind the poster from my now defunct campaign, in front of people who had put their faith—and often their money—into my race. I was achingly aware of the similarities between my father's first campaign, in 1982, and this one of mine, twenty years later. We both fought the Democratic Party machine. We both ran against the political bosses' favored candidate. We both believed that we were the best person to lead the State of New York.

But the differences were painful. My father had won his Democratic primary and bested his Republican opponent in the general election.

I, on the other hand, had failed in trying to persuade New Yorkers that I, and not my opponent, Carl McCall, should carry the Democratic banner in the November 2002 election. Instead, I'd come to be viewed as an arrogant upstart whose campaign lurched from week to week with no clear purpose.

McCall had won. The state's longtime comptroller, he was New York's senior Democrat, the first African American candidate for governor, a beloved statesman. As the Democratic Party's designee, he would now face New York's sitting governor, a Republican, George Pataki, the same man who, in 1994, had beaten my father out of a fourth term.

I'd had days to absorb the descent of my dreams and to accept that the work of the past year and a half was futile.

I scanned the faces in the Hilton ballroom and began reading the words I had carefully written. "I can't tell you how much fun this campaign has been," I said with false cheer. "It's been over eighteen months, and I enjoyed every day on the trail. And we did good work, we accomplished great things. . . ."

That had been true in real time, but today, at the end of my campaign, I couldn't recapture it. Inside, I was in agony, felled by the profound public humiliation. Politics was all encompassing for me. For two decades it had defined me, my self-worth, my connection to my father, my place in my family, my marriage, my friendships, my career—my entire life.

Now I needed Bill Clinton and Charlie Rangel to help clean up my mistakes in the arena where I had always excelled.

I'd started the campaign with plans to bring renewed vitality to New York, the state where I was born and had lived most of my life. The campaign had burst out of the gate with a generous head start. In February 2001, I led McCall in the polls, 45 percent to 25 percent. In July 2002, I was still up by 15 percentage points. But by mid-August, with the September 10 primary less than a month away, my popularity had dropped. My advisers said that to close the gap, we would have to run negative TV ads. "That is something I don't want to do, and I will not do," I told the crowd gathered before me. "If we were to now spend $2 million this week on an acrimonious campaign, we would only guarantee a bloody and broke Democratic nominee, whoever won. And the ultimate success for Governor Pataki in November would be assured. Maybe we could win the battle, but we would lose the war, my friends. And that's not what this is about."

I was eager to be innovative. While traveling around the country for HUD, I'd seen effective programs and examples of creative government that I wanted to bring back to New York. And after eight years of gridlocked, moribund state government, I wanted to push a progressive agenda forward, to restore the state's legacy of bold leadership under past governors like Theodore Roosevelt, Al Smith, Franklin Roosevelt, and Mario Cuomo.

But I'd squandered these opportunities in a poorly executed campaign.

The press had portrayed the race as a classic Shakespearean drama: I ran for election to avenge my father's defeat at the hands of George Pataki.

At the end of the play, not only is the father dead: the son is also dead.

The press narrative was clear: young son of a governor, married to a Kennedy, entitled, assuming, overly ambitious, gets his comeuppance.

"I believe in President Clinton's One America," I told the crowd. "I believe in Mario Cuomo's legacy of the family of New York"—the idea he invoked as governor that we take care of society's most vulnerable members; that we share in one another's good fortune and pain, regardless of differences in color or creed.

"I believe in Robert Kennedy's spirit of brotherhood," I continued. "That is my political philosophy. That is what this campaign has been about—bringing people together in community and sharing and helping. And I'm not going to start dividing now. I will not close a gap in an election by opening one in the body politic.

"That's why, while it is harder for me to step back than to fight forward, today I step back and withdraw from the race. I believe the banner we carry is more important than the person who carries the banner.

"Today is a special day for me," I said. "Kerry and I brought our children to the first day of school. . . . They were born when I was working in the Clinton administration, you see. And when you worked in the Clinton administration, you worked. The taxpayers got their money's worth. . . . So I'll have a little more time to spend with them and that's a good thing. And tonight their daddy will be home with them to do their first day of homework. And that to me is still the most important job in the State of New York."

I glanced at my compact block-lettered handwriting and raced for the finish.

"Tomorrow I will set out to work with Carl McCall and Democrats all across this state," I said. "To do what this Democratic Party is all about and make this State of New York a stronger, a sweeter, a better State of New York. We're going to do it together! Thank you, and God bless."

It had been one of the most torturous ten minutes, twenty seconds of my life.

I remained on the stage while Charlie Rangel and Bill Clinton spoke, but I was hardly listening. I felt I was standing outside myself watching the proceedings, almost as if this were a bad film about someone else's life. Rangel, who had wanted me out of the race, because he had backed his friend Carl McCall, was generous. "I am a Korean combat veteran," he said, "and I know courage when I see it, and Andrew, you exhibited that kind of courage. It's very difficult for people who are not actively involved in politics to understand how difficult it is for a candidate to do what Andrew Cuomo has done today. It is very difficult for people to understand what goes into a campaign. It's not just the money, it's not just the hours, but it is the sincere belief that you can make a difference. . . . The good thing that comes out of this is that we can still make the difference."

I wanted to get back into my car, go home, and be alone. I'd disappointed my wife, my parents, my supporters, myself. I hated feeling like a public spectacle. As I stood onstage, I felt my last bit of dignity drain out.

President Clinton told the audience, "I know that in many ways this is a sad day. I have probably run for office more times than anybody in this room. . . . I suffered two searing defeats in my life. But I can tell you that today is the day you should be very, very proud of Andrew, your husband, son, and brother. He has been great today. You know, there are some great virtues in being term-limited out, one of which is that you can commit candor. So I will make you a prediction. I am the only person standing on this stage whose political career is over."

Drawing on all his years of success and setbacks, Clinton was saying that all things for me were still possible.

Generous and touching as his words were, I felt they were not true. My political epitaph had just been written.

I had composed it myself.

Part I

RISE

CHAPTER 1

The Fighting 69

The Cuomo family in Holliswood, November 1978.

I heard the yelling before I looked outside.

"Out of the living room!" I shouted to my three sisters, Margaret, Maria, and Madeline. "Get Mom! Go to the basement! Take Christopher!"

"I want to watch," said Maria.

"Go," I said. "Now!"

It was hard not to look. Outside the huge bay window, three dozen protesters, men and women, were marching in front of our house in Queens, holding up signs demanding, DON'T RUIN OUR NEIGHBORHOOD! and NO PROJECT—NO WAY! This was the first time I had experienced "protesters," an almost bizarre occurrence in the middle of this residential community.

The protesters were from Forest Hills, a white, mostly Jewish neighborhood in Queens with a low crime rate and top-ranked public schools, where New York City mayor John Lindsay had recently broken ground for a vast low-income housing project, the Forest Hills Cooperative. Their urgent effort to stop construction had driven them to our quiet little block in Holliswood, a solidly middle-class pocket of Queens that looked and felt more like the suburbs, with well-tended garden apartments and 1950s redbrick houses. With five children, my house-proud mother, Matilda, kept our home pristine, inside and out. She put plastic slipcovers over the living room couch and chairs to make certain they stayed clean.

Queens today is celebrated for its incredible diversity, but in 1972, when this fight was unfolding, there weren't nearly as many people crossing the Fifty-Ninth Street Bridge from Manhattan to eat authentic Indian or Greek or Peruvian food. The country was churning with black power and white flight, and despite its liberal veneer, New York was a city full of ethnic tensions. It's telling that *All in the Family*, set in Queens, was the country's number one television show for five years in a row. Archie Bunker got away with calling people "dagos" and "wops"—ugly labels that were unheard of on network TV at that time. But in real life, people stereotyped one another and voiced their prejudices routinely.

I'd absorbed my immigrant grandmother Immaculata's story about moving to Holliswood from Jamaica, Queens, in 1949. It was just three miles—a short drive by car—but a map couldn't account for the social and economic distance she and my grandfather Andrea had traveled with my father, then seventeen, and his older brother and sister. Instead of Italians, their new neighbors were white Anglo-Saxon Protestants. My grandmother cried each time she recalled how a well-dressed woman had stopped her on the sidewalk as the family was settling in. "Don't bring your garbage cans to the curb until trash day," she said. "And make sure you put the lids on tightly."

What my grandmother believed the woman was really saying was, You Italians are dirty and ignorant. And my grandmother was so intent on proving her new neighbor wrong that she kept her house and yard spotless. Twenty-five years later, long after the neighbor had died, my grandmother was still trying to show her. As I cut her grass, she followed behind me with scissors in hand to make sure her front walk was neatly trimmed.

Queens had Italian neighborhoods, Jewish neighborhoods, Puerto Rican neighborhoods, and there was tension. Two blocks from one neighborhood could suddenly seem like the other side of the world. There were kids who were attacked because they rode their bikes into the wrong area or dated someone from an unapproved background. Different neighborhoods had different ethnicities, and young toughs who wanted to protect their "turf."

But it was the protesters from Forest Hills who brought the city's roiling unrest to our doorstep.

Looking back forty years later I realize that in addition to feeling physically threatened, what I found so frightening about the protesters was how irrational they seemed. They didn't come to our block to have a civil conversation or to compromise. They didn't come to discuss. They were angry and they wanted to vent. They came to scream.

I now know too well the state of irrationality that can develop on both sides of the political spectrum.

But at fourteen, I didn't yet understand the bitterness and fear that brought people to these extremes. I was only seeing for the first time the real effect that government, however well-intentioned, can have on people's lives.

By that time my role in our family was set. I am an acute example of the theory that birth order shapes your personality. As the older boy in my family, I had an instinct to protect and defend my sisters and two-year-old brother, Christopher. Just as I helped my mother with chores around the house, it was my responsibility to help the two younger girls—Madeline, eight, and Maria, ten. Margaret was seventeen, three years older than I was, but I was the man of the house when my father was out.

Facing down an eager date or a school bully was different from confronting dozens of adults. I had no idea what the demonstrators might do, and I hated that my mother and sisters were being exposed to their rage.

As I watched the protesters through the window, I was debating what to do when a couple of NYPD squad cars, sirens wailing, blue lights flashing, pulled up and idled at the top of the street.

The irony of the situation was that my father, Mario, the man the protesters had come to confront, wasn't home. An appellate lawyer and community activist whom Mayor Lindsay had appointed to help mediate the housing dispute, my father was also a man of his hardworking postwar generation. He often left before my sisters and I got up and came back after we were asleep. To make their point, the demonstrators would have had to march at 7 P.M. on a Sunday, the one time of the week that my mother insisted he be home for dinner. And when he was home, he was usually working.

I learned early that if I wanted to spend time with my father I had to tag along. Sometimes I'd sit in the library at his law firm in Brooklyn, doing my homework or trying to decode one of the books that lined the walls, unable to resist rubbing my fingers along the embossed leather bindings. And on weekends, we'd drive to Corona, a 1.25-square-mile section of northern Queens that F. Scott Fitzgerald described in *The Great Gatsby* as "the valley of ashes." The members of the Corona community were mostly Italian American like my family but less assimilated or less financially comfortable. They lived in small single-family or semidetached houses that were often hand-built and passed down through three generations. The men played boccie in their spare time, and it was hard to find a front yard without a grape arbor or Madonna statue. It was almost as if they were living in Italy instead of New York. The residents reminded me of my grandparents—hardworking immigrants steeped in traditional values, with a fierce pride. My grandfather Andrea, after whom I'm named, used to say, "When you're gone, your legacy is your kids and what you built."

My father and I traveled to Corona because the city government under John Lindsay, New York's liberal, Republican mayor, was shaking Corona's foundations, literally. And the battle that unfolded there goes a long way toward explaining why the angry mob eventually traveled from Forest Hills to our block in Holliswood.

In 1966, Mayor Lindsay's administration approved a vacant lot in Corona for a new subsidized housing project to move poor African Americans into stable neighborhoods. The effort was part of Lyndon Johnson's sweeping Great Society agenda to reshape the country into one that would fulfill its promises to all Americans, advancing civil rights and eradicating poverty. National grief over John Kennedy's death, a strong desire to finish what Kennedy had started, a flush postwar economy, and LBJ's legendary powers of persuasion made for a potent mix that left no social engineering stone unturned. It took the White House and Congress just a few months to establish monumental programs like Head Start, Model Cities, Medicare and Medicaid, and the Job Corps, and to pass the Elementary and Secondary Education Act that gave federal money to public schools for the first time. Democrats and liberals had a bedrock belief in the idea that the government could correct even the most otherwise intractable problems. They passed laws and established initiatives to ban literacy tests at the polls, wipe out rural poverty, stop the perpetuation of inner-city ghettos, and force integration. The gospel was that government could solve all.

But while congressional Republicans in the 1960s shared many of the Great Society's goals, they opposed the creation of new government programs. In many ways the classic Democrat-versus-Republican argument hasn't changed much. The gist of their argument was—and still is—"These are nice ideas you talk about, Democrats, but government is not the answer; a robust private economy is the answer, and each time government tries to help, it only makes the situation worse. Your intentions may be good, but your government is overreaching and incompetent. I'm telling you, you can't do it. It's impossible."

The residents of Corona didn't want the low-income housing project. They argued that the fourteen-story, five-hundred-unit apartment complex would destroy the village-like character of their neighborhood and overload public facilities. Mayor Lindsay's new, untested administration acted quickly to quiet their loud and public objections.

The City Planning Board cobbled together a swap: it would build North Queens High School, originally slated for nearby Forest Hills, on a vacant lot at Lewis Avenue and 100th Street in Corona, and it would move the low-income housing project to Forest Hills, where a square-block parcel in a densely populated section near the Long Island Expressway sat empty. Though the lot was once used as a driving range, its high water table made it unattractive to private real estate developers.

Ignoring the poor condition of the land, the planners reasoned that since Forest Hills was already a neighborhood of high-rises, the housing project would blend into the local skyline. (In its move from Corona, the project grew in size from one building to seven, ranging in height from ten to twenty-two stories.) They believed that the predominantly middle-class, Democratic Jewish neighbors would embrace a project designed to lift up the poor. They assumed that since most of the residents were renters, they wouldn't complain that public housing would lower property values.

They assumed wrong.

The people of Forest Hills didn't want a housing project any more than those of Corona. Six years later, my father would be the mediator called on to help mitigate the city's obvious mistake in Forest Hills.

But what happened in Corona came first. In October 1966, the residents cheered their future high school. Four Corona houses would have to be demolished to make way for the new construction, but that didn't stop residents from crowding into St. Leo's Roman Catholic Church on Forty-Ninth Street to thank God for their good fortune. Queens borough president Mario Cariello told reporters, "It's a victory for everything that is good and visionary."

The community's euphoria was short-lived.

Five months later, in March 1967, the city altered its plans a second time. Instead of putting the high school on four and a half acres and tearing down four houses, the commissioners of the Site Selection Board dreamed big, demanding eight more acres—twelve and a half total—to add an adjacent athletic field. The cost to Corona was now very steep: a bulldozer would take down sixty-nine one- and two-family houses. The 100-plus families who'd be displaced had no idea where they would move. That's how eminent domain works. The government can seize private property for public use in return for just compensation. How "just" it was for the government to pay $10,000 for houses worth $60,000 on the open market is debatable. But the sufficiency of the payment wasn't the issue. These were their homes, often the only ones they ever knew.

This news would be disastrous for any community. Relatives, neighbors, and lifelong friends would soon be homeless—for the sake of a ball field that could be built any-where. So while the community was gaining a high school, it was losing families to help fill the school.

Banding together as a group nicknamed the "Fighting 69"—for the sixty-nine houses—Corona's residents begged my father to save their neighborhood. It was big government with its high ideals trampling the little people. This was his first high-profile foray into politics, and he sided with the homeowners, against the government in its theoretical pur-suit of progress.

My father and I spent many weekend afternoons in the basement of Corona's Veterans of Foreign Wars Hall or in other, similar hot, crowded meeting places. I'd never seen such a show of emotion from adults as I did at those meet-ings. The women sobbed, "We have no place to go!" and the men shouted the same questions over and over: "What are we going to do? How are we going to survive?" "Why are they doing this to us?" "Don't they have any respect for taxpay-ers?" I remember one wrinkled man saying, "Do you mean to tell me that I fought in World War II so they can take my house away?"

"The Lindsay administration must not have thought the situation through," my father told my mother, my sisters, and me between bites of baked chicken a few Sunday nights later. "But we've found a new site for the ball field less than a block from the school. I'm sure when we meet with the New York City Site Selection Board and explain the mistake, they'll redraw their plans and the controversy will be over."

The meeting didn't go as expected. And neither did the one after that. Over time, the city rejected eleven alternative sites. "The educational values involved in an athletic field adjoining the building far exceed the disadvantages and discomfort to the families involved," a school board official explained to a newspaper reporter. One word from Lindsay could have put an end to Corona's misery, but he said nothing. "Charismatic bastard!" the Corona women called him, spitting out the words as though trying to get rid of a bad taste in their mouths.

New York's young, Hollywood-handsome mayor wasn't deaf to all New Yorkers. In 1968, after the Reverend Dr. Martin Luther King Jr. was shot, Lindsay walked through Harlem in his shirtsleeves to shake hands and offer condolences to the emotionally devastated community. And in doing so, he helped forestall the kind of violence that would engulf Washington, D.C., Baltimore, and Chicago.

But Lindsay had begun to gain a reputation for favoring the city's richest and its poorest voters while disregarding the white ethnic middle class in between. After a blizzard paralyzed the city in February 1969, he quickly cleared the streets of Manhattan but left Queens under fifteen inches of snow for days. His attitude seemed to be: It's Queens. They have shovels. They're strong. They'll figure it out.

But as kids we were mostly sheltered from the political storms around us. During Lindsay's first term, taxes, crime, and the welfare rolls shot up, while city services stalled and jobs evaporated. On his first day in office the mayor faced a transit strike that made getting to work inconvenient for residents of Park Avenue but impossible for workers who had to commute from northern Manhattan, Brooklyn, Queens, the Bronx, and Staten Island. His first initiative—a civilian complaint review board to investigate police brutality charges—allayed tension in African American communities but stirred resentment among the civil servants who were our neighbors.

As time went on, members of Corona's Fighting 69 grew more frantic. They showed up at our house at night, on weekends, and once on Christmas Eve, while my sisters and I waited to open our presents, to plot the next legal maneuver with my father. He went to court more than two dozen times to try to block the city's actions. The Corona residents had been double-crossed by the one entity they'd believed was on their side. Not only were they victims of an abusive government but they had an immigrant's faith in the United States as the land of opportunity. The painful lesson they were being forced to come to terms with was how hard it was to fight City Hall.

Because my father gave away so much time and legal advice to the Fighting 69, he didn't make nearly as much money in his law practice as he could have. It didn't occur to me until later that this was why we lived where we did. He was the only professional among the stonemasons, contractors, firefighters, and cops in Holliswood. Money was never his goal. The dominant ethos in our house, which he took from the Catholic Church and emphasized at Sunday dinner, was, What have you done to help others?

The Fighting 69 did what they could to repay him: the men painted our house and the women babysat. On Sundays, the baker dropped off Italian pastries. These people exalted my father like a savior, and their stories about his good deeds expanded my view of him, making him seem bigger than life. I saw him as a warrior for justice, a great fighter. I was impressed by his occasional mention in the *New York Times*, which, for people in Queens, was usually a onetime event: their paid obituary.

And I realized that he was Corona's only hope.

After the court of appeals ruled against Corona in 1969, the homeowners seemed to have exhausted every option. The city had condemned their houses. As they waited for the eviction notices to be processed, they had to pay rent to the city to live in their own homes. I couldn't believe how unfair it was. Even if my father had been able to persuade Lindsay to change his mind, it would take a special vote by the New York State Legislature and the signature of Governor Nelson Rockefeller to undo the condemnation. But my father didn't give up. He held brainstorming meetings at the VFW and rallied city and state legislators to bring pressure against Lindsay.

Then the impossible happened. One Sunday night in the fall of 1970, the sharp-tongued, celebrated New York columnist Jimmy Breslin, who was a Queens resident, dropped in for a meeting at Corona's volunteer ambulance headquarters.

Breslin was best known for columns evoking the details of everyday people at the heart of major events, and for his investigations of mobsters and corrupt New York City cops. Iconic and powerful, he used his political connections to champion pet causes. In 1969 he ran for president of the City Council on a ticket with the author Norman Mailer, who ran for mayor. The main plank of their platform was the secession of New York City from New York State.

Breslin immediately became a defender of Corona. "The athletic field could house the Green Bay Packers," he told a *New York Times* reporter.

Within days of hearing about Corona's plight, Breslin arranged for my father to meet with the deputy mayor, Richard Aurelio. After a four-year struggle, it took Aurelio only a couple of weeks to persuade his boss to shrink the size of the field. In December 1970, Mayor Lindsay announced the "Corona Compromise," a deal that would save thirty-one houses in their original locations. The owners of the remaining twenty-eight could choose to have their houses moved to a new foundation or torn down. All that was left to do was to win legislative approval for the compromise in Albany. Soon my father's work in Corona would be finished.

Breslin and my father became instant friends. Breslin and Jack Newfield, a reporter for the *Village Voice*, often sat around our blue Formica kitchen table drinking coffee and talking for hours. Newfield, like Breslin, fought for the underdog. A liberal activist who had been a close friend and biographer of Robert F. Kennedy (and who had been with

Kennedy when he died), Newfield was a vocal critic of the Vietnam War and a leader in the movement to persuade LBJ not to run for reelection.

These men had made careers of fanning public outrage against injustice, and their articles often forced the government to remedy whatever problem they focused on—a far cry from some of today's "news outlets," which are just proxies for knee-jerk ideological perspectives. They were a strong influence on me, and it's no surprise that my brother, Chris, grew up to become a journalist.

Sitting in our cramped kitchen, Breslin and Newfield had epic conversations with my father about abuses of power, mainly by Lindsay; about the Muhammad Ali–Joe Frazier rivalry; and about why the Dodgers had left Brooklyn. I loved to pull up a chair and listen.

When anyone called the house, my father would answer the phone saying, "Yep. Yep." So when I picked up, I'd do the same. Breslin would be off and running: "You know what that fuckin' Lindsay did?"

I'd let him go on with a string of curses for a while before saying, "Oh, Mr. Breslin, I guess you want my father."

He'd say, "You little shit!" and hang up.

Today my father talks about how much he regrets the time work took him away from our family. If he could redo those years, he says, he'd strike a better balance. At the time the absence was hard. Much responsibility fell to me as the "man" of the house, and his absence when other fathers were present at Boy Scouts and Little League was palpable. But I saw his hard work as a function of his passionate belief in what he was doing, and I was proud of the personal skill and courage he showed. There were so many times that he could have given up on Corona. Instead, he scouted alternative sites, negotiated new hearings with the city, and, in repeatedly taking the case to court, delayed condemnation for more than two years. Watching him persevere long after most other people would have quit taught me that the good fight is still a fight—the fact that the battle you're waging is noble doesn't mean success will come easily, or at all.

Adding to my father's frustration, in 1970, after he and Lindsay worked out the Corona Compromise, a renegade faction of neighborhood homeowners rejected the deal, trying to force the city to abandon the entire plan—not just the field but also the school. They wanted the neighborhood left alone, not tampered with by Great Society apologists.

"This phase of the Corona struggle was to prove even more excruciating than the first," my father wrote in his book *Forest Hills Diary*. The rebel group, led by Vito Battista, a Republican assemblyman who represented Brooklyn, not Queens, persuaded the New York Assembly to defeat the compromise bill, despite a personal plea by Governor Rockefeller to pass it.

Breslin weighed in, telling the *Long Island Press* that there must be "an evaluation of the spiritual condition of everyone in Albany who's involved in this issue."

He added, "Apparently, the last thought on anybody's mind is those people living in Corona who now face again the torture of having their lives picked apart in public."

Because the splinter group hadn't accepted the compromise, Corona residents were back where they had started. Once again, all sixty-nine houses were to be bulldozed. Still fighting, my father went to court one more time to delay condemnation while he tried to broker a new resolution.

During the delay my father and the Corona homeowners negotiated a better deal with the city. Finally, in June 1972, on the day a second compromise bill was set to expire, Rockefeller signed it, moving the ball field to a less destructive place and returning the houses to their owners. In the end thirteen houses were demolished.

Summarizing the struggle in a letter to the homeowners, my father wrote:

> *A mistake was made. Everyone knew it. The question was: Would the System be big enough to confess and correct its own blunder? And the System did . . . not because it was forced to by vast political strength—we had none of that . . . not because of the financial power of our group—because we were all practically beggars. In the end all we had on our side was the rightness of what we were saying. And in the end it was rightness that prevailed.*

My father took me to the party at Jeantet's Restaurant on Roosevelt Avenue in Corona to celebrate the unbelievable journey the little community had taken over the past six years. I ate veal parmigiana and toasted the triumph with 7-Up. Lindsay thanked everyone who'd worked on the settlement, including my father. The restaurant was as packed and overheated as the VFW Hall had been, but relief had replaced desperation, and you could hear laughter above the din.

My father and Lindsay stood talking in front of the buffet table. Corona had just reached a happy conclusion after years of hundred-hour workweeks. It was a moment when my father and the rest of my family might have relaxed. But by that time, he had turned his attention to the housing controversy in Forest Hills.

Just as the city planners tried to steamroller the Corona homeowners—and essentially steal their houses—they were far too nonchalant about the impact of a large low-income project in the Forest Hills community.

However liberal-leaning the residents were, their penchant for reform was more easily applied to other communities, not to what happened on their own front stoops. They complained that the influx would overwhelm their already crowded schools and subways. They said the swampy subsoil couldn't bear the weight of the federally funded buildings without sending construction costs soaring. This was true, but it was an absurd excuse, given that the money was coming out of the government till, not their pockets.

A Rutgers economist and housing expert named George Sternlieb called such pretexts "the dance of the seven veils." "Remove the tax veil and the school veil and the sewer veil," the *New York Times* wrote, summarizing Sternlieb's view, "and the true reason for the opposition is revealed: People do not want blacks in their neighborhoods."

For four years, while the Corona saga unfolded, both the

Housing and Urban Development (HUD)–funded public-housing project and neighborhood resistance to it in Forest Hills lay dormant. Lack of visible activity combined with wishful thinking had lulled its residents into believing that the plans had been shelved. In fact, architects were redrawing the design to lower the cost and accommodate the spongy soil. What they came up with was three 24-story buildings with 840 apartments.

Just before Thanksgiving 1971, construction trailers arrived on the vacant lot, and the opposition sprang into action. Members of the Forest Hills Residents Association staged a revolt, led by a local realtor named Jerry Birbach. About five hundred people marched in a torchlight procession, hurled rocks through the windows of the trailers, threatened to burn them down, and blocked traffic for hours on the nearby Long Island Expressway. *Time* magazine reported, "The anger, the curses, the denunciation of public officials, the rock throwing—all evoked memories of Little Rock and Selma. But this was not the South revisiting racial integration. This was New York, that reputed citadel of liberalism."

The comparison was more apt than perhaps the *Time* writers realized. In the late 1960s and early 1970s, racial equality issues were pushing southern voters into the Republican Party. At the same time, Lindsay's "limousine liberalism"—a term coined by one of his opponents in the 1969 New York City mayoral race to describe his championing of the poor—cost him white, ethnic working-class support. He left the Republican Party in 1971 in hopes of winning the Democratic nomination in the upcoming presidential election. But his political career was sinking fast. The Forest Hills Residents Association petitioned Governor Rockefeller to impeach the mayor for bringing the city to its "lowest ebb." Hecklers dogged Lindsay everywhere he went, from his official residence at Gracie Mansion on Manhattan's Upper East Side to his presidential swings through Florida and Wisconsin, dooming his campaign.

Lindsay didn't budge on Forest Hills. There seemed no reason to. The plans had survived the scrutiny of New York State judges, an investigation by the federal General Accounting Office, and a review by Housing and Urban Development secretary George Romney, the father of 2012 Republican presidential nominee Mitt Romney. The state legislature voted to kill the project, but Rockefeller vetoed the bill. The Residents Association's efforts to lobby President Nixon brought no reprieve. Construction crews were driving in massive support pilings at the site.

And then, in May 1972, Lindsay called my father to ask if he would consider mediating the dispute as an "independent agent." It took my father just an hour to call the mayor back and say yes. "It was now an undeniably dangerous situation," he wrote in *Forest Hills Diary*. "The dispute was being interpreted as a battle between the Jews and the blacks. . . . The protests from Forest Hills became louder and more anguished. The dangers could not be ignored."

My father's role in Forest Hills was different from what it had been in Corona. There, he'd been a crusader trying to save a close-knit community whose residents were being evicted from their homes and had everything to lose. In Forest Hills, he was a mediator between warring factions.

The goal was to avert a full-scale conflagration at a time when American cities were racial tinderboxes and anything could be the match. The poor for whom the Forest Hills Cooperative was being built were not in such a different spot from the residents of Corona. They needed a place to live. The waiting list for public housing in New York City was 100,000 people deep. But what was at stake for the Forest Hills apartment dwellers was psychological, not tangible, and therefore more difficult to pinpoint. Their sense of security was being challenged, and it amplified their fear of change. Working to strike a balance, my father conceded that the odds against coming up with a compromise that satisfied both sides were "very long." But, he told my family, "It's worth a try."

He'd already been trying to mediate Forest Hills for several weeks when we went to the Corona victory party at Jeantet's. As we left the restaurant, we saw a hundred pickets standing in front, shouting angrily, and waving placards: NO WELFARE TOWERS IN FOREST HILLS! Fifty police officers rushed to surround Lindsay and escort him to his waiting car. As soon as the car door shut behind him, the protesters closed in, booing the mayor and yelling. "Lindsay, you bastard!"

The protesters' other target that night was my father. "You're a fraud!" Birbach, the leader of the Forest Hills Residents Association, screamed as we hurried past. "Your appointment is nothing but a political ploy."

Forest Hills had passionate absolutists on both sides. Outspoken members of the Forest Hills Residents Association said, "No how, no way, are you bringing in all those poor people." On the other side, pressing for the project, some African American groups said, "All white people are racists. Jewish people are racists. You're all racists." Instead of having a civil conversation, people from opposite poles were screaming at one another. Neither side was right, but their voices drowned out any other opinions.

I had walked around Forest Hills with my father a couple of times and listened to him talk with enough residents to know that most people weren't on the extremes. They told him, "It's not up to me to tell people where they can and can't live." They understood that the city had to try to accommodate everyone. But they were afraid to vocalize their assent to the apartments publicly for fear of being denounced. As the *New York Times* wrote, they were, "if not a silent majority, at least a thoroughly outshouted minority."

If you stripped away the noise and accusations, there was a real debate to be had. Most people in Forest Hills were racially tolerant but afraid of the projects. It would have sounded something like this: I know we need to take care of our poor, but the projects are an example of good government gone bad. The government is trying to help by getting people out of the slums.

Its intentions are good, but it's going to wind up building *another* ghetto. It'll just be warehousing the poor. The people the government is trying to help are actually going to be hurt, the project will be expensive, and when it fails it will destroy the surrounding neighborhood.

I know, but we should help.

I'm telling you that you can't. It's impossible.

A description by the writer and urban activist Jane Jacobs summed up the problem: "Low-income projects . . . become worse centers of delinquency, vandalism, and general social hopelessness than the slums they were supposed to replace." Living in New York City, people had seen the projects built and saw neighborhoods suffer. Much of the "white flight" to the suburbs was based on fear of the projects.

But as Lindsay's independent agent, my father wasn't there to hold a debate on the project's merits. He was there to mediate. After two months of discussions with city, state, and federal officials; community, civic, and religious groups; and neighborhood residents, he submitted his recommendation to Mayor Lindsay. Instead of three 24-story buildings with 840 apartments, he proposed three 12-story buildings containing 432 units. He also suggested setting aside more units for senior citizens, since they, too, were lacking proper housing and would be a stabilizing force for the community.

With its height halved, the project would fit the architectural scale of Forest Hills, whose buildings ranged from seven to fifteen stories. And while decreasing the overall size would lighten the load on a community worried about overcrowding, the complex would still be large enough to "obviate the charge of tokenism," as my father wrote in his report to the mayor.

Among the downsides was that lower buildings involved a higher cost per unit; the apartment cost would increase from $35,000—barely within federal funding guidelines—to $50,000. That's "the cost of new luxury apartments in New York City," one reporter wrote. The city would have to make up the multimillion-dollar shortfall.

No one was entirely happy with the recommendation— "the mark of a good compromise," my father said. Counterproposals, speeches, and protests followed. In the end, Mayor

Lindsay accepted my father's plan. To quell neighborhood anxiety, 40 percent of the complex was designated for elderly residents, and, at the suggestion of Queens borough president Donald Manes, city leaders voted to make the project a co-op—residents were given ownership shares—making it the first such public housing facility in the country. A few months later, in the face of suburban hostility toward housing desegregation, a fivefold increase in subsidies, and a scandal involving HUD employees, Richard Nixon declared a freeze on new public housing, although it didn't affect Forest Hills. The shutdown wasn't lifted until Jimmy Carter became president.

The Forest Hills Cooperative opened its doors in 1975, two years after Lindsay left political office for good. In 1981, the federal government stopped building new public housing projects. In a twist of fate, I would visit the complex in 1999 as HUD secretary to give it a management award for excellence.

So after all that, did anyone ever hear the crack of the bat on that Corona ball field? No, because government simply could not get its act together. The school and ball field were never built, because of the city's growing financial constraints in the mid-1970s. How ironic—not only was government misguided in its policy directive; it was then incompetent in its execution!

After marching and shouting in front of our house for a couple of hours that afternoon in the summer of 1972, the protesters got tired of waiting for my father and left. But I continue to draw lessons from Forest Hills, and from Corona, to this day.

As attorney general and governor, I've often been asked why I got into politics. People see the overarching ambition it takes to attain higher office, and they assume that, at its core, it's a desire for the title and the trappings and the power of the office. And in my case, because I am a Cuomo, they conclude that my interest was fanned by lullabies when I was in the cradle; that what led me here was my father's rise in New York politics, his years as governor when I was in my twenties, and the proximity to power I experienced at a young age.

It was none of those. What drew me in were the battles that my father waged outside our front door. These bookends to my earliest civics education directed me not to politics per se, but to pursuing a life of public service.

So much of 1960s liberalism was based on a conviction that government was infallible. But watching my father on the other side of the fight, as a lawyer and mediator, taught me that both government's pursuits and their implementation can go terribly wrong. Worse than being graceless, government can be arrogant, its callousness resulting in the tears of the Corona housewives who would cry to my mother, and in the anguished faces of the plumbers who came to our house to help my father unclog a drain. He must have felt overwhelmed as he tried again and again to go up against a powerful, almost unstoppable force.

In the early 1970s, when the fight moved to Forest Hills, I got a frightening glimpse of the volatile combination of race, class, and community; of the ways that raised voices on the extremes, left and right, can thwart compromise; of how readily fear and hope can collide and explode; of how complex and nuanced these problems were; and of how humble one had to be about government's ability to solve them. Of course it makes sense only looking back, but these became my earliest insights into what I would later learn was called "urban policy"—a body of ideas filled with both promise and peril not only for New York but for all of America.

I've since realized that the best teacher isn't theory but practice. Yes, the vision can sound good on paper or in a speech. Yes, it can inspire. But a good theory does not automatically lead to a good policy. I saw then how dangerous it can be for politicians, Democrats or Republicans, to wage political arguments from on high, with little knowledge of the ultimate consequences of their actions and decisions— and I hold fast to the memory now.

And so when I'm asked today about why I run for office, why I chose the brutal business of politics, I think about two neighborhoods just a few miles from where I grew up— Corona and Forest Hills—about what it took to wage and win the fight for what was right against a government that at times showed itself to be wrongheaded and heavy-handed; how dangerous and divisive the extremes can be; and, as I learned from my father's experiences, why the poetry of politics can fail, at times, in the prose of governing.

CHAPTER 2

A Hopelessly Quixotic Battle

Tim Russert, my dad, me, and John Iaccio at the
Democratic National Convention, San Francisco, 1984.

The work of resolving the Corona and Forest Hills housing controversies transformed my father from private practice lawyer to dedicated public servant. He realized that for him, ideally, government, not business, could be the arena where big goals could be accomplished. As he wrote in *Diaries of Mario M. Cuomo: The Campaign for Governor,* he'd rather spend his energy "trying to help people than trying to make money with them."

But first he had to get the job.

He considered entering the New York City Democratic mayoral primary in 1973, when there was a broad field that included the two-term city comptroller Abraham Beame (the eventual winner) and three other candidates. After hosting a few breakfasts for potential donors, my father realized he lacked both the financing and the personal commitment he'd need to win.

But a year later he felt ready. He ran for lieutenant governor against Mary Anne Krupsak, a former New York State Assembly member and first-time state senator from central New York.

In some states the governor chooses the lieutenant governor, but in New York the two offices are treated separately. The candidates for each office have their own line on the primary ballot, and the winner for governor from each party is paired with the winner for lieutenant governor from that party. They then run as a team in the general election.

My father's campaign against Krupsak, when I was sixteen, was my first political volunteer job, and my desire to help outpaced my skills. I spent my after-school hours and all summer answering phones, handing out leaflets, pouring coffee, and driving my father to campaign events. Looking back, I wonder if his advisers lobbied against putting the candidate in a car with a newly licensed teenage chauffeur.

Each night from sundown to sunup, a few energetic friends and I drove around Brooklyn, Queens, and Manhattan, stapling CUOMO FOR LIEUTENANT GOVERNOR posters back-to-back around light and traffic poles so people could read the message from either side. It took Krupsak's people a couple of days to tear the posters down, and then we'd start again.

The poster crew was more successful than the race. Krupsak trounced my father, a loss he attributed to the feminist fervor rocking New York and other parts of the country. He joked that even my mother, Matilda, had probably voted for Krupsak. Despite his visible disappointment, he had taken what was often a necessary first step into politics. The election substantially upped his statewide profile, and that would pay off almost immediately.

After sixteen years of Republican rule in New York, the 1974, post-Watergate, Democratic current swept Hugh Carey into the governor's office, pushing out incumbent Malcolm Wilson.

Carey, an Irish Catholic whose wife, Helen, died of cancer during the campaign, was a seven-time U.S. congressman from Brooklyn and a friend of my father's from St. John's University. He offered my father his choice of jobs in the new administration. My father chose secretary of state. It was considered a cushy assignment—its prestige disproportionate to its workload. The secretary of state registered corporations, and licensed barbers and other professionals. Whenever I went for a haircut, I'd scan the wall in front of the barber's chair for my father's scrawling signature.

Previous secretaries of state kept their regular jobs and juggled them with the light official duties. But that wasn't my father's way. Worried about the appearance of a conflict of interest, he resigned from his law firm and his part-time teaching post at St. John's Law School.

The moral high ground did not come with a pay raise. His annual salary had reached $100,000 months before, and now, at $47,800, he'd cut his income by more than half. His pro bono work in Corona and Forest Hills had already given my siblings and me the message that what matters is helping people and making a difference, not money. But here was a refresher course—good pay is less important than good work.

With Carey's encouragement, my father redefined the job of secretary of state. He expanded his role, becoming a close adviser to the governor and a cabinet-level ombudsman, setting up a phone line for citizens' complaints. He put the mediating skills he'd honed in Forest Hills to use, traveling through New York State as liaison between local officials, citizens, and the state to heal badly bruised trust in government. He settled a rent strike at Co-op City, an apartment complex in the Bronx; interceded in a land dispute between the state and the Mohawk Indians; and launched an investigation into a state nursing home scandal.

The mid-1970s were a tough time for New York City. John Lindsay; his City Hall predecessor, Robert Wagner; and Governor Nelson Rockefeller were free-spending politicians who lavished funds on projects that would help them amass political support and stave off strikes by the public employee unions. In 1974, when Abe Beame took over as mayor, New York was operating on a multimillion-dollar (by some calculations, a multibillion-dollar) budget deficit. By May 1975,

Wall Street was no longer willing to sell city bonds. Without the ability to raise revenue, the city couldn't pay its bills.

Carey, who opened his 1975 inaugural address by saying, "This government will begin today the painful, difficult, imperative process of learning to live within its means," moved quickly to establish the Municipal Assistance Corporation (MAC), an independent entity led by investment banker Felix Rohatyn. MAC was created to sell state-backed bonds in return for layoffs, a subway-fare hike, and a freeze on municipal wages and welfare payments, among other city cost-cutting measures. A few months later, he created the Emergency Financial Control Board—essentially putting the city into receivership—and gave the board the power to fire city officials and reject budgets.

Despite the governor's aggressive efforts, in October 1975 Mayor Beame's office announced that the city would have to declare bankruptcy. Only a last-second concession by the teachers' union kept this from happening.

Although Gerald Ford said he would veto congressional legislation for a bailout, prompting the famous *Daily News* headline: "Ford to City: Drop Dead," the federal government eventually gave New York City $2.3 billion.

The infusion didn't fix every problem. To retaliate for layoffs, the innocuous-sounding Council for Public Safety—made up of New York City firefighters and police—printed and distributed thousands of copies of "Welcome to Fear City: A Survival Guide for Visitors to the City of New York." Designed to crush the tourism industry, it featured a skull and warned visitors to stay off the streets after 6 P.M., avoid the subway, and not even think about leaving Manhattan for the supposedly riskier outer boroughs.

New Yorkers were fed up with Mayor Beame. In 1977, *six* candidates challenged the unpopular incumbent in the Democratic primary. One was Bella Abzug, the three-term congressional representative of the West Side known for her wide-brim hats and her leftist politics. Somewhat less liberal and more obscure, Ed Koch, a four-term U.S. congressman who lived in Greenwich Village, was another.

Media strategist David Garth tried for months to persuade my father to enter the race. Garth, an ornery, cigar-smoking New Yorker and a friend of my father's, pioneered political advertising in the early years of television. He had a genius for turning a candidate's minuses into pluses. He'd helped put Carey in the statehouse. Before that, when Mayor Lindsay lost the Republican primary in 1969 and went on to run on the Liberal Party ticket, Garth recast the candidate by making a commercial that had a powerful effect on the voters. Lindsay in shirtsleeves on the porch of Gracie Mansion laid out his mistakes and asked for another term to correct them. David was always kind to me and I learned much from him.

But in May 1977, it was Governor Carey, not Garth, who finally persuaded my father to run for mayor. Carey wanted an ally and a strong fiscal manager in City Hall and believed that my father could deliver. But by that time, Garth had signed on with Koch, whose chance of winning the mayoralty Garth put at twenty to one. The veteran political operative persuaded Koch to lose twenty pounds and crafted a double-barreled tagline: "After eight years of charisma" (a swipe at Lindsay), "and four years of the clubhouse" (aimed at Beame), "why not try competence."

My father made the decision to run in the spring of 1977. But first he asked all the family members for our opinions. We talked about the pros and cons over Sunday dinner. I saw only the pros. "There's no one in the race who wants to help people as much as you do, Pop. They just want to make a name for themselves," I said. "You should run." Unfortunately, my father's procrastination had put him at a disadvantage, more than he initially realized.

When my father named me his Bronx campaign manager, I was a nineteen-year-old college junior, living at home and commuting to Fordham University, a Jesuit school in the heart of the Bronx. In my walk to campus from the subway, I'd pass vacant lots and boarded-up stores, so I knew how much help the area needed.

Two crises—an epidemic of heroin addiction and the city's economic collapse—had hollowed out most of the South Bronx. A huge number of buildings had been burned out by arsonists or abandoned by landlords losing money because of rent control.

Our storefront campaign headquarters was on Arthur Avenue, a rare stretch that had retained its original Italian character. We were the newcomers on the block, which included a butcher shop that sold thirty different kinds of Italian hams and a bakery that sold loaves hot from the oven.

I was thrilled that between the previous campaign and this one, my father had promoted me from chief photocopier to borough manager. And flattered. I knew he could trust me with the jobs that, done right, can raise a candidate's standing. Done wrong, they can sink a campaign.

I had campaign fever. I kept in touch with district leaders, handled the local press, organized political rallies, and supervised the advance team. Since a call to the right home or a leaflet in the right hands could mean locking in a vote, I kept the phone banks staffed and had volunteers handing out campaign literature at subway stops and street corners during the morning and evening rush hours.

That adrenaline and the belief that we could help change New York City were essential. Besides its financial woes, the city was stirred by unrest. The crime rate, which had been rising in both the city and the state since the mid-1960s, had left most of us with a pervasive sense of vulnerability. We never imagined that it would take twenty years to start seeing the crime rate turn around.

New Yorkers—including myself—were worried about one criminal in particular, a serial killer who called himself Son of Sam. He was a specific, palpable, and growing threat who had shot his first victim with a .44-caliber gun in July 1976 and had continued targeting young women, primarily brunettes, and couples, most often in Queens. Some of the murders happened in places I was familiar with. It was terrifying, and you couldn't help looking over your shoulder when you were on the street. The danger shook our collective sense of stability. He evaded the police for thirteen months. It was the first time I remember thinking that something can come along that no one can fix. By the time David Berkowitz was caught in August, he had killed six people and wounded eight.

An already insecure city became more so on July 13, when lightning struck a Consolidated Edison substation, causing a chain reaction that ultimately shut down the main generator. The city went dark at 9:34 P.M. and stayed dark for twenty-five hours and five minutes before power was restored.

Thousands of people streamed out into the summer darkness. Windows were smashed and buildings were set on fire. Looters stole all kinds of things, including items that seemed too unwieldy to walk away with—TVs, washing machines. They even stole fifty new Pontiacs from a Bronx car dealership.

Twenty years later the *New York Post* said the blackout pushed the city "from hardship to chaos." *Time* called it "a night of terror." Entire neighborhoods were devastated. The looting spree showed how lawless the city had become. Of course, this sense of chaos can have a profound effect on politics and what voters expect from their political leaders. America has always stressed and argued over the tensions between liberty and order, freedom and certainty. When disorder prevails, the premium becomes high for ideas that can, or seem to, promise a return to stability and safety.

Against this backdrop, crime and punishment became the must-address topic for the candidates. Even though mayors have no say in capital punishment cases or laws, expanding the death sentence became a hot-button topic in the race. In 1977, 75 percent of registered Democrats in the city supported using the electric chair, which was then the method of execution in New York State. But the state permitted capital punishment only when an inmate serving a life sentence committed murder in prison.

Koch made his support of expanded use of the electric chair a key part of his outer-boroughs campaign. It was one of the "five reasons all New Yorkers need Ed Koch" listed in his campaign brochure that was handed out in Queens, Brooklyn, the Bronx, and Staten Island. It was not mentioned in the materials distributed in politically and socially progressive Manhattan. Targeted advertising was new, and while Garth hadn't invented it, he put it to good use.

On the last day of July Son of Sam committed his final murder—a young blond secretary named Stacy Moskowitz. Koch's popularity jumped 8 percentage points, from 6 percent to 14 percent. Beame also responded to the terror induced by Son of Sam to call for expanding the death penalty.

My father called Beame's stance in favor of the electric chair "political garbage" and accused Koch of reading opinion polls to determine his position. Strongly influenced by his Roman Catholicism, my father believed that state-sanctioned killing appealed to our worst impulses. He said the city needed more cops on the streets, experienced judges, and an overhaul of the criminal justice system, not a simplistic solution that wouldn't deter violent crime.

He was right as a matter of policy, but wrong as a matter of politics. His mother, Immaculata, urged him to tell voters he'd changed his mind. After he won the election, she said, he could do whatever he wanted about capital punishment.

My father did the opposite. There were times when he could easily have omitted his opinion. But he went out of his way to make sure voters knew he was anti–electric chair. "If you disagree with me on this," he said at numerous campaign events, "you should vote for someone else." I got the message: never trade values for expediency.

His stand against the death penalty cost him the vote of someone whose opinion really mattered. Rupert Murdoch, who'd recently acquired the *New York Post*, ran a front-page endorsement of Koch and pro-Koch articles. Let's just say that at that time at the *Post*, the editorials bled into the news coverage. Some *Post* staffers actually resigned rather than slant the news. That did not dampen their boss's positive effect on Koch's electoral fortunes.

Gradually, my father and Koch overtook Beame and Abzug in the race. When the primary votes were tallied on September 8, Koch led with 20 percent, followed by my father, with 19 percent. Since New York City campaign law dictates a runoff if no candidate wins more than 40 percent of the primary vote, the runoff was scheduled for ten days later. What had been a free-for-all campaign, with Jewish, African American, female, Latino, and outer-borough white middle-class candidates, was winnowed to two men. Success hinged on forming alliances.

Koch's years as a congressman had made him a master of institutional, organizational politics. He was willing to trade political deals for patronage and City Hall positions to forge coalitions. He quickly picked up blocs of support and won the September 19 runoff with a 10-point margin, 55 percent to 45 percent. It was a crushing loss for my father.

In most states, a runoff means game over. But New York allows a candidate to be the nominee of more than one party and to appear on the ballot multiple times. Before the primary, my father had picked up the endorsement of the Liberal Party, which fields its ticket from the existing pool of candidates, selected for their progressive values, regardless of their party affiliation. My father was its candidate, and he was determined to stay in the race, just as Lindsay had done in 1969 after losing the Republican mayoral primary. It was the same perseverance I'd seen my father show when he was trying to save the houses in Corona from being bulldozed, so I wasn't surprised that he was intent on going another round.

Governor Carey was livid. As the head of the state Democratic Party, he demanded that my father drop out of the race. The conversation, with Carey and Ray Harding, the Liberal Party leader, was heated. "It's OK," Harding told my father. "We'll let you off the hook."

"Ray," my father answered, "I wouldn't think of going back on my word. I made a pledge to you, and I intend to keep it." The Liberal Party and Ray Harding would be a fixture in New York politics and Cuomo politics for decades to come.

Carey switched his endorsement to Koch, who won the November general election with 50 percent of the vote. My father had 41 percent.

Looking back, I believe my father's candidacy was doomed from the moment of his late entry. It was his first real race, and his campaign was amateurish. No one was in charge. The people he found to run it were political junkies with good intentions and poor execution. He micromanaged decisions—agonizing over the wording of a press release. He was a nervous and brittle candidate, a far cry from the Mario

Cuomo who would make history at the 1984 Democratic National Convention.

But his passion for political service was far from quenched.

The payoff for his strong performance at the polls came a year later. In 1978, when Carey was up for reelection, his approval rating had dropped to 30 percent. Part of the problem was the governor's detachment from constituents and other politicians. His triumph in saving New York City had also contributed to his undoing. Upstate and Long Island voters felt like children who'd been cast aside while a dazzling but troubled sibling got all the attention. Moreover, after Jimmy Carter's two years in the White House, his approval rating had dipped to 39 percent, and, as happens in politics, every Democrat running in the midterm election year was in trouble by association. The third blow came when Carey's lieutenant governor, Mary Anne Krupsak, announced just before the Democratic state convention in Niagara Falls that she was challenging Carey, throwing his campaign into disarray.

Carey implored my father to run for lieutenant governor, hoping his proven popularity in the mayoral race could pull the governor to victory.

My father is not a man who reconfigures himself to fit someone else's agenda. He agreed reluctantly. As he told my mom, Democrats could fight to hold on to the governorship or hand it to Carey's likely Republican opponent, State Assembly Minority Leader Perry Duryea, a businessman from Long Island.

For the first time my father and I were allied with David Garth, Carey's media adviser. This alliance was ideal for me.

I was able to observe Garth strategize, and I became friends with Carey's son Donald, who was helping with his father's reelection and with whom I remain close.

My father made me field director. He was running unopposed in the primary, so the stakes were low, but he phoned several times a day with questions: "What's happening? What do you know? Who have you spoken with?"

In the general election, my father and I worked together to craft what turned out to be an effective message against Duryea and his running mate, Bruce Caputo, a U.S. congressman from Yonkers: "Let's look at the record." Carey rescued New York City. He cut state taxes. He launched the "I Love New York" campaign that brought back tourists and started a ripple of pride among native New Yorkers. I ♥ NY became iconic.

Having voted against Carey's rescue of New York City, Duryea had few concrete achievements to tout other than his voting record against Medicaid funding for abortions—funding that Carey had supported. He ran on a plan to reverse the loss of manufacturing upstate, cut more taxes, and reinstate a broader death penalty. Recognizing that Carey's soft spot was his personality, Duryea hammered him relentlessly, calling him "the governor no one knows." Our counter-message that Carey was a poor politician but a great governor gained traction. We ran a clean campaign—no innuendos or empty charges—but when our opposition research uncovered a tax issue for Duryea, we made it public. Duryea then refused to release his income tax returns.

As with any campaign, luck was the unpredictable element. In August 1978, two of the three New York City newspapers went on strike. This was a benefit for Carey, whose aloof manner extended to the press and had colored its reporting. Fortunately for Carey, the strike was not settled until November. With few journalists covering the campaign, the governor's remarks didn't make the papers. His message was primarily delivered via carefully produced advertising. Carey and my father beat Duryea and Caputo, winning by about 230,000 votes.

Soon after their swearing in, in 1979, their marriage of convenience soured, and my father's initial hesitancy to pair with Carey seemed justified. "Life as lieutenant governor," he wrote in his *Diaries*, ". . . was about what most of us had expected it to be. . . . There was clearly no room for me at the governor's side on any regular basis." In addition to presiding over the state Senate, one of his few constitutional duties, he resumed his role as ombudsman, though from a new, well-appointed office on the third floor of the statehouse.

I learned from his experience. There has to be trust between the governor and lieutenant governor for the relationship to work. It's all or nothing. As governor, believe me, you have enough sparring partners. You don't want toxic dynamics within your own administration.

I started Albany Law School in the fall of 1979.

In the 1980 Democratic presidential race, Carey, who'd considered running himself, supported Ted Kennedy. My father led Jimmy Carter's New York primary bid. This time the fissure between Carey and my father was too obvious to be concealed from the public. It was heresy for a lieutenant governor to endorse any candidate other than the governor's.

Ted Kennedy carried New York in the March 25 Democratic primary, along with nine other states and the District of Columbia. It was a tough blow, even though Carter, who was embroiled in the Iranian hostage crisis, took thirty-seven, including Puerto Rico.

The first day of the Democratic National Convention in Madison Square Garden, August 11, gave me a close-up view of political machinations. Delegates voted on a proposal to do away with the "open" convention, a practice of long standing, which released them from their prior commitment to a given candidate. That's the proposal we supported. If it won, Carter would be the nominee. If it lost, the delegates could then throw their votes behind another candidate, and Kennedy would be the likely winner. Carey was an open-convention advocate. His reason was transparent. He hoped that in a stalemate, he would be the go-to choice to head the Democratic Party's national ticket.

The delegates voted against an open convention, and Carter prevailed as the nominee.

By the time Carter lost to Ronald Reagan in the general election, I was back at law school in Albany for my second year. It was also my second year living at the shabby but comfortable Wellington Hotel, just down the hill from the capitol. Although I was 152 miles from home, I was still very much in my father's orbit. As lieutenant governor, he worked mainly out of the governor's office in the World Trade Center in Manhattan, but when he overnighted in Albany—during the legislative session, this was usually a couple of times a week—he stayed with me.

My father would never tell me when he was coming to Albany. But I had a secret ally in his secretary, who'd phone me to say that he was on his way. Two hours and forty-five minutes later, he'd burst through my door and find me sitting at a little wooden folding card table, poring over a textbook. I'd look up casually and say, "Oh, hey, Pop. Just in time. I'm reading Evidence." As the father of three daughters, with two in college, I show up at their dorm rooms unannounced from time to time. I can't help myself. I always find them studying. I think it's because they're dedicated students. But maybe they've persuaded my secretary to act as their advance warning system, too.

I do know that all three girls—Cara, Mariah, and Michaela—have a better sense of style than I did. My living room showpiece was a glow-in-the-dark white stallion rearing up against a black velvet backdrop. "What's this?" my father asked the first time he saw it. He loved to tell people, apocryphally, that when he stayed in Albany he'd take the stallion down and replace it with a photo of "Andrew Mark's blessed mother," only to find that the stallion was back on the wall the following week.

Those Albany visits helped forge a close bond between us. In many ways our time together made up for the absences in the earlier years. We'd sit at the card table, where we'd eat reheated lasagna that my mom sent up, drink Chianti, and talk politics. My father told stories—some funny, some sad, some infuriating, some triumphant—about the people who ran the state.

As our conversations began to center on the upcoming 1982 election, my father never mentioned that he had any particular confidence in my political acumen. Expressing feelings and pride in their children was not something the men of his generation did. But I'd worked on each of his campaigns, and he'd seen that I was quick to size up a situation and was fast at solutions. Those experiences left us with a vacuum-sealed sense of trust.

We were almost certain that Carey would try for a third term but were less sure he'd ask my father to be his running mate.

Hugh Carey had a truly remarkable accomplishment in saving New York City from bankruptcy during the fiscal crisis. He rallied the unions to "chip in" to save the city money and provided innovative bond financing. But his personal negatives were mounting as the years went on. Jimmy Breslin referred to the governor as "Society Carey." The sixty-two-year-old Carey had begun dyeing his hair and courting wealthy women, one of whom he married after a three-month romance. Soon after his wedding to Evangeline Gouletas, who'd made millions in Chicago real estate, Carey—and the rest of the newspaper-reading public—learned that she'd lied about the number of times she'd been married.

Could my father successfully challenge the sitting governor in the New York Democratic primary?

I was honest. "I think it's a bad idea, Pop," I said. "You don't have a solid political reason for splitting with him.

You'd look like a whiner and give Carey ammunition against you."

He held the possibility open.

In the spring of 1981, my father rented a one-room office in the World Trade Center and began to hold a weekly Saturday-morning meeting with a pared-down contingent from his lieutenant governor's office to go over the organizational aspects of a potential campaign. I drove down every Friday to attend. I'd spend the rest of the weekend driving a tow truck for the Esso station where I'd pumped gas and fixed cars as a kid. Towing was a good deal more lucrative. I made about $300 during the graveyard shift—enough to cover my rent and expenses.

My father hadn't decided whether or not to run, and Hugh Carey hadn't announced his plans. We spent the next six months not so quietly testing the political waters. A poll we commissioned said that my father had a better chance than Carey of beating a Republican opponent. We threw a $500-a-plate fund-raiser, with the hope of raising $50,000 from one hundred people. Instead, the event, headlined by former vice president Walter Mondale, drew five hundred people and raised $250,000. Ed Koch revved up the crowd, telling them that Mario Cuomo would make a good governor.

Koch's endorsement was a welcome surprise. In the four years since he and my father had run against each other, neither had made overtures to end their rivalry.

We had money in the war chest, a poll saying that Mario Cuomo could win, and the support of the party. The machine wants to back the candidate with the best chance. So we moved ahead. It seemed all but certain my father would run, but even I didn't know if he'd made up his mind 100 percent.

Carey must have taken stock of his dismal standing. On January 15, he called a press conference, to which my father was not invited, and announced that he wouldn't seek a third term. All of the pressure that had been mounting over the past fifteen months disappeared. Speaking with reporters that afternoon, my father said that he was running. Though a formal announcement wouldn't be made until March, every voter who read the paper or watched TV news knew it was game on. It was a strategic and necessary move. With Carey out, the field of contenders would be crowded. New York Assembly Speaker Stanley Fink, New York City Council President Carol Bellamy, and New York Attorney General Robert Abrams were considering a run. One person who wasn't on the short list: Ed Koch.

In the fall of 1981, Koch had become the only candidate in New York City mayoral history to take both the Democratic and the Republican primaries. The city didn't yet have term limits, but Koch was explicit: he asked voters for three terms to turn the city around and volunteered that he wouldn't run a fourth time. Serving the people of the greatest city in the world was his highest aspiration, he said.

My father was sitting at home on a Sunday afternoon in mid-February when the phone rang. It was Koch, calling to say he was entering the governor's race. "I don't know what you'll do," Koch said. "I'm surprised to hear that," my father replied. "Of course, I'm running."

No one had expected Koch to jump into the gubernatorial race. For one thing, this was only his second term in City

Hall. A more compelling reason was that, while he loved Manhattan, he'd shown no affinity for the rest of the state. "Have you ever lived in the suburbs?" Mayor Koch told *Playboy* magazine. "It's sterile. It's nothing. It's wasting your life, and people do not wish to waste their lives once they've seen New York [City]! . . . This rural American thing—I'm telling you, it's a joke."

What or who could have persuaded him to enter the race?

The answer: Rupert Murdoch.

In late January 1982, while Mayor Koch was on a ten-day vacation in Spain, with media strategist Garth, Murdoch, the owner of the *New York Post*, launched a "Draft Koch for Governor" campaign in the paper. It included a clip-out coupon for readers. Similar to a "Do you like me?" note passed around by sixth graders, it provided a "check yes" box. Murdoch had used editorials and clout to push Koch in the 1977 mayoral race. Now he wanted a repeat in the gubernatorial race.

No chief executive of New York City had successfully used City Hall as a launching pad for higher office. Garth, who'd been ready to work with my father as soon as he returned from vacation, tried to dissuade Koch, advising his client that going back on his word to the voters of New York City could be costly.

When Koch wouldn't listen, Garth dropped my father and joined Team Koch. Party regulars switched allegiances. Only Mayor Erastus Corning of Albany, whose longtime friendship with my father was stronger than the Democratic Party's iron domination, stood with us.

Fink, Bellamy, and Abrams took themselves out of the running. So too did most of the supporters who, only weeks before, had been telling my father, "Go for it" and "I'm with you."

The party is not sentimental.

My father was stoic. He knew the Democratic machine was fickle. He expected it to unleash its well-organized power. Anyone in the state's Democratic political circle who came near us could expect to be persona non grata. It was as if the machine had turned fire hoses on us, trying to knock us off our feet and keep us down.

The challenge was to remain upright.

At the regular Saturday-morning meeting in early March, a couple of weeks before his formal announcement, my father said, "I'm thinking of naming Andrew as my campaign manager."

He hadn't told me, but it wasn't a complete surprise. Our campaign was such a nonentity that no top-tier people were willing to take the job.

"If anyone has a better idea," my father said, before concluding the meeting, "Tell me next week."

At the next Saturday meeting the staff arrived with sixty names of possible campaign managers. Sixty! The message: *anyone* is more qualified than Andrew. From their perspective they might have been right.

Their reaction turned out to be not about confidence but about appearance. The staffers believed that if my father said, "My campaign manager is my twenty-four-year old son," the press would mock the campaign even more than it already was doing. They were right.

I was at the age when most people are just getting started in politics, and in life. It would look as though my father had handed me the job, and I'd be up against political operatives twice as old, with four times my experience. I was a full-time law student.

We spent the meeting going down the list.

In the end, I was named campaign director to avoid the appearance that I was running the day-to-day show, and no one was given the title "manager."

No matter what I was called, assigning me to the job was an enormous risk on my father's part. This was the most significant fight of his life—and his last chance at elected office. If he lost now, or stepped aside, he'd be seen as an inveterate loser.

I would never have considered turning him down. I found his strong showing of trust and confidence tremendously gratifying. Besides, I learned growing up in Queens, the standard was clear: sons help their fathers. We were Cuomo & Son. And my father and I had a relationship that exceeded the usual parental-filial bond. This would mean five campaigns in eight years. We'd spent hours dissecting what went wrong in the 1977 mayoral election. I wanted to help him correct those mistakes. This time he knew I'd have his back so that he wouldn't have to manage the campaign. Although we generally agreed on strategy, I nevertheless wouldn't be afraid to challenge his ideas if my father couldn't back them. He could lose his temper with me, and I wouldn't quit. When a situation gets tough I fight.

My father formally announced his candidacy, as planned, on March 16, 1982, at the Halloran House, a hotel on Manhattan's East Side. He spoke about the need to reconcile the interests of a diverse state and to fight for middle-class, family-oriented values. "No one knows the whole state better, no one loves the whole state more than I do," he said, getting in a dig at Koch. "I particularly liked the Mayor and supported him, believing that he would serve for twelve years," my father said. "He promised to serve the city for twelve years."

He introduced the two-for-one deal that he repeated during the six months of the campaign: "If you like the Mayor, keep him mayor, and elect Cuomo governor."

With my mother, Matilda, and my sisters and brother and me in the audience, my father laid out his philosophy and platform. "I have made a commitment to my family as well as to myself to conduct a personal, relentless effort to bring down the grotesque crime rate in this state."

He vowed to control the state's expenditures, striking a compassionate note that would be the hallmark of his campaign. "Fiscal soundness is essential," he said. "However, I believe that the ultimate purpose of government is to improve the condition of people's lives. If government fails to do that, it fails utterly no matter how neatly balanced the columns of its ledgers."

Before Koch those remarks would have played big. After Koch they received diluted attention. The day after his speech the *New York Times* wrote my father off as the "generally acknowledged underdog."

As Ken Auletta later wrote in *The New Yorker*, the Cuomo campaign was "generally considered a hopelessly quixotic battle."

They were understating the case.

Koch had everything: money, name recognition, endorsements, Garth, and a surge of popular support. A poll taken at the time showed us where we stood: 35 points behind the front-runner.

Even my grandmother, Immaculata, put the odds on Koch.

My first undertaking was to find a space for our campaign headquarters. Not easy. Our long-shot status was no secret. Prospective landlords worried that there would be reprisals from the mayor if they leased us a storefront.

Finally I scouted a shabby loft in the garment district, on West Thirty-Ninth Street between Fifth and Sixth avenues. The conduits were exposed, and the paint was peeling. The landlord accepted us on two conditions: six months' rent up front and no MARIO CUOMO FOR GOVERNOR posters in the windows.

A couple of days after we set up our shop, I walked in carrying buckets of white paint. "Stop what you're doing, pick up a roller, and let's get this place in shape," I told the few people who were there.

Looking back, I'm amazed at what I figured out. I wanted our group to be proud of what we were creating, and being proficient even at something as simple as painting an office can give you the confidence to move forward with more demanding tasks. Creating the perception of competence is one way to build real competence. Belief in yourself, in turn, can shape reality. Also, a coat of paint would make our outfit look more credible.

But a new coat of paint couldn't mask the fact that the party pols and the press treated the Cuomo campaign as a joke. We were outmanned and outgunned, put together with paper clips and chewing gum. We had only three full-time staffers on our payroll. My father referred to them as "Andrew's young tigers": my law school pal Gary Eisenman; Mark Gordon, who took a leave from writing his doctoral dissertation on Soviet foreign relations to help with data and polling information; and Royce Mulholland, a high school classmate of my sister Maria. He came from hardworking stock, was tireless, and put great effort into everything he was asked to do.

We hired some pros who worked as needed. President Carter's pollster, Pat Caddell, came over as our pollster. Finance Chairman Bill Stern was our one, true, in-house grown-up. He was good at raising money, with a real business mind, and used the word "no" judiciously. Bill Haddad, our gray beard, and Harvey Cohen, our ad genius. There are only three parts to a campaign: politics, operations, and money. Money is the hardest part. Bill kept our shoestring campaign solvent. He also gave us day-to-day credibility because the rest of Team Cuomo was made up of my twentysomething friends—many outsiders, oddballs, reformers, idealists, and young people with no political ties.

We shared inexperience and tenacity, and accepted that we didn't know what we didn't know. And in many ways, that ignorance was our greatest asset. We didn't know that winning was nearly impossible. We didn't know what we didn't know. We believed that voters would respond to my father's commonsense approach.

The unions didn't care about electing my father as much as they wanted to teach Koch, who had reined in their city contracts, a lesson. Norman Adler ran the political committee for District Council 37 of the American Federation of State, County, and Municipal Employees. It was the city's largest labor union, representing the clerical, technical, and maintenance workers at schools, courts, libraries, and hospitals. Adler took an office in our headquarters. He wielded a lot of influence, and workers from unions formed the backbone of our campaign operations. One young staffer, Howard Glaser, was indefatigable, and this was the start of a thirty-plus-year friendship.

Outrunning the competition took every second of every day. I spent most of my time on the phone trying to win back defectors to the Koch camp. If we couldn't secure their backing, contributions would dry up and the campaign would never get under way. Few people returned my calls and even fewer promised to support us.

Other calls were to gather intelligence. As lieutenant governor, my father had people working for him who represented different parts of the state, and we were able to use them on the ground as political touchstones: Louise Slaughter, now a longtime member of Congress, from Rochester, was one. Congresswoman Nita Lowey, a great lady and talent from Westchester County, was another. I'd ask them the same questions my father asked me: "What's going on? What do you hear? What do you know?"

Youth was on my side. I'd make call upon call until I was satisfied I had the answers.

The second piece of my job was handling my father's schedule. Every day was maximized. We had to put him in front of as many voters as possible. Fortunately, he was inexhaustible. And my mom, a natural on the stump, crisscrossed the state almost as much as he did, often speaking about my father's agenda without notes.

Much of my energy went into keeping up my father's spirits. In the early days, the New York media's "C" team didn't bother to cover our press conferences. So we faked it. We'd set up chairs, fill them with volunteers, and hand out notepads and pens. It's hard to believe that my father was fooled, but I know that it made a huge psychological difference to see that his words weren't echoing in an empty hall.

No matter how well I did my job, I was aware that everyone was taking my measure, from deep-pocketed dilettantes to longshoremen from the seafarers' union, rough men who appeared to have been plucked from the cast of *On the Waterfront*. I had to win over the former and act tough with the latter.

It was all hard. Politics always was and still is a contact sport. You need to have the strength, capacity, and conviction to deal with confrontation.

Plus, this was my father running. I couldn't stomach letting him down. He might not win the governor's seat, but if we lost, it wouldn't be without a fight.

The first battle was the New York Democratic convention in Syracuse, a scaled-down, less theatrical version of the party's national convention, which took place in mid-June.

It is the first contest that reporters and insiders watch to measure the campaigns' strength. There are two ways to qualify for the New York gubernatorial primary. The first is for a candidate to win 25 percent of the state delegates' votes. The other, which takes more organization and money, is to gather 15,000 signatures from across the state on a petition.

Koch controlled the New York City leaders and had the strong support of the Democratic machine, including state-wide chairmen and committee people. He sent the most delegates.

The convention was to be his coronation. Koch had already been mentioned as Walter Mondale's running mate in the presidential election of 1984, two years away. The next stop after that: the first Jewish president of the United States. That was the machine's plan.

The party wanted to humiliate my father. Its position was, We'll tell you when it's your time to run. You don't tell us. You had the audacity to challenge the wisdom of the Democratic chieftains? You will now be squashed.

Koch had a top-of-the-line bus with a generator that powered his staff's walkie-talkies inside the convention center. I was impressed. We were driving an old camper—a clunker my sister's friend Royce had hand repainted with the Cuomo campaign logo. Gary and Royce drove the Cuomo Mobile to Syracuse. We'd put in an advance request for a parking permit downtown, but the mayor, Lee Alexander, who was on Koch's short list for lieutenant governor, turned us down.

Jockeying for a parking spot was a small worry. We were losing on every angle. When I arrived in town a day later, the guys filled me in. "They're beating us, man."

To the extent that we had delegate support, it was from the local renegades, the few who would disagree with their chairman and vote against his direction. They were an odd lot and unpredictable. I didn't want them subjected to direct, sustained pressure from their local boss at the convention. They were, for the moment, supporting us, but a few intimidating words from their chairman—"You know your brother works for me?"—and they would flip.

To safeguard our small band of delegates I rented a party boat. The night before the convention opened, my father took them for a dinner cruise on Lake Onondaga. They were removed from the grasp of their chairman, and their solidarity gave them strength.

While my father was on the lake, I stayed back at Hotel Syracuse. I'd been summoned by the New York City Democratic bosses: Meade Esposito from Brooklyn, Donald Manes from Queens, and Stanley Friedman from the Bronx.

"Sit," Esposito said.

Friedman and Manes were my father's contemporaries; Esposito was my grandfather's age. It really was a smoke-filled back room. Each man was nursing a fat cigar.

It seemed surreal, as if I were looking at the situation as an observer. They must have had ninety years' political experience among them. I thought, I'm twenty-four years old. I have no business being in this room. Our campaign still wasn't even a credible operation.

"Koch said we're giving your father the 25 percent he needs to get on the ballot," Manes said.

I knew they weren't doing this to be nice. They were doing it to avoid a backlash. Voters don't like the party machine telling them who to vote for. This was the worst outcome for us. This way Ed Koch would leave the convention looking like a mensch, and we'd look hopelessly weak—as if we couldn't get on the ballot without help. That would be death for us. Better for my father to get locked out of the convention and come across as the rebel. It would make a stronger impression with voters. There is drama and a message in "going to the people" with petitions.

I looked at Manes and said, "I don't want your votes."

"What do you mean you don't want our votes?" he barked. "That's the only way you'll get on the Democratic ballot."

"I'd rather get shut out by the convention," I said. "Then I could say the Democratic bosses shut us out." They knew it was true, but brazen to articulate.

"Kid, nobody's asking you. We're telling you. You've only got enough delegates to take fifteen to twenty percent of the votes. We're going to make up the difference."

"Our delegates will cast enough Cuomo votes to get you to twenty-five percent. Do you understand, kid?" Manes said.

I said, "Well, I don't accept it."

"It's not up to you," Esposito said.

"What do you mean, it's not up to me?"

"We're going to have our people vote for you."

I said, "I won't accept their votes."

He said, "Nobody's asking if you accept."

"I'll reject their votes at the convention."

"There's no way to reject votes."

I said, "Well, if you are going to have your people vote for us, I will have my people vote for you."

Now Esposito was upset. This was supposed to be a ten-second conversation. I'm sure he was thinking, Why are we wasting our time on this kid? He's dense and crazy. We should've just given Mario the extra five or ten percent without telling the kid.

They dismissed me.

I had no idea how it would play out. The next day the vote opened. The roll call always starts with Suffolk County on the tip of Long Island and runs west and north through the state, assembly district by assembly district. Koch had forty-two of Suffolk's fifty delegates locked in. The remaining eight delegates were for Mario Cuomo.

One by one, the people I knew were Koch delegates stood and said, "I vote for Mario Cuomo." So it was clear to me the Koch party leaders were giving us the 25 percent by having their delegates vote for Mario Cuomo. But I had made them nervous the night before so they were going to give us the 25 right at the beginning of the vote count. The roll call was a slow process. You could walk up to anyone on the floor. Seeing the Koch delegates were switching votes, I went to our delegates and said, "Vote for Ed Koch."

It was a crazy thing to do on one level. We didn't have votes to spare. But we couldn't get to twenty-five percent on our own anyway, so in some ways it couldn't be worse.

As their turns came, our delegates stood and voted for Ed Koch.

I could see the leaders looking at one another. They knew something was wrong. They must have said, "This lunatic kid doesn't have a delegate to spare, and he's giving away his votes so he can be under twenty-five percent and say he got shut out by the party bosses." This bizarre turn of events made them anxious.

They paused the roll call.

The vote count is a labyrinthine process, and now they had to calculate how to get us to 25 percent if all our delegates voted for Koch. It was a whole new calculation. They decided their safest strategy was to give us all their votes until we hit 25 percent. Koch person after Koch person stood and said, "I vote for Mario Cuomo."

Cuomo person after Cuomo person stood and said, "I vote for Ed Koch."

They must have thought I'd keep going and have all our people vote for Koch.

Once the Koch forces had succeeded in giving 25 percent of the votes to my father, they shifted to cast the rest of their votes for Koch. It was too late for them. We also shifted, and our remaining delegates voted for Cuomo. They had already given us too many votes. We wound up with a much larger percentage of the vote than anyone had imagined.

The final count was 61 percent for Koch to 39 percent for Cuomo. We'd caught the Democratic machine so flat-footed that it couldn't explain how my father had received an additional 14 percent when nearly everyone in the room was for Koch. And it couldn't admit publicly that it had attempted to hand us the 25 percent but blew it.

Winning 39 percent didn't change the fact that Koch was the party favorite, but it was a huge victory for us. We proved that we didn't need the machine, and that it was more vulnerable than the party regulars thought. The news coming out of the convention was that my father showed surprising strength.

Koch and my father were running on a similar platform: increasing public safety and decreasing state spending. But my father sought to characterize himself as the traditional liberal, while tying Koch to the Republican Party. In 1980, while my father had backed Carter, Koch had hosted Ronald Reagan at Gracie Mansion and praised Reaganomics. I'm sure he was only looking out for New York City in case Reagan won. But then, in 1981, Koch had run for mayor on both the Republican and the Democratic tickets.

At the end of the convention, when my father addressed the delegates, he took a jab at Koch's political wavering, saying, "The body of this party will not long survive without its soul."

He was so impassioned, so articulate, that he won the hearts of many people in the convention hall. It was the moment of conversion. We were still 16 points behind Koch in the polls and way behind in the money. But the convention was a turning point. We escaped political death, and went into the summer with renewed energy.

Amusingly, Koch's state-of-the-art bus broke down during the convention, whereas our little mobile headquarters sputtered along, parking tickets and all—a metaphor for our changing fortunes.

In early July, the night before the first debate, which was sponsored by the *New York Post*, I went to the Sheraton Centre in Manhattan to negotiate the rules with Rupert Murdoch's representative. We wanted to make sure the debate had a semblance of fairness. My father felt that the allotted short-answer-and-rebuttal periods put him at a disadvantage. The debate was a big deal, and my father was nervous. It was like trying to get a racehorse into the gate; he didn't want to get locked in. I pressed for more time. The *Post* guy said, "We're not giving you anything."

I called my father from the Sheraton ballroom.

"They won't budge on the format," I reported.

"Then we're not going," my father said. It was about eight o'clock in the evening. I thought this was an overreaction and that he would calm down later.

I turned to the rep. "He's not doing the debate."

The rep started screaming, "What do you mean, he's not doing the debate? I have six hundred people showing up here at seven o'clock tomorrow morning."

Our negotiation continued, but I didn't get my way on a single point. Finally, I left.

My father and I talked until midnight. He remained firm.

My phone rang at six o'clock the next morning.

"Maybe we should go," my father said, before I said hello.

"Yeah, I think we should," I said.

Because he wasn't scheduled to go the night before, I'd made no arrangements to pick him up in Holliswood, a long way from midtown Manhattan during the morning rush hour. There was a delay in getting him a car so he left late. We've all come to depend on smartphones for instant communication, but at that time I couldn't text or e-mail ahead to tell the *Post* people my father was coming. The *Post* still believed my father was a no-show and told Koch he would be alone onstage. We arrived at the hotel late. The ballroom was filled with about six hundred people at tables of ten. Koch was already onstage, ready to have a softball Q&A with a mostly friendly audience.

My father was walking in from the back of the room, which caused a commotion as people saw him. It was like a wave crashing to shore. Then "our" people in the room, maybe 150 union people, started banging the tables with their fists. As my father got closer to the stage, the banging grew louder. To everyone's surprise it was Mario Cuomo! In the next day's paper, the *Post* called our supporters "Cuomo's Claque," delivering the message that they were a bunch of rowdy, unwashed union types. But the entire episode unnerved Koch.

In 1982, debate prep didn't mean holing up in Florida for two weeks to rehearse responses to every possible question, as I did with Al Gore in 1996. To prepare for the *Post* debate, my father and I had quickly reviewed a few talking points.

Standing in the back of the ballroom that morning, I was like a nervous parent at a school play. My father's a talented debater, but early on in his career he could come across as arrogant. When that happens it doesn't matter what you say; people remember only the superior attitude. We knew this because that's what had happened during the 1977 mayoral debates.

This time, he used humor. After Koch won the coin toss, my father grabbed the microphone and said, "No wonder he's for casino gambling."

Except for opposing stances on broadening the death penalty—as in 1977, Koch was for and my father was against it—the contest was shaping up to be about which candidate had the credentials to best lead the state.

Koch said my father had "no record of executive leadership."

My father cast himself as the candidate who, as secretary of state and now lieutenant governor, knew the state and would bring the people of New York together. He reminded the audience that Reagan had visited Gracie Mansion in 1980 and worked hard to tie Koch to Reaganomics: "Acquiescence was acceptance," my father said, "and acceptance was wrong."

Partly because Koch was unnerved—"more subdued than is his custom," as the *New York Times* put it—I thought my father outperformed him. The media didn't declare a winner. The *New York Times* wrote: "After it was over, everyone was asking who had won. The experts who decide such matters certainly had different debating styles to choose between. In the hour that they argued, Mr. Cuomo sprinkled in quotes from Edmund Burke and the prophet Isaiah. Mr. Koch's quotes were from Felix Rohatyn and The New York Times."

But media and public perceptions about my father were slowly changing. A new poll after the debate showed us only 8 points behind Koch and, for the first time, ahead among likely voters.

But the underdog fight never stopped.

A week out from the primary, new punches were thrown. Hugh Carey announced that he was endorsing Koch over his own lieutenant governor. The rejection shouldn't have surprised us but we'd expected the governor to stay neutral. This was personally hurtful and potentially devastating to the campaign.

Two days later the *New York Times* published its own endorsement of Koch, noting, "Ed Koch has proved that he can govern."

The *Times* went on, "Lieut. Gov. Mario Cuomo offers no comparable experience or record. . . . He has held only undemanding state offices, which leaves him at a disadvantage." The *Times* was never really comfortable with the outer-borough, middle-class, so-called moderate candidate Mario Cuomo. At that time, the *New York Times* editorial was thought to be gospel, especially in a Democratic primary.

As upset as we were, we couldn't allow ourselves to be distracted from our goal. The "young tigers" and Howard and I made another pot of coffee and ordered another round of bacon cheeseburgers from the Greek coffee shop across the street. We worked until 2 A.M. I grabbed three hours of sleep. I was at my desk before 7 A.M.

We studied voter rolls to see how constituents had voted in past elections. We used the information on Election Day to decide where to make phone calls urging people to vote. This was all done by hand. Today this information is computerized. You press a button. You get the answers.

I held tight to my conviction that we could win, on the theory of the best man will win. My father was the best man to govern the state. And accomplishing something no one else believes you can accomplish is a huge motivator. I embrace the idea that you can change destiny by believing in yourself and outworking everyone. And that's what we were trying to do.

But on September 23, the day before the primary, it seemed certain that, despite everything, we were going to lose, as a *New York Post* poll showed us down by 18 points. I knew the poll was wrong, and I suspect they did too, but it was their last piece of propaganda to dispirit our supporters.

On primary day, I was at Cuomo headquarters, while my father and the rest of my family were at home. We'd positioned people around the state to make sure the pro-Cuomo voters we'd identified went to the polls. We had a massive GOTV (get out the vote) operation, with thousands of people on the ground ringing doorbells and driving people to the polls. Then we braced ourselves for the outcome.

That evening, my family and I waited at the Halloran House, hoping there would be a celebration and fearing a wake. When the votes were counted, we were stunned. Cuomo beat Koch by 53 percent to 47 percent. My father had hoped that Carl McCall would win for lieutenant governor. But he lost to Alfred DelBello, who had campaigned with Koch.

Koch conceded at 11:30 P.M. We headed downstairs for my father to say a few words. The theme song from *Rocky* was blaring, and supporters were shouting, "Mario! Mario!"

It was one of the great nights of my life.

We took fifty-four of New York's sixty-two counties. Koch won New York City and its four adjacent suburban counties.

The reason Koch was able to gather support at the start of the race worked against him in the end. Koch was the face of the city. And upstate New York at that time was alienated from New York City, and feared a New York City mayor running the state. In case anyone forgot, my father wore two campaign buttons, one that read KEEP THE MAYOR MAYOR and a second that read CUOMO FOR GOVERNOR. Upstate voters felt that if Koch won, the city would receive all the spoils.

We also benefited from the mistake Koch made in *Playboy*, degrading upstate.

Only Koch could beat Koch, and he did.

Without taking a day off, we headed into the general election. Our opposition was Lew Lehrman, a plainspoken Republican who campaigned in red suspenders. He'd made millions transforming his family grocery business into the Rite Aid drugstore chain. A fiscal and social conservative, Lehrman favored trickle-down economics, promising a 40 percent tax cut over ten years to spur economic growth. He called for "tougher" judges and broader use of the electric chair, and opposed the government-funded abortions that my father had consistently supported.

Our theme was "Jobs and Justice." Rather than tax cuts, my father called for capping state spending and bringing back jobs that he said belonged in New York. For instance, New York City's subway cars were being assembled in Japan, where the work could be done more cheaply.

In early October, my father's effort to tie Lehrman to Reagan's failed economic policies got a boost when the unemployment rate hit 10 percent. We were ahead, 51 percent to 36 percent.

Lehrman outspent us three to one, $13.9 million to $4.8 million. He used much of his budget on a fusillade of TV advertising and direct mail. His tough-on-crime message began to stick.

"Is there a television watcher in the state who has not yet

seen the man in the red suspenders tell how tough he would be on crime, or how he would try to invigorate the state's economy?" a *New York Times* editorial asked.

A *New Yorker* cartoon showed a parrot next to a TV. The parrot says, "I'm Lew Lehrman. Lew Lehrman for governor!"

Our lead began to dissipate. Pat Caddell's final internal poll showed us only 5 points ahead.

Lehrman wanted my father's supporters to defect. Many did. But we won over some big names. The *New York Times*— the newspaper that at the beginning of the race had written my father off as a long shot—endorsed him. Of course it is nearly impossible for the *Times* to endorse a Republican. "Mario Cuomo offers no imaginative new agenda," its editors wrote. "But he does forcefully advocate the humane values of the old one."

We billed my father as having "experience money can't buy." We also had a not-so-secret weapon: my mother.

We put her on TV. My mom is emotional, empathetic, and people-oriented. Her authenticity and sweetness came through the lens. My father, who can come across as overly intellectual, was softened by association. One sixty-second commercial showed her at a backyard barbecue—the quintessential middle-class mom. She looked into the camera and talked about our family's traditional values. She could have been any mother in Brooklyn or Buffalo. Toward the end of the campaign, we aired her spot more often than my father's. She was that effective.

People almost always talk about a father's influence on his son, but rarely talk about a mother's, especially in my case, since I followed my father into politics. But their influence on me was around fifty-fifty; I inherited traits from each.

In the final days, the force of our on-the-ground political organization carried us. Union halls became phone banks. Each volunteer had a list of likely supporters and a script: "Hi, did you vote yet? No? I'm calling to remind you to vote." If the voter was reluctant, we would say, "We're sending someone to take you to the polls and bring you back." In a close election, a superior get-out-the-vote effort can give you 2 to 3 points.

Would that be enough to put us over the top?

At four o'clock in the morning on November 2, West Thirty-Ninth Street was empty except for a neighborhood eccentric outside campaign headquarters bleating out a tune on a bagpipe. The polls would open in three hours. I lay down on top of my desk, closed my eyes, listened to the music waft up, and thought, I have done everything I can possibly do.

Election Day. I had a phone stuck to my ear, constantly checking on people in the field: "What are you doing? What are you hearing?" Everyone was optimistic, but wishful thinking is a campaign hazard. I was edgy, bracing for the worst.

That night, when the results came in, my father had won, 51 percent to 48 percent. It didn't matter to us that the margin of victory was narrow.

When my father gave his acceptance speech at the Sheraton Centre, I joined him onstage with the rest of our family. He reached out his hand to shake mine. I will never forget the joy and excitement on his face. In retrospect, I think I was happier for his victory than for mine years later. I don't think I would have ever forgiven myself if he had lost. He was the right man for the job, and a loss would have been a tragedy. Many said he shouldn't have put a son in that position in the first place, but in victory it was all vindicated.

In the summer of 2013, we unveiled my father's official portrait as the fifty-second governor of New York at the state capitol in Albany before 150 invited guests. I was struck by how many people from the 1982 campaign, including at least a dozen members of my staff, are still part of our close family circle. I attribute these lasting relationships to our improbable victory and also to the caliber of the people. Working hard on a common goal, as we did in 1982, binds people together. We were fighting the good fight and we were proud of our efforts. It was a good feeling. The campaign instilled in me a need to be fully engaged in a cause much greater than myself.

It's an unlikely comparison, but when I think today about the 1982 campaign, I'm reminded of the speech King Henry makes in Shakespeare's *Henry V*, exhorting his troops at the legendary Battle of Agincourt against the French:

> *From this day to the ending of the world,*
> *. . . we in it shall be remembered;*
> *We few, we happy few, we band of brothers;*
> *For he to-day that sheds his blood with me*
> *Shall be my brother; . . .*
> *And gentlemen in England, now a-bed*
> *Shall think themselves accursed they were not here,*

And hold their manhoods cheap whiles any speaks
That fought with us upon Saint Crispin's Day.

The portrait unveiling was a celebration of my father's accomplishments. Many aspects of his life make him an extraordinary man and public servant. But observing him as he
interacted with old friends at the capitol that day, I was reminded that the older I become, the more one characteristic of
his stands out to me. He is a truly self-grounded individual, at
peace with himself and his view of the world. He has debated
the issues, fought the fights, been bloodied and victorious. He
believes what he believes. It doesn't matter what anyone else
thinks—even the public at large. As a kid, I heard his poll-
sters telling him that he would lose because of his view on the
death penalty, but he remained strong and defiant. The same
happened in 1982, when I told him that a poll showed 70 percent of the people wanted the death penalty. His response was,
"They are all wrong!" How beautiful.

Nothing and no one can shake him. Public affection or
disaffection doesn't move him. Wealth doesn't define him.
During his adult life, he has owned one small house in
Queens and one modest apartment. He has never spoken to
me about money. He's never asked me what a poll shows on
an issue we're discussing—or if I can get a bill passed we're
proposing to the legislature. His sense of right and wrong
and his pursuit of principle are paramount. He is exactly in
private as he is in public. There is no "public persona." It's
just him.

The ultimate fight is being at peace with oneself. My father
had won that battle before he ever began.

CHAPTER 3

HELP

Me in front of HELP I in East New York, 1986.

When Walter Mondale, the Democratic presidential candidate, asked my father to give the keynote address at the 1984 Democratic National Convention in San Francisco, my father's impulse was to turn him down.

Today, in the age of Jumbotrons and tweets, a convention speaker doesn't have to do much to grab attention. But in the low-tech days, he had to sway the audience with his voice. A solid performance didn't guarantee the speaker's advancement, but a bad speech could be a career-ender.

But Mondale persisted, calling him personally. Repeatedly. The keynote was a way to thank my father for helping him win the April 2 New York Democratic primary against Gary Hart and Jesse Jackson.

The Democratic Party of the early 1980s was trying to juxtapose its progressive vision—a philosophy of opportunity and shared success for all—with the Republican idea of attenuated government and survival of the fittest, embodied by Ronald Reagan. No one articulated the Democrats' dream more beautifully, or the differences between Republicans and Democrats more forcefully, than my father. His 1982 gubernatorial victory had proved that some risks are worth taking, and I encouraged him to say yes.

So did Tim Russert. Before he went into the news business, Tim was my father's counselor, communications director/ spokesperson, and close adviser. He and I had spent hours watching, rewinding, and rewatching videotapes of past convention keynote speakers. They had a common element: no one listened. Shots panning the crowds caught people in midyawn, dozing, wandering, and chatting with seatmates. How the convention audience responds to a candidate colors the way the TV audience will react. If the people who love the process enough to wear foam fingers, patriotic hats, and donkey ears look bored, the people watching at home are flipping channels.

To steer the collective focus to my father we introduced him with a six-minute video about his childhood in New York. We hoped darkening the room would work like the flickering light that tells theatergoers intermission is over and the show is about to resume. We didn't expect a ground-swell of applause, but we hoped that when my father walked onstage, the audience would appear focused.

The "speech preparation" process for my father was exhausting. Days were spent on discerning the ideas, the logic of the case, then outlines, then language, and then reordering and rewriting. The convention speech, although in many ways a "best of Mario Cuomo" compendium, must have gone through sixty drafts before he was comfortable. We sat around the dining table at the governor's mansion listening to him read successive drafts of his speech and made next-to-last-minute revisions in the convention hall.

My father didn't like to be away from the state for any length of time. He also liked to sleep in his own bed. So quick trips were his stock-in-trade. We flew to San Francisco to do the speech and did a rehearsal in the empty hall to get him accustomed to the room. He was nervous. I went to make some phone calls and met him backstage a short while before he was to go on.

"How do I look?" he asked—not a typical question.

"Fine," I said, "you just need a little makeup and you will look great."

He looked at me suddenly, confused. "Makeup, I just had makeup put on," he said.

"Oh well, it will be great. Don't worry, we didn't get here on looks," I said. We smiled and relaxed.

Watching from the floor on the night of July 16, I willed the best to happen.

My father opened with a reference to President Reagan's comment that the country is a "shining city on a hill":

"A shining city is perhaps all the President sees from the portico of the White House and the verandah of his ranch, where everyone seems to be doing well," my father said.

"But there's another part of the city, the part where some people can't pay their mortgages and most young people can't afford one, where students can't afford the education they need and middle-class parents watch the dreams they hold for their children evaporate.

"In this part of the city there are more poor than ever, more families in trouble. More and more people who need help but can't find it. . . ."

My father's powerful words and impassioned delivery electrified the live audience as well as the 79 million viewers watching on television. And they transformed him into a national political figure.

When he finally walked down the steps from the stage after a thunderous ovation, he was trying to absorb the response. "How did it go?" he asked.

"They love you!" I said, clasping his shoulders.

For the first time since my father had run for public office a decade earlier, my existence wasn't tied to his rising star. I needed a break from politics. It had been an amazing experience. I'd learned to manage people, to solve problems, to broker agreements, to tell people things they didn't want to hear. Maybe most important, I'd learned to listen.

Some lessons had been painful and we had made mistakes. After he won in 1982, my father made me his transition director. I know it's because he trusted me, but I didn't fit the usual mold. Heading a government transition is a huge job that usually goes to a nonpolitical government professional—an éminence grise. I was young and, except for politics, inexperienced. Besides the appearance of incongruity from the establishment, it fed the perception that my father didn't trust many people and was insular. It also made me the political target.

There was also a basic disconnect in Albany. Because the governorship was being handed from one Democrat to another, Hugh Carey's staffers expected my father to keep them in their jobs. The incumbent Democrats did not think this was the equivalent of a hostile takeover; it wasn't a Republican winning, as it was Democrat to Democrat. Also, Mario Cuomo was the lieutenant governor in their administration. My father had very different assumptions. That set up untenable dynamics.

Many people lost their jobs who never saw it coming. As I was "transition director," people assumed I was making the personnel decisions. They were wrong, but I became the lightning rod for dozens of people out of work. There was nothing good in it for anyone. The newly unemployed didn't lash out at my father. They blamed the messenger. The Albany media dubbed me "Prince of Darkness," "Darth Vader," and Mario's "hatchet man."

Welcome to Albany! While there is a sophistication in the size and extent of its government, there is a small-town-gossip quality and a culture of negativity. I was in Albany for only nine months, a $1-a-year Special Assistant to the Governor. I then headed up an extensive campaign to persuade voters to approve a $1.25 billion transportation bond issue to rebuild New York's roads and bridges. It worked, and it made New York State a better place to live. I then ran Mondale's New York presidential primary, knowing that when it was over I would try something new. I'd passed the New York bar. At twenty-six, I was ready to walk my own path.

I was interested in going to work at either the U.S. attorney's office or the Manhattan district attorney's office. Both were prestigious legal positions. I went for a job interview at the New York City appeals bureau with longtime Manhattan district attorney Robert Morgenthau.

The imposing art deco building on Centre Street had the patina of legacy and heritage. Climbing the stone steps, I felt as if I were walking onto a movie set. Morgenthau's office could have been a Smithsonian exhibition of extraordinary political memorabilia, including a letter Eleanor Roosevelt wrote to him when he was at prep school—his father, Henry Morgenthau Jr., was FDR's secretary of the treasury.

I had ten days between Mondale's primary win and my swearing in as an assistant district attorney. During my time in the DA's office, I developed a lifelong admiration for

Robert Morgenthau. He is an example of public service done with integrity and decorum.

During World War II, when his torpedoed naval destroyer sank, Morgenthau promised his Maker that if he was rescued, he'd spend his life working for the public good. He kept his lifetime promise, retiring in 2009, at age ninety. He had overseen 3.5 million cases in thirty-five years, a longer tenure than that of any other DA in New York City history. During that time Morgenthau took on Wall Street, street gangs, and vigilantes. He established the first sex crimes unit in the country and pursued systemic public corruption and white-collar crime. His case against the Bank of Credit and Commerce International (BCCI) for fraud in 1991 remains the largest prosecution against a financial institution. Eighty-one of his hires have become judges. One is Supreme Court justice Sonia Sotomayor. His work and work ethic have been such a clear example that, in my own life of public service, I push to hold myself to his standard.

As one of thirty young lawyers in the appeals bureau, I wrote appellate briefs and argued to uphold the conviction of defendants before a bench of judges. The job provided me with a high volume of legal experience. We worked on large, complex cases. And while my salary of $23,500 didn't make me middle class, it was a $23,499 raise.

During my year there, I was assigned to fifteen appellate cases and won all of them. But each victory felt less rewarding than the one before. The odds favored the state prosecution and there was an uncomfortable sameness about the cases the system was handling. Invariably the defendants were young men who'd been born into broken families and raised in public housing. Most had dropped out of school, been convicted of drug possession as juveniles, served time, been released, been rearrested, and been released again. Each had committed a felony and was now on his way to serving decades in prison. The alibi was always some version of: "I was with my girlfriend." The girlfriend would flub her testimony and contradict the story.

It was clear that we were locking up too many young people—condemning them for the rest of their lives; setting them up for failure when they were finally released. There had to be a better way.

I knew what hadn't worked: the harsh drug laws named for Nelson Rockefeller. For most of his fifteen years as New York governor, from 1959 to 1973, Rockefeller argued that drug addiction was a social ill. A liberal Republican, he favored rehabilitation, not jail. But a combination of presidential ambition—he had to prove to conservatives that he was tough on crime—an escalating heroin epidemic, and rising treatment costs led him to reverse his long-standing position. In January 1973, Rockefeller called a press conference to introduce a new concept: mandatory sentencing of fifteen years to life for drug dealers and users. This included those caught with small amounts of marijuana. The number of drug convictions shot up immediately—with no corresponding drop in crime.

When my year with Morgenthau was up, I was asked to join Blutrich, Falcone & Miller, a small, general practice firm on

Park Avenue, as a partner. While I was still unsure about what I wanted to do with my career, this felt like a homecoming of sorts. My father's protégé and an early political adviser, Jerry Weiss, originally founded the firm, and I'd interned for him one summer during my years at law school. My then-girlfriend, Lucille Falcone, was a partner, and the other partners were longtime friends, and peers. Lucille had been intimately involved in my father's gubernatorial campaign and served as finance director, so she knew my whole world.

It wasn't the safe haven I'd hoped for. There were no ethical or legal mandates prohibiting family members—or elected officials themselves—from representing clients before the state. But I wanted to go further, so the firm had, at my request, agreed that we'd avoid controversy by turning down any representation before the state. Still, there was speculation and gossip. And the Albany media loves to foment "scandals." My father's enemies were constantly pushing a conflict story. Their attack was, in essence, "Well, you're not representing clients before the state but they may interact with the state on their own or with other attorneys." By that standard you can't represent anyone with a driver's license. The innuendo was infuriating and political, but there was nothing I could do: it's impossible to refute an innuendo.

I'd admired the legal profession since childhood, when my father showed me that the justice system was a critical tool for keeping government abuses in check. But now, working in my fourteenth-floor office, I spent my days helping negotiate real estate deals for developers of strip malls and shopping centers. It didn't fulfill me, and there was a void in my life that was growing. I missed the feeling of doing something meaningful. I started to become more interested in a developing phenomenon: the new homeless problem.

Except during the Great Depression and at the end of World War II, when many Americans lacked permanent housing, homelessness was usually a problem of society's misfits—alcoholics, drug addicts, runaways, and prostitutes who bunked in seedy hotels on skid row.

By the early 1980s, there were an estimated 60,000 to 80,000 people sleeping in doorways, in grossly overcrowded shelters, or in welfare hotels on any given night in New York City. But no one living in the city needed statistics to realize that homelessness was soaring. In 1985, walking to and from work was like seeing a Charles Dickens novel come to life. Commuters wearing fur coats and Rolex watches stepped around tattered, hopeless human beings lying on subway grates and sleeping in boxes to stay warm. I looked at them, and myself, in disbelief. We'd all started out as somebody's child. Some of us grew up to have enough. Some didn't. These were the abandoned people. Some were addicts, some were delusional, some had AIDS, some were just poor. How had the rest of us become numb to all this? What had our society become that we could see people suffering and look away?

Two societal changes led us to this shameful place.

Before the mid-1950s, mental hospitals were primarily state-run, and they were horror shows. Patients were, in many cases, barely cared for; instead they were locked up, tied down, sedated, and, in some places, abused. Often the staff was poorly trained, and the facilities were unsanitary. But in 1955, the introduction of the antipsychotic medication Thorazine launched a movement that crossed party lines to release the nation's approximately 560,000 institutionalized mental patients.

Liberals and conservatives saw the pharmaceutical solution and mass release of patients as a way to shutter an apparently unfixable system that warehoused some of the nation's sickest people. Liberals believed that the drugs and deinstitutionalization would restore the basic rights the patients had been denied in state warehousing. Republicans embraced deinstitutionalization as a way to cut a big budget item that grew in proportion to the rising mentally ill population each year.

In October 1963, three weeks before his assassination, President John Kennedy signed a law to replace state mental hospitals with two thousand federally funded community mental health centers. For Kennedy quality of care was important. His sister Rosemary, who suffered a brain injury at birth, was lobotomized at twenty-three. After the tragically unsuccessful operation, she was transferred to a small, private, Catholic facility in Wisconsin, where she was cared for until she died at eighty-six.

By 1977, about 340,000 mentally ill patients had been released. New York closed most of its mental institutions a year later. But between 1963 and 1980 only about a quarter of the community health centers were built. The clinics that opened often offered inadequate care. And the act didn't provide long-term operating funds. In 1981, President Reagan reduced funding for mental health programs by 30 percent and folded the money into state block grants—money given with only general guidelines on how it should be spent—relieving the federal government of responsibility for the mentally ill.

Health-care professionals told people, "If you take this pill you're going to be fine." That optimistic prediction was rarely on target. The effectiveness of psychotropic medications had been exaggerated.

The broken promises meant that mentally ill people, including many with schizophrenia, often went unmedicated and unseen by health-care professionals. They weren't being monitored by medical workers. Their compliance with the prescriptions was unknown. There was no way to track the effectiveness of the medication or when prescriptions expired. This left tens of thousands of people with mental disorders—a third of the nation's homeless population—wandering the streets.

A second event occurred in 1981. The country was in a recession, and, for the first time, the homeless included a new group not previously seen on the streets: families. They were working people who'd been able to hold on until a child got sick, a breadwinner was deported, or a job was lost. They were people who got a predatory loan to tide them over and within weeks were crushed by compounded interest. They were people on a years-long waiting list for low-income housing. When they were without a home, the armature of their lives collapsed. The small treasures that reminded them of who they were—snapshots, the baby's outgrown booties, birth certificates—were toted around in garbage bags. The essentials—the crib, pots and pans, a table—were, if they were lucky, in a neighbor's basement. More likely, these had been put out on the curb and lost to scavengers or rain. As they tucked their children into shelter cots in a communal room where addicts were fighting with one other and the mentally ill were fighting with their demons, their bad times became infinitely worse.

By the start of the 1980s the pressing question became: What can we do to turn the tide?

In a January 1984 interview with Ronald Reagan, *Good Morning America* anchor David Hartman asked the president what he would say to the nation's poor. Reagan answered, "The people who are sleeping on the grates, the homeless . . . are homeless, you might say, by choice." It became a flash point.

People do not live on the street, lose toes to frostbite, get attacked in the night, or eat from garbage cans out of choice. People do not sleep outside in the cold with a toddler in their arms for any reason except that they have no other option.

Democrats and Republicans have perfected the "he said–she said" dance around so many issues. The point is not to fix the problem or even to debate it. The point is for politicians from both parties to burrow deeper into their entrenched positions while lobbing blame at the other side. This allows them to continue the decades-old argument over how big government should be and whether or not our taxes should be used to pay for the poor.

In the 1980s, homelessness was the proxy for that argument.

Liberals, urban twenty- and thirtysomethings, and Hollywood stars adopted homelessness as their cause célèbre, and insisted that the solution was simple: build more permanent housing.

The Republicans maintained that the silver bullet was jobs. If people didn't want to be homeless, they should work. Then they'd have money to pay rent. If they were in need, then charities should help.

Liberals pinned the surge in homelessness on Ronald Reagan. In his first year as president, he sliced the budget for public housing in half. By the end of his presidency, the cuts totaled 80 percent. Programs for the poor were axed to fund a tax break for the wealthy and to expand the defense program. Eligibility standards for low-income housing were further tightened. Plenty of people were still poor, but they no longer qualified for federal housing subsidies. There were 3.3 million fewer apartments than families who needed them.

Blaming Reagan was correct but also was the simple answer. The reality, I found out, was more complex. A friend of mine worked with a homeless advocacy group and was eager for me to visit the "welfare hotels" with him to see what the state government was doing.

I visited Hotel Martinique at West Thirty-Second Street and Broadway. Built in 1910 to serve Broadway theatergoers and well-heeled shoppers, the sixteen-story, French Renaissance masterpiece had a mansard roof, and a dining room that was a replica of the ornate Apollo Gallery at the Louvre. When the Martinique opened, an overnight stay cost $3.50. When I visited seventy-five years later, the room rate at New York City's forty-six welfare hotels was as high as the landlords could get away with—usually around $100 a night— and the city, state, and federal governments sharing the bill weren't getting much for their money. The Martinique was reputed to be among the worst, but all of the welfare hotels were dangerous, rat-infested warehouses for homeless families.

Following the manager from floor to floor, I took in as little air as possible, holding my breath for as long as I could. The stench of garbage, sweat, and urine was overwhelming. Doors were spray-painted with graffiti. Lead paint was peeling from the ceiling and raining onto the floor. Toilets were broken. Drugs were being openly used and sold. The railing had fallen off the once grand staircase and the stairs weren't fenced in until a child fell and died.

The welfare hotels' rules seemed designed to impede even the smallest steps toward a healthier life. They were designed for transients, not families who stayed a year or longer. Tenants couldn't prepare fresh food because they had no kitchen. But having a hot plate was a fire hazard that could get you thrown out. The security guards traded sexual services in exchange for not reporting the women who owned hot plates to management. How desperate these women must have felt to submit to abuse so they could give their children warmed-up canned spaghetti.

The rooms were so tiny there wasn't space for babies to crawl. Their older siblings didn't have room to play. The children had little hope of escaping poverty. Doing homework must seem futile when you're hungry and have no place to sit, no pencils, and no paper. All around you people were shouting and swearing.

As we walked through the building I saw how naive I was to be musing over schoolwork.

Down one hallway I saw a little girl, about five, staring into an open doorway, apparently transfixed. What's she staring at? I wondered. Why was she in the hall? Surely, it had to be better inside her apartment. Then I saw what she was watching.

A woman—her mother, I guessed—was having sex inside the room. "I'm sorry," the building manager said to me, flustered, as she rushed to slam the door shut, leaving the child alone in the hall. "I'm so sorry."

That was when this shifted from policy to personal for me. That young girl could have been one of my sisters. Even the mothers were young girls themselves, eighteen or nineteen. What a tragedy. Somehow I knew that I could use everything I had learned in law and government about fighting for the underdog, about the need to bring fresh thinking and new ideas to achieve progressive ends; I hoped. I felt in that moment determined to come up with an answer that she, and the city's roughly 3,500 homeless families, could live with. My father was the governor. Certainly this gross injustice could be addressed.

Hotel Martinique and the city's other welfare hotels were prime examples of how city, state, and federal government failed.

The state government's answer was that the problem arose from a federal government rule that went back to the New Deal, when Aid to Families with Dependent Children (AFDC)—what most people usually call "welfare"— was established to give assistance to women and children when the man of the house was dead or absent. It was state-administered federal money that by law could be used only to pay rent for temporary or emergency housing. It couldn't be used to build permanent housing for the homeless. The reasoning was that AFDC was a social service program. Subsidies for permanent housing came from the Department of Housing and Urban Development.

OK, I understood the rule, but while well intentioned, it was completely backfiring. You take a lot of money from good, hardworking people and do very little with it. You cram families—children—into miserable, unsafe, rodent-infested rooms in a welfare hotel, and you're paying $36,000 a year per room. Rooms no one else would pay a dollar to stay in. The only thing you've done successfully is to turn the owners of the welfare hotels into kings!

And contrary to the stated rule, the money was actually being used as a housing program—we were just paying it to a hotel owner instead of actually paying for a decently maintained apartment. The AFDC rule created a mini industry: landlords who wanted to receive government money bought hotels strictly to house the homeless. This made them terrible places.

I spent a lot of time asking myself what could be done. So it didn't really help that my father was the governor; there were federal rules.

I wasn't convinced that the liberals' answer—just provide government housing—was better than the conservatives' blame. I didn't believe that you could simply pick people up from grates, install them in apartments in a remote new neighborhood, and call the job finished. Victims of domestic violence needed support services. Drug addicts needed rehab. The jobless needed to find work. Parents needed child care.

Research led me to a different approach: build temporary housing for the homeless and provide the social services they need to succeed. I knew that ultimately we'd have to grapple with the scarcity of permanent, subsidized housing for this population, but without this radically new intervention, I was concerned that more housing would not really solve the problem.

I put together a white paper about the AFDC law and better alternatives that I presented to the *New York Times* editorial board—the same group of editors I'd met with numerous times over the years to discuss my father's political views. "I have an idea," I said, "and I'm hoping you'll publish an editorial about it. If someone would build a transitional place for families to live, the housing complex would qualify for funding under AFDC. The sponsors could bring government and private enterprise together to form a not-for-profit corporation and secure land and a low-interest government loan."

Jack Rosenthal, the paper's smart editorial page editor, asked a few questions.

"The landlords have no incentive to provide tenants with even basic services," I said. "You can provide a family with temporary housing and services such as drug and alcohol treatment, domestic abuse counseling, job training, and day care, and actually save money as opposed to the current cost of a welfare hotel room. Families would live in a clean, safe environment, and they'd be ready to transition in six to nine months." Even more, it could all be done for less money than we were currently paying the hotels. It was better services for the homeless, at less cost to the taxpayer.

"Andrew," Rosenthal said, "you've made a persuasive case. If you're so convinced your model will work, why don't *you* do it?" I was shocked by the response but intrigued. There is no better communication method than actually demonstrating the concept.

I accepted the challenge I'd meant for someone else.

Early in 1986, I formed a new, private nonprofit named HELP—an acronym for Housing Enterprise for the Less Privileged. "If it's OK with you, I'd like to build a demonstration project, pro bono, to show what can be done," I told my partners at Blutrich, Falcone. "I'll do this on the side, along with my regular client work. If it's successful, other groups can use the model. If it's not, I'll see the flaws."

They were in.

I thought about Mother Teresa's philosophy: "Help one person at a time." That had worked for her. "Maybe if I didn't pick up one person," she said, "I wouldn't have picked up forty-two thousand."

I named the project HELP I.

It's not the idea that stymies most people; it's the implementation. I put together a coalition of bankers, developers, and contractors. In this case knowing the inner workings of New York State government helped me.

The city located a site and the state condemned an empty city-owned square-block lot in East New York, a predominantly African American and Hispanic area, through eminent domain, the same process that John Lindsay used in 1967 to seize the Corona homeowners' property. The difference was that this was in an isolated section of Brooklyn, and we weren't tearing anything down. We were building something.

Today parts of East New York have co-ops with granite countertops and Sub-Zero refrigerators selling for $300,000. But in those days, it didn't seem there was even a remote possibility that such a down-and-out neighborhood could ever be reclaimed. In 1990, the New York Police Department's Seventy-Fifth Precinct, including East New York, had about 60,000 residents and 109 murders, while Boston, with a population of roughly 575,000 people—nearly ten times larger— had 152 murders.

In the mid-1980s, East New York almost never made the newspapers except in articles written about the latest murder. The media typically described the area as "crime-ridden." I couldn't deny that. No matter the hour of the day, it was not uncommon to hear gunshots.

New York State's Housing Finance Agency issued $14 million in low-interest bonds. Jerry Speyer, who was a founder of the major New York–based real estate firm Tishman Speyer Development Corporation and a Blutrich, Falcone & Miller client, agreed to build the two-hundred-unit complex at no profit.

Alex Cooper, a New York architect and urban designer, had gone into private practice after years as a city planner. He was public-spirited and creative. I asked him to handle the design.

"I want something safe and utilitarian, because thousands of families will pass through," I said. "But it has to be inviting. Even though it's temporary, it will be their home. We need to inspire the residents to put their lives back together. We want the facility to feel like a community. And we need to answer the critics who say that none of this can be done."

Details can make a huge difference in any endeavor. In 1982, when I asked our skeleton campaign staff to paint our headquarters, my instincts told me that fresh paint would give us all a sense that the bigger job was important. For HELP I, I believed that living in a pleasant environment could help these beaten-down people stand up taller and begin to believe in themselves and the possibility of a better life.

It was a skyscraper-tall order. The only models we had were HUD public housing, an architectural style that bore a resemblance to maximum-security prisons. It was unbelievably exciting to transform an idea—transitional housing—into a tangible, three-dimensional form.

Alex had a real feel for what we were trying to accomplish. "I've figured out a way to use prefabricated materials to keep construction costs down," he told me.

The first time he unrolled his drawings for my board, and me, it was obvious he'd hit the mark. He spread out a rendering of two 3-story buildings facing one another, as if in conversation, across a landscaped courtyard filled with playground equipment. Like a 1960s motel, the apartments opened onto a common balcony that doubled as a walkway. We chose exterior corridors in the belief that what you can't see can hurt you. Literal transparency lowered the chances that bad things would happen. I imagined mothers leaning against the railing, chatting, as they kept an eye on their kids playing below. There weren't many fathers present in the homeless community, and our rule was that couples had to be married to live together at HELP I.

Each family would live in an identically furnished two-room apartment with a bathroom and tiny kitchen. No more storing milk on the windowsill or depending on the corner bodega for Pop-Tarts and Lunchables. Now the tenants would be able to cook.

The third wing, a one-story building, would house a day-care center and rooms for community meetings and counseling sessions.

We moved forward rapidly. In February 1986 I gave a joint press conference at City Hall with my father and Mayor Koch to announce the project. They had put aside the animosity of the 1982 governor's race and had basically been working well enough together as governor and mayor for three years. We laid out an ambitious timetable: construction would begin in April, and we'd receive the first families by the end of the year. Given the squalor the moms and kids were living in, we didn't have a New York minute to waste.

But not everyone was pleased. The Coalition for the Homeless in 1981 called me "a card-carrying member of The Heritage Foundation," the conservative Washington think tank. The homeless advocates felt that admitting that homelessness was a complex problem, and that the individuals had issues to deal with, would cost the cause political support. And acknowledging addiction problems would play into the Republicans' homeless-by-choice argument. The advocates were deaf to my point that their own "solution," of "housing, housing, housing," was unrealistic.

The prefabricated materials would lower building costs by

20 percent compared with a conventional building and cut five months off the construction time. But I didn't anticipate that the saving would cause a ferocious labor dispute with the trade unions. Just the opposite. I thought it was a double win, because going modular would mean jobs for an upstate manufacturing plant.

The unions objected because the prefab panels meant we'd employ only about half the number of on-site construction workers the project would need.

Instead of breaking ground, I spent the spring—and summer and fall—meeting with union leaders. Having never done this before, as I ran into this obstacle, I started to feel that I might not be able to turn my concept paper into a working model. In many ways, this was the first major setback I'd experienced in my career, where I had something I was deeply invested in and couldn't make happen. I lay awake at night worrying that the first big thing I tried to do on my own was going to flop, leaving the families I wanted to help no better off.

After several months of negotiations, we compromised. I agreed to lower the ratio of prefab materials to on-site materials to on-site building on this job and to use traditional construction of future projects. The construction crews agreed to go to work. The delay cost us almost $3 million. Worse, the months that the lot lay fallow meant more months that families in the Martinique and the city's forty-five other welfare hotels had to hold their breaths, metaphorically and literally.

————————————

My father and Mayor Koch attended the opening-day ribbon cutting for HELP I on December 22, 1987. The mood was triumphant. We'd decorated the courtyard with Christmas trees, and the complex shone.

But the greater joy had come the day before when the first fifteen families moved in. We asked the city to send us the families who'd been in welfare hotels the longest—mothers and kids who, in some cases, had endured years of distress. They arrived, hauling their meager belongings. We met them at the entrance on Blake Avenue. The just-hired Red Cross staff helped us give each family a welcome box filled with essentials—bedding, pots and pans, Fantastik and other donated cleaning supplies, toothbrushes and toothpaste. We wanted them to feel that someone cared about them. And judging by the tears I saw in some of the women's eyes, I think they did.

Reviewing HELP I in the *New York Times* in March 1988, the paper's architecture critic, Paul Goldberger, wrote, "To anyone who has seen the accommodations given to families at hotels like the Martinique and the Prince George, these buildings seem not like excessive luxury at all, but merely like the arrival, at long last, of simple decency."

That's exactly what I'd been striving for.

Building HELP I turned out to be the easy part.

Taking the welfare hotels' longer-term residents turned out to be a bad idea. The more time you had spent there, the more problems it meant you had. If the families had any money, relatives to turn to, or the ability to rebound on their own, they wouldn't have submitted to the crushing indignities of living in a hotel room, cooking on a hot plate, for years. And even those who didn't have major issues when they moved into a welfare hotel did when they left. It was nearly impossible not to be crippled by the experience. As a result, there was a lot that the residents needed to unlearn. And there was a huge amount that we, as administrators, counselors, guards, and complex managers needed to learn. Fast.

We wanted HELP I to be a place where people got a chance to turn their lives around. If we bent the rules at all the place would sink.

HELP I had a social compact. In exchange for comfort, safety, and a place of their own, residents had to sign in and out and adhere to a strict 10 P.M. curfew. Many women didn't want to sign the contract. We stood firm. Without a signature, they didn't get past the front desk.

When we found residents with drugs they were evicted.

The classes and counseling sessions they needed to reboot their lives were mandatory.

We had one entrance and a firm no-guest policy—except in the reception area, at certain times of the day. Outsiders, including boyfriends, were not allowed inside the apartments. If you broke the rule, you lost your apartment. This didn't stop women from trying—a group stood on the balcony and called to their boyfriends outside the gate, "Here I am. Jump the fence!" It was *Romeo and Juliet*, urban style.

The depth of the residents' problems created an overwhelming workload. If each resident had one problem, that still meant eight hundred issues to deal with in a day. Most residents had many more than one.

I made it through the early years of HELP I the same way I survived my father's 1982 gubernatorial race: by not knowing what I couldn't do. I discovered that there's no gain in running away, and that if there are failures, this doesn't necessarily mean there are no successes. The important things are *always* daunting.

I'd been naive thinking that nonnegotiable rules would keep crime out of the complex. Many of the women who came to live at HELP I were addicted to crack. It gives an intense, fifteen-minute high and creates an insatiable need for more. Feeding their drug problem led to other crimes.

We moved residents in as the apartments were finished. One day I looked up and saw a line of men on the third-floor balcony. A resident was charging construction workers $3 for oral sex—a money-for-drugs scheme. Fortunately for her she hadn't yet bought the drugs. We told her: leave or go to drug treatment. She went for the treatment, and I redoubled my effort to understand what made her, and others like her, self-destruct.

One of the starkest incidents was when a new resident—one of the few men—unhooked the bathroom sink and toilet from his unit and sold them on the street for $5 apiece to buy crack. He didn't just need a place to live; he needed substance abuse treatment.

I sat in on 12-step meetings at the facility and saw how easy it was for people to lose control of their lives and how hard it is to get back on track. Rehabilitation for substance abuse is an incredibly difficult proposition, and the recidivism rate is as high as 66 percent. Sometimes the effort seemed futile. I witnessed residents with substance abuse go into and out of rehab. Like prison, it was another revolving door. I remember one woman whom we had placed at least seven times. It was a terribly damaging pattern. I had to hope against reason, Maybe this time will be different. Maybe this time they'll get it. Some did. Some never would. But there was no alternative but to try, again and again and again.

For some residents the devil they knew was less scary than being on their own. I was so pleased to watch a young victim of domestic violence who'd received counseling leave her destructive relationship. "Yes!" I thought. "She gets it!"

Three weeks later, I saw her holding hands with another man whom I knew to be abusive.

Just as I'd been my sisters' protector growing up, I now felt responsible for our youngest residents, those children born unlucky. There was a lost seventeen-year-old girl who'd been eleven when her mother's boyfriend raped her. Now she was pregnant.

We couldn't order up a different past for the children, but we did work on the present, giving them some of the attention and experiences that most kids their age get without asking. One way was Saturday-morning Little League. The HELP I Mets had maroon-and-yellow uniforms—a point of huge pride to these children who so desperately wanted to belong to something and who, in many cases, had never had a new piece of clothing. I got some of my buddies to coach with me, and my father, a onetime minor league center fielder for the Pittsburgh Pirates, visited a few times and proudly wore his HELP I Mets warm-up jacket.

One eight-year-old boy, Robbie, was one of the worst athletes I'd ever seen. He swung at every ball that came near the plate without connecting—even once. We stuck him in left field, where we were sure a ball wouldn't come his way. After a couple of games I asked a friend to give Robbie some pointers. They'd worked together only a few minutes when my buddy walked over to me. "Hey, Andrew," he said. "I don't think Robbie's a bad athlete. I think he can't see worth a damn."

The next Monday I took Robbie to a clinic for an eye exam. He was borderline legally blind. I was dumbfounded. How had I missed that? How had his mother? His school?

I later figured out how he'd gone undiagnosed. His mother was a drug addict who'd moved frequently, and Robbie had changed schools just as often. The entire system had failed him.

The HELP I Mets had the worst record in the league, and possibly the worst in baseball history. Our motto was, "We never won a game, but we never lost a fight."

Well, we did win one game. The other team didn't show up. We lost twenty-six. But it didn't matter. We had an award ceremony and everyone got a trophy. It was so important that these children had a sense of achievement and pride.

Although our team's record was not exemplary, our HELP I program was. In March 1988, we hosted a congressional hearing called by two New York Democrats: Daniel Patrick Moynihan, the state's senior U.S. senator; and Tom Downey, a longtime U.S. representative from the South Shore of Long Island and a longer-time friend. We met in response to President Reagan's plans to put a thirty-day limit on emergency aid for homeless families in each twelve-month period. One after another, the elected officials testified against the change in the law: Ed Koch; Harlem congressman Charlie Rangel; Al Gore, then a U.S. senator; and Massachusetts governor Michael Dukakis, who, like Gore, was running for president.

Even so, Congress made HELP I a national demonstration project for putting AFDC funding to good use.

I measured success in increments. I knew that the children staying at HELP I were in a better place than they'd been in the night before, and I felt good about that. I knew the mothers were in a better place than they had been in the night before. I felt good about that, too.

Having helped one, as Mother Teresa suggested, I thought it was time now to help another. I'd built the first facility as a demonstration project, sure that others would see that it worked and replicate it, in New York and around the country. The need was growing at warp speed. But most not-for-profits didn't have the necessary financial capacity or expertise. I had first-rate architects and builders I could access.

In 1988 Westchester County, a wealthy suburb north of the Bronx, had roughly four thousand homeless people—the largest suburban homeless population in the country. As in New York City, the solution was to put them up in local hotels. Andrew O'Rourke, the Republican county executive, who challenged my father in the 1986 gubernatorial race and lost, was, on this issue, looking for a solution. O'Rourke was a moderate in the Rockefeller-Pataki New York school of Republicans. That was before the ultraconservatives had grown in the Republican Party. Interestingly, O'Rourke agreed to work with me and help. It was a big gesture on his part on the heels of a nasty election. I had a lot of respect for him. He agreed to donate county land on which transitional housing complexes could be built if the local towns would provide zoning and approvals. He correctly saw the solution as a way to save the county money and free up the hotels for business travelers.

Among the towns that came forward were Greenburgh and Mount Vernon. Greenburgh's eight-term town supervisor, Anthony Veteran, a seventy-one-year-old Democrat, had chosen the ideal site. It was on the grounds of Westchester Community College, in the old-trees, old-money hamlet of Knollwood. About a mile from the Knollwood Country Club, the proposed site was isolated. The residents wouldn't disturb the neighbors.

When HELP I opened in East New York, the locals barely took notice of their new neighbors. I knew that Westchester's well-heeled homeowners wouldn't regard us as benign. NIMBY—"not in my backyard"—was a swift and vocal sentiment. And no one wanted transitional housing less than Greenburgh, a town of 85,000 people.

Soon after Veteran announced the project in mid-January 1988, he called me. "The neighbors have some questions, Andrew," he said. "It would be good to host a community meeting."

A few nights later, a HELP intern and I drove up from Manhattan to do the presentation. We were going to meet at Woodlands High School. The intern was twenty-one. At thirty, I was the senior guy in the car. "I'm going to show you a trick," I said.

We pulled into a Dunkin' Donuts and bought a box of to-go coffee and two dozen doughnuts. "Coffee and doughnuts will change the whole tone of the meeting," I assured him. "It's a simple act, but it conveys cordiality and changes the whole tone."

The intern had a little notebook. He wrote down what I'd said.

When we arrived at the high school, the parking lot was packed. "There must be a basketball game or something going on," I said.

I pulled the car up to the front of the school where someone from Tony Veteran's office was waiting. "What's our competition?" I called out my window. "Is it parents' night?"

"Seven hundred people showed up," she said. "They all came to see you. They're jammed into the auditorium. And they're mad."

I parked the car. "We're ready," the intern said. "I've got the doughnuts."

Twenty-four doughnuts for seven hundred people. "Leave the doughnuts, leave the doughnuts," I said.

The lesson I'd inadvertently taught him was that old guys don't always know what they're talking about.

Inside, I explained the project. "We see the complex as one hundred and eight apartments spread over two six-story buildings, linked by a community center. There will be an open field and a playground in the center."

Greenburgh residents shouted objections. Property values

would nose-dive. Schools would become overcrowded. And the biggest fear of all: the project would bring in unwanted male visitors, crime, and drugs.

"We have a serious human problem here," Veteran told the booing audience. "How would you like to live in a room with one child or two children and no cooking facilities?"

"Oooooo," they yelled, oozing sarcasm.

The complex will be well-maintained, with security and an excellent fire prevention program, we promised.

"Let it burn!" a woman shrieked.

To bolster their opposition, some Westchester residents had researched the police files on HELP I in Brooklyn. They found good ammunition: there had been dozens of calls for police assistance. I'd initially hired minimum-wage security guards, but the job was more than they could handle. All they did was call the police. Now I tried to keep the number of 911 calls down by telling our staff to call me before calling the police unless a situation was imminently dangerous. I slept with what I called my Batphone by my bed. When it rang, no matter how late or how early, I talked through the situation before authorizing a police call, or I would go to the site myself. The trip from Manhattan to Brooklyn was about thirty-five minutes without traffic. Fridays and Saturdays were givens. I got the same urgent call five nights running: a man was trying to stab his wife with a kitchen knife. Nothing really prepares you to go mano a mano with a drunk, irate husband wielding a ten-inch steel blade. I was lucky that the few men in the complex tended to listen to me. I was more afraid of being outmaneuvered by the Westchester op-position than I was of getting hurt at HELP.

The more I learned about how to help the homeless, the more questions I had. Over the summer, I rented a Win-nebago with two buddies and drove cross-country to look at innovative homeless facilities between New York and Cal-ifornia. The trip showed me that the problems were bigger and more complex in New York. That distinction had fueled our social services, making them much more sophisticated than the national norm. We stopped at one mission billed as having a twenty-eight-day detox program. When I told the director I'd like to see it, he took me down to the base-ment and stopped in front of a door with a Master padlock. After fumbling with the key, he was able to open the door. I couldn't believe what I was seeing. Thirty guys were lying on bunk beds in front of a single TV. The detox program was, if you agreed to the program: you're in that room, you watch the TV, and you can't get out for twenty-eight days.

I realized that in spite of all the false starts, our concept of transitional housing, with social services, was the right answer. The fact that it didn't always work was proof that what I'd thought from the beginning was true: housing alone would almost never work. Even with services, going from being homeless to being productive was an uphill road, and I had severely underestimated the difficulty of the journey. Without services these people had almost no chance of pull-ing themselves together.

In three years I had taken HELP I from an idea to a working program. Overall, I was pleased, especially when I thought about all those people who doubted I would have the fortitude to see it through. My experience at HELP liberated me from the usual debate. It shifted the question about how to fix homelessness from the theoretical to the practical. Instead of just a handed-down decree saying what people *thought* worked, now there was an answer. There were facts. A right and a wrong.

In September, I got outside affirmation. After a tense three-hour meeting the Mount Vernon town council in Westchester County approved a forty-six-unit complex.

By October I knew that I could no longer straddle two jobs. My partners at Blutrich, Falcone had allowed me to bill fewer hours than they did and to operate my not-for-profit out of the law firm for years longer than any of us had anticipated. I had just opened my second HELP project, a small complex in Albany, with twenty-four apartments. There was no doubt that my passion was with HELP and less at the firm, and my choice was clear. But it was a big change. HELP was a small not-for-profit with no real financial security and myriad challenges. My salary was downsized from $150,000 a year to $50,000. I moved into a small apartment on East Fifty-Third Street. I'd rented a no-frills loft office at West Thirty-Ninth Street and Sixth Avenue.

Until then the HELP staff had consisted of an unpaid intern, a secretary, and myself. Now I finally hired another member: a young, talented guy named Marc Altheim. His job was to help me accelerate HELP's build-out. Besides the projects I was trying to coax through in Westchester, I'd just announced the approval for two complexes in the Bronx. I was talking to officials on Long Island, in Suffolk County. We did so much in a short period of time.

One of the most prominent skeptics regarding my project was Mike McAlary, the New York *Daily News* columnist. He'd been asking about my work, and finally someone told him, "You ought to go out to East New York with Andrew and see for yourself what he does." He decided he wanted to write a story on HELP I, and at dusk one Friday evening we drove out to East New York.

Mike was a bigger-than-life character. He worshipped Jimmy Breslin and Pete Hamill, and had fashioned himself as the next generation of street reporter and the voice of the little guy. He wanted to say Cuomo's son was helping the homeless as a cynical launch to a political career—a mandatory first step of activism. His skepticism was obvious, and I felt he had his column written when he got into my truck.

Parking in front of HELP I, we saw the silhouettes of people on the roof next door. As soon as we walked into the reception area, a worried night staffer rushed up to me and said people were throwing cinder blocks from the adjoining six-story roof down onto the corrugated metal roof of HELP's single-story community center.

"Have you called the police?" I asked.

"Three times," she said. "They never came."

"You stay here," I said to McAlary. "Let me go and see what's going on."

McAlary insisted, "I'm coming with you."

"Then it's off the record," I said.

After we entered the dilapidated building next door, we had to climb over men sleeping in the stairwells. The building reeked of urine. We hiked six flights up to the roof.

As soon as we opened the door, we saw a bunch of teenagers sitting around, drinking beer and smoking marijuana. Drunk and stoned, they were tossing the cinder blocks. Just for fun. Each time a block hit, it sounded like a bomb had exploded, and they'd burst into laughter. As soon as they saw us, the kids ran away.

It was not the impression I'd hoped HELP I would make.

When Mike wrote his column, he honored the "off the record." Instead he asked what we should think about "Andrew Cuomo, lawyer in exile. Is he doing this just because it is right or because it is right for him? How about maybe it doesn't matter why."

Then he wrote about something else he witnessed:

On Friday, a Red Cross worker led a homeless woman toward an apartment door. The woman turned a key, pushed the door and looked at a room all smart and clean. Then she began to weep.

Andrew Cuomo kicked an expensive black shoe on the sidewalk.

"This is not just some goo-goo liberalism," Andrew Cuomo said.

For a moment, you thought maybe he would cry, too.

Mike McAlary wasn't the only person I took to see HELP I. I was proud of creating something new and was eager to show it off—and I hoped it might impress a pretty brown-eyed blonde. I'd met Kerry Kennedy at a Democratic fund-raiser in Manhattan. She was living outside Boston, where she had just founded the Robert F. Kennedy Center for Human

Rights. A nonprofit to promote social change around the world, it was named in honor of her father, who had been assassinated when she was eight.

I told her that HELP I wasn't far from the Bedford-Stuyvesant Restoration Corporation, a trailblazing public-private community development model her father created in 1967, to reinvigorate the decaying Brooklyn neighborhood.

"You might find it really interesting," I said.

"I'm flying back to Boston tomorrow morning," Kerry said. "Is there any way we could go before I leave?"

"I'll pick you up at 7:30 A.M., give you the grand tour, and drop you off at La Guardia Airport in time to catch your flight," I said. "I'll be on my Harley. I hope you don't mind having helmet hair."

During the next months, I wooed the residents of Greenburgh. On the weekends, I wooed Kerry, with more success. She was engaging and spontaneous, and I was enthralled. We dated for several months and managed to avoid the "scene." But she really wanted me to visit the Kennedy family's compound in Hyannis Port, and I'd run out of excuses.

I'd never been to Hyannis and had no idea what to expect. I was working in Manhattan and went to a men's shop to get the right clothing. I explained to the store's owner where I was going. "I want the best," I said. I was outfitted with every high-style summer garment. I had polo shirts with multiple logos and windbreakers with fluorescent colors and designer loafers. My bathing suit was the latest in men's swimwear—colorful, knee-length, loose fitting.

I was ready to meet Kerry's family.

I arrived in Hyannis on a Saturday morning around eleven and pulled into the driveway. Just then a gaggle of people piled out of the house—adults, kids, teens, neighbors, dogs, and Kerry. She kissed me hello and introduced me to her mother, Ethel, who personified energy and exuberance. She waved as she walked. "Come on," she called, "We're going sailing."

"That's OK," I said. "I'll unpack and see you when you get back."

I didn't know the protocol. Ethel stopped and turned around to face me. "Oh, no. You have to come sailing."

Kerry looked at me.

"OK, let me change." I'm sure I sounded as tentative as I felt.

"Hurry."

I ran inside, found a bathroom, put on my new clothes, and hurried to catch up. The group was already trooping down the block toward the water. When we reached the dock, I wondered where the boat was. There were ten of us, not counting two dogs, and all I saw were dinghies and small boats. Just then everyone scrambled into a small blue sailboat—the *Resolute*. It reminded me of that commercial where a dozen people cram into a Volkswagen Bug. Every space was taken up. People and dogs were standing, crouching, lying. Ethel patted the only empty spot. It was next to her. "Come sit here, Andrew," she said.

I obeyed. I was uncomfortable—a cat in a dog pound. First, I was dressed all wrong. These people were wearing cut-off denim shorts, ragged T-shirts, and no shoes. I looked like a designer logo smorgasbord. Not to mention the baggy psychedelic bathing suit and loafers. This was *Saturday Night Fever* meets Hyannis Port. Kerry's brothers looked at me with either pity or scorn. I couldn't tell which.

I'd been around motorboats all my life, but I am not a sailor. Ethel is. Soon we were cutting through the waves with a passion that would make one think we were competing in the America's Cup. Boat heeling, water splashing over the sides, Ethel yelling commands, dogs barking—it was mayhem on the high seas. After a while, Michael, one of Kerry's brothers, took out a thick rope, attached one end to the stern, and tossed out the line. At last, I thought: a safety device. Thank God someone's anticipating the likelihood of man, woman, teen, child, or canine going overboard. At least they might have a chance of grabbing on.

Not a minute later Michael fell in.

Grabbing the line as it zoomed by, he was now being dragged through the water like a torpedo. Ethel looked at me and said, "Andrew! Quick! Help Michael!"

Many thoughts went through my mind, but I looked at Kerry's face and knew this was not the time for small talk. I jumped in. Luckily I too caught hold of the rope. I saw Michael at the far end and started working my way down the rope, hand over hand. I'm not a great swimmer and we were going fast, but bit by bit I got closer and closer to Michael, still managing to hang on and to breathe, despite the salt water I swallowed. Finally I reached him. I felt so relieved. I threw my arm around his chest and pulled him close. "Don't worry, buddy," I said, gasping, "I have you. You'll be OK."

Michael, his face not three inches from mine, smirked at me and said, "What are you doing? This is called dragging. It's fun. I'm fine. Take your hands off me."

With that, he scampered up the rope like a squirrel on a telephone line and heaved himself over the stern into the boat. I was mortified. I'd had no idea he was doing that for fun. I clung to the rope, too embarrassed to do anything else. After a few minutes my arms started to get tired. Kerry was yelling, "Come back to the boat, Andrew!" I started to work my way up the line, but the force of the water was so great that my baggy bathing suit was inching down my legs, headed back to Queens. I needed one hand to hold the suit up. Pulling myself along the rope was a two-handed job. A conundrum.

"I'm having a great time!" I called back. "I want to stay out!" Somehow I held on until Ethel slowed near the mooring, and I could swim back.

I learned more about dragging, a favorite Kennedy pastime, than I wanted to that day. But the more lasting memories had to do with Ethel. Telling me to jump in served two purposes: First, it was a test to see if I would. Second, she knew we were going too fast for Michael to hold on to the rope. Adding my considerable bulk would slow the sailboat down to a point where Michael would be comfortable. It would have been easier, and a lot safer, to slow the boat by turning it out of the wind. But it would have sacrificed the excitement of the sail.

That's Ethel. An adventurer who courts challenges and has an infectious love of life. We became instant pals and developed a beautiful friendship. Seeing Kerry so relaxed around her family made me even more smitten with her. The next time I went to Hyannis Port I jettisoned the fancy clothes.

Little by little, as we invited ourselves into people's kitchens for coffee and persuasion, Marc and I were making progress in Westchester. "Greenburgh has a crisis—a homeless population of one thousand people. We have a solution," I said over and over. "After ten years, the facility will be turned over to the town to use as senior housing." We assumed that during that time other people would have stepped in to fill the nation's housing gaps.

We leafleted the town, and ran public-service announcements on the radio. "As county taxpayers, you'll spend $54 million for welfare motels this year," I told Westchester radio listeners. "Our project will save you county tax dollars."

Most townspeople were coming around. But neighbors in the two Greenburgh communities Mayfair and Knollwood, closest to the proposed West HELP site, organized themselves into the Coalition of United Peoples and declared war on West HELP Greenburgh. Some didn't want their children in the same schools with homeless children, and some didn't want to pay for the increased school costs to educate the West HELP children. The hostility brought back the ghosts of Forest Hills. After one public meeting, a man came up to me in a parking lot and started cursing. I got nasty letters. One read, "Mr. Cuomo. You should die . . . slowly." The threats grew so vitriolic that the police had to come to the community meetings.

The community's fears were grounded in past national

housing disasters, including the twenty-seven-story cinder block bunkers the federal government built between the 1930s and 1960s—which quickly devolved into ghettos tanking the surrounding neighborhoods. John Lindsay's poorly executed city planning in Queens in the 1960s and 1970s had been the next generation of good intentions implemented badly.

"You're promising to do this project differently, the Mayfair and Knollwood residents said. You're telling us that it won't bring down our neighborhoods. Well, we don't believe you. Many of these people had lived in the Bronx and had seen the decline that caused their flight to the suburbs. They would not allow us to bring the Bronx's problems to Greenburgh.

Mayfair and Knollwood were resourceful. This was no usual NIMBY fight. They sued to secede from the town of Greenburgh and incorporate into their own village, Mayfair-Knollwood. Carving out a separate government entity would enable them to establish zoning rules prohibiting such a project.

We countersued on the basis of a civil rights violation. Since Mayfair-Knollwood's population would be white, its formation would dilute the voting rights of minorities, who would become 0.001 percent of the vote.

Over the next three years, we held eight public meetings and fended off five lawsuits by the opposition. One suit claimed that West HELP's policy of housing only mothers and children discriminated against certain groups, including people without families, the mentally ill, and drug addicts. This case was dismissed.

Another lawsuit alleged that we had violated New York State environmental law by not considering different locations and a different footprint. After we revised our initial study, the state supreme court justice hearing the case said the real environmental damage would be the "loss of housing for impoverished women and children."

I didn't let Mayfair's and Knollwood's excuses sidetrack me from other projects. AIDS had become a full-blown crisis that intertwined with homelessness. We still didn't know exactly how the HIV virus was transmitted, and the general public was terrified of the mysterious, and still relatively new, disease. In those days, contracting AIDS meant a death sentence, and we opened a facility in the Bronx tailored to patients who'd run out of money and friends and had nowhere else to go.

Ultimately the effort by the Greenburgh opposition to reduce the number of apartments from 108 to 75 was voted down by the county board of legislators, but, as a compromise, we redesigned the complex as twelve 2-story buildings. We agreed to hire twenty-four-hour security guards and install a barbed-wire-topped fence around the site. At HELP I we'd added a fence to keep the residents safe from the dangers of the neighborhood. In Greenburgh, it was the opposite: the neighbors were afraid of the women and children inside. To reduce the burden on the school district, we guaranteed that only families with preschool children would stay there.

For some, no compromise was enough. One afternoon, when Marc and I were heading to a meeting, we turned off the Cross-Westchester Expressway onto Knollwood Road and were met with about a hundred mint-green ribbons tied around the trees, a takeoff on the yellow ribbons Americans had tied around trees during the Iranian hostage crisis (and, later, during the Gulf War, to welcome home the troops). But now the message was: Unwelcome. Not your home.

On June 9, 1990, Kerry and I were married in Washington, near her family's home, Hickory Hill, in McLean, Virginia.

We were in love. I was sure that we were going to be a lifetime match. In Queens, marriages always were.

Our families, all loyal Democrats who believed that government service was an honor and an obligation, did not run in the same circles. The Cuomos were middle-class New Yorkers. The Kennedys were regarded as American royalty. Although they had many of the same friends and attended many of the same events, my father and Kerry's uncle, Ted Kennedy, didn't meet until the wedding. Kerry and I were a little anxious about how that would go—they were very different sorts—but we shouldn't have worried. The two men got on like old friends.

Standing in front of the altar, with my brother, Christopher, as best man, I watched our wedding party take their places. The bridesmaids and ushers were mainly family, but I also asked a couple of my close friends to stand with me, including Mike McAlary.

Kerry and I stood small, under the soaring dome, watched over by a thirty-five-foot mosaic of the apostle Matthew, the patron saint of civil servants. We recited the vows we had written to reflect our shared values. Besides agreeing to love and to cherish one another, we pledged to help "the people who have disappeared in El Salvador, the children in shelters in New York." I put a band on top of the emerald-cut diamond I'd given her when I'd proposed on Valentine's Day and kissed my bride. Twenty-seven years earlier, St. Matthew's had been the site of President Kennedy's funeral Mass. Her family remembered, but today the church was filled with joy.

Kerry moved into my bachelor apartment on East Fifty-Third Street and set up her offices one floor above HELP.

I'd met, courted, and married Kerry in less time than it took to get West HELP Greenburgh off the ground.

Shortly after construction began, I got a call that the site was on fire. We never found out what, or who, had started the blaze. But we lost materials and time and had to begin again.

We opened Greenburgh in January 1991 to rave reviews: "The $10 million housing is also the most lavish Mr. Cuomo has built," the *New York Times* wrote. "The shelter's lobby, with a sun-filled rotunda and potted palms, could just as well belong to an Upper East Side apartment building."

Some passersby who didn't know better stopped to ask about the new condominiums. The praise was gratifying. Not that the griping went away immediately. Neighbors complained that the residents who pushed baby strollers on Knollwood Road didn't look as though they "belonged" in the community. I took that as an endorsement. It was a tremendous improvement over the rapists and arsonists they feared in all likelihood would show up.

The project did come at a price, as all great battles do. Tony Veteran lost the next election for town supervisor. Doing the right thing cost him. There are a few Tony Veterans in each generation, but these heroes are rare in politics. Many politicians eat a lot of rubber-chicken dinners to develop political capital that they then don't want to spend. How shortsighted. At the end of your career, the only thing that matters is the lasting effect of your actions. Otherwise, what's the point? You have to be willing to incur opposition if you actually want to get something meaningful done. All the difficult issues are controversial, by definition. But that's the point of public service and what separates the statesmen from the journeymen in my opinion. Tony Veteran was a statesman.

What had begun as an experiment had become my passion. I'd stopped thinking of the HELP facilities as individual projects; I now saw them as part of a "continuum of care" against homelessness. Transitional housing like HELP I and West HELP Greenburgh was the first step.

Step number two was government-subsidized permanent housing with on-site social services financed by a new state-city program called Permanent Housing for the Homeless to fill the financing gap left by AFDC. By the time the Greenburgh facility opened, Alex Cooper had completed an architect's model of our first permanent housing complex. Genesis Homes, named to signify the new start it would mean for the tenants, would be built on Blake Avenue, across the street from HELP I in Brooklyn.

Four stories tall with a tan brick exterior, the complex was

designed like our HELP complexes, with the same open balconies, landscaped courtyard and play area, and single entrance. The apartments ranged from one to four bedrooms
and cost $400 to $700 a month.

Half of the 150 apartments would be reserved for formerly
homeless families who'd come through our other facilities
and put their lives on track. The other half would be for
low- and moderate-income residents, stable people who were
managing their lives, but, financially, were close to the cusp.
We knew these tenants needed more than four walls and a
roof. When you're on the economic fringe, access to day care
and job training can be the difference between moving forward and bottoming out.

We took steps to help give future tenants pride in their
new home. We added elegant architectural touches—cupolas
and turrets—and a provision in the lease for a management
role in the complex.

As I began my fifth year at HELP in the spring of 1991,
Genesis Homes was on track, slated to open in May 1992. But
I'd yet to build in Manhattan, which posed challenges differ-
ent from, and larger than, those in Brooklyn and the Bronx.
Land use in Manhattan is complicated, and high-rises are
tricky.

I was determined to prove that affordable housing could
be provided with grace and that the tenants could live with
dignity in a high-density middle- to upper-middle-class, established neighborhood. In other words, I wanted to do what
John Lindsay could have done from the outset in Forest Hills
in 1972. The timing for this project was right. New York's
new mayor, David Dinkins, who had replaced three-time

mayor Ed Koch in 1989, had promised New Yorkers he would "renew the quest for social justice."

I found a vacant city-owned lot that ran from East Fourteenth Street to East Thirteenth Street, between a nightclub and a nineteenth-century landmark restaurant named Lüchow's.

I wasn't the only person with an eye on the lot. The New York City Housing Authority wanted it for two hundred units of public housing, an admirable idea but not one that the housing authority had, in the past, done well. On the other end of the financial spectrum was a developer named Jeffrey Glick, who saw the parcel as the ideal spot for luxury housing and a mega–retail project.

My plan melded the two concepts. Like Genesis, it would be mixed housing—half for graduates of transitional housing facilities and half for people who needed low-income housing but it would have extensive retail space on the first floor. I called the project Genesis Apartments at Union Square to make it indistinguishable from the neighborhood's luxury apartments. A posh condominium complex—four 29-story buildings named Zeckendorf Towers—had upped the income level of the neighborhood.

Because the city was transferring the land, the Fourteenth Street–Union Square Local Development Corporation (LDC), an umbrella group of area community organizations and businesses, had to determine the best land use and approve the project. I started talking with the LDC cochairs, Jonathan Fanton, the distinguished president of the New School, and Rob Walsh, a businessman who had worked to transform the Union Square area from a drug-ridden wasteland. A local resident named Joanna Underwood formed the Thirteenth Street Community Association, ostensibly to challenge the high cost of construction ($143,000 per apartment). The group claimed—in court—that it was about twice the cost of a gut-renovated, 100 percent low-income building. But really they just didn't want what Underwood called a "vertical ghetto" in the neighborhood. I had learned from the past. This time I knew I was in for a fight. This wasn't just about a piece of land; it was about the soul of the city.

In September 1991, while I tried to nudge my idea forward, Mayor Dinkins asked me to head a commission to come up with a citywide plan for homelessness that became known as the Cuomo Commission.

"I'll expect to see your findings in five months," the mayor said.

Even for someone who thrives under pressure, this was a tight timetable. The temptation was to rush forward. With HELP and West HELP we'd developed a working formula. But would it work as well when we supersized it?

We also wanted to depoliticize the argument before it started. For this, we needed to go back to the laboratory. We needed to take the city's fragmented, patchwork-quilt way of dealing with homelessness and turn it into a system. We started to document and quantify the need: How many people were stoned? How many were drunk? Which not-for-profit is doing what? What gaps did we need to fill?

"This isn't about theory," I told the commission in our first meeting. "It's not about rhetoric. It doesn't matter who we *think* the homeless are. What matters is reality. The facts. That will point us to solutions."

We started in an armory shelter that routinely slept as many as a thousand people. The line to the men's bathroom was more than two hundred deep, all waiting to take drug tests. "Pee in the cup," a health worker told each one.

The test was anonymous, a way for us to gauge how many people in the vast "congregate" shelters were addicts. The numbers were staggering. Eighty percent of single people tested positive for drugs or alcohol—as compared with 65 percent of those in smaller shelters. But among homeless adults with children the number dropped to 30 percent.

Between November and January, the Cuomo Commission held five hearings at City Hall. Presiding over them taught me a new level of political patience. We heard from shelter administrators, church leaders, advocates for the homeless, the head of the New York Civil Liberties Union, the commissioner from the New York State Office of Mental Health, U.S. Senator Daniel Patrick Moynihan, and—perhaps most important—homeless people from New York City's streets. We asked, debated, and answered questions. Housing was a legal right in New York. Should it be? Who qualifies? Where should it be? How do we protect the children? What should we do about the people with AIDS?

An AIDS activist came to a hearing wearing a skeleton costume and throwing bags of water he'd dyed red to signify tainted blood.

The final report, called "The Way Home: A New Direction in Social Policy," emphasized a practical approach without a political bent and called for an overhaul of the city's homeless services. For a decade, the approach to homelessness had been to wait for people to be on the street and then try to find housing for them. In the report we examined cause and effect to try to prevent this problem. People in transition— those being released from prison or a hospital or aging out of foster care—are the most vulnerable group. The solution was to be proactive—to spend money at the front end to maintain their housing arrangements rather than when they hit bottom.

To help those already on the street, we suggested creating more small shelters with social services. Moreover, the city would supply permanent housing to people only after they successfully completed training or treatment specific to their individual vulnerability. The issue that most upset the status quo was our recommendation to take away responsibility from the colossal—and colossally incompetent—Human Resources Administration established by John Lindsay in the 1960s. We urged that Mayor Dinkins create a new, more nimble agency to administer homeless shelters and to hire nonprofits to provide services, including job training, and drug treatment.

The mayor endorsed our plan, but members of his administration turned it into a turf war. Dinkins announced that he'd consider all sides and reveal his decision in eighteen months. One commission member, George McDonald, who founded the Doe Fund, a nonprofit group that helps homeless single men find work in New York City, satirized the delay, telling a *Times* reporter: "I'm going to reserve comment while I study and analyze the city's plan to study and analyze the commission's plan."

I was as glad for McDonald's sense of humor as I had been for his intellectual heft and breadth of experience while we conducted our research. But it didn't make me any less disheartened about Dinkins's delay. With the number of homeless families in the city rising, I felt we needed answers now.

To my relief, in September, many months ahead of schedule, Mayor Dinkins accepted the Cuomo Commission's recommendations for treatment-based housing. It was a triumph. "At its heart," the *New York Times* later wrote, "the Mayor's plan would profoundly change the philosophy that animates the system." In the winter of 2011, when I took office as governor, Mary Brosnahan, the current executive director of the Coalition for the Homeless—the group that had once said we were undermining the homeless by acknowledging that their problems were more than not having a home—published a letter in the organization's newsletter that affirmed the work the Cuomo Commission had done:

> *The dirty secret of homelessness policy is that we know what works. Dozens of studies since the Cuomo Commission, plus the experience of cities across the country, have proven Cuomo right: by transitioning homeless Americans into housing that they can afford and giving them the support and the services they need, hundreds of thousands have successfully rebuilt their lives.*

While I was building housing, both transitional and permanent, for the homeless, Kerry and I were also building a life together. She was traveling internationally for the RFK

Center for Human Rights, and I was ricocheting between HELP projects. But on weekends, we went house hunting. We found a house on Grosvenor Street in Douglas Manor, Queens. We both felt at home in the "garden suburb" on the tip of a peninsula fronting Little Neck Bay. The neighborhood was within the city limits (my wish) and felt secluded (hers). It was a twenty-five-minute drive to our offices.

While the Cuomo Commission worked on the Dinkins report, plans for the Genesis Apartments at Union Square moved along in one-step-forward, two-steps-sideways fashion, orchestrated by those for and those against. Marc Altheim helped shepherd the project. Finally, in August 1992, a New York City Council subcommittee green-lighted the apartments on Union Square. On the day of the vote, a dozen angry Union Square residents picketed on the steps of City Hall. WE WANT ANSWERS FROM ANDREW, one sign read. SAY NO TO CUOMO. One critic told the media, "We already live in a sea of drugs and prostitution."

Shortly after the 1992 election, I got a call from Congressman Tom Downey. "Andrew," he said, "Bill Clinton asked me to chair the health and housing cluster as part of his transition team. I don't know anything about housing. Why don't you come to Washington and help me?"

His timing was ideal. During my six years at HELP, we had housed roughly five thousand families and spent $100 million on construction. We employed more than five hundred people. I had immersed myself in so many broken lives that I was emotionally exhausted.

I planned to stay in Washington for six weeks. But after meeting Bill Clinton and Clinton's appointed HUD secretary, Henry Cisneros, the young, charismatic Latino former mayor of San Antonio, Texas, I was offered a position at the agency. I thought about all I could accomplish if I joined it.

My father counseled me against the move. He was suspicious of Washington and felt I would get lost in the bureaucracy. I heard him. But I believed that it was the place to nationalize the approach to homelessness we'd pioneered in New York. I was also ready to leave the New York goldfish bowl.

Clinton's election generated renewed hope and excitement among Democrats across the country, replacing the malaise brought on by twelve years of Ronald Reagan and George H. W. Bush. Bill Clinton and Al Gore were the next generation. They made government cool again.

My sister Maria Cuomo Cole took over HELP, so I left New York knowing the organization in which I had invested my soul could meet all challenges. Maria is a superstar. She has natural charm. She is also organized and tenacious. There were constant challenges at HELP. After ground was broken for the Genesis Apartments, Joanna Underwood's Thirteenth Street Community Association pressed forward with its lawsuit against HELP for the illegal use of public funds, appealing to the then-incoming mayor, Rudolph Giuliani, to stop construction. But the City Council's approval was final.

In March 1995, tenants moved into what we had officially named the Genesis Robert F. Kennedy Apartments. I traveled back from Washington with Vice President Gore for the event. It was thrilling to see the relief and happiness the new tenants felt, but for me the greatest approbation came months later, when Joanna Underwood publicly said the building "is as clean as can be. There is not a spot of dirt, there is no disruption. The building has been absolutely no problem on the block."

Vindication!

What I learned during the HELP years provided me with important insights that have served me well in my career. I understood how the private sector in New York could view government as the enemy. I saw how complicated regulations increased the cost of doing business. Real estate development in New York City and New York State trained me in dealing with the frustration of layers of government bureaucracy and taught me how to negotiate my way forward when time really is money.

HELP also showed me the shallowness of the political debate and how hard it is to actually achieve a solution. It also showed me that only results matter. The pundits and ideologues will opine and argue as an ongoing occupation. Someone or something must conclude and act. To act requires skill.

That's why I tell young people who want to go into government: the desire to do good is not the same as doing good. Sure, it's nice that you want to help. But it's better to have the *capacity* to help. Learn something. Master a skill. Become a financial, construction, housing, management, or social services expert—whatever. You have to be able to show results. That is the real gift to the community.

This wasn't as true for my father's generation. At that time, the Democratic Party had to persuade the voters of the correctness of their position, to stand up for civil rights and women's rights. The Democrats won the argument: the public slowly accepted the dream of social justice, as articulated by great progressive leaders like my father, Ted Kennedy, Martin Luther King Jr., and others.

But the goal has shifted, and the Democratic Party of that era had failed to prove conclusively that government can be an efficient and effective vehicle for realizing the dream. Conservatives argue about the problem not the solution. Progressives must now demonstrate that we can do what we preach; that we can deliver the product we presold. The difference between my father's operating style and mine is more by design than by personality or temperament. I have to reflect a different ethos for a different time. The Democrats' vision of government must show it can work and produce.

And in the mid-1980s, when I first became passionate about homelessness, that is exactly where we were. Governments were spending millions and voters were not getting the results they were promised.

Sure, it stung to have liberal advocates tell me that I was hurting the cause by admitting how complex the homelessness problem really was, to be a Cuomo yet labeled a conservative for daring to suggest that there might be a far more effective way to help the homeless.

But the experience of creating HELP solidified the conviction: If you are not willing to withstand criticism, at times quite harsh, then you shouldn't seek to be an agent of change, to lead a cause, to create a new and better way. And a willingness to rethink and reform matters now more than ever, as Americans' faith in government is at record lows. Public housing was a virtual billboard for government failure in every city across the country. Years of waste and abuse, from food stamps to procurement excesses at the Pentagon, from lax oversight of the financial sector to huge cost overruns in the building of roads and bridges, have given taxpayers hundreds of reasons to distrust the government.

Despite the skepticism, if we are willing to put ideas ahead of ideology, buck convention, create new models of change, like HELP, and relentlessly focus on results, I still believe that all things are possible.

CHAPTER 4

The Perfect Metaphor

*Hard at work on-site for Habitat for Humanity's
"The House That Congress Built" project in June 1997, as
secretary of Housing and Urban Development.*

Ten floors of basement."

That's how Jack Kemp, a former Department of Housing and Urban Development secretary, under George H. W.

Bush, described HUD's headquarters to me after President Clinton nominated me to become assistant secretary of community planning and development. Kemp was right.

Outside, the poured concrete building has small, indented windows. Inside, it has gray, linoleum-tiled floors and all the charm of a prison.

Designed by Marcel Breuer, a master of the modern American architectural movement, it was of the moment. But the moment was 1968, and the look did not age well. It is sadly a perfect metaphor for the country's story of low-income housing.

As I roamed the dim halls, on my way to my first meeting with HUD secretary Henry Cisneros, the building reminded me of the many ways public housing had gone wrong. Subsidized housing started in the 1930s as a way to help the working poor and people devastated by the Depression get out of urban slums. As time passed, the government provided "public housing" as temporary homes so people could pull themselves up and into self-reliance. But somewhere along the way the system failed. The government-sponsored projects became run-down, overcrowded places of concentrated poverty and crime. What was meant to keep people afloat while they built their lives became housing of the last resort. By 1965, when HUD was created to replace the Housing and Home Finance Agency—meant to be the pinnacle of Lyndon Johnson's Great Society—it was inheriting a disaster.

HUD was the monument to the great Democratic vision: help the poor, rebuild the inner cities, use government to advance social justice. It was the hallmark of every great Democrat's finest speech. John Kennedy, LBJ, Mario Cuomo, Ted

Kennedy—all advocated for the essence of the HUD mission. But HUD had failed to deliver its mandate.

In the six years I'd built housing in New York, I'd never looked to the federal housing agency for guidance or assistance. HUD seemed to be a place of failed solutions. I joked that if failure brings opportunity, I could take comfort in knowing my opportunities were boundless.

My job as assistant secretary at HUD had me in charge of community development, homelessness, and economic initiatives. I knew President Clinton was looking to take nationwide the ideas that had worked on a small scale in communities and states. Because we arrived in Washington at the last minute, we temporarily moved into Kerry's magnificent childhood home, Hickory Hill, with her mother, Ethel. Hickory Hill is on the west bank of the Potomac River, in McLean, Virginia, thirteen miles from the U.S. Capitol. The original Georgian manor, built shortly after the Civil War, was home to Robert Jackson, who was appointed U.S. attorney general and a Supreme Court justice by FDR and who served as chief U.S. prosecutor at the Nuremberg trials after World War II. After Jackson's death, his widow sold it to John and Jacqueline Kennedy, who lived there briefly before Kerry's parents bought it in 1956 and expanded it to make room for their eleven children. Painted white, the thirteen-bedroom brick house sits on five and a half acres with a tennis court and pool.

Life with the Kennedys was not at all like life with the Cuomos. When I was growing up, my family life was largely insular. Life-loving and generous, Kerry's mother is the quintessential extrovert and, especially in those days, an ardent entertainer. Before I got to know Ethel, I thought Washington's political relationships were episodic and fleeting, but she was one of a rare breed who held friends dear. When Kerry and I moved in, Ethel's husband, Bobby, had been gone twenty-five years. But Ethel still graciously hosted anyone who had helped him during his brief and remarkable career as a U.S. attorney general, U.S. senator, and presidential candidate.

Ethel and I grew close. She was a lot of fun to be around. One day I was in a meeting at HUD when my assistant interrupted. "Ethel Kennedy is on the phone for you," she announced.

"Do you mind asking if it's urgent, or if I can call her back?" I asked.

Seconds later, my assistant returned. "Mrs. Kennedy says she's at the vet because your dog, Cisco, attacked her dog, Rowser, and the vet wants to castrate your dog."

I hotfooted it to the phone, and Ethel was still laughing.

As assistant secretary, I had a staff of about two thousand and a budget of roughly $10 billion. My goal was to make Community Planning and Development (CPD) far more effective and relevant in communities that needed it.

We got a big assist from President Clinton, who, unlike Republican presidents before him, had a keen interest in taking on the country's large-scale urban ills. Early in 1993, he signed an executive order directing HUD to break the cycle of homelessness in America. At Henry Cisneros's direction, I took the lead in an interagency effort involving HUD, the Department of Health and Human Services (HHS), the Department of Veterans Affairs, and others to research and

draft a report on the causes of homelessness—and how to
fix it. My team held forums in cities and towns across the
country.

Getting out of New York was a great experience for me. I
was in every state multiple times, and in more than six hundred cities. I saw the best ideas out there. I was surprised to
find anti–New York sentiment outside my home state and so
many stylistic differences between New York and everywhere
else. I was young and supercharged, but I quickly realized
that my approach struck many people in other parts of the
country as brusque. In my new surroundings, people often
invited me to "visit." There is no New York analogue to "visiting." "Visiting" seemed to be a purely social meeting to just
"catch up" with no apparent agenda or purpose. It took me
a while to understand that these social exchanges really did
have a purpose, helping cement what would become long-
term relationships. But they were alien to my young, driven
self. It was an invaluable experience.

We started with a groundbreaking report, "Priority:
Home! The Federal Plan to End Homelessness." It went to
President Clinton in February 1994 and to the press and advocates soon after. In many ways it was the federal version
of the report I had done for Mayor Dinkins. It was well received. It "really does say what we've been trying to say for
a long time," the director of the National Coalition for the
Homeless told the *New York Times*.

"Priority: Home!" made public the fact that about 7 million
Americans had experienced homelessness in recent years.
Using this empirical number in a federal report was un-
precedented. The reasons for homelessness were as varied as

those we'd uncovered during the Dinkins years. The causes weren't just those the Republicans emphasized: mental illness and substance abuse. Chronic poverty, racism, neglect of our country's veterans, and federal cuts in the budget for housing were also to blame.

The federal government had poured millions of dollars into abating homelessness, but that was nowhere close to the amount of money needed. And the government's fragmented approach had made already awful circumstances a lot worse. Four federal homelessness programs administered 1,500 grant applications from around the country. The applications were graded and selected on their merits with no preference for location. Theoretically twenty projects in Memphis, Tennessee; one in New York City; and two in Sioux Falls, South Dakota, could be approved for funding. What no one at HUD was asking was, Does this make sense? The first year I was there, one project received almost half the money budgeted for homelessness programs. It was a beautiful project. Exquisite, even. But if our goal was to use federal funding to leverage local support and help the nation to meet the challenge of homelessness, no single project deserved 50 percent of the money when all fifty states had compelling needs.

Our new formula was proportionate. Densely populated cities like New York, Los Angeles, and Chicago had the largest homeless populations, so they were eligible to compete for the highest percentages of funding. Next, we said that advocates within the same communities had to work together to come up with a single, coordinated plan. If there were twenty groups in Cleveland, then instead of competing against one another they had to team up and apply for a single grant. Then they could divide up and decide who would be in charge of what. One organization would handle domestic violence treatment; another would supply beds; a third would offer job training and child care. Duplicating services wasted money needed to help homeless people become self-sufficient.

Would-be recipients had to do an inventory of need and available social services, design a system, and coordinate, and they had to compete—so performance mattered. The new approach was my first attempt to use federal resources strategically, to incentivize top-notch government performance, rather than simply hand out grants. The approach also applied the program model I knew well. It was the same "continuum of care" that I began at HELP and that Mayor Dinkins approved for New York City. Under President Clinton, we extended the practice to all fifty states. First we stabilized the homeless in transitional housing, providing them with services through public-private partnerships; then we moved people into permanent housing. What had become routine to me was new to the rest of the country. "I can't believe what started with one facility in Brooklyn six years ago has gone national," I told Kerry. "It feels like we've really accomplished something." In retrospect, this success showed me that change on a national scale was indeed possible, albeit difficult. We had redesigned major multibillion-dollar programs in entrenched venues and made them work.

In a follow-up assessment that we commissioned, Columbia University's Barnard-Columbia Center for Urban Policy found that the Continuum of Care was helping hundreds of thousands of people reestablish their lives—fourteen times more in 1995 than in 1992. During the same period the congressional budget went from $404 million to $1.1 billion. Congress now felt it was getting its money's worth.

Harvard University recognized the model with its prestigious award for "innovations in government"—the government equivalent of a Pulitzer Prize or an Oscar.

While I was at HUD, the Internet was just taking off, and I was intrigued by the fact that for the first time technology could link the average citizen to the local government, making it accessible to anyone with a computer and a phone jack. What was happening in local government no longer had to seem remote from individuals' lives. We posted online each city's long-term goals, consisting of its housing, economic, and social development plans, called its "consolidated plan," and for the first time, those who lived there could comment on how the money was being spent and the practices and plan that their government had established.

We made great progress with the Continuum of Care and consolidating planning initiatives, but it was our community development work in urban and rural areas that was most visible. As HUD secretary, Jack Kemp had championed free-market "enterprise zones," which offered tax incentives to businesses that invested in blighted inner cities. His theory was: reduce taxes and regulations, and businesses will flourish.

President Clinton upped the ante. His idea, known as Empowerment Zones (EZs), was as much about personal development for local residents as about business development in the communities that were selected. Bill Clinton believed—as

I believe—that job creation and training were the keys to helping the country's poorest neighborhoods prosper. He promised $100 million over ten years to a total of ten winning cities, rural areas, and Indian reservations that would be chosen on the basis of their communities' wants, needs, and plans, explaining how *they* would achieve the transformation. Up to a hundred others would receive smaller economic packages.

President Clinton believed in helping people help themselves, not in handouts with no expectations. On the flip side, he gave the participants a lot of autonomy. As one EZ coordinator told the *Philadelphia Inquirer,* "Model Cities said, 'Bring me your poor, and I'll solve your problems.' Empowerment Zones say, 'Show me your capacity, your vision and ability to get things done, and we'll give you seed money to get there.'"

The Empowerment Zones model was an ambitious undertaking going right to the heart of urban poverty and seeking life in the cemetery of Democratic initiatives. Clinton had wisely taken the best of Republican principles—the private sector, not government, creates jobs and wealth—and combined it with the Democrats' philosophy: you can't pull yourself up by your own bootstraps when you are stuck in the mud. You need government assistance with education, training, social services, and so on, and an incentive to make the market go where it otherwise wouldn't go. This "best of both" policy making was what we believed, and it also defeated the political polarization that dooms so many efforts. Usually one side of the aisle behaves as if it must prove the other wrong. This approach allowed both to claim victory.

Clinton enjoyed sharing credit. Galvanized by President Clinton's mission, I worked seven days a week. Kerry was traveling like crazy to promote human rights around the world. After we'd lived in Washington a few months, *Time* included us in a humorous ranking of Washington's power couples, saying that we worked too hard to join the Georgetown social scene: "Not much fun," the article quipped, "but great last names."

With the consolidated planning initiative, the Empowerment Zones, and the reinvented homelessness program, it was more than a full plate. These were all big, high-profile, national programs. They are where I learned firsthand the importance of working with a group of talented people. One person's capacity in a sprawling bureaucracy is only as good as his or her ability to assemble a team. I like and need the ability to perform and accomplish many intricate projects, so group dynamics are vital. I hate yes-men. They are dangerous. I need independent managers to accomplish their own projects. I like strong-minded people who can take risks, solve problems, and exercise authority, and are confident enough to deal with the consequences of their success or failures. As assistant secretary, I had some stars. Jacquie Lawing had worked for Al Gore when he was in the Senate, on his 1992 vice presidential campaign, and at the White House. She came to work at HUD because she was committed to helping the poor. I admired her passion and commitment. A Southerner from Tennessee and a longtime Washingtonian, she had taught me about the ways of my new city. Howard Glaser had been stalwart during the cheeseburger-and-fries days of my father's 1982 campaign. Karen Hinton, a Mississippi native, had a deep dedication to social issues and racial justice. Joe Percoco, who'd worked for my father while he was governor and had joined me at HUD after George Pataki won in 1994, was the total package: trained as a lawyer, he had the guts, brains, and stick-to-itiveness necessary to attack any project—hard. Joe had another trait that served us well: during the worst of times he could make us laugh. Mark Gordon, a brilliant Columbia-educated lawyer, came down from New York. He was disciplined, effective, goal oriented. Other key players on my staff were Kenneth Williams, deputy assistant secretary, and Fred Karnas, deputy assistant secretary for homelessness.

Committed leadership also helps. Vice President Gore was one of the biggest assets of the Empowerment Zones program. After my staff and I sorted through applications from six hundred cities to choose six EZ winners—Atlanta, Baltimore, Chicago, Detroit, New York, and Philadelphia—he headlined a number of our events. It turned out that he and I had several connecting points, including that we were both sons of well-known political fathers. Another was our friend Tom Downey, the former U.S. congressman from Long Island who had brought me to Washington to help on the Clinton transition. The three of us often shot pool together and debated topics of the day, including the 1994 midterm elections and how to reform poverty programs in ways that would make them more effective and win the long-term support of the middle class.

It was always a worthwhile discussion. Al was a wonk first and a politician second. I mean that as a compliment. He is wicked smart, with a scientific and engineering mind. He loves talking policy. President Clinton put him in charge of a major program called the National Performance Review (later renamed the National Partnership for Reinventing Government). Guided by the bestselling *Reinventing Government: How the Entrepreneurial Spirit Is Transforming the Public Sector* by David Osborne and Ted Gaebler, Al and a rotating staff canvassed federal agencies to find ways to streamline the government, making it considerably more efficient and less bloated. Everyone beyond a certain age remembers the Pentagon's $640 toilet seat and Al's hilarious appearance with David Letterman on *Late Show*. The Pentagon had an insane rule that if an ashtray dropped, it had to break. Dave and Al sat there flinging and breaking ashtrays. It was a great way to poke fun at this goofy directive and to tell viewers that the government's wasteful days were ending.

"I know you break ties in the Senate," Letterman joked. "I didn't know about this."

Letterman also played up the veep's caricature as a stiff politician. Let me say for the record: This is inaccurate. Al Gore is, in fact, thoughtful, warm, easygoing and funny—attributes that didn't come across on television.

And effective. He and his team came up with 1,200 recommendations to cut $100 billion in waste, while simultaneously making government user-friendly. Many of the changes were overdue. We were on the cusp of a new millennium, operating with 1950s machinery. While Bill Clinton repositioned government politically and rhetorically, Al fine-tuned it for the next generation. And in doing so, he became my third mentor. The other two were my father and Bill Clinton.

The Clinton years were some of Kerry's and my best. We

bought a spacious five-bedroom house that sat on the top of a hill, overlooking a quiet street in suburban Virginia, a few miles from Hickory Hill. Much of our family time was spent in the kitchen, where we did a little cooking and lots of talking. The gift of gab is one trait that the Cuomos and the Kennedys share.

I received the greatest gifts of my life while we were living in Washington: our children were born. The twins came first, on a bone-chilling day in January 1995. Their deliveries were a family affair: my mother; Kerry's mother; my brother, Chris; and her sister Rory all cheered Kerry on. We honored our mothers by naming the twin girls for them: Cara Ethel and Mariah Matilda.

Holding these tiny beings for the first time was one of the most profound moments of my life. Another came two years later when our third child, Michaela, was born. The connection is immediate and unseverable.

Before we left the hospital with our new family, the floor nurse gave us some advice: "Just get them on the same schedule, and you'll be fine."

She neglected to tell us how difficult it is to get one baby on a schedule. With two, it's impossible. The combination of babies who ate and slept at different times and my new-parent nerves ensured that I was an attentive father—often overly so. Nights lasted forever. Even when the babies slept through, I didn't. I'd hover over their bassinets, straining to hear them breathing.

I was so sleep-deprived during the girls' first year of life that once I dozed off at an event with Gore. I was sitting on-stage while he addressed the audience. Suddenly he said my name: "Blah, blah, blah, Andrew?" I snapped out of my daze, completely disoriented.

Al covered for me. "Andrew and his wife, Kerry, recently had twins, so he isn't really sleeping much," he told the crowd, drawing appreciative laughs.

When the twins were about nine months old, Kerry and I planned a rare date night. The babysitter was a competent, no-nonsense woman who had helped take care of Cara and Mariah from their first day at home. Kerry and I had a relaxing dinner, letting off steam and laughing at the inanities of trying to diaper and feed two squirming babies at once.

When we arrived home after dinner, a police car was parked in front of the house, and the officer said Mariah had been taken to the hospital. She had crawled to a filtered water dispenser we kept in the kitchen, with a big, plastic bottle on top. She was just learning how to stand and reached to pull herself up. As she did, she grabbed the red knob that dispensed hot water. The water ran down her arm and chest, burning her soft skin so that it peeled like wet tissue paper. The burn was extensive. In the hospital the doctors were trying to explain the ramifications. I kept asking for a plastic surgeon to advise us on scarring. Finally the lead doctor grew impatient. "Mr. Cuomo," he said, "the question isn't one of scarring but of 'viability.'"

I couldn't process the word. Viability? What was he trying to say?

Then I understood. My legs went weak. I went to the hospital chapel and prayed. I had never felt such fear in my life.

Kerry and I spent two weeks in the children's burn unit.

In the halls we met other distressed parents and heard their stories. We became familiar with the threatening burns children experience at home: "Spaghetti" burn—"S" shapes seared into a child who pulled a pot off the stove; the pasta that stuck to skin produced burns even more severe than the boiling water, which moved over arms, legs, and torso in seconds. Silverware poked into electric outlets. Water heaters with the temperature set too high.

I have never been more grateful and relieved than I was when we learned Mariah was going to be OK. Parenthood made me hyperaware of dangers I'd never thought of before. We saw so much during our daughter's hospital stay that I promised myself HUD would start an initiative to teach people to childproof their homes. This became the Healthy Homes project.

When I was a new father, someone told me that with children, the days are long but the years fly by. That was true for me with parenthood and work. In what seemed like three and a half weeks, not three and a half years, Clinton and Gore were up for reelection, this time against Republicans Bob Dole and Jack Kemp. Bill and Hillary Clinton and Al and Tipper Gore were reprising their famous bus trip from the 1992 campaign.

Clinton and Dole had two debates, but Al would face off against Jack Kemp in a onetime, winner-take-all contest. It was a tremendous honor, and an even huger amount of pressure, when Al asked me to take charge of his vice presidential debate prep for the October 9 event in Saint Petersburg, Florida. The hardest part of a political debate falls on the candidates, because they're the ones who have to think on their feet. But the better versed they are on the issues, the easier it is for them to press a point to their advantage.

A small campaign staff and I put together notebooks on every issue that might arise: affirmative action, the economy, the Family and Medical Leave Act, foreign policy. It was also my job to make sure Al was culturally current. Could he discuss the hit movie *Fargo*? I knew he was familiar with the "Macarena," because he'd performed it at the Democratic National Convention in Chicago. But was he up on popular singer Tracy Chapman and the hit band Everything But the Girl? Did he have opinions on the bestselling books *Men Are from Mars, Women Are from Venus* or *Primary Colors*?

Al was a hands-on public servant and naturally curious, so nothing we covered was new to him. But ninety minutes is a long time to be under bright lights with an opponent who's playing gotcha. As vice president he needed to be able to reel off the fine points that would help frame Bill Clinton's accomplishments. I spent a dozen hours thinking of tough questions and a dozen more critiquing Al's rehearsals. Did he misstate a fact? Was his tone off? Did he hesitate before answering? How the vice presidential contenders square off adds to the narrative that builds around the presidential candidates. I appreciated Gore's faith in me. He knew I would tell the truth about his performance.

I have had a stomach flip or two when I've faced a tough crowd. But I have never been as anxious about anyone's performance as I was waiting for Al Gore to answer the first debate question at the Mahaffey Theater in Saint Petersburg.

Wasted worry. Al refused to get ruffled. I thought he came

off as smart and decisive. For the most part the media con-curred. One observer wrote, "As with past veep face-offs, the event was not expected to shake up the presidential contest, and it didn't. But the match probably helped the Clinton campaign more than the Dole effort."

I later used the skills I picked up as Al's debate coach to help my daughters prep for school plays. Together we have memorized the lines for the mean-spirited orphanage matron Miss Hannigan in *Annie*, and I can probably still sing "Memory" from the musical *Cats*. Watching my daugh-ters perform always filled me with both pride and nerves.

On Election Night 1996, with 49 percent of the popular vote to Dole's 41 percent (and Ross Perot's 8 percent), Bill Clinton became the only Democratic president in the twen-tieth century besides Franklin Roosevelt to win reelection.

Even before the election I had started thinking about what I might do next. Henry Cisneros had announced his plan to resign as secretary of HUD. Henry was a superstar. He was a natural: handsome, brilliant, charismatic. He was a hero of the Hispanic community. I believe he could well have been Al Gore's running mate in 2000 had he not had the unfortunate political handicap of a "special prosecutor" dogging him. He had been under investigation by an independent counsel since 1995 over allegations that he had lied to the FBI during his background check about payments to a former mistress. Indicted in 1997, he pleaded guilty to a misdemeanor and was later pardoned by President Clinton. The "independent counsels" were one of the tactics of the partisan Republican

Congress. I also believe that if Henry had been the candidate for vice president on the ticket, Gore would have won the presidency. Henry was that good. And he was good to me. He was a patient teacher, and I learned much from him. I thought I'd done a good job as assistant secretary, but I thought it was unlikely that Bill Clinton would tap me to become secretary—and I was unlikely to stay if he didn't. I had to plan a new life.

About a week before Christmas, I got a surprise phone call. "Andrew," President Clinton said, "I'd like you to take the helm at HUD." The political strategist James Carville has said that when speaking with a president, you should always make sure you have the last three words. I remembered to use that strategy in this conversation: "Yes, Mr. President," I said.

I hung up, elated because of—and in spite of—the job ahead. At best, HUD was chronically dysfunctional and terribly managed for decades; at worst, it was corrupt. It hadn't had a clean financial audit since its start. Its programs were too often ineffective and outdated, many performing far below what taxpayers should reasonably expect—and what communities and residents deserved. Its buildings were often government-sponsored ghettos. It took the higher ideals articulated by Democrats and destroyed them on the cold reality of failed execution.

In 1994, as part of their conservative revolution, Republicans wanted to dismantle the agency. HUD was a political lightning rod: as Democrats embraced it, conservatives wanted to discredit it. Just before becoming Speaker of the House, Newt Gingrich told the *Washington Post*: "You could abolish HUD tomorrow morning and improve life in most of America." Even Cisneros had admitted that HUD "allowed itself to evolve into a bureaucracy far more attentive to process than to results, characterized by slavish loyalty to non-performing programs and insufficient trust in the initiatives of local leaders."

The failure was due in part to a flawed program design and in part to the people who ran it before Cisneros. The worst offender was Ronald Reagan's two-term HUD secretary, Samuel Pierce. Pierce spent eight years in his office watching soap operas and out of his office on taxpayer-paid overseas junkets. Under his watch billions of dollars were lost to fraud, theft, mismanagement, and favoritism.

In the early 1990s, HUD's inspector general described the agency's future as "dim," and for three consecutive years the nonpartisan General Accounting Office (GAO), which investigates how tax dollars are spent and reports to Congress, had designated HUD "a high-risk area for waste, fraud, and abuse." Usually the GAO gives this label to a single program or division. HUD was the only cabinet-level agency in its entirety to receive the rating. Not one or two bad apples spoiling the barrel—the GAO said the whole barrel was rotten. It was a dubious and dangerous distinction because if the agency remained "high-risk," it would inevitably be shuttered. The GAO report pinpointed four long-standing department-wide deficiencies: "weak internal controls, an ineffective organizational structure, an insufficient mix of staff with the proper skills, and inadequate information and financial management systems." HUD's weaknesses made hundreds of billions of dollars in insured mortgages, housing subsidies, and community development vulnerable to loss and improper payments.

Given this abysmal track record and the damning evaluation from the government's top watchdog, in 1996, Republican presidential candidate Bob Dole, who called public housing authorities "landlords of misery," promised to eliminate the department if he won the White House.

Putting a fine and painful exclamation point on all this, just two weeks before Election Day the *New York Times Magazine* ran a cover story about subsidized housing, noting that before Ronald Reagan became president, some 400,000 Americans received subsidized housing. But the budget passed by Congress that President Clinton signed in 1996 provided not one new affordable unit. "The death of affordable housing—what a strange notion in a nation as spectacularly housed as this one," the *Times* wrote. It was a searing commentary on the agency whose fundamental legal mission was "a decent home and a suitable living environment for every American family."

HUD, the *Times* added, was a "discredited bureaucracy with an unpopular cause." Not exactly the description you'd fantasize about for the agency you were nominated to take over.

The question to me as a "next generation" Democrat was simple but profound. Was the dream that HUD was meant to embody just a pretty speech and a fanciful vision, or could it actually be realized and if so could government realize it?

The odds seemed tremendously adverse. After all, there was a thirty-year history of failed attempts.

Either a "next generation" Democrat must admit past government failings, resolve the issues, and make government work, or the conservatives were right. Could we "reinvent" HUD, and actually realize its vision efficiently and effectively? Could we reform a massive bureaucracy to perform with competence and integrity? The nation wanted to know. Congress wanted to know. I wanted to know. This was the place and time to find out.

Although the agency's prospects were bleak, I was excited and charged to the bone. If confirmed, I would be one of the youngest cabinet secretaries in our country's history. I was ready for the job. And around that same time I received other, more life-changing news: Kerry was pregnant with our third child.

Life was good.

In January 1997 I sat at a table across from the members of the Senate Banking, Housing, and Urban Affairs Committee for my confirmation hearing. A sizable crowd of Cuomos and Kennedys were on hand to silently (and, with two-year-old Cara there, not so silently) cheer me on. Mariah had had a meltdown as we were leaving the house and stayed home with a babysitter. "Mariah heard that the Section 8 renewal issue was going to come up," I joked with committee members.

It was a proud day for me. A fellow New Yorker, Senator Daniel Patrick Moynihan, who was chairman of the powerful Senate Finance Committee, made a guest appearance to introduce me. Senator Moynihan was a hero of mine. I had watched him when I was a young man. He was an effective role model—smart and principled. His eloquence and powers of persuasion made him a New York legend. It was an honor to have his stamp on my nomination.

Before he became a senator, Moynihan, who trained as a sociologist, was an assistant secretary during the Kennedy and Johnson administrations at the U.S. Department of Labor, where he was one of the architects of the War on Poverty. His controversial landmark 1965 report, "The Negro Family: The Case for National Action," usually known as the "Moynihan Report," argued that the prevalence of single-mother families in African American society was slowing its economic progress. He went on to become a U.S. ambassador and then a four-term senator known for speaking his mind.

Referring to a conversation we had had a few days earlier about public housing, Senator Moynihan told the committee I had shown "the beginning of all wisdom."

Senator Ted Kennedy, Kerry's uncle, was very helpful in the confirmation. During our time in Washington I developed a warm relationship with him. A big part of my job as assistant secretary was seeing firsthand how different communities were faring. I got a lot of opportunities to watch Ted in action in his home state, Massachusetts. He was one of the country's all-time great retail politicians: no community was too small for him to visit. He always took the time to shake hands and have his photo snapped. He knew the importance of showing up, of letting people know that government was working for them and that he was bringing home the bacon.

On the day I was confirmed as secretary, he sent me a gift. It was a flag that had flown over the Capitol that morning. Today it is a treasured keepsake.

The senators were cordial. Senator Al D'Amato was chair of the Senate Committee on Banking, Housing, and Urban affairs that oversaw HUD. We had been political opponents in New York, but Al knew that there was no reason to stop my confirmation and that confirming a New Yorker was good for the state. He was personally supportive, but it was clear that the Republican senators had little time or patience for HUD, and they took turns warning me about the quagmire I faced. I gathered that they did not think I—or anyone— could fix the agency.

"HUD has problems, both financial and operational," said Richard Shelby, a Republican from Alabama. "Mr. Cuomo knows that. Money is not the answer."

Another Republican, Lauch Faircloth, from North Carolina, said: "We spent billions of dollars on the cities, and yet we have to ask ourselves a very fundamental question: Are the cities better off than they were thirty years ago? And I think we would have to say, no. . . . HUD has, so far, lost the ability to manage itself, which is going to present an enormous challenge to you, Mr. Cuomo."

The senators cited the intractable poverty in every region of the country and repeatedly reported the many ways HUD had made the bad worse. They never challenged the goal of HUD—helping the poor—they challenged only the means and the results.

An hour and twenty minutes later when I got to speak I didn't try to defend the indefensible. I said:

If we were allowed to make a decision between fiscal prudence and meeting the needs of these Americans, it would be a tough choice. But in truth we don't have that choice. We have an undeniable responsibility to balance the budget. No one would argue that. But at the same time we have an equally undeniable responsibility to meet the needs of troubled Americans. We have to do both. . . . With a government that is smarter, smaller, and better. As the president said, we have to do more with less. . . . We must recognize that the role of government in the private sector has to be looked at in terms of partnerships that can be forged. I understand this in a very personal way. . . . I entered this field not as a government official, but as a builder and operator, a manager responsible for meeting the payroll and balancing a budget. I learned that the object of our efforts must be the development of self-sufficiency, not the perpetuation of government programs. My experience taught me that the pride and dignity of having a job and earning one's own bread is still the best social services program that exists. I learned that the private sector is the engine that's going to drive the rebirth of a community, and that the real solutions are not going to be found in Washington, are not going to be found within the Beltway, but will be found when we unleash the potential of local communities across this country. I will look to these experiences to guide me as I seek to fulfill HUD's mission.

I'm certain that the senators on the Banking Committee were expecting me to be a hard-charging liberal who would say the Republicans were wrong and would insist that HUD ran like a well-oiled machine. They thought I'd say that anyone who opposed HUD was a racist, classist conservative. I knew that's what they were prepared to hear because that's what Democrats had said for twenty years. They thought that since I was a New York Democrat, I would worship at the altar of big government.

Instead my response, in essence, was, If you're right you're right—we must be willing to admit that some programs don't work. If HUD couldn't be fixed, then we should stop trying, and I would sign the letter dismantling it.

Either it works or it doesn't.

Having traveled around the country and seen poverty and suffering that were much worse than anything in New York, I was deeply committed to HUD's mission. As assistant secretary I had visited the Chicago Housing Authority with a group of bureaucrats in suits. The public housing in the Windy City had become the worst symbol of our seemingly futile quest to deal with urban poverty. It is also entirely government-created: built, subsidized, and perpetuated. When we came up the staircase of one high-rise, I spotted an African American girl, maybe six years old, on the landing. She was looking through a filthy window covered with thick iron bars—it was as if she were looking through a prison window. The cinder block walls had been painted beige, and the dimples in the cement were filled with grime. The girl turned around and looked at us impassively. Ten years had passed since I'd visited the Martinique Hotel in New York, but this brought me right back. I thought it could be the same child I saw in the hall watching her mother turn tricks. This youngster was long past despair. She looked resigned. Her eyes were blank, as if she'd seen so many awful things that she could no longer feel. Nothing could surprise her.

I'm especially sensitive to the problems and challenges of young girls because of my daughters. I'm brought back to my role as protector and caregiver for my three sisters. There can be no greater cause than to improve the lives of children in need.

Once confirmed, I gathered my senior team in the secretary's conference room. Many who were with me as assistant secretary stayed, including Karen Hinton, my press secretary; Howard Glaser, deputy general counsel; Jacquie Lawing, deputy chief of staff; and Joe Percoco, special assistant to the secretary. They were joined by Jon Cowan, my new chief of staff, who had been a valued adviser to Henry Cisneros and acting assistant secretary for public affairs. He was from California and one of the bright young stars who came to revolutionize Washington. He was a pioneer and Generation X leader. Rhoda Glickman and her husband, Dan, who served as secretary of agriculture under Bill Clinton, were close friends from my time in Washington. Rhoda had been crucial in preparing me for my confirmation hearings, and I knew that as a senior adviser she would pay close attention to our critical congressional relationships and push our agenda.

Saul Ramirez, who took my spot as assistant secretary in community planning and development, had been the longtime mayor of Laredo, Texas, and had a great deal of experience. Also on my team were Alvin Brown, special adviser; Joe Hacala, adviser for faith outreach; Bill Apgar, the head of the Federal Housing Administration; Gail Laster, general counsel; Mercedes Marquez, senior counsel for civil rights and fair housing; Jacqueline Johnson, liaison for Indian affairs; Michael Steadman, assistant secretary for policy research and development; Chris Lehane, special counsel; and Christine Pelosi, special assistant.

Henry Cisneros had taken significant steps toward fixing HUD. Under a program called HOPE VI, he'd dynamited some of the worst public housing and began replacing it with attractive, small-scale, mixed-income apartments that blended into the community. He'd started streamlining the agency, downsizing the staff, and consolidating programs and departments. He made great progress, but more was left to do. "Compassion without competence has failed HUD and the people we are here to serve," I told my new staff.

We discussed a phased plan. First, get our own house in order. Design programs that would work to provide housing and develop communities that would accomplished the mission. This included finding the right role for government and the private sector that would be efficient and fraud resistant. Second, test and prove the progressive model and then deploy it and make a difference on the ground. Third, build public support for the agency's mission.

With one caveat: Step One can kill you! "The hours will be long," I said. "We'll be working weekends. But when you resent coming in at nine o'clock on a Saturday morning, remember that the people we're helping have it far worse.

Second, this is not just about fixing an agency. This is about proving a vision that reaches back to FDR. HUD is the poster child for incompetence now. But in two years, we will be the poster child for reinvention."

We met with the Government Accounting Office, read its reports, and interviewed hundreds of civil servants. When anyone said that something had been done because "that's the way it's always done," we'd come back with, "Why?" The expression we used was "Peel the onion." Ask the next question and the next and the next. Even if it makes you cry! We looked at computer systems, federal housing subsidies, accounting systems, public housing, grant programs, and job classifications. Everyplace you looked you found problems.

For example, there was no staffing plan for the department. HUD had some ten thousand employees, but there was often a shortage of people assigned to the most important jobs. There had been no realignment of staff in decades.

It was too late to tinker. We had to replace the engine. Once we knew fundamental reorganization was our only option, I called a meeting with the head of HUD Council 222 of the American Federation of Government Employees (AFGE), the union that represented thousands of HUD employees. "So we're clear," he said, "if you're going to try to move desks and reconfigure offices, that's something we're going to have to talk about, because that's going to be very disruptive."

"The distance from the person's desk to the window?" I asked. "We're talking about a whole different magnitude of change here."

It became clear that union opposition would deal us a major blow in advancing our agenda. The union people didn't just want to tweak it; they wanted to crush it. If they succeeded, they would stop the bulk of our plan. The lesson I learned is that you can't just have a well-thought-out strategy—you also have to make sure you've done your homework to get buy-in. We needed to upend the culture, and I needed to communicate that I was not just another in a series of secretaries happy with the status quo. So we went back at it, determined to win over as many employees as we could and take on the union where we had to.

We eliminated every position in the department and replaced each one with a new job description in a new organization. Over the long term, we planned to decrease the payroll by three thousand jobs. HUD employees stayed seventeen years on average, and I understood why they went ballistic over our reform plan. But I also knew this: if we didn't save HUD from extinction, *everyone* would be out of work.

I brought together department heads for coffees and had one-on-one conversations and group meetings. I made speeches that were broadcast to the entire department, and my senior staff members spent extensive time talking to their employees. The message was the same and delivered over and over: we believe deeply in your commitment and talent as civil servants; but not only to save the agency but to save your jobs, we're going to have to rethink how HUD operates.

We painted a picture of how this new structure would work—why it would allow them to do their jobs more effectively, what the logic was behind our strategy, how each of our proposals worked. We also made clear that the days of denial and half measures were over. We preached and sold and cajoled, arguing that it just wouldn't work anymore to say no; it was time to say yes, to embrace change, however daunting, and that change must touch every corner of the agency. All of us needed to get behind this plan, and that would require them to press their union leadership to back it, as this was very likely the final chance that HUD had to really turn itself around and get off the high-risk list: "Every day, every month, every year, we are on that list, your job is also at risk, so the stakes for you, for the people you passionately serve, and the cause we are all fighting for couldn't be higher."

The union took us to court. I'm not antiunion, so I hated having to fight against it. But the HUD mission had become so twisted that it was as though the vendors and the unions had become our programs' beneficiaries. That was not the point. Taxes were to be used not to fund a bureaucracy but to help the poor.

The mismanagement of HUD was staggering. At one point, I asked to see a list of HUD's properties throughout the country.

The incredible response: "We don't have a list."

I was dumbfounded. "HUD is the largest landlord in the country, owning tens of thousands of buildings outright and funding tens of thousands of private units," I said. "And we don't have a record of what and where they are?" We did have the names of the Section 8 landlords to whom we mailed checks. (Section 8 is a program by which landlords rent to tenants who receive a government housing subsidy.) Most of them had been private developers who had built apartment houses in the 1970s and agreed to accept Section 8 tenants in return for twenty-year contracts with the federal government. It was a guaranteed revenue stream that lasted longer than it took to raise a child. In exchange, the landlords were supposed to keep the buildings well maintained.

But no one from HUD ever followed up. The agency paid the subsidy to the owner every month, and over time actually lost the information on the location of the buildings. HUD didn't know where they were—not to mention the condition, compliance, etc.

We started at square one, calling the landlords to ask where the apartments were located. From the addresses we had on file, it seemed as though a great many of the buildings were in Florida. But we learned that wasn't the case. Florida was where a huge number of landlords had retired and were receiving their subsidy checks.

Every year property managers were required to submit their building's financials. HUD had rooms filled with these tax forms, each one quite thick—thousands upon thousands stacked in boxes that were stacked on more boxes, under years of accumulated dust. No one had read them. Ever. Our job was to provide tenants with a clean, decent place to live. We had no idea if the landlords were ripping us off or if the tenants were eligible for subsidies.

Our solution was to establish the HUD Real Estate Assessment Center (REAC). One of my advisers, Gary Eisenman, whom I'd known since law school, went to the U.S. Department of Energy, which had created a handheld device for assessing nuclear reactors—a rudimentary precursor to an electronic tablet not unlike what UPS uses to track packages. We asked the department to reconfigure the device for our

purposes and then sent hundreds of newly hired HUD in-
spectors into the field to score buildings against an electronic
checklist, read by a central computer. Next we mailed a questionnaire asking tenants to rate their satisfaction with their
buildings: plumbing, upkeep, cleanliness, etc. This was the
first time any of them had been asked. It was unconsciona-
ble that the federal government was operating in a way that
would sink even a mom-and-pop shop.

Taking an inventory of our properties was a significant
first step, but when we found scandalous abuse, the agency
didn't have the authority to press criminal charges. Our only
option was to file civil suits for unscrupulous behavior, but
unless we had an airtight case, it was as good as letting bad
landlords off the hook.

In its thirty-odd years, HUD had brought only a handful of
fraud cases. There was no expectation that HUD would even
check the landlords' financial reports. That had to change.
We had to do a better job of protecting the agency's funds. I
called Louis Freeh at the Federal Bureau of Investigation and
posed an unusual question: "Would you consider assigning
an agent to HUD to head a new enforcement unit?" He sent
us a top-shelf, white-collar career investigator named Ed
Krauss. Ed helped us to establish an enforcement center and
create fraud-detection software. We stopped accepting the
paper financials that had been piling up. When an electronic
form came back, we could tell how much money landlords
were getting paid, what their maintenance costs were, and
what profit they were making. If the numbers didn't add up,
the system would spit those forms out for more scrutiny. And
most important, Ed and the new enforcement center would

ensure that we could not only gather the information and track wrongdoing, but then also assemble a solid case for the Department of Justice to pursue criminal fraud charges. Instead of looking the other way, we would now be a real threat to anyone thinking of ripping off the government.

To announce the changes, I told my staff, "Let's get an invitation for the annual landlord conference. I want to alert the entire industry to this crackdown."

"I wouldn't do that, Andrew," Jon Cowan said. "There's going to be a huge backlash. The quieter we are about this, the better. These people are politically connected. They will call the White House. You don't want that." Jon is a perfectionist with balance, judgment, and an unerring sense of how things will play out in any given situation. I was lucky to be working with someone who was both a big-picture and a little-picture guy. Ordinarily I listened to him. But not this time.

"I don't mind," I said. "We should be kicking up dust. Some of these guys have gotten away with bad behavior for twenty years. I don't want my message to be, 'Tsk, tsk.' I want them to know that things are different now. Half of enforcement is posting warnings. When you see a sign that says 'No Speeding/Photo Enforced,' you slow down. You don't have to see a cop with a radar gun. You just have to *think* he's there and you slow down. That's human nature.

"At HUD the opposite has been true," I said. "Landlords know no one's checking up on them. My message to them is: 'Watch your step.'"

And that's what I did. I stood before hundreds of people in Washington's convention center. "There's a new sheriff in town," I said. "I've recruited an FBI agent to make sure you're doing what you say. Bad actors spoil it for everyone," I went on. "We're going to make it good for the rest of you. If you're taking care of your property, you don't need to worry. But if you haven't been treating your tenants properly, make no mistake. We will come after you. The days of nonenforcement are over."

No one gave me a standing ovation. The landlords were offended. To them my takeaway message sounded like, You're all crooks. But my point was that when you have no system to determine who's good and who's bad, everyone is suspect.

I understood their reaction, but I didn't let it get to me—or impede the new program. We weren't trying to be popular; we were just trying to be productive.

Even the physical space at HUD was dysfunctional. We decided early on to bring the offices down to street level. "HUD Next Door" opened bright, accessible storefronts in cities across the country. We installed kiosks in high-traffic areas so that if it was after 5 P.M. and the storefront office was closed homeless people looking for a place to sleep could find the closest shelter. Someone who needed a housing subsidy could find the number for the local housing authority.

The HUD workforce had been in government so long that they had not experienced many of the latest economic, housing, and community development practices. We needed new blood desperately. The problem was that no one wanted to go to work for HUD. Nor did I want career bureaucrats. I wanted people current in the field who could bring practical, state-of-the-art knowledge. We designed a midcareer program and required a two-year commitment. We also offered a program supervised by Harvard's Kennedy School that would give a Certification in Housing and Urban Development. We likened it to the Peace Corps, and Sargent Shriver was a spokesperson for the program. Shriver was a genuine inspiration and a present-day reminder of the magic of the 1960s, when he had headed the fledgling Peace Corps.

When you make changes you make many people angry. In my first couple of years as secretary, the Republican Congress held one hearing after another on HUD. The Republicans were suspicious of everything we tried. The *Washington Times*, a conservative newspaper started in 1982 by the Unification Church's founder, the Reverend Sun Myung Moon, to counteract liberal newspapers, called community builders "HUD's biggest fiasco in recent years. . . . Styled as an 'urban peace corps.'"

Washington was my first exposure to the conservative media machine. Fox News, which was launched in 1996, was the TV equivalent of the *Washington Times*. For months the *Times* ran a series of vicious articles attacking HUD, fed by members of the Gingrich-led House of Representatives. "Facts" were often misstated. Successes were overlooked. I made our case to the editorial board, but the following Sunday I woke up to another front-page story about dysfunction at HUD. Either my powers of persuasion had failed, or the editors were determined not to be persuaded. But we were making progress where it counted. We prevailed against the union in court. We also took our case to union members, over the heads of their leadership.

The GAO hadn't yet taken us off the high-risk list, but in

May 1998, David Osborne, coauthor of *Reinventing Government*, evaluated our reform plan, HUD 2020. "HUD today is a different place than it was a year ago," he wrote, adding, "The agency that was a symbol for government scandal in the 1980s could very well be a model for reinvention in the 1990s."

Two years later the GAO reported that HUD had made "credible progress in overhauling its operations to correct its management deficiencies." When I took over as secretary in February 1997, our annual budget was $19.4 billion. We knew we'd made progress when, in 1999, Congress increased our budget to $25.2 billion, and, after turning down our requests for four years, funded 50,000 new housing vouchers. This was life-changing for families who would finally get off waiting lists and into homes and a symbolic turning point in the debate about the future of HUD.

If you work in Washington, one of the first things you notice when you walk into any federal building, even the West Wing of the White House, is a wall of sixteen-by-twenty photos promoting the successes of that agency—smiling cabinet secretaries cutting ribbons or surrounded by children. I thought, You never see the failures. At the NASA building you see pictures of the latest rocket being launched, not the ones that exploded. The federal highway administration doesn't show the bridges that collapsed. Health and Human Services doesn't show pictures of people on food stamps. I decided to do something different.

The economy was booming. A record number of jobs were

being created. Unemployment was at a historic low. About 7 million Americans had been lifted out of poverty.

But not everyone was part of the bounce-back. So when visitors walked into HUD, they faced a two-story wall filled with jumbo photos of places and people in need. Latino families in the *colonias* in Texas, near the Mexican border, living in poverty without running water or electricity; neighborhoods destroyed by floods or hurricanes; Indian reservations in Alaska; living conditions that looked like those in a developing country, not America on the cusp of the twenty-first century. When visitors asked the receptionists why HUD showcased these images, they would answer: because we want to remind employees that we're here not to pat ourselves on the back for the work that's been done but to focus on all that's left to do.

Drawing attention to "the people and places left behind" was crucial, and, happily, I worked for a president who felt the same. Clinton, having grown up in Arkansas, with little money and no father, was tuned in to the nation's poverty. As he said in his 1999 State of the Union Address, "Our greatest untapped markets are not overseas—they are right here at home." That summer I accompanied him on a "new markets" tour, along with a delegation of senators, entrepreneurs, bankers, my family, and an overflow press plane. We stopped in places like Detroit and East St. Louis, Illinois— on-the-edge places that could go either way. They had the potential to change for the better, or to become the next Mississippi Delta, overwhelmed by circumstances and overlooked by policy makers. East St. Louis, across the Mississippi River from its better-known Missouri counterpart, had been a thriving blue-collar town whose fortunes plummeted when railroad and meatpacking jobs went elsewhere. A new freeway sliced through once-cohesive neighborhoods. By the 1990s the city's population had dropped by half, to around forty thousand people. Residents lived in such extreme poverty that there wasn't enough money in the town's coffers to put gas in its police cars. Sewers overflowed. Garbage pickup stopped. In 1998, the *New York Times* called it "the epitome of a dying town." With only one store, a grocery store, it was also a retail desert. We realized that income and jobs and business opportunities were being lost in places like these, where townspeople had to go outside the city limits to buy anything. Our stop highlighted the opening of a new Walgreens drugstore, funded in part by HUD community block grant money and built by a developer who understood that the people who live there need the same services as anybody else, rich or poor.

We also visited Pine Ridge Indian Reservation in South Dakota, the second-largest reservation in the country. HUD had been working with the Oglala Sioux there for more than a year. Rugged and isolated, it is a place of weather extremes: 116 degrees in summer and 40 degrees below zero in winter. Pine Ridge is the rural equivalent of the Chicago Housing Authority. It is a place overwhelmed by alcohol, drug abuse, unemployment, teen suicide, and a violent crime rate three times the national average. We were working on home ownership as a way to develop community stability.

Not a simple task. Questions about land ownership made it hard to get loans from the local bank. If you understood the culture you could see why. Native Americans traditionally believe that the Earth owns the land. The tribal elders board believed it owned the land. The bank's question was: If a loan goes bad, who's accountable? Mother Earth didn't qualify and collecting a bad debt from the reservation was not a reasonable expectation. Our solution was to start a nonprofit and provide a staffer to work with banks and homeowners. We recruited potential homeowners with the means to pay a mortgage. Then we arranged a deal with a prefab homebuilder.

Bill Clinton understood the power of the office: a presidential drop-in makes even the worst situations—a tornado in Arkansas, an African village hit hard by AIDS, a school in the wake of gun violence—feel fixable. It gives victims hope, and sometimes hope is enough to cause change.

Since the beginning of his second term, President Clinton had invited me to join his Wednesday-night group at the White House. This standing get-together was more relaxed than other meetings the president attended. We gathered in the "Yellow Oval," a sitting room in the family's private quarters, above the Oval Office. It got its nickname from its wall color and shape. Our neckties loosened, we'd go over new polling data and discuss what we heard and saw as we traveled around the country. President Clinton was wary of the Washington bubble. It was important to him to know how his policies were being received beyond the Beltway. At times these meetings took place against a backdrop of the personal troubles that beset his presidency.

In the 1960s and '70s, HUD worked with the World Bank and the United Nations in developing countries. We resumed that earlier mission under Clinton, assisting Mexico and countries in Central America and the Caribbean. To-gether we focused on four areas: housing finance, technol-ogy, community development, and urban planning. In 1998 I traveled to China, where I met with government officials and agreed to help them with two pilot projects—one on af-fordable housing and the other on mortgage securitization.

A year later I was thrilled to represent the United States on a binational commission with President Nelson Mandela's post-apartheid government in South Africa. One of Mande-la's campaign issues five years earlier was a promise of new affordable housing. Better living conditions would help close the housing gap between whites and people of color. Because white bankers had a history of refusing to give mortgages to black people, Housing Minister Sankie Mthembi-Mahanyele and I discussed how to introduce and enforce fair-housing and lending practices. In 2000, when the South African parliament passed a mortgage disclosure act to protect the poor from discrimination, the Housing Ministry publicly ac-knowledged HUD's help.

Housing discrimination was also on HUD's agenda at home. Almost thirty years had passed since the Fair Hous-ing Act became law. Enacted by LBJ in 1968, one week after the Reverend Dr. Martin Luther King Jr.'s death, it prohibits discrimination in the sale, rental, and financing of homes and apartments on the basis of race, sex, religion, national origin, family status, or disability. The law had a terrific impact, but there were still weak spots. To counter this, Pres-ident Clinton challenged our agency to double the number of Fair Housing enforcement actions that were brought against violators during his first term. Some of the hate crimes we investigated—incidents we called "discrimination with a fist"—such as cross burnings in people's front yards made us feel that we were back in the Jim Crow South. Other violators had modernized to "cyberhate." One case of housing discrimination via the Internet came to our attention in 1998 after Bonnie Jouhari, a fair-housing advocate in Reading, Pennsylvania, found a flyer on her car that read "Race Traitor Beware." It was illustrated with a picture of a Klansman and noose. Roy Frankhouser, a self-described chaplain and grand dragon of the United Klans of America, was making threatening phone calls and stalking Jouhari, sitting outside her office and snapping photos of her, which he displayed on his weekly cable access call-in show, *White Forum*. At the same time, Ryan Wilson, a white supremacist, ran her picture on his hate group's website holding a threat she'd received in the mail from Frankhouser with the message: "Traitors like this should beware, for in our day, they will be hung from the nearest tree or lamp post." Wilson called Jouhari's biracial daughter, Pilar Danielle Horton, a "mongrel," adding another hateful message: "If those people are still alive when the political tide swings back to the right . . . they will find our wrath something to be dealt with."

Jouhari and her daughter fled Reading for Seattle, but the KKK threats followed them across the country. They received harassing phone calls and, at one point, found a dead rabbit on their doorstep, and they had to move again.

We brought—and won—a fair-housing case on the grounds that the white supremacists were interfering with the right of Jouhari and her daughter to live in a community. The white supremacist Wilson was fined $1 million. Besides paying damages to Jouhari, Frankhouser agreed to publicly apologize to the women, attend eighty hours of sensitivity training, perform one thousand hours of community service, and broadcast fair-housing public service announcements on his KKK TV show. He also had to post a HUD fair-housing poster on the outside of his house. I was pleased that Frankhouser could no longer spread hate, though I don't think he thought so highly of me. He told a reporter: "Andrew Cuomo can kiss my rebel derriere."

And while we renewed the agency's commitment to fully enforcing the nation's fair-housing laws, we also focused on helping more Americans get their piece of the dream and buy a home. For decades, through the Federal Housing Administration and in its oversight of mortgage lenders Fannie Mae and Freddie Mac, HUD had been a leading player in home ownership. When President Clinton made raising the U.S. homeownership rate a signature goal, he challenged us to add as many as 8 million new homeowners to the rolls between 1995 and 2000. We worked hard to help make that happen, enabling millions more Americans to afford a home of their own and raising the rate from 64.2 percent to 67.7 percent.

In the wake of the Great Recession, from 2007 to 2009, some critics tried to pin the blame for the foreclosure crisis on my time at HUD in the late 1990s, but that was an inaccurate rewriting of history. While we were passionate about raising the homeownership rate, we were also increasingly concerned about the growth of subprime lending and its effect on borrowers. As HUD secretary, I held a series of public hearings around the country to examine lending issues and concluded that too many in the banking industry were beginning to fuel risky residential lending with insufficient oversight. In 2000 these hearings culminated in a major 120-page report, "Curbing Predatory Home Mortgage Lending," which outlined sweeping recommendations to help stop banks from ramping up risky lending. Had our warnings been heeded, many home buyers would have avoided the toxic loans and foreclosures that began to swell in 2007. Instead the Bush administration ignored the report, loosening rather than tightening financial regulation. It wasn't until 2010 that the bulk of recommendations were adopted when President Obama signed the financial reform act that overhauled the nation's financial system. Similarly, when I ran for governor, the *Wall Street Journal* asserted that "in the wake of Mr. Cuomo's agitation, Fannie and Freddie's purchases of subprime loans skyrocketed." I left HUD in 2001, and Fannie Mae and Freddie Mac did not step up their purchases of subprime assets until after 2004, when the Bush administration allowed the companies to triple their subprime securities holdings. As a direct consequence of the Bush administration's aggressively pushing Fannie and Freddie into the subprime market, the companies purchased or guaranteed more loans from risky borrowers from 2005 to 2008 than in all prior years combined.

The Working Group on Financial Markets, established by Ronald Reagan after the 1987 stock market crash, got the history right when, in 2008, it conclusively stated that "the turmoil in the financial markets clearly was triggered by a dramatic weakening of underwriting standards for U.S. subprime mortgages, beginning in late 2004 and extending into

2007." The disastrous decline in standards occurred years after President Clinton's and my time in Washington. The Bush administration discarded badly needed protections. One glaring example: on its watch, Fannie and Freddie no longer had to fully document a borrower's ability to repay, undoing the significant underwriting standards that we had put in place at HUD.

I knew Al Gore counted on my help in the presidential race of 2000, and I knew the country would benefit if he were elected. When I hit the road to campaign for him, those par- allel thoughts pushed me past exhaustion. The last ten days before the election were a flat-out run. Flying from one swing state to another, we hit Virginia and Florida, made our case in Camden and Newark, New Jersey, and then did three stops in Pennsylvania—a big rally in Pittsburgh, Scranton, and State College—before Philly on Sunday. On Monday night, we were revving up the vote in Cincinnati.

Campaigns are insular and full of adrenaline. And as much as politicians say they don't pay attention to the polls, when the numbers are tilted toward a win, the gung-ho, full- speed-ahead energy they create is contagious. Some final polls showed Al Gore and George W. Bush in a statistical tie. Bush was up in Gore's home state of Tennessee. Gore was up in Florida, where Bush's brother Jeb was governor.

On Election Day the first good news came at 8 P.M. On the basis of projections from exit polls, the Associated Press and all of the major news networks—CNN, NBC, Fox, CBS, MSNBC, and ABC—declared that Gore had carried Florida.

By 10 P.M., the networks had retracted their prediction and placed Florida back in the "undecided" column.

At 2:30 the next morning the networks made their third declaration. They called Florida and, with it, the presidency, for Bush.

Al Gore spoke to Bush and congratulated him on the win. Then, on the way to deliver his concession speech, he was called back. The count was too close for him to surrender. He telephoned George Bush and retracted his earlier call conceding the election.

I joined Gore and other top aides in a seventh-floor suite at the Loews Vanderbilt Hotel. It was the middle of the night, and everyone was on the phone. We flipped between CNN and NBC, where my old pal Tim Russert was using a whiteboard that read "Florida, Florida, Florida" to explain the goings-on. A recount was a given.

It had been a week of almost no sleep at all, and an Election Day of hope replaced by despair and now, renewed hope. Both campaigns were thrown into chaos, but we were confident.

The candidates put together chad teams for the recount. Gore had Clinton's former secretary of state Warren Christopher. Bush brought in James Baker, the former secretary of state and utility player from his father's administration.

Optimistic at HUD, we proceeded as if transitioning to a Gore administration, but we were caught in limbo. No one in the White House was talking transition. All we could do was continue to function and to prepare for the end of the year as if things were the way we trusted they would be when the decision was made.

But with each day, the situation got uglier. The recount introduced a new low for cutthroat politics. After Thanksgiving we started to have doubts. Frustration also doubled by the day. After five contentious weeks the U.S. Supreme Court stopped the recount, not because it was right or wrong but because it could not be completed by the December 12 deadline. Gore disagreed with the Court's decision but said, "For the sake of our unity as a people and the strength of our democracy, I offer my concession."

A lingering death, it turns out, is much worse than a clean loss.

I wanted to be professional. I called my senior staff at HUD together. There were ten of us at a table for twenty. "We gave it the good fight," I said. "I want to do this right. Let's show the Bush people we're pros."

In the end we all felt bruised. I would have loved to stay as HUD secretary. There had been talk that maybe I would go to the White House to help Gore. The unfairness got to me personally. But it was worse for the country. You could feel the divide. The media wrote daily about how the votes were counted. Which votes counted, which were pitched and why, and which candidate would have won if hanging chads, butterfly ballots, the timing of absentee ballots, and questionable voting machines hadn't been in the mix—all this is still debated today.

Now as I replay the loss in my mind I don't spend much time on the rights or wrongs of the Florida system. Instead I think about what could have been done differently. Gore was a much better man than the public knew. The campaign did not do him justice. In a relay race, it's not enough to have two runners who are very fast. They have to transition well. The problem, as I see it, is that the baton pass was bobbled.

During the four years I was HUD secretary, I learned the valuable lesson that the concept of change is universally appealing in the abstract and personally frightening in reality. People go to great lengths to deny, deflect, and defend rather than to admit and resolve. Change is destabilizing. People feel more comfortable when they know what's coming.

But if change is hard for one person, it is nearly insurmountable for a group, even in situations where staying put is clearly detrimental.

Niccolò Machiavelli wrote prophetically: "There is nothing more difficult to take in hand, more perilous to conduct, or more uncertain in its success, than to take the lead in the introduction of a new order of things."

We are surrounded by examples. The American public education system is a stump-speech staple. We say that educating our children is a national priority. But we're teaching our children the same way we did fifty years ago. We school them from 8:30 A.M. to 3 P.M., while other countries have longer and fuller agendas. We take summers off because of the country's agrarian tradition of 150 years ago. We take away recess despite research showing that children learn as much from play as from work. We know that different children learn in different ways, but we teach to only one learning style. Technology in the classroom, which could revolutionize individualized learning, is proceeding glacially. We're only starting to measure teachers' performance to incentivize excellence and to help those who need it.

Bureaucracy repels change. The political system automatically protects the status quo.

Our health-care system is similar. Whether or not you agree with the Affordable Care Act, it's indisputable that our previous system wasn't working.

HELP, HUD, practicing law, and successful and unsuccessful campaigns have taught me that change must be approached with moon-landing precision. HUD was a good training ground because it posed the greatest challenge. A long-term massive bureaucracy, the difficult political system, and the status quo were certainly unsustainable. The agency involved the most entrenched unions. It clung to the worst ideologies. It taught me many lessons and it gave me confidence that even large flawed systems could be changed.

When George W. Bush came in, his administration closed down many of our programs, including Empowerment Zones and Community Builders. It was difficult to see our good work undone. But the Republicans couldn't take away all that we had achieved.

In January 2001, after observing us for four years, the GAO reported that HUD had made real progress, and it narrowed the agency's high-risk designation to just two areas: single-family mortgage insurance and rental housing assistance programs. HUD as an agency was now officially off the "high risk" list and no longer a target for elimination. In fact, some of the same Republicans who'd talked about closing the agency were now investing in it. I answered the question I set out to answer for the Democratic Party, for the nation, and for myself: government could work even where dysfunction had prevailed for decades. We had proved that compassion and competence were not in tension, but could be bound together, each essential to the effective pursuit of social justice.

PART II

FALL

CHAPTER 5

A Broken Man

*With President Clinton by my side, I withdrew
from the 2002 New York State gubernatorial race one
week before the Democratic primary.*

I stayed in Washington until the last day of the Clinton administration. I wanted to end things properly. Even though the election didn't go our way, I didn't want to do a disservice to the HUD transition or to the administration.

We moved to New York, and I unofficially announced my intention to run for governor. Kerry and I had a combination welcome home/announcement event at my brother-in-law Kenneth Cole's chic store on Fifth Avenue. Some 250 guests went upstairs to the store, where waiters passed seafood canapés and champagne on silver platters. But I barely ate. I shook so many hands and was hugged by so many people that it took me a half hour to make my way to the podium.

Martin Luther King III, a close friend and head of the Southern Christian Leadership Conference, whom I got to know while I was at HUD, opened the program. "I'm supposed to be brief, but I come from a family of Baptist preachers," he said, drawing laughs. "When I think of Andrew, most of all I think of his character. As Martin Luther King Jr. said, the ultimate measure of a man is not where he stands in comfort and convenience, but when issues are tough. I had the opportunity about ten times to work with Andrew . . . to end discrimination in housing."

Then Kerry spoke. "Our daughter Cara's teacher asked me to come to class and talk about human rights and Martin Luther King [Jr.]," she told the crowd. "Just as I was asking myself how I was going to explain [such a big topic] to a group of six-year-olds, Cara stood up and said, 'A long time ago, blacks and whites couldn't drink from the same water fountain, and they had to live in different houses, and Martin Luther King worked hard to bring them together. But Martin Luther King couldn't do it alone, so my grandpa [Robert F. Kennedy] helped him. But they're both dead. So my daddy has to do it now.'"

Kerry paused. "Of course, on the way home I said, 'Daddy and Mommy!'"

I looked at my wife and Martin King, and thought: The three of us were raised by men of courage—men who had taken the hard way and appealed to Americans' better natures, men who were convinced our country could live up to—even exceed—our founding fathers' original concept of freedom and justice for all. They worked to right the inequities in our country and had faith that there were enough good, honorable people who would back them up. Tens of thousands did. Standing together for civil rights and against other wrongs, they reached the tipping point.

But that drive had grown shaky in New York by the end of the twentieth century. Now, at the dawn of the new millennium, I believed that our state needed to recapture the commitment to improve education, job opportunities, and living conditions for all its citizens.

"Remember when you trusted government and wanted to be part of it?" I asked the crowd.

Next I announced my immediate and future plans. "I'm going to get a good bagel, a slice of pizza, an egg roll, and some ribs. And then, my friends and family, I want you to know I intend to run for governor of the State of New York."

The crowd broke out applauding and cheering. Until that moment the only people I'd seriously discussed the idea with were Kerry and my parents.

I wasn't the only member of Bill Clinton's cabinet to return home to run for a state's top office. Former attorney general Janet Reno from Florida, and Bill Richardson, the former energy secretary, from New Mexico, were doing the same. (Reno would lose the 2002 Florida Democratic primary, and Richardson would be elected to two terms.)

I thought I could win against George Pataki, the moderate, pro-choice Republican who had bested my father in 1994, and I felt certain that running the Department of Housing and Urban Development had given me the experience I'd need to lead New York State. Traveling around the country, I'd seen how innovative, modern ideas—using the tax code to spur development; offering constituent services online; establishing new models of public-private partnerships; attracting bright, young people into public service—and hard work had revived the economy in many places. Bill Clinton and Al Gore's push to reinvent government led to greater efficiency and creativity in programs nationwide. I wanted to put this sort of thinking to work in New York, particularly upstate. There, as in some of the economically pressed places I'd visited with President Clinton, the residents had been stripped of hope.

The New York State government had basically ceased to function. The Democratic Assembly and the Republican Senate fought, and the governor jousted with both. It was long-term gridlock. Paralysis hurts everyone. The state was falling behind, and the government that had once been a national model of innovation was now a model of dysfunction. This wasn't the state's history when New York governor DeWitt Clinton proposed a waterway, the Erie Canal, to stretch from Albany, on the Hudson River, to Rochester, on Lake Erie. Thomas Jefferson had called the idea a "little short of madness."

Canals had been popular and successful in England and

continental Europe and, in this country, carried George Washington's imprimatur. In 1784, before the U.S. Constitution was drafted, Washington had begun pushing to use the Potomac River as the basis for a navigable waterway he called the Patowmack Canal, to reach from the Atlantic Ocean to the Ohio Valley. The canal, which opened in 1802, three years after the first president's death, proved indispensable for moving large quantities of merchandise from the East Coast westward to the interior. But because of wide fluctuations in the water level it was navigable only a couple of months a year.

In New York, Governor Clinton prevailed against critics, persuading the state legislature to approve $7 million in building funds for a rival canal. In 1825, when the project was completed, on time and on budget, detractors called it "Clinton's Folly" and "Clinton's Ditch." But the governor had the final word. The 363-mile Erie Canal immediately became the gateway to the West, forcing the Patowmack into bankruptcy. It meant that New York City quickly trumped Philadelphia as the East Coast's busiest port, and the canal transformed Albany, Syracuse, Rochester, and Buffalo into boomtowns. When the Erie Canal was at its busiest, in 1855, some 33,000 cargo ships traveled from the Atlantic Ocean to the Great Lakes. The C&O Canal in Washington, built to supplant the Patowmack, never enjoyed the same success.

But even DeWitt Clinton could not guess that one day a web of railroads and interstate highways would supplant the waterway or that deindustrialization would send the region's manufacturing economy into permanent decline. Harsh winters and inordinately high taxes didn't help. Upstate New

York was falling farther behind New York City year by year. By 2001, Buffalo's steel industry, Corning's fiber optics industry, Binghamton's electronics industry, and Syracuse's machine tools industry had experienced mass layoffs, bankruptcies, plant relocations, and closings. The state did little to stem the tide.

New York's gridlock was much earlier and in many ways worse than that of Washington. The annual budget set the scene. The state constitution dictated that the legislature and governor deliver the budget by April 1. But it had been late each year since 1983, my father's first in office. Sometimes it was late not just by days or weeks, but by months. Allegations of financial corruption in the capital were legion. In 1999, the tobacco company Philip Morris was fined $75,000 for underreporting the amount it had spent lobbying state lawmakers. In a related story, the Albany *Times-Union* commented: "The state Legislature has to face up to its collective shame for allowing special interests to prevail in Albany at the expense of the public good."

Against this backdrop, I saw myself as a radical reformer—one who would dramatically shift state government from moribund to modern and energized. I would make the government work and give citizens real leadership. The overarching theme of my campaign would be renewal: a "new" New York. Standing before my strongest supporters at our welcome-home party, I leaned toward the microphone. "New York was always the first," I said, building to a peak. "It was always the best. We always led the way. We have lost that position. . . . We will make New York NUMBER ONE again. We will make the Empire State the Empire State again.

My hope was that by announcing now, in January 2001, I'd forestall media speculation and lay out all my plans up front, clear and concise, and set a "tell it like it is" tone for my race.

The media played my gubernatorial bid as an effort to avenge my father's loss to Pataki in 1994. But my aspiration to become governor was not born of a personal vendetta— not at all.

My father never thought, "Pataki beat me." He thought, "I lost the race." Just as only Koch could beat Koch in 1982, only Cuomo could beat Cuomo in 1994. My father was swept out by the sentiment of that midterm election cycle: an anti-incumbent, anti-Democratic sentiment that handed Republicans both houses of Congress and the majority of statehouses. The nation's mood for change was embodied by Newt Gingrich's ten-point Contract with America, which promised to scale back the size and role of the federal government. Pataki fashioned a similar but more trenchant message, which the *New York Times* aptly summed up as: "down with taxes, up with the death penalty, out with Cuomo." On top of it all, after twelve years my father's team was tired. Twelve years is a long time in politics.

There were other reasons my father lost. How voters feel about the economy almost always determines the incumbent's fortunes, and people in upstate New York, where businesses were sputtering, wanted to see a new face in the statehouse. My father raised $12 million in campaign contributions, compared with Pataki's $25 million. Pataki spent more than half his money on advertising. Attack ads ran rampant that year—the worst on the radio. Pataki's negative ads appealed to voters' anxiety. The tagline of one was: Mario Cuomo "needs to go home, live as we do, to understand the fear we have for our loved ones."

I write all this with tremendous guilt.

My father had asked me to manage that campaign. He knew he was in trouble and he had no one around him who could run it effectively. My father enjoyed the intellectual and had little time for the operational. Now things had to happen. I agonized over the choice. I'd been assistant secretary at HUD for only two years. We had bought a house and started a family. I was deeply passionate about the work on homelessness, empowerment, and economic development that we were doing. I still had a lot I wanted to accomplish.

Watching my father's campaign unfold was like watching a slow-motion automobile crash. As the election neared, I thought about it often. I knew that he relied on me, and I had let him down. Finally, two weeks before Election Day, I used vacation days to come up to New York to help out.

The most important thing that happened that week was that Rudy Giuliani, New York City's Republican mayor, endorsed my father. In a surprise announcement Giuliani said Pataki was indifferent to New York City. Suddenly everything soared. What had been a deficit of 7 percentage points for my father became a 13-point lead.

Pataki deftly turned Giuliani's support into a negative, suggesting that a deal had been cut between the governor and the mayor, and that New York City would reap the benefits at upstate New York's expense—as if the Hudson River ran green with money flowing downstate. Ironically, what hurt Mayor Koch was now hurting my father with Mayor Giuliani. Giuliani went on to become "America's Mayor" after 9/11, and I always respected his willingness to cross party lines.

On Election Day, Tim Russert, who had become NBC's Washington bureau chief and the host of *Meet the Press*, and remained a close friend, phoned me with updates on exit poll numbers. At 4 P.M., Tim felt he had enough information based on traditional turnout models to project a win. "It looks like your father's going to take Pataki by five to six points," he said.

The next few hours were a happy blur. At the desk in his suite at the Sheraton Centre, my father wrote his acceptance speech while my mother, sisters, and brother, Chris, relaxed. "The polls close at nine o'clock," my father said. "We'll wait for Pataki to call me and concede. Then we'll go down to the ballroom. From now until the networks call the race, I'm going to take a rest."

He took a nap. I paced. My family ate dinner, watched TV, and changed into dress clothes.

Tim called again at about 9:15 P.M.

"Listen, Andrew," he said. "Turnout was higher than we expected in Republican areas. Mario's going to lose by three points."

I put the phone back in its cradle, and I thought I was going to be sick to my stomach.

I opened the bedroom door. My father was lying on top of the bedspread, fully dressed, stiff because he didn't want to

wrinkle his suit. His eyes were closed. The pages of his acceptance speech were lying on top of his chest. I stood over him.

I couldn't make myself say the words. Instead I backed
into the message.

"Pop," I said, clearing my throat. "We're going to need a
different speech."

My father opened his eyes but didn't say a thing. He was
stunned.

The final tally was Cuomo, 45.4 percent; Pataki, 48.8 percent. Later my father said, "If you had run the campaign, I
would have won."

I believe that. So I can see why people thought when I was
running for governor that I was really returning to win one
for my father. But he wouldn't have wanted that. And neither
would I.

Before I could run against Pataki, I had to face Carl McCall,
the Democratic comptroller, who also wanted to head the
state's Democratic ticket. I hoped that getting out in front of
McCall and taking a commanding lead would persuade him
to sit out the race.

I respected Carl, whom I'd known for twenty years. He
had risen from Harlem's Democratic clubhouses to become
deputy ambassador to the United Nations under Andrew
Young during the Carter administration. In 1982, McCall
was my father's choice for lieutenant governor, but he lost
the primary to Ed Koch's candidate, Al DelBello. After that,
Carl left politics, working at Citibank as a vice president for
almost a decade. But public service was still in his system.

For two years, beginning in 1991, he served as president of the New York City Board of Education. He became state comptroller in 1993 when the state legislature voted him in to fill the vacancy after Edward Regan resigned to become the president of Bard College. Carl had been elected to the comptroller post twice, in 1994 and 1998. At sixty-five, he was the highest-ranking Democrat in state politics and the first African American to hold statewide office.

His credentials were solid. But I thought I'd make a better governor.

If I was elected, Albany would no longer be hostage to what my father's friend Jack Newfield, the *Village Voice* writer, called "the permanent government"—a coalition of industries, including education and health care—vested in the status quo. I would deliver on-time budgets. I would end the "pay-to-play" system that tied the awarding of government contracts to companies that made the highest campaign contributions.

I filed my official election papers with the New York State Board of Elections on January 30, the day after the welcome-home party. Carl announced his gubernatorial bid two days later, on February 1, and filed his election papers midmonth.

I had a two-pronged strategy: to win over party regulars and to keep the campaign focused on Pataki. McCall had a similar plan. In his announcement, he ignored my entrance into the race, taking aim at Pataki's "aimless lethargy" and "detachment." I started out as the front-runner among potential Democratic voters, leading in the polls 45 percent to McCall's 25 percent.

But no matter how good I looked on paper, I'd forgotten the first lesson of politics—it's all local. I was a national player, but I had laid no groundwork among the state's Democratic leaders. I had made no courtesy calls. I had neglected to touch base. Not so Carl; in fact, quite the opposite. He'd been working hard for the people of New York for three decades. He had built and held on to relationships. He knew the rank and file and went out of his way to thank those who supported him. He had a track record of helping his constituents. The Democrat Party regulars were cheering for him. During eight years of Pataki, when they were the "out" party, the Democrats clung together—a small group of true believers who had no real power but who kept the candle lit. Carl had been their leader during that time. He had gone to their county dinners, Rotary Club functions, and wakes when no other senior Democrats were showing up.

And as the state's first African American candidate for governor, he was making a historic run. Understandably, the party was in his corner.

"I'm supposed to be neutral," Denny Farrell, a Manhattan assemblyman who chaired the state Democratic Party, told me early on. "But McCall was with us while you were gone. You're young, Andrew. Four years go by fast. Leaders around the state like you very much. You give a good speech. You're a pro. You're smart. But come on, you're forty-four years old. You need to sit out the race and run next time."

A few others echoed Farrell's sentiments, but I had made up my mind. My father and I had discussed the pros and cons. As always, he supported me. He had run against the party machine in 1982, and I thought I was following the pattern. I neglected to take into account the sharp differences between my father's campaign and mine. He had been Hugh Carey's lieutenant governor and before that, secretary of state. My father's "family of New York" concept—the idea that we take care of one another—resonated with voters. I thought my work as a cabinet secretary would mean something to New Yorkers. I didn't realize that I had more to prove—and would ultimately craft a less compelling message—than my father.

As the child of a politician, you inherit positives and negatives, with a larger serving of the latter. You receive built-in political training: you see what it takes to organize a campaign operation, how to connect with crowds, how to articulate your message in a way that makes sense to voters, and the value of public service and the good you can do. At the same time, people resent you. This country doesn't like political dynasties. People assume that you had it easy—that you were born with the proverbial silver spoon in your mouth. The truth was that for much of my childhood my father was an outer-borough lawyer, and I was raised in middle-class Queens, so it was more as though I'd been born with a plastic fork in my mouth. But perception is reality.

My father had been an extraordinarily effective, popular three-term governor, but when Pataki ousted him in 1994, some Democratic officials felt he'd let them down. Their attitude was: Your father didn't help us after he lost. He wasn't even attentive when he was here. They were correct in saying that my father had never been a cheerleader for the state Democratic Party. Though he'd won against the machine and become the titular head of the New York Democrats, he still thought of himself as an outsider. He never went out of his way to acknowledge the local chairmen or to attend their county dinners or feed the party with patronage.

And because he'd lost in 1994, state Democrats believed that our shared last name meant I couldn't win, either.

Others had a distaste for me left over from the 1982 transition, when my father took over the governorship from Hugh Carey. There was a sentiment that could be expressed as "Oh, now Andy wants to come around." Two decades later, some party insiders weren't so much pulling for Carl as pulling against me.

Months after I made my announcement at Kenneth Cole's store, I realized how wrongheaded it had been to launch a populist political campaign at a celebrity-studded, invitation-only event. It showed how off-kilter my perceptions were. In my mind I'd been a New Yorker who had an out-of-town job. We were back and forth often—to visit friends and family, to check up on HELP. I worked for a popular Democratic president. I was wholly engaged in politics. Then Kerry and I returned to my home state. We'd found a hundred-year-old farmhouse abutting a six-hundred-acre woodland preserve in Mount Kisco. It was an hour's drive from the city, in Westchester County, down the block from Kerry's brother Bobby.

But the state party talked about me as though I had been living on Saturn. It was similar to Saul Steinberg's *New Yorker* cover—if you're not in New York you don't exist. I was dumbfounded to realize that, although I was a native New Yorker, the party saw me as a carpetbagger.

In the early months, I was scrambling to launch my campaign. Raising money was the most pressing task. One morning, when I was walking into the office of a potential donor, he introduced me to a man walking out. "Andrew Cuomo, meet Andrew Farkas," he said.

"Andrew Farkas," I repeated. "Why do I know your name?"

"Because you sued me at HUD and almost destroyed my life," he replied, raising his voice to a near-shout, "for a politically inspired lawsuit. That's why."

"If you'd like to talk about it, please feel free to call me," I said. "Let me give you my number."

"No, no," he said. "If you want to talk about it, you come to my office and meet the people whose lives you ruined."

"OK, I will."

Before I went to see him, I had to learn what had happened in the lawsuit. Its roots predated me as secretary.

Starting in the early 1990s, Farkas was running a company called Insignia Financial Services, a conglomerate that bought up small real estate management companies and consolidated them in a "roll up." To him, the deals were paper transactions, like buying stock. He rarely saw what he bought. In 1995, HUD took control of one of the properties—the Sierra Nevada Arms in Las Vegas—where a broken sewer pipe was contaminating the playground. Two years later HUD filed a civil suit. Farkas settled with HUD, paying $7.4 million in fines, and immediately sold his residential properties.

I called Farkas a couple of days after we ran into each other. I sat at a conference room table with him and his partners, and we delved into the lawsuit—sometimes contentiously.

We agreed to disagree but heard each other out. Then we shook hands and I left.

Not long afterward, Farkas called me up. "I disagree with what you did at HUD," he said, "but I respect that you sat down with us. I never thought you would have the guts to do that. I'd like to take you to dinner."

I didn't know what to expect when we met at an Italian restaurant. But over gnocchi and risotto, we discovered that we had a lot in common. We're about the same age and have a similar get-the-job-done approach. By the time our coffee arrived, I was telling him about what I planned to accomplish as governor, and he was sharing his thoughts on the real estate business.

With contributions coming in, it wasn't long before I was outraising McCall. Still, I needed to establish a fingerhold with party regulars. We took the offensive. Kerry, our kids, and a few campaign staffers spent summer weekends attending rural county picnics and barbecue dinners. I shook hands, made speeches, and ate a lot of chicken.

In mid-August 2001, Pataki was ahead of me in the polls, 51 percent to 35 percent. He also led Carl, 51 to 31 percent. Significantly, nearly 50 percent of New York voters indicated that they were ready for new leadership. That was huge! Now I just had to persuade them that I was the right candidate to replace Pataki. Among Democrats, I was still ahead of Carl, 38 percent to 32 percent, with the rest of the voters undecided.

But no pollster could have predicted what happened next.

As with Pearl Harbor and the assassination of JFK, people

beyond a certain age will always remember where they were and what they were doing on the morning of September 11, 2001, when the World Trade towers fell, the Pentagon was struck, and a United Airlines jet crash-landed in a field in Pennsylvania.

Kerry and I were driving to the city from our new home in Mount Kisco.

She had meetings that day, and I was dropping her off on my way to work, in the financial district, at the lower tip of Manhattan. We were listening to the radio, when we heard that a plane had slammed into the World Trade Center.

Like many people, I thought at first that there had been an accident.

Kerry turned to NPR's *Morning Edition*. Bob Edwards sounded shell-shocked: "Breaking news from New York City, where planes—two planes, have hit both towers of the World Trade Center in Lower Manhattan," he reported. Kerry gasped.

Edwards continued, "The upper floors of the World Trade Center—110 floors high—each tower. Television networks were showing pictures of the first crash so that everyone watching that picture saw a second plane hit a second tower."

"Oh, my God," Kerry said. "We have to get to the girls."

We made a quick U-turn and headed for the children's preschool. Intellectually I knew Mariah, Cara, and Michaela were safe, but your first instinct is: Where's my family? Are they OK? We needed to see our kids. Hug them. Tell them we loved them.

On the radio, an eyewitness who had seen the first plane

strike the North Tower reported, "Papers flying everywhere; people falling out of the building. Ten minutes later: another boom. You can't imagine."

He was right. I couldn't fathom it. The Bruckner Expressway in the Bronx was as I'd never heard it before or since: utterly quiet. I drove as if on autopilot. Like everyone else, we were scrambling to process the inconceivable. A few minutes later, NPR played a tape of President Bush saying that the planes were "an apparent terrorist attack on our country." And adding, "Terrorism against our nation will not stand."

The sense of vulnerability and of loss of control brought back my recollection of the government-recommended nuclear-bomb drills that terrified me when I was in grammar school in Queens in 1963. The nuns at St. Gerard's instructed us that as soon as we heard a siren blare we were to stop everything and crawl under our desks, knees up, heads tucked in between. The terrorizing message was that bombs can explode at any minute, and even at age six I was pretty sure our desks were poor protection. I dwelled on obvious questions. How would I get home if that were to happen for real? Where would I find my parents? Would we be safe? Who would still be alive? The drills traumatized a generation. But the Cold War had ended. The Soviet Union was gone. I hadn't experienced the same fear since—until I listened to accounts of this coordinated terrorist attack. And this time, the situation didn't come with the reassurance that it was only a drill.

Now I was frantic to call my mother and father, my sisters, my brother, our friends in Manhattan. Kerry wanted to call her mom at home in northern Virginia. But nearly everyone in the city was doing the same. Cell phone systems were overwhelmed. Our phones were useless. Suddenly being unable to reach family members and having no idea if the attack would continue pulled us up short. Most people, including us, had no emergency plan.

Kerry and I arrived at school, joined the stampede of parents inside, and found our children sitting quietly in their reading circles. Michaela, four, was home with the babysitter. Mariah and Cara didn't ask questions—they were distracted by the novelty of an unexpected day with Mommy and Daddy—and they were too young to be told the details of what had happened. "There was an accident with some airplanes," I said, trying not to betray my anxiety.

By the time we got home, we'd heard about the third plane smashing into the Pentagon and the fourth plane plowing into a field instead of reaching its unknown target in Washington. Kerry didn't say what we both were thinking—the Pentagon is only ten miles from Hickory Hill. We kept the TV off and cooked grilled cheese sandwiches for lunch. We took a long walk in the woods next to our house, gripping our daughters' hands, and then played the kids' board game "Candyland." Later, Kerry and I took turns stealing a few minutes away to flip on CNN and dial phone numbers that rarely connected. That night we found out that several of our daughters' schoolmates had lost parents who worked at the World Trade Center. Although the odds were that we would know people who died, the reality shocked us. The idea that mothers and fathers went to work one day and didn't come home to their children was too unthinkable to take in.

An editorial in the next day's *New York Times* summed

up our collective understanding: "We look back at sunrise yesterday through pillars of smoke and dust, down streets snowed under with the atomized debris of the skyline, and we understand that everything has changed."

In the days and weeks after 9/11, everything we had taken for granted seemed more tenuous. What had preoccupied us when we woke up on the cloudless morning of September 11—mainly, the nation's shaky economy—seemed trivial. Relationships felt more tender, more fragile, and more important than ever. That was true for me as a father, son, sibling, and husband.

It also transformed the race, though that was far less important. In August Pataki had a 61 percent approval rating. After 9/11 it shot up to 81 percent. Just as Americans gravitated toward family and comfort in the weeks after the terrorist attack, they looked for direction from the country's existing leadership. Voting had already begun for the New York City mayoral primary on the morning of September 11. Two weeks later, when the rescheduled primary election took place, some voters wrote in Rudy Giuliani on the ballot. In the aftermath of 9/11, the two-term Republican, who had acquired the nickname "America's Mayor," sought to extend his mayoralty to help the devastated city transition to a new administration. Two of the three major candidates approved the idea, but the modification, which required legislative approval, lacked support in the heavily Democratic state Assembly.

Navigating the aftermath of 9/11 was complicated. Do you raise funds, or don't you? Do you campaign, or don't you? My staffers and I debated those questions endlessly, along with what we thought the post-9/11 zeitgeist would be. One theory was that the collective trauma would raise voters' expectations—they would demand greater competence from government—reinforcing my campaign message. But we couldn't guess. There were no precedents for what we were going through. Ever.

I kept fund-raising and my few appearances low-key. The city was quiet through the holidays. How different this new landscape was.

By the New Year, people were slowly getting back to business.

The Democratic Rural Conference (DRC) straw poll was our first test. The conference, representing forty-one rural counties, was established in 1996 to counteract the heavy Republican influence upstate. McCall himself and most of the party regulars believed that the straw poll, the bellwether for the state Democratic convention in New York City in May, was his to lose. In early January I called my small campaign staff together and laid out my plan for winning. We would adhere to my mantra, "Do it right, or don't do it at all." We would follow up on every delegate lead, and we would make sure that these hardworking women and men knew their concerns had been heard. We would make conference members feel special. When we started visiting delegates that month, we figured out that of the conference's 128 total votes, we'd locked in only 30, to McCall's 98. To win, we would have to hold on to the delegates we had and get 35 more votes. My deputy campaign manager, Joe Percoco, who had started working for my father at nineteen and later joined my HUD staff, drove with me from county to county, while I made phone calls to delegates: "Hi, I'm Andrew Cuomo. I'm running for governor." I did a lot of listening. Then I'd make my case. It was like the phone offensive I'd orchestrated twenty years earlier, when I was my father's campaign manager. I'd say, "I agree with you on this and this. I disagree with you on that. Let's agree to disagree. I'd like your vote."

Between us, Joe and I called every conference member, every week, and kept notes. Joe was great, a natural leader and manager. We spoke with some chairmen who had never heard from a candidate before. After a few conversations, I knew it all—whose uncle had broken his leg, who'd lost a job, and whose kid had been cast in the high school production of *Oklahoma!* I also knew this: there was little hard support in the Democratic Rural Conference for Carl McCall. Some of the people I spoke with became our lieutenants. They'd say, "I had a conversation with so and so. She's really not too sold on Carl. She's open to hearing from you."

Spending time on the road with Joe reminded me of the all-encompassing nature of politics. Running for office, or governing, is not something you do from 9 A.M. to 6 P.M. and then go home, pop open a beer, turn on the TV, and relax. Trying to understand other people's problems and helping them get to know what you stand for require your all. You're constantly analyzing how to make the next stop or the next day go better. You're operating on adrenaline.

I also couldn't help thinking about upstate New York's unique history—man-made and geological. One turning point in the American War of Independence took place in 1777 at Saratoga, where an American victory persuaded the French to enter the fight as our ally, tipping the war's outcome in favor of the Continental Army. In the Adirondack Mountains, where I've loved to camp and fish since I was a teenager, we were looking at billion-year-old stone that the Ice Age had hammered into peaks. We went as far west as Niagara County, home of the magnificent roaring falls.

Despite these treasures, the rural counties were suffering from a difficult reversal of fortune. Upstaters had handed Pataki his victory against my father, but he had done little to spark the regional economy. I lobbed my attacks at him, not at McCall, telling DRC members that Pataki had "made the Empire State the caboose on the economic train."

A month out from the straw poll, McCall still led, 75 to 53 votes, but we were steadily gaining momentum. Each week we sent the delegates mail on my campaign issues. "Upstate New York doesn't have to be this way," I told them. "The Erie Canal was created because of one man's vision. We will build on that going forward." To prove my point, I pledged that as governor, I would give $100 million in state money to venture capital firms to invest in small businesses. "Small businesses are the engine of growth of the New York economy," I said. They create "eight out of ten new jobs each year, and we need to invest in them to help them grow."

The Democratic Rural Conference straw poll was held on March 23. I was excited and anxious going in, but I knew my staff and I hadn't missed a chance to connect with people. I had shaken their hands and shared pots of coffee in their kitchens. We'd handed out ANDREW CUOMO mugs filled with candy, New York State wine from the Finger Lakes district, maple syrup, and North Country cheese as a show of respect. We'd learned that some counties had delegate vacancies and read the rulebook to find out how to fill them. We knew who was coming from which county and who was sending a niece or neighbor as a proxy. To make sure I had done everything possible, I called in reinforcements. My mother and father; Kerry; and her uncle, Ted Kennedy, phoned DRC members and asked them to vote for me.

The weekend of the conference, statewide candidates and groups sponsor breakfasts, lunches, and dinners. We commandeered the delegates right after the Friday-night dinner, with dessert. Instead of serving a slice of apple pie and coffee with powdered creamer in a bland ballroom, we went all out. We brought in balloons, a dessert buffet, a DJ, and a photographer. We showed the delegates such a good time that many skipped the late night dance and stayed on. Even people who weren't for us joined in.

We went into the Saturday vote with the understanding that if everyone kept his or her word we would win, but we couldn't be sure. The poll was taken by secret ballot. When the votes were counted, I had won, receiving 67 votes to Carl's 61. I took our success as a good omen. It was one of our sweetest victories.

My announcement at the Kenneth Cole store had signaled my intention to run. I formally launched my campaign on April 16, 2002, with a four-day, twelve-stop bus tour that we named "Ideas, Energy, Action." I was pumped up. Coming off the Democratic Rural Conference triumph, I felt that we had picked up real momentum. To evoke the progressive reform spirit of my campaign we began on the steps of the historic Nassau County Courthouse, whose cornerstone had been laid by Governor Theodore Roosevelt in 1901.

Next, we went to HELP I in Brooklyn, the site of what Kerry and I now thought of as our first date. Introducing me, Kerry recalled how I'd picked her up on my motorcycle. "I knew this was going to be no ordinary ride!" she said.

At each stop, I attacked Pataki.

I had hit my groove.

"Pataki is doing less with more than any governor in New York history," I told applauding crowds. "Government represents special interests better than the interests of regular people. It's our government, and we want it back."

I promised to cut taxes, improve public education, and kick-start the upstate economy.

Finally, we ended Day One in Albany on a high.

The next day our itinerary was Utica, Syracuse, and Buffalo.

Sitting in my "Ideas, Energy, Action" bus, traveling between Utica and Syracuse, I regaled the media covering my campaign with freewheeling banter on my experiences during the Clinton years. Later, pulling onto the New York Thruway en route to Buffalo, I switched to other stories. I told reporters what I had seen in the days after the World

Trade Center fell. "There was one leader for 9/11. It was Rudy Giuliani," I said. "[George Pataki] stood behind the leader. He held the leader's coat. He was a great assistant to the leader, but he was not the leader."

A few weeks earlier, McCall and I had attended the West-chester County Democrats' spring dinner, held by News 4 and the local Gannett newspaper. McCall went on first. He said, George Pataki is high in the polls now, but he's high only because of his association with 9/11. But in truth Pataki didn't do anything for 9/11. He was just the tallest guy in the photo next to Giuliani.

When it was my turn, I said, "Carl McCall says George Pataki didn't do anything on 9/11. That's not fair, Carl. He did do something. He was there to hold Giuliani's coat."

The Westchester audience had laughed. But now, weeks later, the reporters on the bus did not. They jumped on their cell phones and started pounding the keys on their laptops. By the time the bus rolled into Buffalo, we knew we had a serious problem.

That afternoon, when a reporter read him my comments, Pataki reportedly asked, "He actually said that?" He went on to say, "There are things I can say, but I don't think it's appropriate. . . . I'm just stunned by the comments. I just think it's very sad."

The *New York Times*' political reporter, Adam Nagourney, who'd been on my bus, wrote in the next day's paper: "Mr. Cuomo's remarks startled some politicians, given the passions stirred by the topic. . . . Rarely has the Sept. 11 attack been invoked to discredit a political opponent." Adam was an Albany veteran, and Tim Russert and I had many battles with him. He knew what he was doing.

Over the next seventy-two hours, I didn't get to talk about reforming Albany, improving public schools, cutting taxes, or creating ten thousand new jobs upstate. The headlines of the multiday story were blunt: "Criticism Grows as Cuomo Sticks by Criticism of Pataki," "Cuomo's Coat Tale Is Short on Truth," "Cuomo-Cide: Storm of Outrage Greets Andy over Big 9/11 Gaffe."

We live in an era of gotcha politics, when rival candidates exploit any sound bite they can to mischaracterize the opposition. What I'd said as a quip—a throwaway—handed them an opening. My "coat holder" comment, as communicated by the media, sounded dissonant in our post-9/11 world. It was a sharp reminder that you can say something in one context that translates differently in another.

Republicans and Democrats pounced on the comment, and Pataki skillfully mobilized his forces against me, manipulating the situation so that he became a victim. His people orchestrated a symphony of criticism. Rudy Giuliani said, "The reality is that the governor was a full and complete partner and I held his coat as often as he held mine. We supported each other."

McCall was eager to pile on: "Our political dialogue should be at a higher level. The tragedy of Sept. 11 should not be used to score political points."

Union leaders representing firefighters and cops vowed not to endorse me. Peter Gorman, president of the Uniformed Fire Officers Association, said, "It's an outrage that someone like Andrew Cuomo . . . [would] criticize Gov. Pataki, who attended dozens of funerals, who was there every time we needed him and who has spent countless hours helping the families." Mayor Bloomberg said there was no need for Pataki to defend his actions, "They speak for themselves." And Denis Hughes, president of the New York State AFL-CIO, said he had "nothing but admiration for the way Gov. Pataki handled this."

A couple of weeks later I was marching in the Salute to Israel Parade when a spectator yelled, "Hold my coat, Andrew." One stupid remark on the most sensitive topic in a generation communicated one thing: arrogance.

Even my staunchest supporters, including my father, said, "Forget it. If you have to explain something you'll never be able to make people see it your way." I dropped it, but the sour impression it left in voters' minds hung over my campaign.

During my Democratic Rural Conference swing, I'd converted several party leaders from McCall's endorsement column to mine. I had secured many of the upstate counties. But rather than giving me an edge going into the state convention in New York City as I'd hoped, the straw poll had the opposite effect. It had been a wake-up for McCall, who clamped down on the Democratic leadership.

As in my father's day, candidates had to win 25 percent of the delegates' votes to get on the primary ballot. McCall, who had secured commitments from almost all of the delegates, made it clear I wouldn't get the requisite 25 percent.

I would go through the convention and come up short. To force a primary on September 10, I'd have to take the alternative route—securing fifteen thousand signatures on petitions circulated in the state.

We made a calculated move. "Fine," we told the McCall people. "You take the convention. We'll skip that and take our campaign directly to the people."

In distancing myself from the convention, I wanted to emphasize the obvious: I wasn't the candidate of the party machine. I thought it proved my ability to do something unorthodox to get the job done—an approach that had served me well in my father's campaigns and at HELP and HUD. Circulating petitions was a legitimate, albeit expensive and time-consuming, path to the primary. Plus, it was my only shot.

It was only later that I realized that what I'd thought was a bold move was actually a big miscalculation. No one read my boycott the way I'd intended: as a grassroots effort, rejecting the status quo. Instead of projecting myself as an outsider, I created the impression that I was petulant and arrogant. The unintended message was: I will play your game only if I can win. I alienated the Democratic Party faithful. I had picked up delegates at the DRC and now they were left in the lurch, without a candidate to support. When it was reported that I hadn't received a single vote from the 353 convention delegates, the truth, as with the "coat holder" line, was too difficult to explain in a sound bite.

I later collected 100,000 signatures, 85,000 more than I needed to force a primary. I was pleased with my strong showing. But the number was meaningless to New York voters.

A poll released on August 15 showed that McCall and I had flipped positions since the race had begun. He was now leading, 47 percent to 31 percent, among likely Democratic voters, whereas just six weeks earlier, I'd been in the lead, 47 percent to McCall's 32 percent. Instead of gaining traction, I was rolling backward.

At the end of August I went to the New York State Fair in Syracuse, a must-do for statewide politicians. It's an event heavy on livestock and maple syrup, with a largely rural turnout. The fair tests a candidate's mettle. It can be a humiliating affair. I'd walk up to people and say, "Hi, I'm Andrew Cuomo. I'm running for governor." Many walked away, leaving my unshaken hand in midair.

That day, it was even easier to ignore me. Former president Bill Clinton and U.S. senator Hillary Clinton were also working the fair. They were the star attraction. If I registered with people at all, I came somewhere behind the Ferris wheel and the funnel cakes.

With the combined firepower of a former president and a U.S. senator, the Clintons were the de facto heads of the New York Democratic Party, and they were officially neutral in the primary race. They didn't go out of their way to say hello, and they left before I could make my way over to them. The press took this to mean that they were now leaning toward McCall. An Associated Press story that ran a few days later said: "The trio didn't even manage a photo together."

Months later, I learned that the Clintons were already poised to shift to McCall. Some of their advisers, fund-raisers, and staff had quietly moved over to help him. It made sense. Along with Rangel, McCall's support had been indispensable to Hillary's 2000 Senate race.

In the meantime my campaign seemed to be imploding without outside help. My staff and I had been watching the polls. I still had more money in my campaign coffers than McCall, and some of my advisers had suggested that I blitz him with negative TV advertising. "If you do that, Andrew," they said, "you'll win the primary." But on the day of the fair, I'd directed some of my senior people to call Charlie Rangel on my behalf. The topic: what would it take to negotiate a graceful exit from the race?

I hadn't made up my mind, but over the weekend, my negatives continued to stack up. The *New York Times* acknowledged that I had brought "dynamism and energy to the campaign trail" and praised my "willingness to put a spotlight on Albany's dysfunction." But, the paper's editorial board said, the ideal candidate would be someone with my "spirit" and McCall's "experience and gravitas." Being called dynamic and energetic is good in itself. But when I put it next to the *Times'* praise for McCall, I knew what a beauty pageant contestant must feel when she wins the Miss Congeniality prize. The *Times* joined the *Daily News* in endorsing McCall, saying that his record on state finance made him the better choice.

I was still considering my options on Labor Day, when the West Indian American Day Carnival Parade in Brooklyn took place. Usually, I enjoy parades, and this one was a must-attend. But on this day, rain was coming down sideways. Spectators were huddled under umbrellas or wearing garbage bags to try to stay dry. I'd worked through a scheduling conflict and heavy traffic to get there, and I arrived more than an hour late. Because of the size of the flatbed truck we were driving we had to let people go in front of us and then follow them at a frustratingly slow pace. We'd hired a DJ, but the music we'd counted on, always a highlight, was canceled. "It's too wet," the DJ told me. "The amps will blow if I plug them in."

From the front seat I saw Hillary Clinton. Next to her was Carl McCall. Together they marched on foot down Eastern Parkway. It didn't matter whether or not Senator Clinton was actually endorsing McCall officially. That's how it looked to the world, including me. The parade was a total disaster for me.

With the primary eight days away, my campaign staff had set up seventy appearances in thirty towns around the state. I was planning to grind through fifteen-hour days. But I'd sat alone in my study over the past several days and thought about what I wanted. I'd had long conversations with both Kerry and my father. I'd done the math and believed that my advisers were right: I could win. But at what cost? Going negative against McCall was indefensible. It would split the party. I was a lifelong Democrat. New York City voters were still feeling bruised by the vitriolic Democratic primary runoff for mayor the year before. The city's former public advocate, Mark Green; and Bronx borough president Fernando Ferrer, the city's first Hispanic mayoral candidate, had pummeled each other. Green won but was too bloodied to effectively fend off Michael Bloomberg in the general election for his first term.

My other option—dropping out of the race—also seemed untenable. It would be admitting failure. As a candidate, you put yourself in front of the public. You spend an almost incomprehensible amount of time and money making sure people recognize you and know what you stand for. You ask for their vote. When you lose, the rejection is personal. And it all plays out in public. You've tried to prove to voters that you can do a good job, and they're saying, We don't think you can.

My family was supportive. "Do whatever you have to do," everyone said.

In my gut, I'd known the answer to this dilemma since Friday. But life-altering decisions usually unfold gradually, not as a lightbulb moment the way they do in cartoons. I wasn't likely to come up with an alternative, but it was also intensely difficult to say to myself that I was leaving the race, let alone go public with an irreversible announcement.

On Monday night, I called Bill Clinton at home in Chappaqua for advice. He confirmed my thinking. "Andrew," he said, "there's no way this ends well. If you win, you lose, and if you lose, you lose."

I'd seen President Clinton's empathy in action dozens of times over the eight years I'd worked for him. But until now, I'd been an observer, not a recipient. "If you drop out," he said, "and you'd find it helpful, I'll come be with you when you make the announcement and give you my public support."

The moment I decided not to go negative on McCall, I felt

better. I'd wanted to disrupt the dysfunction of the state government, but I had not wanted to damage the New York Democratic Party. My agenda for change, which had seemed so right for the times twenty months ago, was completely wrong in a post-9/11 world. But I hadn't fully appreciated this until the past few days when it became apparent that I was losing.

It didn't matter what I'd thought going in or how hard I'd tried. I was devastated. I'd always embraced challenges. I'd sought out one of society's toughest problems—homelessness. We'd left HUD in far better shape than we'd found it. I had never quit. Anything.

My innate political ability had always been a point of pride. Campaigns had dominated my life for nearly three decades. I couldn't grasp that this was where thirty years had brought me.

I had taken on the Democratic machine. But unlike my father, I hadn't run a persuasive campaign. I'd been unable to convince voters that I was the best person to lead them. My impulses had been good, but my implementation had been inexcusable.

I took out a legal pad and handwrote my exit speech. Then I called Joe Percoco. "It's over," I said. "We'll announce tomorrow morning. Can you set it up?"

Once my decision was firm, I had to shut things down quickly.

I left my study to find Kerry. She had just put Cara and Mariah to bed. I dimly remembered that the next day was their first day of kindergarten. I couldn't comprehend beginnings; I could understand only the ending to my own story.

"I'm quitting," I said. They were some of the hardest words I'd ever uttered. It did not get easier when I called my mother and father.

The next day grew more surreal. Everything was done by rote. Picking out my suit and tie that morning felt like dressing for my own funeral. Then I had to meet with my staff and call my key supporters. We'd been talking through the possibilities for several days, so they were not surprised, but they were shaken. Some people had been with me since our welcome-home party. Others had been with me for years. They'd donated money, put their faith in me, and cheered me on. Worse than letting myself down was disappointing them.

In the hours leading up to the press conference at the New York Hilton—and at the event—I did my best to appear upbeat and confident, trying to mask the humiliation I felt. I was all action and no thought. A robot. To be otherwise was too painful.

Bill Clinton and Charlie Rangel stood behind me on the stage. It was the best way to project unity within the party, which would be good for Carl McCall going forward. Rangel's presence signaled that whatever barbs we'd exchanged during the race wouldn't obstruct our future friendship. As kind as their praise was, nothing could have made the situation tolerable for me. When you're dead, you're dead. Who shows up at the funeral doesn't matter.

I had been so set on winning that when I lost, I didn't have a rebound plan.

"What are you going to do now?" Kerry asked the next morning.

"I don't know," I said.

I took ten days to relax, something at which I had little practice. Kerry and I took the girls out of school on a Friday and spent a long family weekend in the Hamptons. Joe and I went fishing one day in Long Island Sound.

In this lull, I began to see my life more clearly. I realized I had put more into my campaign than I put into my family. During the Clinton years, I didn't spend enough time at home or with the kids. I was overtaken with work. I told myself that they were too young to notice. I didn't think about the fact that Kerry was often there alone. For years I came home after they had all already been asleep for hours. This didn't strike me as unbalanced. It's what I had known. Kerry's schedule also had her traveling internationally for her human rights work. I'd wanted so much to believe our relationship was solid that I dismissed the distance that had sprung up between us. Determined to right things, I worked at being a present parent and spouse. I drove the girls to soccer practice and ballet. I pushed them on swings in the park.

Kerry and I had essentially simply set our furniture down after the move from Washington and hit the campaign trail. Now I threw myself into home renovation projects. At the time I didn't see that as a metaphor. I was trying to turn our house into a home. Months later, I realized that what had needed work wasn't our house. It was our marriage.

Not all of my focus was inward. Carl didn't want to speak with me right away. Even though I'd dropped out, he blamed me for hurting his race, because he'd had to spend so much money in the primary and it would hurt him in the general election against Pataki. That's one theory. Another is that his primary win gave him a boost with voters in the general election. As soon as he was willing to take my call, I told him I wanted to help. Although I believed that my political career was over, I wanted to support the Democratic Party, so I tried to raise money and took some of the $1 million in campaign funds I had left to get out the vote in the upstate rural counties. McCall wound up in a three-way race among himself, Pataki, and the Independence Party candidate, Tom Golisano. But with the fear fanned by 9/11 still in the air, there wasn't a question over who would win. On November 5, the once seemingly vulnerable Pataki claimed his third term in the statehouse with 49 percent of the vote, compared with McCall's 33 percent and Golisano's 14 percent.

When the new year came, I tried as best I could to put the election behind me, but I still believed that my campaign message about change had been the right one. The reaction to 9/11 and people's need for stability was right, but the underlying problems did not go away and would need fundamental reform. I began work on a collection of political essays called *Crossroads: The Future of American Politics*, published later that year. The bipartisan book includes works from nearly forty politicians, professors, and other leading Democratic and Republican thinkers, including Bill Clinton, Nancy Pelosi, Peggy Noonan, and pollster Frank Luntz. In my essay, "America at a Crossroads: What Democrats Need to Do to Lead into the Future," I wrote: "It is a fact of politics that the party that best understands the forces of change and can see to the next horizon most clearly becomes the dominant political party." I added: "I believe the left-right debate misses the mark and is a trap for the Democratic Party. The question is not left or right, but forward or backward. . . . True Democrats are aggressive progressives. . . . The essence of the Democratic philosophy is the concept of 'justice' in its fullest sense: social justice, economic justice, and racial justice."

Although I was certain I was out of politics personally, I thought a lot about the American political scene writ large. That spring I took part in the Fellows Program for political practitioners at Harvard University's Institute of Politics, where I led an informal study group. I was as much the student as the teacher. The seminars served as a laboratory for articulating the ideas I set down in *Crossroads*. After my bruising race the previous fall, it was reaffirming to be around politically aware people who yearned to make a positive difference in society. I still believed that government was the best vehicle for change. And as Bob Morgenthau had shown me in the Manhattan DA's office, attracting the brightest and best is crucial. "If you have an opportunity to be in government, take it," I told these smart young people. "Private sector law firms and not-for-profits will always be there. But opportunities to be in government, in positions where you can help make change, are infrequent and fleeting. You never know if you will be offered the chance again."

But it wasn't satisfying for me to urge others to work for the public good. I yearned to be involved myself. I didn't have to search for a cause: 2003 was the thirtieth anniversary of the stringent Rockefeller drug laws, a sad milestone for New York and the country. The statutes had remained essentially unchanged. As an assistant DA, I'd seen the laws' detrimental effects on defendants, and in my gubernatorial race I had campaigned to make them less punitive and more effective. New York's prisons then held about twenty thousand people, 95 percent of whom were African Americans and Latinos, found guilty of drug possession or sales. Most had never been convicted of a violent crime. Besides the steep human cost, the annual bill to New York taxpayers for their incarceration was an exorbitant $700 million.

The hook to attract young people to the cause was easy: a hip-hop concert. I set up a nonprofit called Countdown to Fairness, with Russell Simmons, a friend and fellow Queens native, who had created the music label Def Jam. Russell recognized the power of rap and the artists who performed it. He had recently founded the Hip-Hop Summit Action Network, which used entertainers to press for social change. We brought together an unexpected, and amazing, mix of performers and politicians: Susan Sarandon and Tim Robbins, Mariah Carey, Jay-Z, Sean "Puffy" Combs, 50 Cent, and New York City's former public advocate Mark Green and former comptroller Alan Hevesi, who spoke between acts. Our goal was to mobilize people to press their state representatives for changes in the laws. We wanted a full repeal of mandatory drug sentencing.

One thing I couldn't control was the weather. The concert fell on an unseasonably chilly and uncomfortably wet night. But to my surprise, it still drew thousands.

Our campaign was so successful that Pataki invited Simmons to come meet with him in a closed-door session in Albany, and it revived a vigorous political debate over the drug laws. (Eighteen months later, Pataki signed the Drug

Law Reform Act, which, among other provisions, lowered mandatory sentences from fifteen years to eight for offenders with no prior felonies and allowed prisoners serving drug-related life sentences to apply for lower sentences.)

About three weeks after the concert, Russell and I received word that the state Lobbying Commission was launching an investigation against us for lobbying without a license. I wasn't lobbying: I was using money left over from my campaign to highlight a terrible social injustice. Besides, the money I was spending had been properly disclosed. After my campaign fiasco less than a year earlier, I was horrified to be negatively portrayed in the newspapers again. Too often government officials are looking for a headline at the expense of someone's reputation. The case was eventually dismissed, but the damage was done.

Along with these extracurricular activities, my chief task that spring was to find a paying job. That problem was solved when Andrew Farkas called one day. I knew he was starting a real estate investment bank called Island Capital that would finance various projects from mortgages on commercial property to new development in Europe, the Middle East, and the Caribbean. He asked me to come in as vice president, advising him on his domestic and international deals.

It was an ideal, albeit predictable, job for a former HUD secretary. HUD is, in effect, the nation's largest real estate company.

All of the post-campaign activities I was involved in were gratifying. But I'm certain that, subconsciously, one of the reasons I stayed so busy was that I was afraid to be still. If I kept moving, my unraveling marriage couldn't catch up with me. After the campaign, I thought Kerry and the kids were my safe harbor. I was wrong.

Kerry and I had been seeing a marriage counselor, and I held on to the idea that the relationship was fixable. For me, divorce was not an option. I didn't want our daughters to undergo the trauma of a split family life.

My refusal to budge was rooted in childhood. For Catholics like us divorce was only for extreme situations, and only for someone else. It was presented at school as the ultimate failure. Catholics did not give up on marriage. This was ingrained in me from my childhood. The kids in the neighborhood called an abandoned frame house around the corner from my home in Queens the "divorce house." The family had split; there was a trauma. That explained why the grass grew long, the shutters drooped, and the blue paint peeled.

It surprises me how much of my childhood perceptions were still with me in middle age. The fact that my older sister was divorced did not soften my view. I could not put myself in the same sentence with the word "divorce." Until a reporter did it for me.

I was in my car, driving to Island Capital in midtown, when my cell phone rang. It wasn't a number I recognized. "Hello?" I said, pulling over to the curb.

"Sorry to call about this, Mr. Cuomo," a *New York Times* reporter, Jennifer Steinhauer, said. I had been receiving calls from the *Times* for twenty years. But I never expected what she said next. "I need a comment about your divorce."

"What?"

"I've got your wife's statement," she said. "Can I get your response?"

Steinhauer said, "We're running the story in tomorrow's paper. I need you to comment."

After thirteen years of marriage, and truly stressful times, I knew the ties that bound us together had frayed. But I had hoped we could work through what I saw as a difficult time, not an end. Obviously, I was in denial. In Kerry's mind she had left already.

In a daze I drove to my office, where I called my parents and then the lawyer my sister had used. Next, I phoned my close friend Dan Klores, a public relations consultant and one of the guys I'd shared a birthday party with for a number of years. My father, Dan, and I met at the lawyer's office, with my brother, Chris.

We put out a statement and braced for the worst. The tabloids had a field day. A Kennedy-Cuomo divorce made the gossip pages explode. Coming after the campaign loss, the papers and my political enemies enjoyed throwing dirt on the grave. Like the scene from *The Odd Couple*, I packed my bags and showed up at the Manhattan apartment of my long-time friend Jeff Sachs.

I was sad, angry, scared. Alone. Separately, my political debacle and divorce were each devastating. Together the combination felt dreadful.

Sometimes you have a loss in life, but normally it's isolated and not everyone knows. You get divorced but you go to work and you still like your job. Or you get fired but you go home and you have your family.

This was sweeping across my life. Everybody knew it everywhere. People knew I'd run for office, because I'd just spent $10 million telling them. They knew I'd been knocked on my *tuchus*. They knew I'd been humiliated politically and personally. It was 100 percent awareness of every aspect of my life.

Losing a statewide election is to me like being the guy who fumbled the ball two feet short of the goal line in the last seconds of the Super Bowl. The media replay the whole thing, over and over, in slow motion. My 2002 defeat was trumpeted, analyzed, scrutinized, and reveled in for months.

All the top pundits and reporters pronounced me DOA. Then came my center-stage split from Kerry, and it was generally agreed that no amount of political life support could save me. I thought I was dead too.

One day when the story was still being splashed across the *New York Post* and the *Daily News*, I hailed a cab. I remember getting in, giving my address, and looking out the window for the twenty-minute ride. When we reached the destination, I said to the cabdriver, "How much?"

He said, "It's on me."

I was startled. "Why?" I asked.

He said, "I know who you are, I know what you are going through, and you need it more than me. Good luck, Andrew."

That said it all.

CHAPTER 6

Losing 101

This castle that my grandfather Andrea built in his yard in Queens now sits in my backyard in Mount Kisco, New York.

I stayed in Jeff's apartment for nine months, too broken to do anything else. Even routine decisions were overwhelming. Thinking about where to live—near the girls in Westchester County? in an apartment in the city where I'd be close to work?—seemed beyond my emotional reach. And I didn't know what I could afford until my divorce from Kerry was final.

But these weren't the questions that ripped at me. I'd replay scenes from my marriage, trying to pinpoint when our relationship had become unsalvageable. Many days I didn't have the energy to try to unravel the tangled ball of emotions. What made me decide to take on Carl McCall? Worst: my heart hurt for my daughters. "When are you coming back to live with us, Daddy?" was the one question I couldn't answer or bear.

I was obsessive about seeing them. I couldn't bring the kids to crash on Jeff's couch so in the beginning, before Kerry and I worked out a custody arrangement, I'd leave Island Capital around four o'clock each afternoon and drive forty-five miles from midtown Manhattan to Mount Kisco to pick them up. We'd go to the local diner a couple of nights a week. Cara, Mariah, and Michaela always ordered chicken fingers. The more I saw them the more I ached with remorse. The cost of my failed marriage was huge. We'd paid not through the nose but through the heart.

The world of the politically dead is sparsely populated. "Friends" disappeared, too busy to answer phone calls or go to a Knicks game. Having witnessed the aftershocks of my father's gubernatorial loss in 1994, I should have remembered that when you lose you go from five thousand friends to five. Politics is a zero-sum game.

You can tell a lot about people by the way they handle the "dead." You see the full spectrum: compassion and kindness, pragmatism and vengeance, avoidance and dis-association. Many people I knew—old friends and political acquaintances—were uncomfortable around me. What were they supposed to say? "I'm sorry your life exploded."

I had several real friends who were life savers. You don't need large numbers. You need a few really good people.

But the constant high of political life—the juice; the action; the buzz; even more, the direction and goal—was gone. I always had a purpose that I was proud to pursue. And that pursuit in many ways defined me—maybe too much. Now I needed a total recalibration. Politics was not an option. What do I do? I was lost.

Wading through the remnants of my career and my marriage, I thought back to a time during the HUD years when I experienced being literally lost. Kerry and I were going to spend a few days with my sister Maria and Ken in Martha's Vineyard. She went ahead with the kids and I would follow in our boat. I headed to Pentagon Marina, where we kept our boat. The thirty-three-foot Chris-Craft was the right size for me. I was not really proficient in the open sea, but I love a good challenge, and it was a coastal trip so I tried it.

The two days at sea were uneventful, and the ocean, re-storative. Staying at my sister's house, tucked away on a pond on the northeast corner of the island, was the first time I'd relaxed in months. Sitting in the sunshine on the terrace I reveled in their company and conversation. We went fishing and grilled the day's catch for dinner. Working for the government, I was always looking ahead. With them I was in the present. Catching, cooking, and eating were instant gratification.

Vacation over, I headed south with the boat, planning to split up my return trip. The sea and the weather were fine. I passed Newport, Rhode Island, and pointed toward Block Island. Suddenly, a dense, cold, gray blanket of fog rolled over my boat. I could hardly make out the bow twelve feet in front of me.

I wanted to press on, because slowing down in the middle of nowhere is not a good idea. Foghorns and bells were sounding in the distance, seeming to come first from one direction and then from another. But without visual cues, I couldn't get my bearings. I looked at the loran, a navigational device that gives latitude and longitude coordinates so boaters can plot their positions. The numbers were changing and bouncing erratically. The device was useless. I learned later that heavy fog can interfere with the satellite signal.

My sense of direction disappeared. I couldn't tell if I was facing north, south, east, or west. I couldn't see a horizon. I had no sense of distance. All I knew was that I was alone in the ocean with about sixty feet of salt water beneath me and an impenetrable sky above. If another boat was near, neither captain would know until the crafts collided.

What struck me most was that everything I usually counted on—my hearing, my sight, my instincts, the electronics—was gone. I was plowing forward at moderate speed when the depth gauge suddenly dropped, showing that the boat was in ten feet of water. It couldn't be, because the charts were showing I was at about fifty feet. I sucked in the soupy air and reminded myself that depth gauges are notorious for inaccuracy, especially if there's debris in the water. It wouldn't necessarily be a cause for worry. Sonar can bounce off any obstacle under the boat and give a false reading. I slowed down and reset the gauge.

The needle immediately returned to ten feet. My mind raced through the possibilities.

On a sunny day that would mean you're close to land or over a sandbar. Of course, on a sunny day, my eyes would tell me that. Was the fog affecting the depth finder? Had the moisture thrown off the electronics? Seasoned pilots know what to do when they can't determine direction: trust the instruments.

I couldn't make myself do that.

I was still moving ahead when the fog shifted from solid gray to brownish beige. Vague forms appeared. Faraway fog-horns were drowned out by a roar. Suddenly it became terri-fyingly clear. This wasn't brown fog. It was the side of a cliff. I was about to smash into Block Island. The breaking waves were tossing my boat toward the jagged rocks. Another twenty seconds, and it would be too late. Desperate, I jerked the steering wheel to the left and shoved the throttle forward. I prayed nothing was lurking in the fog ahead.

Giving up control is not something I've done often in my life. But sometimes you have no other choice. I overrode my instincts and adrenaline and headed at idle speed opposite the direction of the land. I bobbed around for what felt like an eternity in the fog, not knowing how much I was drift-ing or in what direction. I braced for the worst. Finally, the fog lifted enough for me to move on. I reached Shinnecock Canal Marina in Hampton Bay, Long Island, in the last bit of daylight. I was wiped out, and my confidence was shot.

Ten years later, in 2003, I had the same feeling that I'd had that day. I realized that my frightening experience on the boat was a clear metaphor for my life after politics and marriage. I felt now as I had then, lost without anything I usually depended on to keep me safe. I knew I needed to get to a place where I could, in a sense, depend on the coordinates—literally and immediately. I needed to let my internal GPS system take me back to where I'd started, to the time before Washington and politics and high stakes and fancy people. Somewhere I took a wrong turn. I needed to retrace my steps to the last place where I knew was the right course.

I would find myself driving back out to Queens from Manhattan. I knew where I was when I was in Queens.

Like Brooklyn, the Bronx, and Staten Island, Queens was always described as an "outer" borough. "Outer" suggests there's an "inner," and although it was not called that, the "inner" borough was Manhattan. In many ways, that's where the insiders lived. Everyone important seemed to think that Manhattan was the star. They considered Queens the star's less attractive sister. In reality, Queens was large enough to be its own city. It had its own personality. Its own worldview.

That's where I'd head. I'd drive the same loop, getting on the Grand Central Parkway or the Long Island Expressway, gambling on traffic. Past the airport and World's Fair to 188th Street. A slow pass by my father's parents' house on Rio Drive to see the spruce tree that, years before, had been uprooted in a storm and replanted by my grandfather, father, and uncle. Still thriving more than half a century later, it was a powerful reminder that family, work, care, and dedication can conquer adverse odds.

From there I'd drive to Pompeii Avenue to see the house

we lived in from the time when I was a few months old and my sister, Margaret, was three.

My childhood was marked by geographic simplicity. My elementary school, St. Gerard's, was a few blocks from home in one direction. My Cuomo grandparents were a few blocks in another direction. In Queens it was common for three generations to live at spitting distance from one another. My father's father, Andrea, went to church on Sundays, but his wife, my grandmother Immaculata, was a daily communicant. I was often the altar boy at the Masses she would attend. He drove her to and from Mass every morning. He may have cursed from time to time, but if he did, it was in Italian, and as a kid I never heard it. Like most men in Queens, Andrea worked to provide. He and Immaculata opened a small grocery store in Jamaica and lived in the apartment upstairs. They worked nearly 24/7, staying open until 11 P.M. and getting up at 2:30 and 4 A.M. to make sandwiches and coffee for truckers starting the day shift. After twenty-five years, they sold the store and used the proceeds to build several small wood-frame houses in Hollis. In 1958, my grandfather sold the cheapest one—my father called it "the runt," because it sat on a triangular piece of property—to my parents for $28,000.

It was a comfortable place to grow up. Our neighbors were union tradesmen and civil servants—cops, firefighters, bus drivers, mail carriers, sanitation workers. They had secure jobs in which you received benefits and a pension, and once hired, you seldom got fired. Being a tradesman—a carpenter, stonemason, auto-body mechanic, electrician, house painter—didn't come with the same perks, but these people commanded respect. There was an honor and an artistry to what they did.

Their children aimed for the same honorable jobs. In those days, Queens parents didn't aspire for their kids to be the president of the United States or president of IBM. They just wanted to raise productive citizens. Even if they could have provided their children with a trust fund, they wouldn't have. Hard work was expected.

My father's public service salary of $47,800 supported the six of us without much surplus. But if we'd been rich, he still would have insisted on hard work. He expected it from himself, and he demanded it from me. I didn't mind then, and I'm grateful for it now. My daughters, whose tuition is more than the average annual salary, may not be. They have endured my frequent lectures. "I worked minimum-wage jobs. That was two dollars an hour!" I say. Then and now I divide the cost of everything by two. "Those jeans cost eighty dollars! That's forty hours of work—almost a week's salary!"

Queens always had a diverse population. It is a residential United Nations Borough and a great experience. But despite diversity, the values were shared. Relationships were real. It wasn't utopia. But on the surface, and to my younger self, life was simple. People had problems, but hardly anyone ever got divorced. There were no scandals. No known infidelities. To me, Queens represented stability.

Driving around the old neighborhood in 2003 I found answers to current and old questions. I'd always wondered why my parents didn't sell the house on 197th Street until five years after my father became governor in 1983. Now I got It. Knowing that the house was there and that they could return anytime kept my father grounded, just as going back was helping me regain my equilibrium.

I thought about my grandfathers, with whom I'd shared a close bond. Different versions of the same model, both men were mechanically minded and gifted at working with their hands. Both exuded common sense. I wondered what their advice would be about my political and marital devastation. I was sure that they would have thought I was Icarus. I over-reached and got too fancy. But I am sure that they would have counseled me to take the long view. Sooner rather than later my life would fit back together. They had given me a strong foundation. That helped heal me.

By the time I knew him, my grandfather Andrea was old, and he had grown cautious. But as a child I'd been steeped in stories about when he was young and brave. He left Tramonti in southwestern Italy in 1926 and came to this country, a skilled craftsman with no prospects and a wife and baby back home. He took a back-cracking job laying sewers in New Jersey to earn the money to bring them to America. It took him twenty-three years to accomplish his goal: owning his own single-family home with a yard.

I've noticed that those who have the courage to leave their extended families and the comforts of home to come to a place where they don't know a soul or the language are often motivated people, with a strong work ethic and determination to succeed. This was certainly true of my grandfathers.

A truly gentle soul, Andrea devoted much of his time to his family. For many years, when my parents owned only one car, which my father drove to work, my grandfather took my mother grocery shopping and my siblings and me wherever we needed to go. You could tell he took pride in being useful.

We'd usually alternate Sunday dinner with my mother's and father's families. My grandfather's palace was a single-family home "unattached," as he was quick to add for people who may not have known. His backyard was often the place where the Cuomo family would get together. During the winter, my grandmother would cook all day Sunday for the "meal," which was more an affair that started at lunch and blended into dinner. Lasagna, sausage, braciole—hearty food, well prepared. The kids would run around outside and the grown-ups would sit, chat, and argue at the table for hours. The summer was my favorite time of year. My grand-father was a talented artisan. He especially enjoyed build-ing with stone. He had built from brick and marble a large outdoor stove with a chimney. He also built a long wooden picnic table that was freshly painted every year and seated about twenty-five. It reminded me of the table in the depic-tion of the Last Supper.

Another project was a concrete fishpond that was probably all of twelve feet in diameter but to me, as a boy, it was the Atlantic Ocean. The pond was filled with clear water so you could see the goldfish. He created a waterfall, powered by a garden hose, which cascaded into the pond.

At either end of the pond were two stone castles. These were my favorites. He built them in his basement during the winter from stones he'd picked up at the beach during the summer. Each stone was round, approximately two inches in diameter, whites and off-whites, and smooth from the water and sand. With these stones he fashioned four-foot-tall miniature cement-and-stone castles. He labored for days on them and was proud of his simple but impressive creation. On the top was a turret from which a miniature American flag flew—a symbol of my grandfather's constant, heartfelt refrain of God Bless America. I was taken with them and could spend hours playing with the fish and just imagining. I thought the whole affair was grand and my grandfather was Michelangelo. This was his expression of his artistic side, a side of his personality that he had the opportunity rarely to show. Life was too practical for him. He was an Italian laborer, a delicatessen operator seven days a week—who had time for art or creativity? It was a luxury—and his life had no space for luxuries. But now in his later life he had his artistic flourish and it was enough for him. And it was enough for all of us. We could have been on the Isle of Capri or on the side of a mountain, and I couldn't have been any more pleased. The simple pleasures for me were always the truest. The bells and whistles and faux sophistication, while initially attractive to me, ultimately left me unfulfilled. I was programmed in Queens; it was hardwired in my DNA. This is utopia. This was the perfect weekend. There were no trips to the Hamptons or Aspen. There was no Martha's Vineyard, and a trip over the George Washington Bridge was semi-exotic. No motorboats, jet skis, or private planes. But there was substance and nourishment for the body and soul. Having spent decades and gone out and had all the fancy Sundays that I thought I was missing when I lived in Queens, I found what I missed most was what I had left behind.

It was how Queens taught me Sundays should be.

And Queens was right.

My mother's father, Charles Raffa, was also an Italian immigrant, from Sicily. A craftsman who built much of the furniture in their home, he understood corners, angles, and how to turn a two-dimensional drawing into a three-dimensional work of art—not that all his projects were beautiful. A natural businessman, Grandfather Raffa earned his living manufacturing custom refrigerated cases for supermarkets. He was a fashionable man who was relatively "rich," or so we felt, or at least upper middle class. He enjoyed his success and what America did for him. He and my grandmother Mary lived in Flatbush, Brooklyn, but owned a second home forty miles from Manhattan on Lake Hopatcong in New Jersey. The lake was hardly farther from the city than most bedroom communities, but when we were there we thought we were in the "country." Built in the 1920s, the home included servants' quarters and a wide porch that overlooked the water and sat on three acres of land. There was a bell under the dining room table that the previous occupants would push when they wanted the butler or maid.

I was most impressed by the two-story boathouse where my grandfather kept his cherished twenty-two-foot Chris-Craft. I thought of it as a floating piece of furniture.

I spent most of my childhood summers and, often, school-year weekends at the lake. My sisters and I would swim for hours, or I'd drop a line off the pier, sometimes catching a pike, pickerel, or bass. We'd take a break only to devour the picnic lunch my mother would bring down from the house.

Grandfather Raffa often took me fishing and boating. My father never came. Looking back I realize he was trying to make up for my father's work-induced absences. He recognized that living in a house full of sisters, I could use some male companionship. Later I did the same with my younger brother, Chris. We swam and fished and laughed with each other and played simple games together. There were no electronic devices, no separate televisions or even radios. We entertained ourselves and each other.

While I loved the summers at the lake, I wanted to become independent and earn my own spending money. As a teenager I tried all kinds of jobs. I did short stints as a hardware store clerk, a tutor, and a security guard.

The summer I was sixteen, Ernie, a mason contractor—a classic first-generation Italian who lived down the street from my parents—said he'd pay me $50 a day, huge money back then, to work for him as a laborer. "It's a hard work," he warned.

"No problem," I said. I weighed about 220 pounds, and I'd been working out and lifting weights. I could pick up small cars. Cinder blocks would be easy.

The first day I jumped into his truck at 5:00 A.M. and we drove for about an hour to a large home on Long Island. Ernie got out, threw down a pick and shovel and a wheelbarrow, and spoke the words I will never forget. In his broken English, he said, "Pudda da driveway atop a da truck."

"What?" I asked.

Ernie repeated, "Pudda da driveway atop a da truck."

"What?" I asked again.

Frustrated by the communication divide, Ernie grabbed the sledgehammer and started pounding the concrete driveway. At first I thought he was angry and was acting out. But then he grabbed the pick and swung it so perfectly that it exactly hit the crack. He lifted a large chunk of concrete about six inches deep, picked it up, and threw it into the top of the dump truck about two feet over his head. "Pudda da driveway atop a da truck."

I got it.

I worked harder that day than I ever had before. When I got home at eight that night I was too tired to eat. I crashed on top of my bed and slept until four the next morning when it would start again.

I was adapting to the schedule and muscle fatigue. But three weeks into the job the temperature hit a hundred degrees. It felt hotter on the black asphalt parking lot of the Jewish Temple on Long Island. The supply trailer was at one end of a long parking lot. Maybe it was one hundred yards from the construction area, but it may as well have been a mile. My job, as the low man on the crew, was to unload the supplies. Ernie grew impatient if I carried less than what felt like several hundred pounds of material per trip. As I made the trek I watched the heat bounce off the asphalt in waves. On what must have been my four-hundredth fetch and carry, I started feeling light-headed. The next thing I remember was lying on my back looking up at Ernie pouring a bucket of water on my body. Once upright, I politely suggested ending my employment.

When I went to face Ernie several days later to get my last

paycheck, the workers all mocked me: this hulking kid who thought he was so tough but couldn't finish the day without fainting. For months I would drive to my house from the other direction just to avoid passing Ernie's home.

The immigrant tradition of hard work is not a myth. Immigrants work at jobs no one else wants. And they do it without unions and health care and lawyers.

They have my total respect.

Thinking about that summer made me remember other jobs. After I left Ernie's crew, I wanted something less strenuous—and the chance to be around kids my age—so I pursued an opening at Baskin-Robbins. I didn't mind scooping ice cream, but my vanity trumped a paycheck. Even with my low fashion quotient, I knew you could not look cool wearing a paper hat. Any gains you made when you gave a young lady a double scoop of fluffernut, a popular peanut-butter-and-marshmallow concoction, were canceled out by the hat. It was a girl repellant.

A couple of weeks later, when I was still refusing to wear that part of the uniform, I was fired.

I kept returning to the gas station where I would work off and on for ten years. It was an Esso Station (later, Exxon) owned by George Haggerty, who first hired me when I was fourteen. I don't think it occurred to my boss or my parents that I didn't have working papers. It was a nonissue.

George was kind and decent to me. He knew I was hard-working and trying to push myself in the right direction. Hollis was hardscrabble, and a number of my peers were already in trouble. There were few secrets. Everyone knew who was drinking too much, was doing drugs, was in a gang, or had dropped out of school. The girl who "got in trouble" and the boy who "got her in trouble." The labor pool was not top-round draft picks. I was reliable and conscientious. As soon as I could, I began buying, fixing up, and selling low-end cars for a few thousand dollars each.

As I got older, the part of the job that I enjoyed the most was manning the tow truck on the 4:00 P.M. to 8:00 A.M. shift while I was in school. The money was so good that during law school, I'd come down from Albany, work a weekend, and make about $300—enough to pay for tuition, rent, gas, and food.

I'd pick up the radio-dispatched truck and go. As long as I could reach a stalled vehicle within twenty minutes it didn't matter where I waited for the call. Sometimes I'd go to a friend's house or on a date, when I could find a girl who didn't mind the smell of gasoline and the rattling of chains! If I'd had a tough week, I'd nap at my parents' house in be-tween calls, leaving the home phone number for the dis-patcher. Although I slept with the phone near my head, often I was so tired I slept through the ring. My father did not. He'd get up and wake me. He was never a soft touch, but he was a good sport about it and appreciated that I was a hard worker. My mother, who has never lost her girlish humor and is always up for anything, would keep me company on some dispatches. She acted as if she was doing it for fun. Now, as a parent myself, I know she rode shotgun to make sure I stayed awake. We had a good time.

I have great memories from those days. I met Damon Runyon–type characters who lived hard lives with hard drinking, hard jobs, hard women, and hard breaks. Salt-of-the-earth people leading real lives. Some who overcame their circumstances and many who were overcome by circumstance.

Friday and Saturday night society could be found at the neighborhood bar. Each neighborhood had its spectrum of quiet, rowdy, pickup, and just bad bars. I could handle the spectrum. Twenty years later I can visit the same bars and meet some of the same people sitting on the same stools. They never left "the neighborhood" and are proud of it.

For boys in Queens, there was a progression. You'd go from a minibike or go-cart to a motorcycle and then a hot rod that was meant for showing off. I bought a minibike at thirteen. Naturally, by eighteen, I'd traded up. My mother and I had equally strong feelings about my new motorcycle. I loved it. She couldn't stand it! I had the advantage. The fact that she had her hands full with my brother and three girls meant that she had a looser grip on me. She was too exhausted to wait up for me at night.

As an adult I've found that a big part of being a successful executive is motivating, cajoling, managing, and rewarding people to act. It led me to become a relationship manager among political forces and factions. But when I need to decompress, I head to the garage—my man cave. (As the father of three daughters, you find that a locked toolbox becomes a man's only true personal space.) There I can work on my 1975 Corvette, my prize, which I bought and fixed up when I was in college. I joke that the daughter who gets the "Blue Angel" when I go to the afterlife will know she was my favorite. A Corvette was always the dream car for a boy from Queens. We were not sophisticated enough for Ferraris or Porches.

Also, we were Americans, and this country made the best, and the best was a Corvette. My 1968 GTO navy blue convertible is also a beauty. And I keep two Harley-Davidsons. My Harley Custom Dyna Glide is a little rough and scratched up, but I've had it a long time. Like me, it shows the scars of battles but survives.

I wouldn't say that I'm an adrenaline junky, but I do like the thrill of speed. I like fast cars. Fast boats. Fast motorcycles.

There's nothing quite like taking a motorcycle into a curve, right up on the edge of its capacity. Everything is wiped clean from your mind. Thoughts of the meeting you have on Monday morning are immediately eclipsed by survival instincts.

I'm still partial to the American muscle car with a hefty eight-cylinder engine where you hear and feel the power. I'm not a four-cylinder foreign-car fan. Nor am I in love with the new cars with their admittedly more sophisticated engineering. The electronics make them feel more like a video game than a mechanical powerhouse. I've had dozens of cars, mostly late 1960s and early '70s models, and they are still works of art to me.

I most enjoy speed on the water. The thrill is the feeling that at any moment Mother Nature could pick you up and flip you like a pancake on a griddle. But when the wind and spray are in your face, and your senses are on overload, it's great. It's one of the things I miss being governor. Having State Police always nearby dampens one's sense of adventure. Diligence and prudence may be words to live by, but they can be boring!

I graduated from high school in the spring of 1975 and went to Fordham University in the fall, living at home and commuting to the Bronx for classes. I still unclogged sinks and mended window screens, attended my sisters' ballet recitals, and took Chris to Boy Scouts and Little League. I couldn't leave and put even more responsibility on my mother.

During law school, I kept my weekend tow truck operator's job. My earnings and loans paid for law school and my share of the apartment I rented with my father, and I graduated with no debt, having paid back what I owed. I moonlighted for AAA until 1982, when my father launched his campaign.

Driving around Queens, looking at the places where I used to work and hang out, was my version of grief therapy. In that quiet time I realized that when you're growing up the message is only about winning. There is no college course called "Losing 101." Commencement addresses exhort graduates to soar. Speakers say things like: "Go for it! The world is your oyster! Dare to succeed! You're limited only by your own dreams!"

No one talks about the flip side: inevitably, we all experience loss. We may do it to ourselves or life may do it to us, but sooner or later loss hits all of us squarely between the eyes. Real, adult loss. You lose your job, get divorced, face a health crisis, have a child with a serious issue, experience the death of a loved one. You can try to insulate yourself, but the reality is that much of life is beyond our control—as frightening as that thought may be.

After my back-to-back debacles, I began to realize that what matters most is how you handle losing. You can wallow in it, or you can push through it. You can choose to let it break you, or you can choose to let it teach you.

Winners are successful losers.

I was so struck by our culture's inability to acknowledge these difficult truths that I considered writing a book on how to deal with loss. My preliminary research turned up astounding examples of people who had lost big and come back better, who failed—sometimes repeatedly—but kept trying and succeeded. Michael Jordan didn't make his high school's varsity basketball team the first time he tried out. Elvis Presley got a C in music. Steve Jobs got fired from Apple. Oprah Winfrey went to Baltimore to coanchor the evening news. Within eight months she was demoted to early morning headline reader. Isaac Newton failed at school. Harry Truman's haberdashery business ended in bankruptcy.

I reread Elisabeth Kübler-Ross's 1969 book, *On Death and Dying*, and from that, I developed my own thoughts about loss.

During my years with HELP I sat in on dozens of counseling sessions, 12-step meetings, and interventions that made me aware of human behavioral patterns. What I took away was that, as with Kübler-Ross's first stage of grief, our initial response to failure is denial. We come up with excuses and blame circumstances or other people. It makes us feel better in the short term. We need a salve. Denial is a buffer when the truth is too painful.

It is natural to claim a no-fault divorce—as in, no fault of mine. Few people will, in the throes of ending their marriage, say, "Yeah, I really screwed up!"

I remembered sitting in HELP 12-step meetings and hearing twenty versions of the same story: "My husband came home. He didn't look at me. It made me feel bad. I had a sip of wine. Once I had the sip of wine . . ."

I wanted to say, "Have you noticed there's a pattern here? Hellooo! It isn't about your husband not looking at you. It's about you. If you don't look inward and become more self-aware, you're going to repeat the same pattern for the rest of your life."

But ironically, my first reaction to my loss—the divorce and the campaign—was what I'd heard at so many HELP sessions: I'm a victim, an innocent bystander. Life conspired to hurt me. Mine was a nightmare come true in tabloid color. And I handled it by being defensive.

I was too hurt to accept any blame, but I was good at blaming others. My friends listened while I listed the reasons I'd lost to Carl McCall. Sometimes I'd say it was the Democratic Party, the political environment, and 9/11. At other times I'd put it on the nasty *New York Times'* reporter, Pataki, and the *New York Post* for exploiting my "coat holder" comment. The trap is that there is a scintilla of truth in all these rationalizations, so the logical mind can seize them.

I try to understand what I went through so that I don't repeat my own pattern. I also talk to my girls about it so they can better understand me and begin to understand themselves. Everyone experiences loss differently, but for me it was in five phases. Here's what I learned—and tell my girls:

In Phase One any excuse is OK. Transferring guilt or blame to a third party is a necessary short-term strategy for intense pain. It allows us time to stabilize and deal with the immediate problem. It's true for people across all situations. The other day one of my daughters was upset about a grade and blamed me for keeping her out so long that she didn't study enough. I was in "Daddy dungeon"—loud music, one-word answers, no eye contact, no laughing at my jokes (this last one also happens when I'm not in the dungeon)—her way of reminding me that she's mad without having to speak. The incarceration can last from a few hours to a few days, depending on my infraction.

I get that. I've done it. Blame buys time. We're all entitled to nurse our wounds, but if we want a different outcome the next time, we have to hold ourselves accountable.

Phase Two is about an honest, accurate assessment of liability. You have to take stock of where you went wrong and stop the behavior. If you do this, you'll grow. If you don't, you'll stagnate. It's that simple and that complicated. Most people spend a lifetime avoiding a frank self-assessment of their strengths and weaknesses. It's hard to scrutinize the person in the mirror. Acknowledging your flaws during the rocky times can be almost impossible. But I knew if I didn't recognize them, I'd never grow past this moment. My personal and political losses had one common denominator: me.

When I considered the emotional cost of the campaign, I concluded that it wasn't wrong for me to have taken on Carl McCall. What was wrong was how I handled it. Instead of methodically laying the foundations for a campaign and proving that I was the better candidate—one with a real shot at defeating George Pataki—I let arrogance get in the way. I was wrong to think that my experience in Washington would count in New York, wrong to think I didn't have to work hard to earn people's respect, and wrong not to lay the groundwork and go to people first, before I acted.

I repeated that mistake in my marriage. My ideas about long-term relationships came from my parents—a union of a different generation and between two different people. My father had been raised to support a family. My mother, to be a stay-at-home mom. But there had been a huge shift in expectations since my parents married in the 1950s.

What I didn't take into account was that a marriage is only as good as two people are willing to continue to make it. Marriage is organic. It breathes. It experiences joy and sorrow. To succeed it must be fed and nurtured. It requires constant effort.

Phase Three: Apologize, truly. Own your part without discounting the other person's liability. In most situations there is shared culpability, but people use the other person's actions to excuse their own. They are two separate situations; own yours. I apologized to Kerry for too much work and not enough downtime, for taking work too seriously and our relationship too lightly. I had a Hallmark-card view of marriage—love magically conquers all.

Blame, acceptance, and apologies do not always happen sequentially. Ten days after I dropped out of the race, I apologized to Carl McCall.

I belatedly realized that when I boycotted the state convention in May 2002 I'd stiffed the Democratic Rural Conference delegates who had gone out on a limb to endorse me. I needed to show the Democratic establishment, including Carl, that I was sorry.

Making good on that promise, Joe Percoco and I had spent a good bit of October crisscrossing the state, going to Democratic committee fund-raisers for local candidates. I went wherever I was invited: a chicken barbecue at a rifle range in Schoharie County; the great buffet at Antuns, in Queens; beer and wings in western New York.

At all the stops, I made the case for Carl. Then I took the county chairs aside and told them, "I put you in a tough spot when I was running for governor, and I'm sorry. I want to make it right for you now."

Some people were angry, but I've always found that it's hard to maintain anger when someone is admitting a mistake: "I know I screwed up, and I'm sorry."

If they didn't forgive me, I didn't try to defend myself. You can't say, "I apologize, but." The "but" negates the apology. It's akin to saying, "I apologize, but you egged me on."

Most people were gracious. They'd say, "Andrew, you're a young guy. You're going to do this again. I'll be there for you."

It was gratifying to hear, but I didn't think I would ever be anything besides Andrew Cuomo, private citizen. I couldn't imagine running again. And I was at peace with it.

Phase Four: Forgive yourself. It's not a new concept, but it's the step I found the most difficult. I was frustrated with myself for botching up my chances at winning a job I really knew I could do well—and for getting divorced.

But when I accepted the obvious—that, like all people, I'm flawed and bound to make mistakes, and that's OK—I became more compassionate. I found that when you forgive yourself, it's easier to forgive others. They're not perfect. Yeah, but I'm not perfect either.

Another thing that has made me more compassionate is being open about my mistakes and about the lessons I learned by making them. When I visit people who have lost their belongings to a flood or have been laid off from their jobs, I speak from firsthand experience. "Life will knock you down," I tell them. "You do what's necessary to fix it. You clean up. You rebuild. You begin again."

I know that they can do it, because I did.

All this has also tempered my expectations for my children. I don't expect my daughters to be flawless. I remind them, "We're human beings, and we're imperfect. You do the best you can. You try to be good. You try to be better every day. The trick is to get back up. Learn from it. And start over."

Phase Five: Move forward.

Holding on to anger is corrosive. Give it up.

Don't regret the past. It will keep you from growing.

Don't resent those who were successful where you weren't. Resentment will keep you from accomplishing the next great thing.

Some religions recognize that to move forward you have to let go of the past. In Judaism you throw bits of bread into a moving body of water, usually on the first day of the Jewish New Year, Rosh Hashanah. This represents the casting off of the previous year's sins. Catholics confess to a priest who then assigns, as a penance, prayers that, when completed, return the penitent to a state of grace. In Islam, supplicants talk directly to God.

Whatever you believe, catharsis is the key.

I never wrote the book on loss.

But I did follow the steps to make my life whole again.

What really got me through was my girls. I did all I could to make amends to my three daughters. I believe divorce hurts kids. It's a painful situation at the time, and a bad legacy later. I also think the theory "Better a divorce than a bad marriage" can sometimes be true but is often a convenient rationalization.

In the spring of 2004, after I signed a lease on a modest two-bedroom apartment in Battery Park City in Lower Manhattan, I piled the girls into my car and drove uptown to ABC Carpet and Home, a store in the Flatiron District that would have everything I needed to furnish the apartment.

When we arrived home, the car was packed with faux gazelle and zebra rugs, beanbag chairs, DIY bunk bed kits, spinning light fixtures, purple sheets, and pink towels. Cara liked one set of dishes; Mariah, another; and Michaela, a third. Rather than decide, I bought all three. My daughters had been through so much that I was willing to do almost anything to make them feel happy and settled, even if this meant the apartment would look as though it had been decorated by three little girls whose combined ages didn't add up to twenty-five.

In Washington and Westchester we had a full-time nanny, so the learning curve was steep for Mr. Mom. The girls stayed with me about 50 percent of the time. The back-and-forth meant chaos, displacement, and hours in the car for them. If one daughter had a soccer game or a birthday party in Mount Kisco, I had to take the other two to Westchester with me. They were troopers, carrying their little suitcases, but they were really too young to pack for themselves as they shuttled between the suburbs and the city. There was an unending chorus of "I left this book here. I left this shirt there. Where's my favorite ——?" Each weekend we were together, I'd have to take them shopping for all the things they forgot. I knew even less about girls' dresses and tights than I did about furnishing an apartment, and I discovered that young girls picking out clothes could be finicky. It didn't help that I had the patience of a gnat.

One thing we got good at was putting dinner on the table. We called. Food was delivered. The family favorite was pizza—served on our mix-and-match dishes.

The days when I didn't have the kids, I often worked until midnight, and I volunteered to spend many of my off-weekends traveling to Europe to negotiate deals for Island Capital. Andrew Farkas could not have been more understanding. He had been divorced and knew what I was going through. He would go out of his way to help me with the kids. When the girls were with me, I left my office by 4 P.M., in time to help with homework. I was glad to have a good job, but after working seventeen-hour days, every day, for my adult life, I found that no activity was more satisfying than spending time with my daughters around the kitchen table. The rule I adhered to then still holds true today: they come first. When I have them with me, I don't go out.

I did everything I could to help my children heal. I didn't expect that doing this would heal me. They became my refuge. When I thought *All is lost*, I countered with *No, all is not lost*. Put your energy over there. It wasn't about me, because it was about them. It was not about my pain; it was about the pain I'd caused them. I was surprised to learn that children can give support to a parent. I thought I was helping them, but it turned out they were helping me.

My parents were another tremendous source of comfort. My father and I didn't talk much about what I'd been through, but we shared a tacit understanding. When he lost the governorship in 1994, my parents moved to a co-op apartment on the East Side of Manhattan. Whenever I had the girls for the weekend, we would go there for a huge traditional Italian Sunday dinner.

My mother is a hands-on grandmother. When I was working at HUD and the girls were babies, she'd come to Virginia to babysit. Now she put them in kid-size aprons and taught them how to make homemade marinara sauce and meatballs. While I sat in the living room with my father, I'd hear the four of them giggling in the kitchen.

My girls got to see the softer side of my father. They'd sit with him on the couch and watch a ball game, something he had done only rarely when I was growing up. The first time I saw a pillow that read, "If I knew grandchildren were going to be this much fun, I would have had them first!" I thought, *That must have been made with my father in mind.*

You don't have to do something many times before children think of it as a ritual. Mariah, Cara, and Michaela were delighted with this new tradition, and I realized how much I'd missed by not spending enough time with my family during my Washington years. Jeff Sachs and my brothers-in-law Brian O'Donoghue, Kenneth Cole, and Howard Maier were tremendous supports. The politics never mattered to them in the first place.

My salvation was my girls, my real friends, and Sandy.

I first met Sandra Lee, a Food Network star in 2005, at a cocktail party in the Hamptons given by a friend and political adviser Alexandra Stanton. I was not a big Food Network watcher at the time. I didn't expect to react like that. Sandy is my opposite: a West Coast girl with expertise in cooking, entertaining, and decorating. A businesswoman who had never heard of New York politics. What a relief! I quickly fell in love with her. Why she got involved with me I don't know. I was not much of a catch.

But Sandy was. Smart, successful, and gorgeous, she had launched her flagship TV show, *Semi-Homemade Cooking with Sandra Lee*, a few years earlier. She has enormous appeal to viewers and to readers of her books and magazine, who lead busy lives and want to put good food on the table quickly. No marketing gimmick, her "smart and simple" approach grew out of her hardscrabble beginnings: the eldest of five children, with an abusive mother and stepfather, Sandy had to shop and cook for the household and take care of her siblings—on welfare and food stamps—starting when she was twelve. Her roots have also inspired her philanthropic work: she has devoted herself to the cause of ending childhood hunger in America.

More than a catch, Sandy was a godsend.

Her drive and hyperorganization make her my temperamental match. But we are different in more ways. She is joyful, spontaneous, and interested in a side of the world that I don't think about without some prodding. She loves traveling, fashion, and art. Being with her has made me think about things that are a realm apart from what I do. That's good, because she balances my obsessive focus on government.

Aware of Sandy's decorating talent, I was intimidated the first time I brought her to see my apartment. With good reason. As soon as I opened the door, she gasped. "Promise me you will throw out the animal skin rugs," she said.

I didn't introduce her to my girls right away, afraid to pile on another adjustment in their lives. But Sandy is an exquisitely kind, loving, and nurturing person with an uncommon ability to connect with people. She was as adept at taking care of three young girls as I was not. My children took to her immediately, and as they've grown older, she has been a significant presence in their lives. We have made a family.

She taught me to make Crock Pot dishes, and I have instilled in her a love of fishing.

OK, that's a stretch. She has taught me to flip the switch on the Crock Pot, and I have persuaded her to come out on my boat. With a good book. I thought of buying her a new motorcycle so that we could go riding together, but that was a nonstarter. Instead, I bought a Harley Electra Glide. It's like a couch on two wheels, and I am her chauffeur.

On one trip out to Queens to recalibrate, I took Sandy. We were getting to know each other and I wanted her to know the "real me" and not be confused with the Manhattan fanciness and past glory.

During the day we stopped in front of my grandfather's old house. We were sitting in the car. I was talking about the history and showing her the now-defunct fishpond and backyard shrine to my grandfather. Sandy said it was a shame that no one took the castles. I explained that they were cemented in, probably weighed several hundred pounds each, and would likely break if you tried to move them. Plus the house had been sold years before and there was a new owner. Sandy is more gutsy than I am in some ways and said I should ring the bell and explain the situation and see what they said. What?! Crazy! How embarrassing. What could I say. "Hi, yes, I'm Andrew Cuomo, grandson of Andrea and Immaculata, and the dummy who was just defeated in the election and went through the messy divorce. Now I'm in the yard art business and I want the castles."

"Fine," she said. "I'll do it."

"That would be even more humiliating!" I said. "What would you say: 'Hi, I'm with the dummy. He's in the car, too afraid to get out.'"

I rang the doorbell.

A woman answered and recognized me. She said that people often look at the house. My father had written a children's book, *The Blue Spruce*, that talks about the tree on the property that was upended and people sometimes came to take pictures of it.

I asked about the castles and she smiled. She got her husband on the phone and he couldn't have been nicer in offering to let me take them. "Of course," he said, "they're your family's. It's your heritage. Take them please. You should have them as mementos." I said I wanted to pay for them. No, no, no. Don't offend me, he said. I forgot where I was for a moment. This was Queens and there is a code. These are not rich people, but they have pride, respect, and honor. This was not about money. Thank you, I said. I will be back for them.

"You'll send someone—they're heavy, you know," he said.

"No, I will come back myself."

The next week, I brought the girls and Sandy. We were armed with shovels and a pick. We started digging around the castles as I was explaining the former glory of my grandfather's creation. The castles now had to be fifty years old. One broke as we dug it out. We removed it in about four pieces and I told the girls we would rebuild it. The girls were dirty and sweaty and their arms were covered with little scratches from the bushes but it was a healthy comforting exhaustion. This was a labor of love. Attempting to take the other castle was too much work for then. I returned another time with my brother, Chris, to get it. It came out in one piece. We brought it to my father for a father's day gift. He teared up when he saw it. I can count on one hand how many times I've seen my father cry.

I put all the pieces of the broken castle in crates to wait for a time to rebuild it. Sandy and I rented a couple of houses in Westchester to be near the girls. As they became older they were more involved with friends and school and I couldn't just drive them to my Manhattan apartment. Too many activities were in their neighborhood. So we rented in their neighborhood. Kerry and I had developed a good and warm relationship. She does much good work in the area of human rights that I try to help her with when I can. She has a very good relationship with Sandy. It's really all about the girls. Divorce, ironically, requires more coordination than marriage. Eventually we moved into a house not far from our old house in Mount Kisco.

It was not a grand home, but a sweet one. My grandfather would have liked it. And it had a small pond in the front yard! I hated living in the Manhattan apartment. I am not an apartment person and didn't like the lack of privacy and the inability to just get space. Everything was in boxes. I didn't know where I would end up. Moving into the house was putting down roots and a foundation. Sandy would talk about a "home base" and "safe environment" and that I was "unsettled." She was right. With the house now I could reestablish my life. All my clothes in one place, my pictures, my books, the evidence of my life was unpacked. I reassembled my tools and garage, where I could fix anything. Or at least at one time I thought I could. Until I learned that control is an illusion and that most of the big things in life are out of your control.

I enlisted the girls and we unpacked the crates with the pieces of the castle. It looked like a big jigsaw puzzle. I went to the store and bought cement, wire mesh, and a trowel. I hadn't seen a trowel in years. In Queens they were in every garage. I rebuilt the castle, piece by piece. I laid the mesh inside the cylinder of the castle's body and applied a new coat of cement, reenforcing the whole thing. It will last for another fifty years. I didn't have my grandfather's natural gifts, but it wasn't bad. And he would be pleased. I moved the entire creation to a select spot in the yard where I could see it from the kitchen window. My grandfather used to watch the squirrels climbing on the castle from his kitchen window. Placing that castle in the yard with Sandy's help was my way of saying, "I'm home." I went through hell and lost my footing for a while but now I'm back. I'm grounded. I made it through the fog. I know my direction and who I am, why I'm here, and what I will pass on. The castle will be there until my children move it, or don't!

The castle stands as a life compass pointing to true North. Whenever I have a question as to what direction I am heading, one look at the castle and I remember.

The second castle that Chris and I salvaged we put on the balcony of my parents' Sutton Place apartment overlooking the East River. It was a beautiful and powerful incongruity. Here among the richest people on the planet with the most sophisticated architecture is this crude roughhewn concrete castle with its little American flag waving in the breeze. Yes, out of place, indeed. But a symbol of values and respect to those who came before. A testament of natural talents and lives that sacrificed their joy and potential for their children. A reminder of who we are at our core, beneath the expensive clothing and the big titles, immigrants who started with nothing and were hardworking and courageous and decent and succeeded because this country helped them to succeed. God Bless America.

Some families pass on homes and estates, jewelry, watches, money. Cuomos pass on values. I'll take a cement castle any day.

People often ask me about the aftermath of my political and personal tribulations. The usual question is, "Did you change?"

The better question, I tell them, is, "Did you grow?"

And the answer is, Boy, did I.

To lose a career and a spouse in a matter of months is a double whammy I wouldn't wish on anyone. But if I were given the chance to erase those experiences, I wouldn't. They happened against my will. They left me devastated. I had to rebuild from the ground up. But what I thought was my undoing saved me. And was what made me the person I am today.

Those two seismic changes made me more empathetic, enabled me to see from different perspectives, and taught me that I am a great deal more resilient than I thought. In the process of working through the bad stuff, I developed simple, unshakable priorities. I dedicated myself to my girls, putting them ahead of work, politics, and myself. My hope is that when I get to the pearly gates and am asked if I was a good father, I will be in very good shape.

Being clear about what matters means that life is simpler for me now. I'm more appreciative of the irreplaceable and the small, powerful moments that make life whole, such as sitting quietly on my favorite rock at Saranac Lake. I've realized that core relationships are as rare as they are essential. These are the people who tell me what they think even when they know I don't want to hear it. And they know there won't be any fallout, because our relationship is based on truth.

When I was younger I put enormous pressure on myself. I was driven to accomplish as much as I could, as fast as I could. I had to prove myself. Now I'm content with myself, and that makes it much easier for me to be content with others. I do the best job I can. I don't dwell on what outsiders say about me. I care about how I measure up for the people I love.

I've come to understand that politics is not the only way I define myself. As important, if not more important, is nurturing my girls and seeing them grow; it's Sandy; it's my parents and siblings; and it's my relationships with the people who stuck by me then and will be there in the decades ahead.

Having gone through loss, I'm better equipped for what turned out to be a second tour of political duty. Losing gave me the chance to reflect on all I did and didn't do. I lamented the what-ifs and the should-have-dones. I am clear about my mission: I am bolder and gutsier this time around. I am focused on people, not politics. I realize that political capital is good to have only if you spend it challenging and changing the status quo. I know that the political business is nasty and filled with demagogues, hypocrites, and self-appointed critics. Popular opinion is mercurial and often shallow. Doing the right thing for the right reasons is all that matters. What "they" say is irrelevant.

Some have suggested that I see my return to political life as a second chance. Not really. I see it as if I had come back from the dead. And I've discovered that being a political Lazarus has a silver lining: when you survive your worst fears, there's very little that can shake you.

Part III

RISE

CHAPTER 7

Bonus Buster

*Introducing my father before my victory speech at the
2006 Democratic primary, when I secured the nomination for
attorney general, alongside my daughters—Cara, Mariah,
and Michaela—and my mother, Matilda.*

July 4, 2004.

Joe Percoco has played a lot of different roles in my
life. He was my father's gubernatorial advance man in the
1990s, my special assistant at HUD, my campaign manager

in 2002, my divorce counselor in 2003, and my fishing buddy on a Fourth of July fishing trip in the Hamptons. We were in Shinnecock Inlet, hosing the salt off my boat, when I said, "Hey, Joe. What would you think if I ran for attorney general?"

"Are you serious?" Joe asked.

"Thinking about it," I said.

"Andrew, why would you do that?"

"Because I don't bounce out of bed every morning anxious to go to work."

"Losing the gubernatorial race was a kick in the teeth. The divorce was a blow to the gut," he said. "But you've just put your life back together. You're making a decent buck. You've got time with the kids. You're single. Why stir that up?"

"It's nice to reach into my pocket and buy whatever I want," I said. "But I can be a good father whether or not I'm making a lot of money. I miss feeling what we were doing made a difference."

"I think you are crazy for wanting to go through it again," Joe said. "But I'm game if that's what you want to do."

Five months earlier, in February 2004, New York Attorney General Eliot Spitzer informally announced that he was running for governor in 2006. I was sleeping in Jeff Sachs's apartment, trying to find my balance. A political comeback wasn't only unlikely—it seemed completely undoable. I was shocked when some party regulars mentioned me for AG.

But by July a campaign—and a win—seemed possible. My life was beginning to stabilize. I started putting out a few feelers, talking to the people we knew, dropping in at a few Democratic dinners. We were taking a Sunday drive, not trying to compete behind the starting line at the Talladega Superspeedway. When anyone asked if I was running, I'd say what I'd said to Joe: "Thinking about it."

My reception among Democrats was mixed. Some Carl McCall allies were holding their grudges. But overall I found people are a forgiving lot. At the end of July, I flew to Boston for the 2004 Democratic National Convention, where John Kerry and John Edwards were accepting the nomination. I held on to my "Thinking about it" line.

I wasn't being coy. I was trying to decide: is this what I want? If it is, can I stand to put my family and myself through another campaign and possible loss?

My parents were still feeling stung by the beating I took in the press in 2002 and 2003. They didn't want me to run for AG. At my low point, my father had said, "After what you've been through, no one could blame you if you sat on a bar stool for the rest of your life and drank gin and tonics."

There were lots of reasons to run. The New York AG's office had been a passive backwater shop that went after scams and high-pressure hustlers selling fake Salvador Dalí lithographs, worthless diamonds, and a scheme to make millions in the supposedly lucrative earthworm market. But Eliot Spitzer had transformed it into a powerful, effective platform.

Spitzer went after Wall Street, forcing settlements against the securities and investment banking industries that had earned him headlines and nicknames like "the patron saint of small investors," "the Sheriff of Wall Street," and "Eliot Ness," after the federal agent who helped bring down Al

Capone. In 2002 he was *Time* magazine's "Crusader of the Year." Spitzer's weapon was a law known as the Martin Act. The "blue-sky" statute was enacted in 1921 to keep swindlers from selling swampland in Florida to New York citizens. Between 1911 and 1933, all but one of the nation's forty-eight states had passed similar laws, but none as strong as in New York. The Martin Act gives the New York attorney general the power to subpoena anyone conducting business in the state, authority to take investigations public or keep them quiet, and sole discretion to file criminal or civil charges. People questioned under the Martin Act have neither a right to a lawyer nor a right to remain silent.

"For three-quarters of a century, an unspoken gentleman's agreement bound the moneymen of Wall Street and the New York attorney general's office," Nicholas Thompson wrote in *Legal Affairs.* "The AG got to use . . . the Martin Act, but not against the big boys."

Spitzer "broke the deal," Thompson wrote. "He took the . . . legal equivalent of King Arthur's Excalibur, and plunged it into the guts of Merrill Lynch."

Spitzer's successor needed to shift what he had done exclusively on Wall Street to include rooting out corruption at the capitol on State Street and helping consumers on Main Street.

In criminal cases, the attorney general's office essentially operated like a DA's office or the U.S. Attorney's Office: as a prosecutor you find the facts. You bring the case. You go to sentencing. You close the book and move on. It's rare for prosecutors to clean up a systemic problem. They typically go after individual lawbreakers, using the office's subpoena

power to prosecute. Even in civil cases, they usually operated on a case-by-case basis, doing whatever came across
their desks. If they got a tip on insider trading, they did insider trading. If the tip involved consumer fraud, they did
that. They'd go after individuals in industries known for bad
practices, hoping to scare the ones that got away into better
behavior.

My vision was to refocus the office—to expose and attack
institutionalized injustices. Rather than doing "one-offs," as
I call them, I wanted to concentrate on areas where there was
widespread evidence of wrongdoing across an industry, and
then not just to punish the players but to devise the solution
and fix the problems. We would do it by leveraging the tremendous horsepower of the AG's office.

I felt I had the right mix of experience to be AG: I'd been a
prosecutor in the New York district attorney's office, worked
with the business and real estate communities during my
HELP years, and overseen 500 lawyers in the fight against
discrimination and housing fraud at HUD. I knew how to
protect consumers while preserving jobs. After four years
of George W. Bush in the White House, New York needed
someone who would take on the areas where the federal government had failed people—corporate abuse, public safety,
and labor rights, to name a few.

I examined my personal rationale. Fundamentally I believe that if you want to accomplish big things, if you want to
make positive social change, the best place to be is government.

My 2002 loss had freed me. Realizing your fears—and
surviving—is the ultimate liberation. Having nothing to lose

gave me tremendous confidence. When you're not afraid, you play your best game. What else could the press and my opponents do? After what I'd experienced, nothing could be awkward. Nothing could be humiliating. I had taken their best shot and gotten up off the canvas. They can't hurt me.

The field was crowded. Including me, seven people were vying to become the Democratic nominee for AG: Charlie King, my running mate in 2002, was a longtime friend whom I'd hired as a regional director at HUD. The group also included Michael Gianaris, a state assemblyman representing Queens; Denise O'Donnell, a former prosecutor from Buffalo; Richard Brodsky, a state assemblyman from Westchester County; and Sean Patrick Maloney, a Clinton administration official.

Mark Green was the most formidable opponent. The former New York City public advocate, Green had the résumé of a classic liberal from Manhattan's Upper West Side: he had been a college activist at Harvard in the 1960s and an acolyte of Ralph Nader in the 1970s. He'd written twenty-two books on politics and consumer advocacy. He was the darling of the *New York Times.*

But in my favor, Green was a perennial candidate, who'd run for office a dozen times and lost more than he'd won. He was abrasive and personally tactless. In 2001, on the eve of the Democratic primary for New York City mayor, polls showed Green ahead of Bronx Borough President Freddy Ferrer, City Comptroller Alan Hevesi, and City Council Speaker Peter Vallone. He was also in front of the Republican mayoral candidate, Michael Bloomberg. But after a series of post-9/11 missteps, Green lost to Bloomberg by two points, 50 percent to 48 percent. It was the closest general election the city had seen in a century.

I took an early lead in the race for AG. In December 2004, the *New York Post* quoted an anonymous source who said, "Right now, the smart money should be on Andrew." I have no idea who anonymous was, but I liked his opinion.

I did things differently than I had in 2002. Every county in New York has a Democratic committee. Every committee holds a couple of annual dinners. The larger ones usually throw galas in the spring and fall; the smaller ones hold summer picnics and fall fund-raisers. I went to them all. I paid my respects to local officials, built a base, and assumed nothing. My gubernatorial race was a stark reminder that all politics is local. I was reaching out to one person at a time—again and again. I sent birthday cards to county chairs and delegates, graduation cards to their children, and called with my condolences when their relatives died. I wanted to make it right.

Most of the people to whom I'd apologized, right after I lost in 2002, responded kindly. "You know what?" they'd say, "I was so touched that you came to see me two years ago, I'm going to support you now."

By the summer of 2005 I'd raised $3 million compared with Green's $1.2 million and collected key endorsements from Democratic officials and unions, including the Service Employees International Union/1199, the health-care workers' union. A few months later the *New York Times*—which was wholly supporting Green—summed up the race: "Democratic Elbows Are Flying, Mostly Aimed at Cuomo."

The Democratic Rural Conference (DRC), the straw vote

held by the state's forty-one rural counties in early March, is the first official event on the election-year calendar. Joe had agreed to be my campaign manager, but with the campaign not yet in full swing, we were still working our day jobs. He'd come to my Island Capital office a couple of evenings a week. We'd eat dinner and work our way down a call list of DRC delegates.

A huge number of the non-supporters said, "I know you're going to win, and I'm going to be for you down the road. But I'm voting for Richard Brodsky because he's from Westchester"—that kind of thing. No one said, "How dare you run? You're a bum."

I was back on track.

With Spitzer running for governor and Hillary Clinton up for reelection in the U.S. Senate, the Democratic Rural Conference was buzzing. But the AG's race was the most contested and drew the most speculation from the press. A lot of people had given me their commitment, but I took nothing for granted. I was thrilled when I won with 79 of 156 possible votes—two votes ahead of my competition. Combined.

My campaign was lean and mean. As reporter Jennifer Senior observed in a *New York* magazine profile, "I'm beginning to think that Cuomo lives in his car," she wrote. "What a comedown—not just to scale back your political ambitions but to live in your car on the campaign trail, and to actually be its driver."

Besides Joe, I had Bridget Siegel, a young, talented, and creative woman who'd proved in the 2002 campaign that she could outraise pros twice her age. Ashley Cotton, another '02

Me, approximately aged three.

To Andrew who makes us so proud.

The Two Men Who Made It All Possible

My two grandfathers, enjoying the view at Lake Hopatcong.

*All dressed up for my photo in the 1975
Archbishop Malloy High School yearbook.*

My father and me at campaign headquarters on December 31, 1982.

(WILLIAM E. SAURO/THE NEW YORK TIMES/REDUX)

Victory! My mother and father after my father's triumph.

Before my father's State of the State Address in 1983. Standing on the left, with glasses, is Gerald Crotty, first assistant counsel. My father is seated at center, talking to Mike Del Giudice, who is standing between me and Tim Russert.

At my swearing-in ceremony for the New York State Bar Association, 1983.

Me, as head of HELP, with John F. Kennedy Jr. during a radio interview in New Rochelle, New York, on May 17, 1989. Kennedy told listeners he would have no complaints if housing for the homeless was arranged in Hyannisport, Massachusetts. (AP PHOTO/GERALD HERBERT)

In a huddle with Bill Clinton and my father, 1992.

Me as Housing and Urban Development secretary, walking with USAID administrator Brian Atwood at the airport in Port-au-Prince, Haiti, on September 30, 1998, to inspect damage from Hurricane Georges.

With President Bill Clinton during the December 20, 1996, ceremony to announce my appointment as Housing and Urban Development secretary.
(CHUCK KENNEDY/AFP/GETTY IMAGES)

At debate camp in October 1996 with Al Gore, who at the time was running for vice president. (OFFICIAL WHITE HOUSE PHOTOGRAPH)

My parents, Mario and Matilda, with one of the castles created by my grandfather Andrea.

Under the hood of my '68 GTO. It embarrasses my daughters, but my brother, Chris, and I love working on American muscle cars.

My first debate in the New York State attorney general's race, on October 15, 2006, against my opponent Jeanine Pirro. (AP PHOTO/JAMES ESTRIN, POOL)

*At my swearing-in ceremony as attorney general
on January 1, 2007, at the New York State capitol in Albany, New York.
My daughter Cara held the Bible.*

Relaxing with my girls, Mariah, Cara, and Michaela.

With my family on the stage. The sign says it all.

Casting my vote in the 2010 election in Mount Kisco, New York, with Sandy and my daughter Michaela. (AP PHOTO/SETH WENIG)

With Lieutenant Governor–elect Robert Duffy on November 2, 2010— Election Night! (AP PHOTO/KATHY WILLENS)

Walking from the Executive Mansion in Albany the day after I was sworn in as governor. From left to right: Cara, me, Sandy, Michaela, Mariah.

My proud parents at my swearing-in ceremony as governor at the Executive Mansion in Albany, New York, on December 31, 2010. (AP PHOTO/MIKE GROLL)

The Cuomo clan's yearly reunion.

*Serving as grand marshal of the 2011 Israeli
Day Parade, with my daughter Cara.*

On August 28, 2011, in the aftermath of
Hurricane Irene, I took this photograph out of my car window
of the floodwater in Margaretville, New York.

I returned to Margaretville three days later to survey the damage
caused by the storm and to monitor the ongoing recovery efforts.

President Obama poses for a photograph with me and my girls after arriving on Air Force One at Buffalo Niagara International Airport in Buffalo, New York, 2013. (AP PHOTO/HEATHER AINSWORTH)

Me in Breezy Point, New York, on October 31, 2012,
assessing the damage from Hurricane Sandy.

In Lindenhurst, New York, on November 3, 2012, surveying
more destruction from Hurricane Sandy and comforting a resident
whose shoreside home was destroyed.

*Fishing on Follensby Pond in the Adirondacks,
July 2013, with Cara and Michaela.*

*I was proud to participate alongside New York's finest in the 2013 9/11
Memorial Bike Ride down the West Side Highway to the World Trade Center
site, the same route taken by firefighters on September 11, 2001.*

veteran, was our drill sergeant, albeit one with plenty of charm, who kept me ahead of the task. I also had Jennifer Cunningham, a real New York professional, who was working with the powerful SEIU Local 1199 and was strategically brilliant.

The next campaign milestone was the New York Democratic Convention in Buffalo at the end of May. With 401 delegates, my call list felt endless. But getting a commitment is just step one. Step two is hanging on to delegates when every candidate is putting on the same full-court press.

The night before the floor vote in 1982 when my father was battling to stay in the game against Ed Koch, we had put our delegates on a boat on Lake Onondaga, out of Koch's reach. This time we went to the other extreme. We rented a big restaurant downtown and threw the best party in Buffalo. It was so packed we had to take over the bar next door.

The nominations were set for the next morning. First Eliot was nominated for governor. AG was next. We had twenty volunteers running around holding up Cuomo signs, making sure we were TV-ready. I knew I was ahead, but sitting with my family in my hotel room waiting for the count, I couldn't watch. I was as nervous as a first-timer.

The convention vote is weighted, with the number of delegates from each assembly district determined as a percentage of voter turnout from the last general election. This automatically means that the more densely populated counties—mostly downstate—have the most delegates. As always the count began with the first district, Montauk, on Long Island, and moved west, then north. By the time we hit the Syracuse area, I was over the 50 percent mark. Once I knew I was going to win the nomination I enjoyed watching the count. By the time the second ballot ended, I'd captured 67 percent of the vote. I was stunned. Even with Green's commanding presence in New York City and O'Donnell's name recognition upstate, I hadn't been shut out of one county. Green came in second, with 19 percent. The others still in the race—King, O'Donnell, and Maloney—divided up the small change. With less than 25 percent of the vote, my opponents would have to circulate petitions to get on the September 12 primary ballot. Green was livid, but those were the rules.

"What a difference four years makes," I said, when it was my turn to address the crowded convention hall. Looking down from the lectern at my mother, father, three daughters, and Sandy in the front row, I added, "I am a smarter, better candidate."

One thing I didn't change was my core team. From Memorial Day to Election Day it was a reunion of Cuomo "alumni." Mike Del Giudice, who'd been my father's secretary during his first term, was a pro at state government. Besides knowing Albany, he could answer the most important question in any campaign: "What does the average person care about?" Drew Zambelli had been my father's top aide in the early 1990s. A marketing guru, he'd worked with some of the best-known companies in the country. Similarly, Howard Glaser had worked with me at HUD. He also worked on the campaign. There was Rich Sirota, who had started with my father in 1973; we grew up together. He handled all the finances in my campaign as treasurer. Harvey Cohen and Jonathan Cronin produced great films. My brother-in-law Brian O'Donoghue, a smart lawyer, took leave to help manage the effort. No one had a title. Each one was a tell-it-as-you-see-it friend—essential in a campaign, and in life. They volunteered their time, meeting once or twice a week to divide up the work. Then they'd go get it done.

It felt like the scene in the movie *The Blues Brothers*. John Belushi says, "Now, who here at this table can honestly say that they played any finer or felt any better than they did when they were with the Blues Brothers?" For me, that sums up what it feels like to work on a campaign and to be in government.

On the stump I highlighted my record at HUD—fighting against the Ku Klux Klan, creating housing for the homeless, promoting gun safety, advocating for civil rights. Apart from defending the state, about 20 percent of the AG job is fighting white-collar crime. The rest is recovering funds for taxpayers. I talked about the office as a vehicle for social, racial, and economic justice. I took a stand in favor of same-sex marriage and against the death penalty.

I campaigned hard, but I didn't lose sight of my top priority: being a father to the twins, eleven, and Michaela, almost nine. One Sunday night during the summer Joe and I were going over my schedule for the week. "The event with the Clintons is this Thursday," he said. "We'll have to arrange a sitter for the girls."

"No we don't," I said. "Thursday's my night with them."

"I understand that, but this is the president and Hillary. Donors will be there. You're the only AG candidate invited, and it will be a good way to get a leg up on the others. I'm sure the press will cover it."

"That's nice," I said. "I'll say yes another time."

"But Andrew, this is important. What if *I* take the kids out for dinner?"

Nope. I had learned the important lessons.

During the Clinton years, two zillion events had seemed like must-attends. I realized belatedly that there are only a few things anyone really *has* to do. You have to be there when it's your night with your kids. You have to be a good parent. You have to be a good son or daughter. Period. I had fear and guilt about the divorce when it came to the kids. It didn't matter who wanted the divorce; they were paying the price. I was committed to doing everything I could to make it up to them. They were number one in my life and they would know it—always.

It was important to keep my eye on the goal. In the last days before the election, we introduced a TV commercial that was the brainchild of Jennifer Cunningham: "Eliot Spitzer is leaving some very big shoes to fill," with prominent Democrats from around the state, including Charlie Rangel, Ed Koch, U.S. Representative Nita Lowey from Westchester County, Bill Thompson, the New York City comptroller, and Albany mayor Jerry Jennings, explaining why I was the person to fill them.

I had a twenty-point lead heading into the election, but I knew that being ahead means little in a New York Democratic primary. Polls don't always reflect who's coming out to vote. Anything could happen.

On the night of the primary, we waited for the election returns in the presidential suite at the Sheraton Centre, the same room where we'd received word of my father's loss to George Pataki in 1994—ultimate proof that I'm not superstitious. By about 9:30, when numbers from the Upper West

Side, Green's redoubt, came in, and they favored me, we knew we'd as much as won. Five minutes later the Associated Press called the race.

I bested Green 53 percent to 33 percent. Sean Maloney came in third, with 10 percent.

Sandy, my parents, my siblings, and my daughters were in the suite with a few close friends—people who'd given me their all for years.

As a parent I now know that what you hope for most in life is your children's happiness. I also know that you're powerless to make that happen. I was straightening my tie, preparing to go downstairs to give my acceptance speech, when I caught my mother's expression in the mirror. I could tell by the way she looked at me that she and my father were finally exhaling. I was touched. They knew I'd be OK, win or lose the general election.

There are only four statewide elected positions in New York. The Democratic ticket I was part of for the general election included Eliot Spitzer for governor, David Paterson for lieutenant governor, and Alan Hevesi for reelection as state comptroller. I did a few events with Spitzer, but I mainly went solo against my Republican opponent Jeanine Pirro. A popular former Westchester DA with wide name recognition and the backing of the business community, Pirro came out kicking. After declaring her intent to run a "positive, issues-oriented campaign," her next line was: "There is no comparison between our records." Her attack strategy was to characterize me as unqualified.

The Democratic ticket had its own drama. In mid-October the state Ethics Commission reported that Comptroller Alan Hevesi had "knowingly and intentionally" violated the law for using government employees to drive his ill wife to medical appointments. Known in the tabloids as "Chauffeur-gate," the findings dogged Hevesi throughout his campaign. Spitzer handed off a criminal investigation to the Albany DA's office and withdrew his endorsement of Hevesi. I had not endorsed him. I said: "I think Alan Hevesi has seriously compromised his ability to do his job."

Pirro's personal saga did not derail her attacks against me. In our first debate, she called me "a junior prosecutor more than twenty-one years ago . . . a non-practicing lawyer, looking to be the top lawyer for the State of New York" and tried to undermine my record at HUD: "You didn't clean up corruption at HUD."

She continually said that prosecutors had concluded she had not had her husband bugged, even though the investigation was ongoing.

In the second debate, I hit back, challenging her to release her tax returns from fourteen years earlier when she had filed jointly with her husband, and citing the investigations she was under, including one, by Eliot Spitzer, to see if she had used her position as DA to protect corrupt officials. "The office she is seeking is investigating her," I said.

Three days before the election, I was leading 61 percent to 33 percent. On Election Night we were back in the Sheraton suite when Joe Percoco's phone rang at 9:35 P.M. It was Pirro. With 90 percent of the numbers in, I'd won 58 percent to 39 percent. She was calling to concede.

I wasn't surprised, but I experienced a surreal moment anyway. It wasn't over winning per se. I felt so lucky that I would get to do what I most wanted—to be back in government.

Standing on the stage at the Sheraton Centre Hotel holding hands with my daughters, I thought, maybe I will get to do this job for four years. Maybe it will be eight years. Maybe I will get a shot at something else after this; maybe I won't. But if what I have is one or two good terms as attorney general, I'll be proud of my career. After I gave my acceptance speech, the campaign staff and family came back to the suite. Spitzer and Paterson had won the statehouse, Hevesi was reelected comptroller, despite his ethics violations, and Hillary Clinton was keeping her U.S. Senate seat. Democrats hadn't held all four statewide positions and two Senate seats since World War II.

Everyone in the suite was giddy. I felt content. "What's great about tonight is all these people in this room," I said. "You invested in me. You didn't give me one chance. You gave me two. Thank you from the bottom of my heart."

The time between being elected and taking office was short and busy. I asked my transition team, headed by Stephen Younger, a commercial litigator, past president of the New York State Bar Association, and friend since our law school days in Albany, to conduct a nationwide talent search for the senior positions. "Politics are irrelevant," I said. "Party affiliation is irrelevant. Whether or not I know them is irrelevant." When I was an assistant DA I'd seen the model set by Bob Morgenthau, who attracted good people, politics aside.

As the "people's lawyer," I could not politicize the AG's office. "Bring me the best of the best," I said. "It will be my job to persuade them to come on board."

We put together a strong bipartisan transfer team and recruited some of the most revered legal academics and professionals in the country. Some names popped up right away. One was Steve Cohen. An assistant U.S. attorney for the Southern District, Steve had been chief of the violent gangs unit. In private practice he'd helped overturn high-profile wrongful conviction cases and represented the online music service Napster over copyright infringement. Steve Cohen's name landed on the list on his merits, so it was a pleasing coincidence that I'd known him well since the early days of my father's governorship. He knew a prosecutor's office and the political environment in New York.

Mylan Denerstein was also recommended by many, but getting her to switch teams was tough. Deputy fire commissioner in charge of NYFD Legal Affairs, Mylan was a former federal prosecutor who was doing innovative work and wasn't job-hunting. I'd never met her, but she and Steve Cohen were friends from the U.S. Attorney's Office, so I asked Steve to ask her to meet us for breakfast. The two Steves—Younger and Cohen—and I met her at a restaurant near her home. Assuming she'd recognize me, I jokingly said, "Hi, I'm Steve Younger." I thought my remark was an amusing icebreaker but, as it turned out, Mylan didn't know me from Mr. Rogers. After shaking my hand, she turned to Steve Younger, and said, "Pleasure to meet you, Mr. Attorney General."

A couple of weeks later, she agreed to come on as executive deputy attorney general for social justice.

I appointed Eric Corngold became executive deputy attorney general for economic justice. Eric, a Yale Law grad and a former assistant U.S. attorney for the Eastern District of New York, had made his name prosecuting high-profile fraud cases. He was a veteran, a legend in the Eastern District. A real coup. Robin Baker was called a superstar by Mary Jo White; a seasoned criminal prosecutor, she agreed to become my executive deputy attorney general for criminal justice. Jenny Rivera, a City University of New York law professor, became special deputy attorney general for civil rights. Barbara Underwood became solicitor general after years of experience under the U.S. solicitor general and as acting U.S. solicitor general, where she'd argued numerous appeals before the U.S. Supreme Court. Leslie Leach, who'd been elected Queens County Supreme Court justice, was persuaded to leave the bench and head the defensive side of the office as state counsel. Katherine "Kit" Kennedy, the new special deputy attorney general for environmental protection, had been senior attorney at the Natural Resources Defense Council, where she stopped the Nuclear Energy Institute from engaging in deceptive advertising and stemmed the tide of illegal water pollution in New York City's sewage treatment plants. An Albany lawyer named Henry "Hank" Greenberg, a state bar association insider and former assistant U.S. attorney known for prosecuting white-collar crime and public corruption, became my legal counsel. Ben Lawsky, also of the Southern District, was previously from the office of U.S. Senator Chuck Schumer. Ben, who led the investigation of two former Goldman Sachs employees involved in insider trading, became my deputy counselor and special assistant. Ben, like Steve, had the legal and government experience to bring a well-rounded perspective. I brought Joe Percoco on board as special counsel and Ashley Cotton in as first deputy director of intergovernmental affairs. Richard Bamberger joined us as communications director. He was talented and a great person. Matt Wing joined the team as a press spokesperson. He too was a great asset to the team and worked around the clock.

In the attorney general's office, like any law enforcement agency, it was important to keep the office above politics. The integrity of the investigations was paramount, and we set an early tone of independence and integrity: Follow the evidence wherever it would lead. The stable of former federal prosecutors I brought on sent the message loud and clear. My management model was honed by my time with campaigns, the law firm, HELP, and HUD. As at each the effectiveness of the "team" is the bottom line. In large organizations with broad responsibility, your capacity is only as good as your team's capacity. I find strong people who make our projects their own. They have to be strong enough to accept responsibility for success or failure.

Collegiality is part of the culture. The people I hire win or lose as a team. A failure is a team failure. A victory is a team victory. While this is difficult to achieve, it's a powerful, positive dynamic. They also have a healthy swagger and confidence. That's essential, because government today is a combat sport. The legislature is a natural competitor, and the public is generally unhappy. The press is increasingly challenged by their changing industry, which has made them desperate to grab scoops and "make" news. Some reporters live to create a scandal to get them on the front page. You are guilty until proven innocent. The team is under unrelenting attack. Their only allies are their teammates and the truth. They need one another.

We held our first staff meeting at transition headquarters in Manhattan in December 2006. I was awed by the talent at the table. "Thank you for joining the team and for your public service," I said. "I don't know if you voted for me, and I don't care. I don't really care if you get along with me. What I do care about is that you are invested in each other and your collective success."

When we took a break, Eric Corngold pulled me aside. "I can assure you that I voted for you in the general election," he said. "Just don't ask me about the primary."

I knew then that Eric and I would get along. And I knew he wasn't kidding!

At the end of December, before we got the keys to the AG suite in the state capitol, Alan Hevesi pleaded guilty in Chauffeur-gate and stepped down. As one of my first acts in office, in January 2007, I announced a partnership with the Albany DA to pursue public integrity matters. Through that we learned of evidence of corruption within Hevesi's former office: he had favored friends and political cronies in deciding which pension fund investments to approve. But it would take a few years for our case against him to unfold.

Another early task my senior staff and I undertook was to write a mission statement. This had never been done in the AG's office, and I felt that it was essential to unite our

650 lawyers and 1,800 staff members around a common goal. Despite the might of the AG's office, as spelled out the prescribed duties seem flexible, and the work tends to reflect the occupant's interests.

Together we pounded out our objectives:

The Attorney General's office should fulfill a unique role in New York State as the "people's lawyer," serving as reformers of government and industry. We report only to the people, whom we represent as taxpayers, citizens, consumers, and individuals. Our mission is to identify and solve systemic injustices, which pose real hardships to New Yorkers. We create new codes of conduct and ethics, with statewide and national scope, and help enact reform legislation on a state and federal level.

It didn't take long for the first unjust situation to appear.

In 2007 there was a lot of low-level grumbling about the multibillion-dollar private-student loan business. But an upstart lender named MyRichUncle had amped up awareness. The previous summer, it had run ads in the *New York Times* and *USA Today* that read: "You should know the truth about financial aid offices. They're supposed to help you choose the best lenders. But in reality, they may steer you towards lenders that benefit them. Not you. Unless you check for yourself, how do YOU know you're getting the best loan?"

"How much do you know?" Ben asked the head of the AG's consumer fraud bureau, a long-timer named Joy Feigenbaum, and another attorney in their first meeting.

"Student loans are an eighty-five-billion-dollar industry,"

Feigenbaum said. "The schools designate certain banks as 'preferred lenders' on the financial-aid resource list they give families who need college loans. Families, naturally, turn to the list when looking for financial aid—about ninety percent use preferred lenders. But these lenders aren't necessarily the best deal for the students. Lenders hold boondoggle conferences for university financial aid departments and give gifts to curry favor. They reward them with a percentage of the loans. The people reaping the benefits are *not* the students."

"How many schools are we talking about?" Ben asked.

"It's standard practice," Feigenbaum said.

When they told me the story, I asked, "Do the schools tell the families that the lenders pay them for the recommendations?"

"No."

Feigenbaum was a top-notch lawyer, but she'd only been given one tool in the toolbox: lawsuits. The thought process in the office was binary: litigate or don't litigate. Investigate or don't investigate. It was this type of narrow thinking that prompted psychologist Abraham Maslow to say, "If you only have a hammer, you tend to see every problem as a nail."

But I ran for AG promising that I wasn't going to be the state's sixty-third DA—there was already one in each county. My mission was broader. Our toolbox had more than hammers and nails. As I'd done at HELP and my team had proved at HUD, asking "why" can take you a long way. Often the answer is: because we've always done it this way. Why? Once you peeled back the onion, you change the ways things are done. Tackling homelessness wasn't building one shelter, it was establishing a continuum of care. Fixing HUD wasn't stacking more boxes of documents on top of other boxes that no one had read. We adapted enforcement tools from other agencies and held landlords accountable. We didn't do business as usual; we changed the model. That's what I wanted to do as AG.

As a consumer, father, and someone who had borrowed money to pay for college myself, I grasped that the quickest route to fixing the student-loan problem was to threaten the schools with sunlight. "As soon as we make this practice public, the universities will stop taking money, trips, and gifts from lenders," I said. "They'll get back to their jobs: educating kids. And once schools agree to do things differently, the lending institutions will have to fall in line. As Supreme Court justice Louis Brandeis said, "Sunlight is said to be the best of disinfectants; electric light the most efficient policeman."

"In the meantime, we need to do an alert to notify people," I told one of the veteran consumer fraud attorneys. "Get an 800 number. Do an advisory to say, 'If you want info about these lenders or how this works, call us.'"

"A lot of people are going to call," the lawyer said.

"That's the idea," I said.

"Who's going to answer those calls?" he asked.

"The people here," I said.

"That would be a lot of work," he said.

Welcome to the bureaucracy, I thought to myself. The same dynamics and culture I'd found at HUD were here.

The next few months were crazy. We learned that the first lender we were looking at, EFP, was doing business with dozens of colleges and universities. We then went to those schools and said, "Tell us not just about EFP but about other lenders."

When they finished telling us we had a list of about twenty-five lenders doing the same shady thing in several states. Next, we went to those lenders to find out which schools they were giving kickbacks to. Now we had 500 schools. The more we asked the more we learned and the more widespread we found the problem to be. As we toggled between universities and lenders the numbers grew exponentially. What became clear was that this was accepted industry practice.

In early March we publicly accused lenders of engaging in an "unholy alliance" in which "deceptive practices—some that may break the law—are widespread." A few weeks later, we subpoenaed Columbia, New York University, University of California-Los Angeles, the University of Texas-Austin, and others, which we were able to do if any New York student was victimized. Lenders, including Citibank Student Loan Corporation, Sallie Mae, and JP Morgan Chase, were also on our subpoena list. We announced a plan to sue EFP.

If we'd gone school by school by school and lender by lender, it would have taken months, if not years, to find all the culprits and hundreds of thousands more families would have been scammed. Instead, to reform the practice and fix the problem, we created a six-point College Loan Code of Conduct, which we sent to all the schools and lenders involved. We said, "Let us know in two weeks if you're in or out. If you're in, great. If you're out, we'll come after you. And it's not going to be pleasant."

By early April, we had agreed to a settlement with seven schools, including the twenty-nine campuses of the State University of New York (SUNY), New York University, Long Island University, Syracuse, Fordham, St. Lawrence, and the

University of Pennsylvania. The universities agreed to sign our conduct code that banned lenders from giving schools anything of value in return for any advantage, prohibited lenders from giving trips and gifts to universities, and barred lenders from staffing school student loan offices. The schools had to repay the families who used preferred lenders. Some were on the hook to pay thousands of dollars. Others paid millions for their prior misbehavior.

We also settled with Citibank, which was affiliated with about 3,000 schools. They signed the code of conduct and agreed to pay $2 million into a fund established by our office to educate families about the student-loan business. Soon the lenders and universities were falling in domino fashion. Sallie Mae, which had loaned money to more than 10 million students and had relationships with 5,600 colleges, signed the code. Next came EFP.

Before we got involved, calls for a review of the student loan industry by the U.S. Department of Education's inspector general had gone unheeded at the agency. But in April 2007, George W. Bush's education secretary, Margaret Spellings, announced a task force to look into regulation of the student-loan industry. It was not a coincidence. I testified the next day before a congressional committee. "The U.S. Department of Education has been asleep at the switch when it comes to conducting oversight over the nation's federal student loan programs," I told the House Education and Labor Committee. "As a result of the Department's lack of oversight, corrupt practices and conflicts of interest that undermine the programs have been allowed to flourish."

We then pushed through legislation that applied to every

college and university in New York. In May, Governor Spitzer signed the Student Lending Accountability, Transparency and Enforcement (SLATE) Act of 2007. Our College Loan Code of Conduct became law.

In the lopsided and ongoing battle between consumers and almighty institutions, this was a big victory for the little guy. It was an important lesson for me. Major institutions—top banks and academic institutions—perpetuated a major consumer fraud. It evolved over time and because "everyone was doing it" it seemed OK. But it wasn't. Also, the lasting contribution and accomplishment was not the attorney general's office finding what was wrong, but even more the attorney general's office establishing the policy that was right—and codifying it.

Like the student-loan industry, health insurance is a concentrated business with tremendous influence on the state legislature. And anyone who has ever had a serious illness knows how hard it is to fight for fair payment. This issue affects so many that I started my term with a determination to make it a fairer process. One of the most common complaints recorded on the AG's health-care consumer hotline was about insurance policies' promise to pay a "reasonable and customary" rate for customers using out-of-network doctors. But the reimbursement never matches up with the medical fee. The patient gets stuck with the hefty remainder of the bill. The voice mails left on the hotline were all a version of: "I'm getting $5 when I should get $60—with no explanation from my health insurer."

Eric Corngold had recruited a top talent, Linda Lacewell, from the U.S. attorney's office for the Eastern District of New York to join us. Linda was a career federal prosecutor who won the drug-trafficking case against Sammy "the Bull" Gravano and had helped indict former executives of Enron Corporation as part of the federal Enron Task Force.

She was the right blend of prosecutor and policy. While the student-loan case was concluding, Linda, who came on as special counsel, assembled a health-care industry task force.

In 2000, the *New York Times* ran an article on health-insurance reimbursements, comparing the amount paid by consumers to out-of-network providers with playing blackjack in a casino. In short, the house always wins. The American Medical Association and others had filed a class-action suit against UnitedHealth, the nation's second-largest insurer, over "reasonable and customary" rates for out-of-network providers.

Six years later not much had changed. During the transition the AG's office got a letter from Mary Reinbolt Jerome, a sixty-two-year-old Yonkers resident with advanced ovarian cancer. She was fighting for her life—and with her insurance company, Oxford, over her out-of-pocket costs for out-of-network treatment at Memorial Sloan-Kettering Cancer Center. The reimbursements were so puny that Jerome owed $80,000 in medical bills. That was bad enough. Worse was knowing that there were 100 million Mary Jeromes. Jumping into this fight was a no-brainer.

Fixing the problem would help more than the Mary Jeromes. Exorbitant health-care costs are the top cause of personal bankruptcy in the United States. When hardworking people go broke because of medical bills, there's a ripple effect in the economy. Stores, charities, and even the government take in less.

From time to time we hear that more payouts would threaten the insurance companies' ability to stay in business. But health insurance industry profits were way up— from $2.41 billion in 2001 to $12.87 billion in 2007, a 466 percent increase. Consumer premiums had at least doubled. At the time 70 percent of working Americans, or 110 million people, had joined health insurance plans that allowed them to go out of network. But getting an explanation of the reimbursement process was difficult. How were the reimbursements determined? Who was making the decisions?

We told insurers that operated in New York to come to our offices. We asked Oxford, UnitedHealth Group, Cigna, Aetna, and Empire BlueCross BlueShield how they set the fair market value of reimbursements. Every time the answer was the same: they relied on a research firm, Ingenix, to figure it out. The Ingenix database set the rates for usual and customary fees nationwide. Lacewell jotted "Ingenix" on her legal pad. "Who owns Ingenix?" she asked.

"We do," the person representing UnitedHealth Group said.

"Where does Ingenix get its data from?" Linda followed.

"From us," said United's rep.

Bingo. Game over. Once again a large powerful industry had quietly and over time evolved into a major fraud against the unsuspecting, powerless consumer. Like student loans, this was a pure conflict of interest affecting millions for billions of dollars. Insurance companies can't own the company that sets the "independent" fair rate of reimbursement based on information that they prorate for themselves. This was at its essence a classic price-fixing case. We'd uncovered a major fraud and undisclosed conflict of interest.

Lacewell and her group determined that the insurance companies were underpricing that out-of-network reimbursement rate by as much as 28 percent statewide for some services.

Ingenix's database contained more than a billion claims from more than 100 insurance carriers. When they received a claim, insurers would compare it against the database and then cut the fee to the "reasonable" amount. While doctors in the metropolitan New York City area typically charged $200 for an office visit, Ingenix calculated the rate at $77. Then, under a typical plan, the insurer would pay 80 percent of the $77, or $62. The patient was left to cover the $138 balance.

Insurance companies, like other like corporations, stand together. To get through you have to crack one of the major players. Over a two-year period, we built cases against twelve health-insurance providers including UnitedHealth.

It's the government's job as regulator to make sure that corporations are operating in an honorable way. It's been proven and reproven that we cannot always count on business to do the right thing. And the competition of the market can lead to abuses. The government must be the watchdog and hold them accountable.

On the flip side, the settlement has to make sense. The goal must be to find balance—that sweet spot that is fair for consumers and is fair for the industry.

To do that we had to figure out what was truly reasonable and customary. The problem was the insurance companies controlled the whole industry. After some brainstorming, we thought: If there's no alternative we'll have to help an independent entity form a company. We made Ingenix divest itself and made the insurers pay $100 million in penalties. We then paid five New York State universities to set up an independent research firm, called Fair Health, to generate the accurate reimbursement data. We accomplished this in a year. UnitedHealth also agreed to pay $350 million—the largest cash settlement for health insurance in history—to settle the class-action suit by the American Medical Association. And in Washington, West Virginia senator Jay Rockefeller took up the cause, inviting Lacewell to a congressional hearing on out-of-network rates.

By early 2009 we had brought the major players in line. I told the press: "The industry reforms that we announce today will bring crucial accuracy, transparency, and independence to a broken system. During these tough economic times, this agreement will keep hundreds of millions of dollars in the pockets of over 100 million Americans."

As we worked our way through these big consumer fraud cases, we had multiple pots on multiple stoves. Just before the July 4, 2007, holiday, I was in my New York City office when Governor Spitzer called. Republican Senate Majority Leader Joe Bruno, he said, was using state-owned aircraft to attend fund-raisers. A news story by reporter James Odato had broken in the *Albany Times-Union* on July 1.

Spitzer and Bruno, chief rivals, had been in a power tug-of-war.

If the allegations were true, it would mean that Bruno had breached the Public Officers Law, which says that no public official can use his position "to secure unwarranted privileges . . . including . . . the misappropriation of property, services or other resources of the state." Violators can be suspended or removed from office and are subject to a civil penalty of up to $10,000.

My staff had disbanded for the holiday, but as AG, you are never on vacation. I set up a conference call with my brain trust. Everyone who dialed in made it immediately clear: taking up this investigation was lose-lose.

The last thing I wanted was a problem with Eliot Spitzer. There was an enormous gap between us. We were both Democrats, but I was six months into my comeback term and he was the most popular guy around. Many thought New York's Governor Spitzer was a couple of campaigns away from becoming the United States' President Spitzer.

We assembled a group of smart professionals and left the investigation to them. Steve Cohen had persuaded veteran prosecutor Ellen Nachtigall Biben to leave the Manhattan DA's office to serve as my special deputy attorney general for public integrity. Ellen was known for her ability to manage teams and to get results in tough state cases. I couldn't do better than Linda Lacewell, whom I borrowed from the health-care task force. Jerry Goldfeder, an election law expert, rounded out the team. "Follow the facts wherever they take you," I said. "But remember, time is not our friend. People will expect this to take months. I want it finished in weeks."

A couple of days later, Bruno flipped the tables on Spitzer. "Investigate me?" he asked publicly outraged. "Investigate him!" Bruno publicly called on me to investigate Spitzer for using the state police for surveillance.

We issued our "Report of Investigation into the Misuse of New York State Aircraft and the Resources of the New York State Police" on July 23, 2007. The fifty-three-page document is almost entirely devoid of adjectives. The evidence the team had gathered was largely indisputable. We found that Bruno had done nothing wrong, largely because there were no real rules for the use of the plane in the first place, and those rules needed to be fixed, which they later were. Spitzer's office orchestrated the *Times-Union* story but told the state police they'd been FOILED—meaning that someone had asked for documents through the New York Freedom of Information Law. When the state police couldn't find all of the requested documents in their records, Spitzer's staff had said to re-create the records from memory—some going back months. It was clearly improper for the Spitzer aides to use the state police for political purposes and to manufacture documents to be presented as originals.

We accused four of Spitzer's aides of ethics violations, including his communications director, Darren Dopp, who had once been a member of my father's staff, and William Howard, assistant secretary for homeland security. Spitzer suspended Dopp without pay and demoted Howard to a job outside the executive chamber. Our report also found that State Police Superintendent Preston Felton helped troopers create records of Bruno's past travel to give to the press, bringing state troopers "squarely into the middle of politics, precisely where they do not belong." Richard Baum, Spitzer's top aide, whom Dopp had e-mailed about his plans to discredit Bruno, knew about the impropriety and appeared to look the other way.

Spitzer had said he knew nothing of the matter, but in late March 2008, Spitzer's former communications director, Darren Dopp, testified that when he asked his boss for the OK to give the Albany *Times-Union* the records of Bruno's use of state aircraft, Spitzer responded: "He said f— him, he's a piece of s—, shove it up his a— with a red-hot poker," Dopp said. It became obvious that Spitzer had known about the events all along.

But by then that truth was irrelevant.

Less than three weeks earlier, the story of Governor Spitzer took an even stranger turn. I was in my office on March 10, when rumors started percolating that Eliot was caught by federal law enforcement arranging to meet a high-priced prostitute at the Mayflower Hotel in Washington. It was so outlandish that I assumed it was some kind of twisted April Fools' Day prank. Only it was March.

Within hours of first hearing the rumors, the *New York Times* was given the story the next day, March 10. Under the anti–money laundering provisions of the Bank Secrecy Act and the Patriot Act, federal investigators had put Spitzer under surveillance and discovered he had paid up to $80,000 to a prostitution ring over several years, while he served as both attorney general and governor.

Ironically, the hotel where they met is three-tenths of a mile from the White House.

Since September 2008, when the country had plunged into an economic crisis, my office had been immersed in examining the fallout from the collapse of a number of investment industry kingpins. One of my lead advisers, Ben Lawsky, brought me a *Financial Times* article about massive bonuses being paid out at Merrill Lynch.

I was appalled. To keep Merrill from going under, the Treasury Department had helped orchestrate a merger between Merrill and Bank of America, giving both banks billions in capital under the federal Troubled Asset Relief Program (TARP). Yet, according to the *FT* article, annual bonuses were still scheduled for hundreds of Merrill employees.

Whoa! If you're a thriving company what you pay employees is between you and your shareholders. But if your company is in trouble and the government is throwing you billions of dollars as a lifeline and it's bonuses as usual, you're misusing the taxpayers' money. Paying for a job poorly done violates a private-sector commandment that I thought was sacred: you pay for performance. If your company is bankrupt, you've underperformed.

Of course, it wasn't only Merrill that was paying out bonuses. Fat compensation packages were and are still integral to the culture of Wall Street, where everyone from traders to CEOs can expect an annual windfall. Financial collapse and government intervention did not make Wall Street change its ways.

In October 2008, we sent letters to nine New York banks that were TARP fund recipients. The letters were to the point. They asked for information about the bonuses they planned to pay.

In December we found out that shortly after the Merrill Lynch/Bank of America merger went through, Merrill Lynch gave out bonuses totaling $3.6 billion—or one-third of its TARP money. Usually Merrill bonuses were distributed in January, following the release of the fourth-quarter results. But Merrill had acted more quickly than usual, setting up the appearance that it was eager to pay out before being subsumed by a new bank. Merrill's chief executive, John Thain, was slated to get $10 million.

It was hard to fathom that the company executives—and many others, it turned out—had taken bailout money to give to themselves.

In February 2009 we reported that nearly 700 Merrill employees received million-dollar bonuses, even though the firm had lost $27 billion. Twenty people were paid more than $8 million apiece, and fifty-three people were each paid more than $5 million.

In March news broke that the insurance giant American International Group (AIG) was doling out $165 million in bonuses. This was the same company that had taken $170 billion in government bailout money—more than any other financial institution. Many of the executives set to receive the bonuses were the same ones who worked in the business unit that had sold high-risk insurance products, thereby bringing AIG to the brink of collapse.

I immediately sent a letter to AIG's chief executive, Edward Liddy, asking for more information about the bonuses, the employees who were to receive them, the contracts for these bonuses, and the names of individuals who developed and negotiated the agreements. "Taxpayers of this country are now supporting AIG, and they deserve at the very least to know how their money is being spent," I wrote. "And we owe it to the taxpayers to take every possible action to stop unwarranted bonus payments to those who caused the AIG meltdown in the first place."

AIG did not respond to my letter. I issued a subpoena for the names of the bonus recipients. The next day, on March 17, I sent a letter to Congressman Barney Frank, a Democrat from Massachusetts and then chairman of the House Financial Services Committee. I pointed out that seventy-three AIG employees were each paid more than $1 million in bonuses. I wrote, "AIG made more than seventy-three millionaires in the unit which lost so much money that it brought the firm to its knees, forcing a taxpayer bailout."

The next day, Liddy testified before Congress.

Ben and I were watching the congressional hearing on television when I realized that public anger could spiral out of control. "We need to ratchet this down," I said.

The best outcome would be for the employees to give their bonuses back. The intense public scrutiny was motivational. We worked our way down the list, starting with the people who would yield the most. By March 23, fifteen of the top twenty executives who received the biggest bonuses had returned the money in full—about $50 million. Of the top ten highest earners, nine had returned their bonuses. Though we had their names, after much consideration we decided against publicizing them. I told a group of reporters on a conference call, "If the person returns the money, I don't think there's a public interest in releasing the names."

We issued a conciliatory statement, which read in part: "I

would like to say this to the individuals who have given the money back. You have done the right thing. You have done what this country now needs and demands. We are living in a new era of corporate and individual responsibility. I thank you for setting an example for the rest of the company."

Our investigation continued. I was working to recover $80 million in bonuses paid to employees in the United States. But another $85 million had gone to those outside the country, many of whom were in the London office that managed AIG's credit-default swaps. I told reporters, "We have a very aggressive theory about our jurisdiction, but we don't have a theory that gets us to London."

At the end of July 2009, we issued a report detailing our nine-month investigation into Wall Street's outrageous compensation system. "No Rhyme or Reason: The 'Heads I Win, Tails You Lose' Bank Bonus Culture" described the annual practices at the nine biggest Wall Street firms, showing that while they all claimed to be doling out bonuses to highly performing employees, the opposite was true. We spelled it out in plain language:

When the banks did well, their employees were paid well. When the banks did poorly, their employees were paid well. And when the banks did very poorly, they were bailed out by taxpayers and their employees were still paid well.

The report garnered national press—and public outrage. *New York* magazine nicknamed me the "Bonus Buster," a moniker I proudly accepted. We'd focused attention on Wall

Street's excesses and sparked a public dialogue about business practices that were unjustifiable in the current economy. It was an example of the tremendous impact the attorney general's office can have on unfair corporate practices that diminish the public's trust and steal from their retirement.

As AG I had to be willing to pull back the curtain on the sacred and powerful, some of whom were friends. I told my staff, "Don't be afraid to go where the evidence takes you." Biben and Lacewell were such a smooth-running team I asked them to work together on other public integrity cases. With the help of Solicitor General Barbara Underwood and her group, Biben and Lacewell painstakingly made their way through the labyrinthine investigation of Alan Hevesi that we had launched soon after I became AG in 2007. As comptroller he had been sole trustee of the state pension fund, valued at the time at $150 billion, larger than the entire New York budget. About $5 billion to $7 billion was invested in private-equity fund and hedge fund deals known as alternative investments. The brokers of these deals earned a 2 percent commission. It sounds small, but when the deals are $100 million, 2 percent is $2 million. The way it works is that the brokers' fees—sometimes nothing more than thinly disguised kickbacks or payoffs—are baked into the pension fund. The defendants said that the brokers' fees didn't affect the fund, but common sense says that can't be true.

For decades the state pension fund had been the subject of allegations of pay-to-play politics and self-dealing, including a famous late-1980s "give to get" memo from a top aide to Edward "Ned" Regan, Republican state comptroller from 1979 to 1993, which suggested that those wanting to "get" state pension money for their investment deals would have to "give" to Regan's campaign.

After interviewing more than a hundred witnesses, poring over roomfuls of documents, and unraveling years of complex investments, the team had convincing evidence showing that Hevesi had put his campaign manager, Hank Morris, in charge of the pension fund's alternative investments. At the same time he had formed his own investment companies, acted as the "broker" in a series of deals, getting millions in kickbacks.

One of his responsibilities was telling chief investment officer David Loglisci which investment proposals to approve or reject. How was this made clear? Loglisci's predecessor had been fired for not following Morris's directions. On the other hand, Morris rewarded political friends, cronies, and donors, melding the political campaign with the state pension fund.

The case was strong but, at first, circumstantial. We needed a witness. We got one when Morris's partner, hedge fund manager Barrett Wissman, signed a plea and cooperation arrangement. In 2009 the grand jury indicted Morris and Loglisci on enterprise corruption charges.

For me the toughest catch was Ray Harding, former head of the state Liberal Party. Ray had helped my father win the 1982 governor's race and helped Rudy Giuliani win the New York City mayor's race. He also gave me the Liberal Party's endorsement in my first run for governor in 2002. When I dropped out of the race, the Liberal Party—which needed

50,000 votes to keep its automatic place on the ballot—lost its line. The Liberal Party never recovered.

In 2009 Harding pleaded guilty to receiving $800,000 in pension fund kickbacks. He told the court that he had backed Hevesi for thirty years in his runs for Assembly, New York City mayor, and the city and state comptroller posts. Morris rewarded this political loyalty by naming Harding as a broker on state pension deals so he could collect the bounce-back money. Harding also admitted helping to clear a seat in the Assembly by finding the incumbent a job so that Hevesi's son, Andrew, could run in and win a special election.

As I said at the time: "They were using the fund as a piggy bank to pay people who were doing them political favors. The brazenness is breathtaking."

Based on Harding's age and shaky health—he weighed at least 300 pounds and had serious lung issues—and his cooperation in the investigation, the judge spared him jail time. A few years later, in 2012, Ray died of cancer at age seventy-seven.

In the beginning, the press and opposition lawyers said the pay-to-play arrangements were business as usual, unsavory perhaps, but not illegal. By the end, we had secured eight guilty pleas, twenty-three settlement agreements, and more than $170 million in recoveries for the pension fund and the state. Loglisci pleaded guilty and cooperated in the investigation. Alan Hevesi didn't wait to be indicted to plead guilty. This happened in October, a month before the 2010 election. Sentenced to one to four years in prison, he served twenty months. The last to plead was Morris. After I became governor Morris was sentenced to one and one-third years to four years in prison. He served twenty-five months before being released in April 2013.

It was a long haul, but for the taxpayers, it was a major victory. We'd used every tool at our disposal. We brought criminal cases, civil cases, and forfeiture cases to recoup the ill-gotten gains. We also designed an industry-wide code of conduct to ban brokers and campaign contributions from pension-fund deals. Our case sparked state and federal investigations of state pension funds across the country. We partnered with the Securities and Exchange Commission, which brought parallel enforcement actions. Our campaign contribution ban became a national regulation. Legendary investigative reporter Wayne Barrett called the public integrity case the most important New York had seen in fifty years.

CHAPTER 8

A Second Chance

*Enjoying a laugh with my dad while
my mom looks on, in May 2013.*

In March 2008, two days after Eliot Spitzer resigned as
governor, Lieutenant Governor David Paterson was cata-
pulted into the state's top job.

Paterson, who had endured a childhood infection that

left him legally blind, had racked up a number of firsts as an adult. He was elected to the state Senate in 1985, representing Harlem and the Upper West Side, the same district that elected his father twenty years before.

In 2002, he became the first nonwhite to be state Senate minority leader and as lieutenant governor became the highest-ranking African American elected official in the history of New York. He was now the state's first African American governor.

I was, and am, a longtime Paterson fan. He's witty and I enjoy his company. Friendly for years, we spoke often, over the phone and in person. And in the summer of 2005, the girls and I joined David and his family camping in the Adirondacks. It was a standout weekend.

Even though he was well regarded by Albany lawmakers, Democrats and Republicans, it was an uphill journey from the start. He was sworn in on St. Patrick's Day, two weeks before the budget was due. The legislature, notorious for gridlock and late budgets, was not given to negotiating with any governor. The almost $4.7 billion deficit made the always contentious Republican-controlled Senate and Democratic-controlled Assembly even less cooperative than usual.

Spitzer, a forceful, aggressive Type A personality, had set the tone for the office. How tough was it? In 2007, Assembly Minority Leader James Tedisco, a Republican from Schenectady, had complained about being cut out of some negotiations. Spitzer's alleged response: "Listen, I'm a f—ing steamroller, and I'll roll over you and anybody else." The exchange was leaked to the *New York Post*. After that, Spitzer's nickname became "the steamroller." And it was not a compliment.

Paterson, by contrast, is mild mannered and deliberative. But he's no wimp. When he flexed his political muscle, people reacted.

His first year in office was rocky. In the summer of 2008, as the nation suffered financial meltdown, Paterson gave a televised address, broadcast locally on the networks. New York was facing its worst fiscal crisis since the 1970s, he said. In August he called an emergency session of the legislature and began slashing the budget. Lawmakers up for reelection were, predictably, unhappy. Media, including the *New York Times*, suggested that David needed to be a lot tougher.

His situation became more complicated when Hillary Clinton left the U.S. Senate, and the governor needed to name the replacement. The media buzzed with possible contenders, including me. David said, "Andrew, if you're interested in the seat, you need to tell me." I filled out a questionnaire, but I was never officially asked and grateful not to be. I'm a manager and executive, not a legislator. And I couldn't have brought myself to move to Washington, D.C., away from my kids.

David seemed eager to showcase the selection process. He'd announced his plan to run for governor in 2010. He needed a powerful ally in Congress, and a good pick would demonstrate his worth.

But the opposite occurred. The governor's process of making the appointment turned into what Republican state senator Martin Golden called a "game show." One of the most prominent names bandied about was my ex-wife's first cousin Caroline Kennedy. But his deliberations were as protracted as they were public, and eventually Kennedy withdrew her name.

Finally, on January 22, Paterson called me late at night. He'd chosen Hillary's replacement: Kirsten Gillibrand, a Democratic congresswoman from Albany, a largely Republican district. She was a strong choice who would be on the ballot in 2010. Gillibrand could deliver votes to him from her district. Kirsten was a friend, and I had brought her to Washington to work at HUD. While she was relatively unknown to most, I knew she would ultimately prove a good pick.

In the winter of 2009 another drama was playing out in Albany. New York State was facing a deficit estimated to be as high as $17 billion, a consequence due, in part, to skyrocketing costs for Medicaid and increases in education spending. But the state's dire fiscal situation was also the fault of a legislature that refused to rein in spending when revenues shrank.

That summer, the state comptroller, Thomas DiNapoli, issued a report showing that revenues, including income tax payments, were falling more precipitously than originally projected. From April through June, revenues fell by more than $4 billion—25 percent more than in the same period the previous year. The nation's economic turmoil had taken a serious toll on New York. The report suggested that midyear cuts to the state budget would be necessary.

The State Senate was in a leadership crisis. Under Republican control for decades, in 2008 the Democrats had taken the Senate by a narrow margin of two seats—32 to 30. But that summer there was a coup. Two Democrats, Hiram Monserrate and Pedro Espada, unexpectedly voted with Republicans to replace the Senate majority leader, Malcolm Smith. This was unheard of even in Albany. Amazingly, then Monserrate flipped back to the Democrats' side, giving each party 31 seats. Now the House was at a stalemate. According to the state's constitution, the lieutenant governor is granted the power to cast a tie-breaking vote in the legislature. But Paterson did not have a lieutenant governor. So, the Senate remained paralyzed for a month. On July 8, Paterson appointed Richard Ravitch lieutenant governor. Ravitch is a businessman and former chair of the Metropolitan Transportation Authority under Governor Hugh Carey, and his fiscal acumen made him a shrewd selection. There was only one problem: in my opinion it was illegal. Under New York State law, lieutenant governor is an elected position, not a political appointment. After Paterson tapped Ravitch, Espada returned to the Democrats in a deal that made Espada the Democratic Senate majority leader. Espada said that he'd never agreed with the Republicans and had switched allegiances to help "end the gridlock, paralysis, secretiveness, threats, and partisan politics" that existed in the Senate under Smith. Sure! This temporarily ended the leadership crisis and restored the Democrats' thirty-two to thirty majority. The events and confusion undermined the governor.

Paterson's popularity was sinking. A January 2009 Siena poll had shown him with a 60 percent favorable and a 23 percent negative rating. By the summer the numbers were reversed. Nearly 70 percent of respondents said they would prefer someone else as governor.

By late February 2010, it was evident that Paterson could not win and he dropped out of the race.

With Paterson out, I was definitely in. But I would not declare my candidacy right away. I needed time to develop a coherent plan. The problem was not going to be if I could win election as governor. It was what I could do if I did win. The state was a mess. I didn't want to win unless I believed I could succeed as governor. To do that, I called the regulars, including Joe Percoco and Steve Cohen; my father's two former top aides, Mike Del Giudice and Drew Zambelli; Spitzer's former budget director Paul Francis; a great lawyer, Jeremy Creelan; and Jim Malatras, one of the great rising stars. I'm a big believer in putting smart people in a room and debating the issues. We'd meet twice a week and invite experts in to talk about ethics, the budget, re-inventing government, campaign finance reform, criminal justice, the environment—whatever we thought needed to be fixed. That year, the state Democratic convention was in Westchester on May 26. During an election year, state delegates assemble to select their nominees. But I was running unopposed by anyone in my own party, so the convention promised little drama. To keep public attention on the campaign and our own energy up, we decided that I'd announce my candidacy on May 22, a few days before the convention.

On a mild spring day, I made my announcement on the steps of the Tweed Courthouse, a stately nineteenth-century building in downtown Manhattan that now houses the city's

Department of Education. I chose the venue not for its current purpose but because it has an interesting, ignoble past. It was built by the infamous William "Boss" Tweed, the corrupt onetime leader of Tammany Hall, the political machine that controlled New York City and state politics for more than a century. Boss Tweed had launched the construction of this courthouse in 1861 as a way to embezzle millions of public dollars. The total cost of construction was estimated at around $13 million—the equivalent of around $178 million today. Almost half of that money—a guesstimated $6 million—came back to Tweed in kickbacks. He was tried for his crimes, ironically, in one of the courtrooms in 1873.

The building represents the sort of graft I had prosecuted as attorney general and everything I was running against as a candidate for governor.

"We stand today next to one of the historic monuments to government corruption," I said before a crowd of about 125 people.

A month earlier, my office had filed suit against Pedro Espada, the former New York Senate majority leader, for embezzling hundreds of thousands of dollars from his non-profit health-care center in the Bronx—including $60,000 spent on sushi and lobster. He was the notorious abuser who almost mocked the law. He would be sentenced to five years in prison in 2013.

"This isn't New York at its best," I said. "I represent the people of the State of New York, and we want our government back."

I knew I would be heard by those in state government—the people I held responsible for Albany's chronic gridlock and corruption. "Our government has failed and the people have the right, indeed the people have the obligation, to act," I said. "Politicians of both parties, Democrats and Republicans, share the blame."

I planned to shake things up.

My campaign team had put together an impressive rollout of my candidacy. For months we had worked on a 200-page bound document that grew out of the twice-weekly meetings. Titled *The New NY Agenda: A Plan for Action*, it detailed my plan to reform Albany and get the economy running. The morning I announced, we delivered a copy of the book to the home of every political reporter in the state. We timed it so that a kid knocked on the door and said, "Here you go. This is from Andrew Cuomo" as they were having their coffee and reading the paper.

That day we also released a twenty-one-minute video on our website. It covered all the fine points that I couldn't reasonably address in my live speech. We filmed it flanked by my books and photographs. I looked into the camera and introduced myself. I outlined my platform and explained my political philosophy—that I was fiscally prudent and socially progressive. But I also touched a personal note. I wanted to speak directly to the New Yorkers who had watched me over the years and followed me through my various ups and downs.

"It's hard to come back," I said. "I saw it in my own life. A few years ago, I ran for governor and I lost. And I then went through a very difficult time in my personal life. It was a public humiliation. People said it was over for me; they said my public service career was finished—there was no way I could come back. Some days even I thought they were right. With the compassion and empathy of New Yorkers, you gave me a second chance."

I would not run a hyperpartisan campaign. In addition to the Democratic Party nomination, the Independence Party had endorsed my candidacy. We were building a broad coalition of support across the state, reaching out to voters who were concerned about the economy and upset with the dysfunction in Albany. I welcomed the support of open-minded Republicans like Onondaga County Executive Joanie Mahoney, a very popular and highly talented official. I tapped Robert Duffy as my running mate for lieutenant governor. Duffy, the mayor of Rochester who had also served as chief of police, is a strong, seasoned leader who substantially improved schools and lowered crime in his city. He had earned wide, bipartisan support, and I was excited to bring his talents to Albany.

I was committed to running a substantive, issues-driven campaign. "The answer is not to get angry and get negative," I told the state convention on May 27. "The answer is to get united and to get smart and to get positive. That's how we move forward."

The Republicans held their convention in early June in Manhattan. Rick Lazio, a congressman from Long Island who had run against Hillary Clinton for U.S. Senate in 2000, won 60 percent of the party's vote. The three other Republican candidates at the convention included Steve Levy, the Suffolk County executive; Myers Mermel, a real estate financing specialist; and Carl Paladino, a far-right wealthy Buffalo businessman who had been publicly shamed a month earlier for forwarding e-mails to friends with racist and pornographic jokes. The delegation gave him only 8 percent of the vote at the convention, but Paladino vowed to spend $10 million of his own money to petition his way onto the primary ballot in September.

My campaign assumed we would face Lazio in the general election. As HUD secretary, I often found myself at odds with Lazio, who served on the House Banking Subcommittee on Housing and Community Opportunity, which oversees the housing agency.

I geared up for an intense summer of campaigning. We took our message to all sixty-two counties in the state. At every stop I explained a five-point plan for a new New York: clean up Albany; get our fiscal house in order; right-size government; make New York the jobs capital of the nation; restore New York's place as a progressive leader. We asked citizens to back me, handing out postcards at each event. "Call your legislator and tell them you join our pledge for a new New York," I told voters. By the end of the summer we'd signed up tens of thousands of people.

I had three extra assistants. My daughters Cara and Mariah, then fifteen, and Michaela, twelve, wanted to experience the campaign trail. We'd done a similar, shorter road trip during my 2002 campaign, but they were too young to remember it well. "It will be a tiring, demanding trip," I told them, "but nothing would make me happier than to have you with me." They were thrilled. In mid-July we rented a decent-size RV—a BTouring Cruiser Gulf Stream model—and took off.

Have you ever been in an RV? It looks like it should be fun. And it is, for the first four miles. Then you realize it's a lot like being inside a mobile toaster oven. It gets hot. Everything rattles. When you make a sharp turn, lunch goes flying off the table; when you hit a bump, the refrigerator door opens and condiments pour out; when you pull into an RV campground parking spot, you have to hook up to the septic tank, which is every bit as gross as it sounds. That's when you say this was really a bad idea.

If the girls were my salvation during the divorce, they were my sense of balance during the campaign. It was difficult to take a low turnout or a negative remark from the opposition too seriously with the girls there. Win or lose, they were my assurance that all would be right in my world.

If our RV was a clunker—and it was—our campaign was a well-oiled machine. Wherever we went, we had a policy book on the local issues. Every statewide topic—environment, energy, crime, gun control, taxes, pension costs for municipalities, state mandates on municipalities—was in our policy books. We were prepped and ready.

The RV made three stops a day, with events at 10 A.M., 12 P.M., and 2 P.M. We might talk to a room of 250 to 300 people in a union hall in Syracuse, or a 100 people, tops, in community rooms in firehouses. The girls would take turns introducing me, which all three loved doing. Michaela would always begin her introduction with the line: "I have lived with this man for my whole life," which always got big laughs.

As we rolled down the highways the girls killed time teasing one another about who'd given the best intro. Fatherhood is like basic training for the diplomatic corps. "Who gave the best intro, Dad?" they'd ask. "You were all great," I'd say. This would last for hours. Then they would play cards. I never knew "Spit" was a contact sport until I saw Mariah, Cara, and Michaela play.

When we were in the North Country, the state's largest geographic region, which borders Canada to the north and Vermont to the east, we went fishing and swimming in Lake Champlain. My brother, Chris, and I spent many happy times in the Adirondacks, when I was in my twenties. I had a ball giving my girls the same experiences in the state I love. It was enormously gratifying to be able to show them how beautiful and diverse it is—the Adirondacks, the Catskills, the Southern Tier, wine country.

We also saw the parts of the state that were in hard times. Upstate New York is a different economic reality than downstate. It has suffered for decades—with little help from the state. Almost all the cities show the decline of older northeast and midwest manufacturing cities, but Buffalo is the worst. It was once the eighth-largest city in the country and is still New York's second-largest city. The Ellicott Square Building on Main Street lost its status as the world's largest office building long ago. Much of the city's elegant architecture, built in the flush times, still stands, but not as proudly as it once did. Over the past five decades, the city has been in a steady decline, and many of the jobs have been shipped overseas.

That summer we saw how the economic crisis had made things worse. Buffalo's poverty rate climbed sharply, growing faster than the nation's, and its median household income fell lower than the national average. I met with unemployed residents who had seen the promise of better times turn to dust. People were leaving the city as businesses shut down, and homeowners were forced to foreclose. Loss begets loss. Economic depression signals psychological depression. Compared with other parts of the state, there was a palpable sense of apathy and disillusionment.

It was time to change that dynamic.

Fall brought a shift on the Republican side. Paladino was outspending Lazio reportedly by more than $3 million— and had collected enough signatures to get himself on the primary ballot. With the Tea Party machine behind him, he roamed the state, often with his pit bull terrier in tow, stoking anger and frustration among the party's conservative base. His language was over the top and often offensive. He vowed to "take a baseball bat to Albany," and called legislators "wimps" and "pigs" and "leeches." He even called the speaker of the New York State Assembly, Sheldon Silver, who is an orthodox Jew, "the Antichrist." He frequently yelled out at his increasingly well-attended press events, "I'm mad as hell, and I'm not going to take it anymore!" His message resonated with Tea Party advocates and extreme social conservatives.

On September 14, the angry conservative candidate trampled Lazio in the Republican primary. This conservative beating the mainstream Republican Party was a shock. New York had essentially a moderate Republican Party. It was heretofore inconceivable that an extreme conservative could win. It was the moment that the Republican Party started its move to the right—mirroring the Washington movement. It quietly opened a new chapter in Republican politics where the tail would wag the dog. Conservatives would dominate the Republican Party.

A week after the convention, a Quinnipiac poll showed that my lead over Paladino had shrunk to six points. I had 49 percent to his 43 percent support among likely voters. These public polls are public relations tools for the schools that sponsor them. They need to make news and are often constructed to do that.

Happily, other polls showed a much larger spread. The same week the Rasmussen poll showed me with 54 percent to his 38 percent.

Campaigning against Paladino gave me the opportunity to examine the Tea Party up close. It is an interesting phenomenon. They are against government, especially the federal government (except national defense), and the louder they say it the better they are received. It's much easier to be "against" something than "for" something. The few ideas Paladino did have bordered on lunacy. He promised a tax-cut equal to one-quarter of the entire state budget and proposed putting juvenile delinquents to work as janitors, turning unused prisons into dormitories for welfare recipients where they could take classes in "personal hygiene." He said that children shouldn't be "brainwashed" into thinking homosexuality is acceptable.

When we thought it couldn't get uglier Paladino issued another bizarre open letter to me. In it he wrote, "It's difficult to understand why you, a polished veteran campaigner, scion of a political dynasty and king-designate, would fear a simple businessman from Buffalo, who candidly has never been in a debate in his life—except maybe in a bar. . . . Frankly, I don't think you have the cojones to face me and the other candidates in an open debate. So Andrew, for the first time in your life, be a man."

On September 20, we had a campaign meeting. Ben Lawsky, Joe, and Steve were there, along with my communications team: Marissa Shorenstein, director of communications for my gubernatorial campaign; Phil Singer, an experienced campaign strategist; and Josh Vlasto. Josh, whom Ben knew from U.S. senator Chuck Schumer's communications shop, was new to Team Cuomo. He was young and supercharged.

Not long after the meeting, Josh got a call on his cell phone. It was from Kenneth Lovett, the political reporter from the New York *Daily News*.

"So, I hear Cuomo held a meeting about how to deal with Paladino," he said.

Josh was flummoxed. "Uh . . . a meeting?" he said.

Lovett began quoting verbatim what had been said in the meeting.

Josh refused to comment. He called Ben in a panic. Ben called me. "We must have a leak," Ben said.

Was someone listening outside the door? Ben half-joked.

Later that night Josh checked his phone log and noticed that a call that had come in during the meeting had been from Lovett. At the time Josh had reached into his pocket and hit ignore, but the call showed up as fifty-two minutes Josh hadn't turned his phone off as he'd thought. His cell-phone gave Lovett a seat at the table. He stayed on the line, listening to everything and writing it down.

The next day, the story ran in the *Daily News*, under the headline: "CAN I 'CALL HIM AN A—HOLE?' ANDREW CUOMO IN TIZZY AFTER GOP FOE CARL PALADINO QUESTIONS HIS MANHOOD."

The story quoted liberally from our "private meeting," saying that we were strategizing counterattacks. It was bad, but I saw it as just a bump on the campaign trail. It was almost funny.

Josh called me offering to resign.

"It was a mistake," I said. "Don't worry about it."

It was a curious stunt by Lovett, given that he was violating the New York criminal law against eavesdropping.

We eventually agreed to debate. The event was held on October 18 at Hofstra University on Long Island. In addition to Paladino and myself, the five fringe candidates running for governor were there: Kristen Davis, the madam at the center of the Eliot Spitzer scandal, who was running on the Anti-Prohibition Party ticket; Jimmy McMillan, the candidate of the Rent Is Too Damn High Party; Charles Barron, a Brooklyn city council member representing the Freedom Party; Howie Hawkins on the Green Party line; and Warren Redlich for the Libertarian Party. It was a true New York gathering. Democracy at work.

We debated the issues that mattered most to New Yorkers—the slumping economy, the ineffective state government, and high taxes—as best we could with so many of us onstage.

I stayed focused and outlined my plan to restore trust and accountability to Albany, to attract and retain jobs across the state, and to reduce property taxes, and I voiced my support for marriage equality. Paladino offered a rambling explanation for his opposition.

There were some memorable one-liners. Davis drew laughs for proclaiming, "Businesses will leave this state quicker than Carl Paladino at a gay bar." I injected my own lightheartedness: "I agree with Jimmy [McMillan]. The rent *is* too damn high." You would think we had felt we were coasting to victory. But you don't tempt the fates by relaxing for a second. You concentrate on the issues, not your opponents. Those last few days before Election Day on November 2 were as intense as any in the campaign. We held rallies across the state. There were few surprises. On November 1, former governor George Pataki came out in support of Paladino, citing his "Republican-Conservative core beliefs." He didn't mention that Paladino once called him a "degenerate idiot."

We paid no attention to this endorsement. It was all background noise.

I cast my vote in Mount Kisco with my daughters and Sandy at my side. I stayed at my office until sometime after 8 P.M. working on two speeches. By then I'd delivered hundreds of speeches during my career. With one exception—the day eight years earlier when I'd stood onstage to withdraw from the 2002 race against Carl McCall—I always looked forward to addressing crowds. If I was fortunate enough to be giving the acceptance speech I would speak from the heart.

As I'd experienced in my own life and seen firsthand, what is true for an individual is true for the collective. I wanted the people of the state to believe their future could be bright. Constructing a new building is easy. Changing hearts and minds is hard. Living without hope is hell on earth. My hope was that I would get to try to lift up the state, to celebrate the parts that were good and revamp the parts that weren't, to persuade New Yorkers that we could be smarter and stronger and better.

A little after 11 P.M., I walked into the ballroom of the Sheraton Hotel at Times Square with Sandy and my daughters. In my acceptance speech before hundreds of supporters, including my mother and father, I said: "We are upstate and downstate but we are one state, because we are New York. Yes we are black and we are white and we are brown but we are one state, because we are New York. Yes, we are rich and we are poor but we are one state because we are New York. Yes, we are gay and we are straight but we are one state because we are New York!"

The crowd erupted. I felt euphoric. As if we had all held our breath during the last few months and were only now exhaling.

CHAPTER 9

Coffee Is for Closers

Announcing the 2014–2015 budget.

People seeing the New York State capitol for the first time rarely feel dispassionate. It's a complex mix of architectural styles—Romanesque, French Renaissance, and Italian

Renaissance. It reflects the tastes of three teams of architects and the committees who hired and fired them over the course of the thirty-two years it took to build, from 1867 to 1899. Each new set of legislators wanted to leave a fingerprint on the project.

The first three floors are in the style of the French Second Empire, with rustic stonework, Doric and Corinthian columns, and arched windows. The fourth-floor exterior is Romanesque. Above that are dormers, a mansard roof, towers, and cornices.

I think the building is an extraordinary piece of architecture—and uniquely *American* in the way it brings together different visions. It's inventive and whimsical, but also majestic and serious, exemplifying all the spectacular forces of the post–Civil War era, when New York was emerging as the nation's economic powerhouse. State government celebrated New Yorkers' good fortune by constructing a monument for the ages.

But with all its grandeur and incongruity, our capitol also embodies Albany's talent for wastefulness and procrastination. In fact, the history of its construction is hilariously prophetic.

It is the most expensive capitol building ever constructed in the United States, having cost the state $25 million, the equivalent of about a half billion dollars today. Handcrafted of granite, marble, mahogany, and oak, the building was painstakingly assembled and enhanced with elaborate carvings. Leading mid-nineteenth-century American artist William Morris Hunt painted two large murals on the forty-foot-high ceiling of the Assembly Chamber. Building the

grandest of the grand staircases took hundreds of stonecut-
ters more than a dozen years, and its price tag earned it the
nickname "Million-Dollar Staircase." In truth, that estimate
was low. The building's meticulous workmanship was held
up by bureaucracy and budget shortfalls and the preferences
of individual governors. In 1877 Governor Lucius Robinson
reportedly hated the half-finished capitol's new executive
wing so much that he kept his office in the old capitol while
griping to the legislature about the project's expense.

Stops, starts, and design changes take time; and time—
especially when it stretches into years—costs money. But the
state had no choice but to keep paying. By the 1880s, the fin-
ishing touch, a huge dome in the style of capitols across the
country, was still years away.

It wasn't until Governor Frank Black was elected in 1896
that the end was in sight. He was appalled that, twenty-nine
years in, the capitol's main entrance—the seventy-seven
stone steps and main door to the eastern entrance, looking
down State Street toward the Hudson River—was still unusable. Governor Black abolished the Capitol Commission, an
eight-member appointed board that oversaw the project, and
transferred authority to the superintendent of public works,
ordering him to get the project done before Black's second
year in office began on January 1, 1898. Determination and
good weather combined to make this possible. After gleefully
ascending the staircase on New Year's morning, Governor
Black was the first to officially open the capitol's front door.

I remember walking inside when my father was governor.
The building's magnificence—its monumentality—was awe-
inspiring.

When I came back to the capitol as attorney general in 2007, I was struck by how run-down it had become. The variance between my memory and reality made me doubt that the building was ever as glorious as I remembered. Perhaps a son's pride in his father and a twentysomething's idealized version of government and public service had made me blind to its shabby appearance.

But even discounting my romantic memory, the decay was palpable and the filth and foul odor were undeniably real.

Technically the building had been "under restoration" since the 1970s, but as with the original project, progress had been made in fits and starts. It took architects and artisans twenty-five years, beginning in 1978, just to refurbish the Senate Chamber, and ten to return the Assembly Chamber's vaulted ceilings, tall windows, and intricate stonework to their 1879 splendor. Elsewhere the plaster was crumbling and the carpets were frayed.

Few people noticed, because few were visiting anymore—a symptom of the government's decline. If they visited, they weren't invited inside. When Governor Pataki took office in 1995, he closed the governor's wing of the capitol to visitors, citing security concerns, and had a ring of concrete barriers erected around the building. Critics mockingly renamed the executive floor Fort Pataki.

Since 2000, scaffolding had covered the capitol's exterior as workers repaired the roof and repointed the stonework, enhancing the building's fortress-like appearance. Inside, where new office space was being added and mezzanines and balconies were being reconstructed, walking under scaffolding was part of the routine. The colossal project, with its relentless hammering and drilling, was scheduled to last until 2015. Hallways, staircases, and offices were caked in dust. Skylights were sealed. The weak light that filtered through cast shadows on the walls, where the paint was peeling. Dank, dark, and grimy, the capitol had all the charm of a 1960s New York City subway station. But even worse, it seemed like the buildings' occupants didn't care or notice. Or if they did they were resigned to the dismal conditions they were in.

My time with HELP and HUD taught me that there's a powerful connection between our physical setting and our state of mind. And I know that living in such degradation impairs self-worth.

The opposite is also true. That's why I gave residents a management role in the Genesis complexes we built during my HELP years. Likewise in my HUD days the design and look of public housing were radically changed. Having pride in your surroundings can be transformative. As Abraham Lincoln said, "I like to see a man proud of the place in which he lives. I like to see a man live so that his place will be proud of him."

The officeholders and journalists who covered state politics had lost respect for their surroundings, felt powerless to change them, or grown inured to the decay. I had run for governor promising to clean up Albany in a figurative sense. The concept was abstract. The building itself offered a visible, practical metaphor: dysfunction in its most tangible form. I also needed to show people change was possible. The capitol insiders are a cynical crew. They had to see things could be improved.

I was determined to avoid a protracted, bureaucratic timetable like the one that had dictated the building's construction, which eventually stopped in 1899 only because Governor Teddy Roosevelt said, Enough is enough. The capitol is done. There will be no dome. A practical, strong-minded leader, he knew how to make a decision and tame the bureaucracy.

One of my first thoughts after winning was, Two years from now, the scaffolding will be gone. The capitol will be restored to its original glory. People will be able to see our progress. But I also wanted to make a statement on Day One. That statement was that we were returning government to the people of New York State.

At noon on Saturday, January 1, we held my inauguration in the capitol's War Room, named for its colorful murals of military conflicts. My parents, Sandy, and my three girls were there for the simple ceremony. Taking the oath of office with my father looking on helped assuage much of the pain we both felt after his 1994 loss. But I intentionally downplayed the usual pageantry. Showiness is often used as a false front to detract from our serious, untended issues. I was not going to soft-pedal our problems. "There's a lot of work ahead," I said. "We'll celebrate when the job is done."

With that, I walked out to the Hall of Governors, a cavernous corridor lined with executive offices and an arbitrary collection of portraits of governors past. There I cut a giant red ribbon. "The public is welcome," I said.

Within minutes, workers were dismantling the barriers outside.

My term as governor had begun.

Becoming governor is a lot like being shot out of a cannon. Everything happens so quickly. You celebrate, you catch your breath, you put together a staff. You have to prepare your State of the State Address, then you have to present your budget, and get it enacted within your first twelve weeks in office, and in the meantime you're just trying to locate the men's room. The first big event is that State of the State.

Traditionally, the annual State of the State speech is given in the Assembly Chamber. It's the largest space in the capitol, but it wasn't big enough for everyone who wanted to attend, so the entire affair was for capitol insiders and legislators. Tickets were precious commodities, given out as political perks. Key donors and lobbyists filled the room. My main message was the opposite. We must return the government to the people, and I will not continue the status quo; change has come and will triumph. I also thought there would be symbolic value in changing the venue. Starting today, the business of New York will not be just a conversation between the legislature and the governor. It will be a conversation with the people.

But the legislative leaders opposed the idea. They told me: "Eliot tried, David tried, even George tried, the legislators won't allow it." I listened and concluded that it was even more important for me to shake things up. I said, "We're holding it at the Convention Center."

I wanted to show that things would be done differently in Albany. And I was starting with the opening act. The Albany establishment had seen many new governors come in thinking they would "change" the culture, only to have the establishment conquer and defeat the new governor. These first days and encounters would be determinative. I would insist we move it and I would not back down.

As in most executive positions, your team is everything. I was lucky to have my core group continue from my time as attorney general. I named my sage adviser Steve Cohen as my top aide; Mylan Denerstein, counsel; "my go-to pro" Linda Lacewell, special counsel; Richard Bamberger, my communications director; and Stephanie Benton, director of the governor's office. Ben Lawsky became chief of staff.

Joe Percoco, executive deputy secretary, and Howard Glaser, director of state operations, had been aides to my father when he was governor. Drew Zambelli, my counselor, had also been a senior aide in my father's administration. I'd known Larry Schwartz, my senior adviser, because he was the Suffolk County deputy executive in the 1980s when I built a HELP facility in Bellport, New York. He'd served as secretary to Governor Paterson and knew Albany outside and in. This was my dream team. I'd relied on their good judgment for years, and in some cases, decades. Long-term relationships are rare in politics. Most are transactional. They are built around a campaign or a short-term stint in government, and the power and status the politician's position brings. But across generations, we were a group of people dedicated to government service. I just happened to be leading the cause. The test of time also developed a group of people with deep core values and talents. I demand performance of players on the team and they demand it of each other. I am a tough boss and proud of it. But even more, the team culture demands performance.

On January 5, I stood on the Convention Center stage, colorful flags of New York's sixty-two counties behind me, and 2,220 cheering New Yorkers before me, "real people" for the first time in decades at a State of the State—and it wasn't held in the legislature's domain. The symbolism was powerful. In the front, sitting on folding chairs, was a group of lawmakers blamed for high taxes, scandals, and chronically late budgets—so much ugly stuff that the New York State Legislature had become a staple joke on late-night television. But that also presented an opportunity. I knew from campaigning that many legislators were dedicated public servants hungry for change. They wanted to be part of a government that worked. They wanted to do good things and have a positive reputation. I am both a realist and an optimist: Of course they wanted to be part of a new day in Albany. But like the voters, they doubted that such a transformation was possible. Failure breeds more failure. But success breeds success, and that was my opportunity.

Politically, they had reason to embrace my ideas. They knew that I knew Albany. My tenure as attorney general told them I was serious: I'd cracked down on one member, former Senate majority leader Pedro Espada, for embezzlement. (He was subsequently sentenced to five years in prison.) I had exposed a fraud in the New York State comptroller's office that changed the system countywide. And I'd won my gubernatorial race against Carl Paladino with a resounding mandate.

On the state Senate side, the new majority leader, Dean Skelos, a Long Islander who had been a state senator since the early 1980s, was determined to maintain a high profile for his Republican caucus and wanted to be part of the solution. He was ready to try to make it work. On the Assembly side, Speaker Sheldon Silver, a Democrat, was the experienced Albany veteran, so I believed he too wanted to change Albany's "dysfunction" label. He knows how the government works and truly leads his conference.

The usual State of the State speech is a combination of vacuous rhetoric and sleep-inducing details. They are usually dreadful. Even my father, who could make reading the side of a milk carton sound interesting, plodded through State of the State speeches. I jettisoned the formula and used PowerPoint technology—a first for a State of the State Address—to show pictures and diagrams.

I delivered the serious message that we were going to fundamentally realign state government—with a touch of humor. One slide showed "Ships Passing in the Night." My face was superimposed over a battleship. Incoming missiles were labeled SPECIAL INTERESTS. Shelly Silver and Dean Skelos were shown as captains of nearby battleships. Corny, I know. But it expressed Albany's method of operation, where the Senate and Assembly opposed each other, and the special interests targeted the new governor and his efforts to change the status quo. My recent predecessors had all proposed reform and were attacked by the commercial interests that control Albany and its $140 billion operation. In each recent case, the Albany interests won. "I know this is how it normally happens," I joked. "But not this year." I said with humor the truth that I could not say directly.

I called for an Emergency Financial Plan to close the $10 billion deficit. We'd do it without raising taxes or borrowing money. We would do it by spending less.

There would be two task forces reforming the main spending areas. The Medicaid Redesign Team (MRT) would be made up of leaders in the health-care industry. It would include executives of major hospitals, doctors, health advocates, and members of the health-care workers' union Service Employees International Union (SEIU) Local 1199, as well as lawmakers and state officials. This twenty-seven-member board would advise the government on how to rein in spending while improving state services. The Spending and Government Efficiency (SAGE) Commission, made up of private sector experts, would find ways to reduce redundancies and bureaucracy. In case that sounds unnecessary, consider that the Department of Health had at least eighty-seven statutorily created administrative units: forty-six councils, seventeen boards, six institutes, six committees, five facilities, two task forces, two offices, two advisory panels, and a work group.

I called for an overhaul of the state's juvenile justice system. Youth prisons were big local employers upstate, but the facilities were half empty. I said, "An incarceration program is not an employment program. If people need jobs, let's get people jobs. Don't put other people in prison to give some people jobs . . . That's not what this state is all about, and that has to end this session."

On the basis of the proven idea that incentives get results, I threw out obsolete practices, promising to make funding for education and economic development commensurate with performance. When I was at HUD, we moved away from block grants—lump sums given to states and cities by the federal government—in favor of competitive grants to spur high achievement. It worked. But New York was still using a model from the 1960s in which a school district received state money whether students were learning or not. The result was that New York schools were spending 71 percent more than the national average but ranked fortieth in graduation rates. School bureaucracies had grown while students' success rates declined.

Economic development had been managed in a similar top-down way, with each city and town receiving a portion of the state budget, regardless of what worked and what didn't work.

Functionally bankrupt cities were facilitated rather than restructured. I was also interested in more community-driven approaches. HUD had taught me that a central-government-knows-best approach rarely produces the best results. This lesson was illustrated in Technicolor when a Native American chief took me on a tour of his Alaskan village. In the first house we visited I noticed that the family was storing dry goods in the kitchen sink and had removed the plumbing fixtures in the bathroom to use it as a closet. I didn't say anything, afraid I would commit a cultural faux pas. But the next house was the same thing, and the next after that. "Why aren't they using their kitchens and bathrooms?" I asked the chief.

"HUD regulations require each house to have a kitchen and one bathroom for every two bedrooms," the chief informed me.

"Right," I said. "What's wrong with that?"

"Nothing, Mr. Secretary, it sounds like a good idea, but our village doesn't have running water."

In my State of the State Address, I announced ten new regional economic councils across New York. They included
the Finger Lakes region, a beautiful area in the central part of
the state just west of Syracuse; the Mohawk Valley, the area
around Schenectady, between the Adirondack and Catskill
mountains; and western New York, encompassing Buffalo,
Rochester, and Niagara Falls. The councils would be established to create jobs for some of the 850,000 out-of-work
New Yorkers and stem the flow of businesses and individuals fleeing the state because of soaring taxes and declining
opportunities. This wasn't a make-work program. It was an
opportunity to give these regions the help they needed—not
the help someone in Albany thought they needed. The economic councils would be public-private partnerships run
by the people who knew their regions best and could spot
untapped areas for job growth. This was a much different
bottom-up policy approach.

As I'd done at each campaign stop across the state, I said,
"We must transform the State of New York from a government of dysfunction, gridlock, and corruption to a government of performance, integrity, and pride. This is not about
budget trimming or cutting; it's about looking at how we can
fix government and make it work for the people. Together,
we must take the significant steps needed to reinvent, reor-
ganize, and redesign government to restore credibility and
to rebuild our economy by creating jobs all across this state.

"Change is not easy," I said, "but we must change to return
to prosperity. We must begin by confronting honestly the
challenges we face."

Drawing on my own experience, I added, "In government,

as in life, you can never solve a problem you refuse to acknowledge. Denial is not a successful life strategy."

The presentation of the state budget is the seminal event each year. Why? For the same reason Willie Sutton robbed banks: that's where the money is. Every lawmaker and advocate has an agenda. Everyone has to feel heard. And everybody wants to leave the party with something.

The budget signals to citizens how well—or poorly—their government manages, what it cares about, how much it will tax, and how much it will spend. And, for the executive—be it president, mayor, or governor—the budget is a test of leadership.

Putting together what was projected to be a budget of about $140 billion in the three-week span between the State of the State Address and the constitutionally mandated February 1 due date is level-ten pain.

In New York State all bills are passed in the Assembly and the state Senate and sent to the governor to be signed or vetoed. But the budget takes the reverse route. It starts with the governor, who determines needs and priorities.

Under what's known as the "no alteration" clause of the New York State constitution, the legislature is allowed to reduce or strike items the governor has proposed but not to increase funding to those items or to substitute its own budget for the governor's.

It wasn't only the Republicans and the Democrats whom I'd need to contend with over the budget. In Albany, there is a third group. I call it the CIP—the Commercial Interest Party.

The CIP is made up of the big-business and big-labor special interests with high-paid lobbyists and sophisticated public relations machines; front groups, political action committees, and operatives. These are the commercial interests that benefit directly from government programs. They have ruled Albany for years. People think government decisions are about differing political ideology. Sometimes they are. But they're just as often about the state money for their programs.

The CIP had pushed the notion that the amount of funding was tantamount to the level of caring: the more you spend, the more good you do. Albany bought that line for decades, and it was a lie. More money does not necessarily equal better services.

For example, more education funding was not necessarily improving students' or teachers' performance. It was about growing the bureaucracy. The state budget is about $140 billion. That's a lot of zeroes. Albany had developed a sophisticated budget machine for the interests that could benefit from it. Lobbyists make millions. The media benefits from ads on radio and TV. A network of front groups argue for their budget item with apparent credibility. Groups with names like "New Yorkers for Better Education" publish reports and data on education policy. But these groups are actually funded by the very interests that would benefit from a budget increase. This elaborate mechanism went into operation every year, and it worked well for those in the business of government. We had lost sight of the point of the government exercise: to help the constituent effectively at the least possible cost to taxpayers.

The CIP created a public relations nightmare each year for any governor who tried to curb spending.

When a governor proposed spending reductions, the big PACs would start running opposition ads on TV that insinuated the cuts would be nothing less than the ruination of society.

The spots showed old people being upended from wheelchairs and blackboards crashing off classroom walls. After Governor David Paterson tried to reduce financial aid to hospitals and other health-care facilities, one ad went as far as having a blind man in a wheelchair ask Paterson, who is legally blind, "Why are you doing this to me?"

Typically during this attack blitz, the legislators would lie in wait. The governor's popularity would drop, and they knew that after he was diminished in the public's eye, the governor would fold. The legislature would then reverse his cuts—known as restorations—and increase spending and taxes. After the legislators reshaped the budget to their satisfaction, they would vote to pass it. If they needed to raise taxes to pay for their pet projects, so be it. The Albany networks of lobbyists, lawyers, and public relations experts would have earned their pay. And once again, New York State would defy the principle that you can't spend more than you have, and the taxpayer and the government's intended beneficiary would have lost. That's how Albany worked.

I'd known about the CIP since childhood. My father's friend, columnist Jack Newfield, called it "the permanent government." Jack would rail about it back in our kitchen in

Queens. It was the business interests that had evolved and developed around government programs and eclipsed the original intent and beneficiaries. He always said it was the lurking danger to effective progressive government.

Besides the external interests, to complete the budget is a practical nightmare. Getting 213 elected officials to agree on thousands of items in one budget document is a serious challenge. For years, there was a pattern. The state constitution requires that the annual balanced budget be approved by April 1. But in 2010 it wasn't passed until August 2. I was campaigning for governor then, and I remember the next day's headline in the *New York Times*: "125 Days Late, a State Budget with New Taxes."

I thought, Wow, this really *is* a joke—and a disaster!

The 2010 budget was one of the latest in New York State history; tardy budgets had become the custom. My father was the last governor to pass a budget before midnight on March 31. That was in 1983. New York State didn't have another on-time budget for twenty-one years. Nearly every year, as the deadline passed, governors would submit temporary extenders that stretched the deadline by a week, two weeks, or a month. The average budget was fifty days late.

Lawmakers not only ignored the deadlines but also disregarded the meaning of "balanced."

For two decades the state government hid the ballooning deficit through a series of accounting tricks. The legislators passed "one-shot" revenue measures. They transferred unspent funds from dedicated projects to cover state operating expenses and borrowed off-budget revenues from state agencies. They delayed payments to contractors and suppliers. The budget looked balanced. But instead of addressing the systemic long-term financial crisis, legislators kicked the problems down the road, creating bigger and bigger shortfalls. In 2010, Paterson's last year in office, the budget deficit leaped by $750 million, to $8.2 billion. It was widely accepted, and often reported, that for the coming fiscal year in 2011, the state would be operating with a $10 billion deficit, calculated as the difference between state revenues and the budget's rate of growth. That's the figure I quoted throughout my campaign.

My first budget needed to be on time and balanced. I needed to slam the door on chronically irresponsible behavior. It had to stop.

Many people believe that to be a progressive you must be a big spender. This is a false creation of the CIP to perpetuate the rationale for spending increases. Progressives have never believed in spending for spending's sake. In 1932, in the worst of the Great Depression, New York governor Franklin Delano Roosevelt ran for president on a platform of fiscal responsibility. He believed that governments should stay within their budgets just as families should. When Roosevelt vetoed a congressional spending bill he declared, "We can afford all that we need, but we cannot afford all that we want." Hugh Carey, Bill Clinton, Mario Cuomo, all believed the same. That's the tradition I come from. It's what experience and responsibility teach any executive. I believe the goal isn't simply to pass bigger budgets; it's to use what we have wisely and achieve greater results. If spending more means more performance that's one thing. But it has come to mean more bureaucracy and more money for the providers. That's not responsible to taxpayers or to the people we are trying to help.

And raising taxes comes at a cost. People and businesses are more mobile than ever before. A state raising taxes on the wealthy doesn't redistribute income; it redistributes people. They can move to another state. If we are ever serious about raising taxes as purely a social or fiscal equity matter, discussions of a high-end tax need to happen at the federal level, or a state puts itself at a competitive disadvantage.

I was primed to pass a real, balanced budget, by March 31. My firm intention was to reclaim executive control. My attitude was, If you guys think you're going to delay the budget I'm going to use all the powers of the state constitution and the court's orders from *Silver v. Pataki*, the court case establishing the extent of the governor's control over the budget. Not in a confrontational way, but matter-of-factly. I'd geared up for this during the campaign. If I held legislators accountable—so that any delays they caused would have consequences—the power in the relationship would flip. My staff and I consulted John Cape, who had been George Pataki's budget director, and Paul Shechtman, the lawyer who represented Pataki in the case he brought before the New York court of appeals challenging the legislature's budget authority. We were ready for either scenario: an on-time amicable budget resolution or budget warfare and a shutdown of government. I had lived through the Clinton-Gingrich budget fight and the ensuing shutdown. I felt comfortable I could handle one. I had to. If you are unwilling to walk away from the table, you can't negotiate because you've already lost.

Although I'm in daily communication with my father, it's not our way to discuss the nitty-gritty of governing. But I'd studied the gridlock and tactics of Albany over the past decade and felt sure I knew the way to solvency. So why was it that every time we had a fiscal meeting I'd come away thinking that I wasn't sophisticated enough to understand what was going on?

I listened to the experts' explanations: "It's not in the budget; it's in permanent law," one would say. And "An increase is not an increase if it's required by law," said another.

I didn't get it.

During my second week as governor I called my budget team to the conference room adjoining my office. Steve Cohen, Ben Lawsky, and Budget Director Bob Megna were there, along with Larry Schwartz, who had helped David Paterson pass his last budget and knew the pitfalls. Larry had agreed to be my point person in negotiations with legislators. We were looking at the education and Medicaid figures. Accounting for nearly half the state budget, they had the worst inefficiencies and the highest costs.

"I need to understand what's driving the $10 billion deficit," I said. "Break it down for me."

"Medicaid is slated to go up by 13 percent this year," Bob said.

"I don't understand that," I said. "The inflation rate is under 2 percent. "Why the steep hike?"

Bob took a deep breath. "It's the inflators," he said.

"What's an inflator?"

"It's complicated," Larry replied.

Larry and Bob explained that an inflator is a formula used to calculate cost projections. There were hundreds woven into the budget—inserted into the law over decades, by lawmakers, at the behest of industries, unions, and lobbyists. The increases weren't based on performance, accountability, or the state's fiscal reality. They were effectively permanent budget increases in select areas. I thought to myself, permanent budget increases—the permanent government had triumphed. To compound the problem, if the governor proposed a budget that did not fund the inflator in the budget permanent law, then it was a "cut." So anything less than a 13 percent increase was a proposed cut by the governor and would be used against him in the CIP's public relations campaign. A 10 percent increase in a program would be portrayed as a 3 percent permanent cut by the mean, callous, uncaring governor.

This meant that Medicaid spending automatically increased each year. And similar formulas were being used to lock in the next year's education spending, which had already soared to $20 billion annually. In 2011 both were slated to automatically rise by 13 percent.

What I heard defied common sense.

Like a man-eating blob in a bad sci-fi film, the inflators appeared and then grew unchecked. What was particularly insidious was that they were permanent—not negotiated each year like the rest of the budget. They were tucked away in arcane places, built-in multipliers that automatically jacked up the budget year after year, causing it to nearly double, from roughly $79 billion in 2001 when I ran unsuccessfully for governor to around $136.5 billion in 2010 when I was elected.

Because of the inflators.

Suddenly I understood that the problem wasn't the numbers; it was the process. I was incredulous. I looked at Larry and Bob. "This is insane! This entire budget is a sham!"

"I know," said Larry. "The whole system is rigged."

When I had delivered my State of the State Address, I knew we would be in for a rough time with the budget because we planned to clamp down on spending. No one likes to be told no—least of all legislators who want to take home spoils to their districts.

But I had no idea how bad it actually was—that the bedrock of our state government was being compromised from the inside.

It is easiest to govern by skating across the surface, but I got into politics because I love the details—and the details are what really matter. That's how Larry, Bob, and I handled the budget. In order to put it together, we first had to take it apart piece by piece.

I knew that eliminating the CIP's formulas would have to be the cornerstone of my proposed budget. It would change the dynamics of the state's fiscal crisis, bringing the deficit to a surmountable level, and effectively transform the structure of public funding.

The CIP would expect me to do what had been done for the past twenty years: give in. But this time, the CIP would be

picking a fight with the wrong governor. I wouldn't buckle.
The inflators had to go.

The best way to treat a wound is to expose it to oxygen.
Remove the Band-Aid and allow the elements to fix it.

Here, the oxygen was fair-minded New Yorkers. The legislature was not going to fix itself, so we launched a campaign
to generate public awareness of the bogus budget process
that forced expenses up and counted on taxpayers to foot the
bill. By taking the facts to the people, we would leave the
lawmakers with no choice but to join the reform.

In truth, many legislators were unaware of the inflators.
They receive a copy of the budget a day or two before the
vote. They don't have time to delve into the details, many
of which are highly technical. So the inflators became a set
piece, and the dysfunction kept on going.

To kick off our campaign, I wrote an opinion piece titled
"The Real Albany Sham: The Budget," explaining how the
automatic inflators were driving the deficit. "As Attorney
General, I uncovered schemes by lenders to exploit students,
plots by insurance companies to defraud patients and attempts by Wall Street to deceive homebuyers," I wrote. "In
the past 30 days, as I have prepared the state's budget, I was
shocked to learn that the state's budget process is a sham that
mirrors the deceptive practices I fought to change in the private sector."

On January 31, the eve of my budget announcement to
the state Assembly and Senate, we circulated the op-ed to

every news outlet in New York. The *New York Post* called it a "bombshell op-ed," and reported it under the headline: "Dirty Secret: Andy Lifts the Lid on How Albany Steals Your Money; Cuomo Exposes Dirty Trick." Nearly every major paper in the state ran it, and it was widely reported on TV. Marcia Kramer, the chief political correspondent for WCBS-TV 2 in New York City, described the inflators as "secret budget rules that for decades have padded funding for special interests and helped push state finances into the red."

There was little reaction from lawmakers. A few were quoted as saying that by framing the budget process as a "sham," I was trying to divert attention away from the painful cuts I was proposing. Both Dean Skelos and Shelly Silver said they wanted to study my budget proposal before commenting. But they bristled at my criticism. Skelos told reporters that formulas are part of normal budgeting, saying, "All budgets have language . . . in them . . . there are certain formulas that can be changed and they are every year—whether it's school aid, Medicaid, all of those. I wouldn't exactly call it a scam."

Silver defended the system, claiming that a genuine need for more spending on schools and Medicaid, and not "made up" formulas, was driving cost projections.

The next day, February 1, I presented my budget at Albany's performing arts theater, called The Egg because of its iconic oval shape. As I had done for my State of the State Address, I used PowerPoint to outline New York's fiscal crisis. The state, I argued, had become "functionally bankrupt." Like a functional alcoholic who gets by pretending to be OK, New York was chronically and systemically in debt.

My proposed budget was $132.9 billion. I crossed out the funding formulas, instead tying the projected costs for Medicaid to objective, fair criteria, such as enrollment numbers, the inflation rate, and the Consumer Price Index, a Bureau of Labor Statistics measurement that estimates changes in prices of household goods and services. We recommended closing or downsizing underused prisons, consolidating state agencies, and freezing state salaries. To show how grave the state's finances were, I wrote an executive order giving my senior staff and myself 5 percent pay cuts. That year my salary was reduced from $179,000 to $170,050, giving me credibility when I warned the public unions—state employees, teachers, and health-care workers—that there would be cuts and layoffs if they didn't agree to pare down their contracts.

With an overall 2.7 percent cut in state government spending, the deficit was reduced to zero—with zero tax increases.

Now, instead of wasting months doing the ineffective dance in which the governor cuts and the legislature restores, the lawmakers had a new model for the state budget, one that did away with the old spend-and-tax routine.

It was now a question of passage. We needed the legislators to support us and my firm belief in politics is to get the people behind you and the politicians will follow. I had to keep speaking to New Yorkers and not just to legislators in Albany. On February 2, the day after I presented my budget to the legislature, we posted a video on YouTube and sent out a press release to every newspaper, magazine, TV station, blogger, and tweeter on our communications list. I made my plans clear: I wanted to close the deficit and get rid of the

inflators to end the cycle of rising deficits. "In the past, the attacks by the special interests and the lobbyists forced the governor to back down and give in. Know this: I will not be intimidated. This is why you elected me, and I will get it done." This was a call to action to lawmakers to forget the lobbyists and special interests and make the tough call and the right decision.

That same day, I launched my budget tour throughout the state. I began by visiting Westchester County. Next up were Buffalo and Long Island.

While I went to the people for support, my message did not demonize or alienate the legislators. I wanted them with me and believed I could get them. In the past governors ran against Albany. They blamed the legislature for everything. "Woe unto the poor governor, he tried, but the legislature is impossible." I called it the governor's "impotence defense." I tried a different way, by inviting the legislators to be part of the reform. I praised elected officials, commending them for their good work and willingness to join our campaign for reform. Together, we called for bipartisanship to end the gridlock. "The climate in Albany has become toxic," I said. "That has to change. We're Democrats. We're Republicans. But we're New Yorkers first and we have to act that way and vote that way."

When a reporter asked me whether it was risky to tackle the unions and business groups, I looked at him and said, "If I don't take them on, I fail for sure. Sometimes the safest course is apparently the biggest risk."

But "taking them on" did not necessarily mean fighting them. Broad public support against the funding formulas and Albany's gridlock neutralized their resistance and I invited them to the table to be part of the process. "You get more flies with honey than with vinegar," my grandfather Charlie Raffa used to say.

We included the leadership of the hospitals through the Greater New York Hospital Association (GNYHA), and they were truly appreciative of the inclusion and knew best how to improve the system. With them we added the health-care union, SEIU Local 1199, in our Medicaid Redesign Team, the health-insurance program for poor and disabled people. Medicaid is a federal law, but it is administered at the state level. In New York, the state government pays providers—doctors, clinics, and hospitals—directly. We were looking for measurable improvement in health outcomes, long-term cost controls, and a more efficient administrative structure. To its credit, once it bought into the changes, SEIU was very helpful. In fact, Local 1199 officially endorsed our Medicaid-spending reduction plan, running television ads that promoted it all through March.

Later we asked the New York State United Teachers (NYSUT) union to help us launch a statewide system to evaluate teachers' performance. With its help, we created a plan that would accelerate teacher evaluations for math and English across the state. We wrote and passed this bill in early March to secure the union's support and mitigate pushback. It would go into effect when the entire budget was passed.

In many ways all these strategies were making the budget process work better than I would ever have anticipated. However, we had wanted major reform, which meant we needed to change the sacred cows. They were the state's income tax code and property taxes.

Much of the tax controversy I faced was about a one-shot tax that Governor Paterson had passed in 2009 to deal with dwindling revenues during the worst recession since the Great Depression. Dubbed the "millionaires' surcharge," it imposed a tax on individuals with incomes above $200,000— $300,000 for couples filing jointly—at a rate of 7.85 percent. A second bracket taxed people with incomes over $500,000 at 8.97 percent. During my campaign I promised not to extend it past its January 1, 2012, expiration date. Now, the liberal, Democratic-dominated Assembly was pushing hard to keep the surcharge, and the more conservative, Republican-led state Senate wanted it gone.

The surcharge generated badly needed revenues. But I saw it as an emblem of the state's propensity to overspend and then raise taxes. It also masked a more serious, systemic problem with the state's tax code. Under the permanent tax code, an individual making a taxable income of $40,000 was paying the same tax rate—6.85 percent—as an individual making $40 million. This "flat tax" had been in place for decades. Republican presidential candidate Steve Forbes ran on the promise of a national flat tax in 1996 and 2000, and it never caught hold for a logical reason: it was regressive. New York's flat tax was a dirty little secret. Few realized the absurdity of our code and its basic unfairness. That was the meaningful and progressive reform I wanted.

I decided to handle the surcharge at the same time as the overhaul of the tax code because a "give" in the surcharge could equal a "get" on fundamental tax code reform. We put them off till later in the year.

We treated another potential wild card—the property tax

cap—the same way. I'd submitted a bill to the legislature in January that would cap local property taxes at 2 percent. The state Senate passed the legislation, but the Assembly was still debating the measure, in part because opposition groups, led by the teachers' union, said a cap could hurt school districts that receive funding from a property tax base. I didn't think it was fair that Long Island, Westchester County, and up-state, suffering from the highest property taxes in the nation, were socked with an average 5.7 percent increase every year. Tax bills in some upper-end communities exceeded $40,000 a year. People, particularly older people on fixed incomes, were being forced out of their homes. A tax cap would help reverse years of economic decline outside New York City.

But the issue was complicated. Assembly Democrats had initially insisted the bill be negotiated in concert with strengthening rent regulations in New York City. I decided to put both issues aside until after we successfully passed a budget and restart my push in the spring. We needed to focus on the budget.

The New York *Daily News* ran a quote by Lawrence Levy, the dean of Hofstra University's National Center on Subur-ban Studies: "This is a big, complicated place, and Cuomo could make a difference if he is prepared to focus like a laser. The danger is when governors stop paying attention. Then they can get eaten up by the legislature and special interests."

I was not too worried about getting eaten up—I felt I had come too far for that to happen—but he was dead on about maintaining laser focus. When people say that politics is a sport, it's usually an insult. But there's a positive side to this cliché. Effective politics, smart politics, and politics that result in improving lives and changing the status quo truly require the concentration and drive of an Olympic athlete.

Negotiating the budget with the legislature is exhausting. The formidable undertaking is sleep deprivation, frustration, and reward all in one. You move methodically from area to area—economic development, education, mental health, criminal justice—asking and answering big, and small, questions. Do you want to close prisons? How many guards should you have? How many inmates per cell? Which roads and bridges should we rebuild? Are these projects fairly distributed across the state? Education funding is negotiated district by district, and there are seven hundred districts. Every competing interest needs to be worked out.

This explains why stalemates happen. We see them in Washington all the time. We had a national shutdown in October 2013, when the federal government closed for two weeks after Congress failed to pass a budget for fiscal year 2014. The Republican-led House of Representatives tied passage of the budget to defunding the Affordable Care Act, President Barack Obama's plan to make health insurance available to all Americans, regardless of income. The Democratic-dominated U.S. Senate refused to sign on. Unable to resolve the dispute before October 1, when the country's new fiscal year begins, they closed the government. The standoff went on for two weeks before the GOP gave in.

When the New York State Legislature was at an impasse in 2010, Governor Paterson extended the budget one week at a time, inserting highly debated proposals into temporary budget bills to force lawmakers to pass sections of the budget or be responsible for a state shutdown. The legislators approved the budget piecemeal over several months, passing the final portion on August 2.

I wasn't going to spend months jockeying with the legislature. "Pass an on-time budget or close down the state," I told lawmakers. It's that simple. "Eliminate the inflators. Hold the line on taxes. Those pieces are nonnegotiable."

Conquering gridlock and passing an on-time budget required the multifaceted approach we had designed and were executing: citizen engagement; an advertising campaign, including stakeholders; preparation for court battles; and courage. But politics is still about people, and I needed the legislators' support. Gridlock is caused by unwillingness to cooperate. If I was going to deliver the reform I promised, I needed the legislators as partners. Also, I wanted them as partners.

How did we do it?

Nine thousand cups of coffee; four thousand plates of cookies; dozens of breakfasts, lunches, dinners, weddings, and bar mitzvahs; jokes, charm, and muscle.

In short, it was through developing and cultivating relationships. I've often been asked if I like retail politics—dealing with individual legislators—because I spend so much time at it. I do like it. But I also see it as my job to make these relationships work. I enjoy getting to know people and figuring out what they need to take away from the table. There is an old Italian saying relevant to negotiation: "Everyone needs a piece of bread"—meaning, everyone needs to eat and therefore everyone needs a "win" to leave the negotiating table.

We opened up the mansion for meetings with lawmakers, something that hadn't been done in years. We started with the caucuses: Republican, Democratic, African American, Puerto Rican, Hispanic, and Asian. We went district by district, inviting local Assembly members and senators for breakfasts and dinners. Over and over people said the same thing: "I've never been here."

One senator was so surprised to be invited to the mansion that he started to leave at the end of the cocktail hour. Steve Cohen had to tell him, "The governor is expecting you to stay for dinner."

I met individually with dozens of legislators in my office at the capitol. Historically their leadership was the only conduit to the governor. Many legislators hadn't sat down one-on-one with a governor in years, if ever.

At every meeting, I offered my visitor a cookie. Ronald Reagan had jelly beans. Bill Clinton had M&M's. An Orthodox Jew? May I offer you kosher rugelach? Gluten intolerant? Have a meringue. Trying to stay healthy? Enjoy an applesauce-sweetened oatmeal bar. Charm does have its place in politics.

Getting down to business, I'd say, "Look, I want to be a friend. We can do this together; we can roll up our sleeves and take this process back. Either the special interests and the apathy and the inertia will swallow us or we can change the culture and pass the first on-time budget in decades and redeem the positive legacy of state government."

I also told legislators that the usual delaying tactics wouldn't work. "Fight me on this," I said, "and I'll use my emergency powers to make deeper cuts. I need you to get on board with this.

Nearly every lawmaker I met with liked the idea of being part of a budget that would fix Albany and overhaul the legislature's dismal reputation.

"I offer you a fresh start," I'd say. "If it works, I'll make you a winner and I'll call you a winner. I'll be with you in your districts, letting your constituents know that you were a big part of this historic reform. If there's criticism, step back and point at me."

I'm not a credit hoarder. It's dishonest and impractical. To get anything—good or bad—to happen in government takes collaboration. Leaders who claim full credit for positive changes make enemies of the people who helped. And when an idea bombs, they wind up bearing inordinate blame. If you share success, everyone has a stake in it, and everyone will be more committed to maintaining it.

I learned much of the art of legislating from Bill Clinton. Once, when I was HUD secretary, I was on my way to Capitol Hill for a meeting with a member of Congress. The president asked me where I was going. I said, "I've got this great initiative that I'm seeking support for in Congress."

"Andrew," he said, putting his arm around my shoulder. "That's not how you get members to side with you. The way to do it is to figure out who you need and go to their districts. They don't get elected here; they get elected in their districts. Even if the member isn't there, when he or she comes back, the constituents will say, 'You know, Cuomo was here. He has this great initiative. You should really support it.' Then, when you go to the Hill, you've already won."

President Clinton also showed me that you can't take anything personally. He spoke from tough experience. The Republicans called him every name in the book. The House of Representatives impeached him. But Clinton was there every day, saying, "How do we get this done?" He had to rally the support of the American people; that was critical. But he also had to enthusiastically work with congressmen and congresswomen who had tried to oust him from office.

There is little that I didn't compromise on. There is no other way. More doctrinaire personalities think if you compromise you lose. Not so! If you compromise, you win.

I had a Republican state Senate and a Democratic Assembly. This meant there were items the right needed and items the left needed, and the final budget had to address both. Anything the conservatives liked the liberals would automatically dislike, and vice versa. Reaching agreement was complicated.

To succeed the budget must see both sides to carve out a solution.

The downside is that you get attacked by both parties. The budget was cutting taxes for businesses and homeowners— the Republicans liked that and the Democrats balked. The budget was closing prisons and had more funding for education and social programs—the Democrats cheered and the Republicans got angry.

In some ways, it's easier to argue from the extremes, because it becomes a purist argument. But extremism does not work in a democracy or, as far as I can see, anywhere if you want to actually get something done. Extremists suggest that to compromise is an abandonment of principle. Not so. The principle is democracy and progress. Our founding fathers put together a highly balanced system predicated on reason, cooperation, and principled compromise. In his farewell address, George Washington said that political parties are the worst enemy. John Adams said it again in the *Federalist Papers*. Ben Franklin, too, loved to talk about how the public good should always take precedence over personal opinion.

All the great acts of the legislature were compromises: Medicaid. Social Security. Civil rights. All compromises!

President Lyndon Johnson used to quote Isaiah: "Come now, and let us reason together."

Let us reason together. We have different opinions, but come to the table and we can figure out how to get to yes. Paralysis and gridlock hurt us all.

We were making progress. The March 31 deadline was nearing. There were ten thousand details that needed to be checked off and there wasn't enough time.

We needed to get it done, we needed to close.

When I was in the AG's office, we routinely quoted from a scene in the movie *Glengarry Glen Ross*. Alec Baldwin plays a manager trying to motivate real estate salesmen and teach them how to close a deal. One of the guys gets up to get a coffee, and Baldwin's character says, "Put the coffee down. Coffee is for closers." We made this our mantra: Coffee is for closers. Anyone in our office who closed a deal got the ceremonial bag of coffee on his or her desk, tagged "Closer Blend." It was our theme: Stay focused. Get the job done.

During the first budget negotiations I'd often call Larry into my office and show him the movie clip. After a while, he would drop by and say, "Let's watch it. I need the motivation."

"Closing" applies to Albany's gridlock. The bureaucracy is anti-closing, pro-process. People don't like to decide, because a decision entails responsibility and liability. This is more true for bureaucrats, so they live in a continuous state of process: *I'm working on it, I'm trying, we're talking, we're thinking.*

To deal with this culture, I use "constructive impatience." It goes like this: I will listen carefully. And I'll consider the nuances of your argument. But then I want answers. Decide. Either you're going to get it done, or you're not going to get it done. Choose which it's going to be.

I admit that what I call "constructively impatient" my staff calls "perpetually annoying."

On March 31, the day of the vote, the capitol felt like the big top, but instead of the man on the flying trapeze and ladies riding bareback we had a thousand protesters lining the halls and the Million-Dollar Stairway. Groups of education activists argued with legislators and complained to the media about cuts in school aid. Others denounced my decision not to extend the tax surcharge. They chanted, "The people united will never be defeated!" and "Hey, hey, ho, ho, these budgets have got to go!" and sang "Give Peace a Chance." We expected everything but the seventy extra-large pizzas they ordered for delivery. It was a circus, but I was pleased that the capitol was again a place for open democracy.

It was after 9 P.M. when the two houses began debating the

four final bills, which included the most controversial ones covering education and health care. Following a handful of sticking points—including a misunderstanding about how much school aid was actually being cut once the district-by-district breakdown was released—the state Senate passed the last bill about 11:30 P.M. I hadn't been a day early as I'd hoped, but being on time was an extraordinary beginning.

We had gathered legislators for a press conference. I took the podium and said: "Tonight the Legislature not only passed an on-time budget, but a historic and transformational budget for the people of the state of New York."

I thanked Shelly and Dean and praised the legislators. It was the first time they'd been applauded in many years, and I could see on their faces that they liked it. Both leaders—Shelly and Dean—had worked overtime and pushed hard. It was as much their accomplishment as mine.

It was over. We had done it. The greatest test and symbol of change.

I put my arm around Larry's shoulders. "You've been up a zillion hours. Go. Get a hot meal. Get a good night's sleep," I said. "And then come back and start all over again tomorrow."

Most lawmakers saw this budget as a turning point for the fiscal health of the state and an end to the acidic culture of Albany. Larry said he sensed a new mood of cooperation. "Maybe it's temporary," he said. "But I have a feeling that after they've tasted triumph, there's no going back." Even the press was grudgingly optimistic.

With our first budget, the odds were against us. We were up against a three-decade pattern of bad behavior. But it was our only chance. One major success could set others in motion. And it did: big time.

Maintaining the momentum, we went to work right away to pass a cap on property taxes, pass ethics reforms, and readjust the millionaires' surcharge. By the end of the year, we partnered with legislators from both parties to overhaul the tax code, making it more progressive and equitable for New York's middle class. There was wrangling over these issues; that is the nature of politics. But after our joint success with the budget, I think lawmakers were invested in bridging party lines to make deeper durable reforms. The cultural changes were echoed by the physical transformation taking place around us. By the end of 2011, the renovation of the capitol was well under way and due to be complete in another year. The scaffolding that had felt like a permanent fixture was coming down. The walls were freshly painted, and the skylights were refurbished and scrubbed clean, allowing light to flow into the capitol, as the architects had originally intended.

The building had been even dirtier than I'd realized. For most of the capitol's life, deals really had been struck in smoke-filled rooms. Smoking, permitted everywhere, had left a grungy yellow-brown film on every surface. Except for the floors, little in the building had been thoroughly cleaned in decades. I remember running my index finger along the impressive stonework of the Million-Dollar Staircase. When I pulled it away the pad of my finger was black, covered with the top layer of a hundred years of crud. The dim lighting

was actually a blessing, but it also lent weariness to the portraits that lined the Hall of Governors, as if these men, also
jaundiced by cigarette smoke, were looking at us with resigned disgust.

In accelerating the schedule, I'd been motivated by the
belief that the capitol that took more than thirty years to
build shouldn't take longer to renovate. Talk about gridlock.

I'd moved the finish date up by two years, committing to
a 2013 deadline. Rather than up the costs, it lowered them.
A small portion of the savings came from striking unnecessary work from the original plans. The big difference came
from not having to pay engineering and design consultants
for twenty-four additional months. Total saved: $2.3 million.
With stepped-up effort and manpower came a new determination.

We cleaned the stonework, the ceilings, the wainscoting,
and the sandstone molding. We repainted the walls in their
original salmon hue—and then repainted again when we realized that hairline cracks in the plaster needed a skim coat. I
say "we" because, in truth, I was never far away. I cared deeply
that this project be done quickly and correctly. After all, I'd
inherited this love for craftsmanship from my grandfathers.
The *New York Times* would later poke fun at my microman-
agement of the restoration. An article said I'd complained
that the paint sheen was too glossy. I admit that I was per-
snickety. One of the terra-cotta tiles from the roof above the
Senate Chamber came loose during cleaning. Etched into its
underside was the name of the man who had originally installed it: JH BUCHANAN 1881. He must have taken real pride

in his work and wanted to leave his mark. This impressed us all, and it said a lot about the artisans who constructed the building.

We also transformed the building from a government office to a museum. I enlisted Harold Holzer, a longtime friend of my father's who is senior vice president at the Metropolitan Museum of Art. First we installed museum-quality, high-efficiency lighting in the Hall of Governors. I remember flipping the switch and marveling at the portrait of Governor Thomas Dewey. He is wearing a crisp blue suit. For years I had assumed it was gray.

We tracked down several of the missing governors' portraits at museums and archives. The portrait of mid-nineteenth-century governor William Henry Seward, who later became secretary of state to Abraham Lincoln and Andrew Johnson, was found in an administrative office in the State Education Building. The one notable absence: Mario Cuomo. I tried to persuade my father to sit for a portrait. He thought it was vain and said no, just as he had when he left office. "We've done this whole reorganization," I said. "You need to sit for a portrait." Unable to change his mind, we had it painted behind his back. We asked a few old friends to contribute. Knowing how my father felt, people gave money but demanded anonymity. "I promise," Steve said repeat-edly. "There's no way Mario will be able to trace the money back to you." We lucked out when the well-known portraitist Simmie Knox agreed to work from a photo.

We unveiled the portrait at an Executive Mansion recep-tion on my father's eightieth birthday. He didn't say much about it. But a couple of days later, he called and asked for the names of the people who'd contributed to the portrait fund. For an instant I thought it was a trick question, figuring he'd want to chastise them for participating in this vanity project.

My father said, "I want to write and thank them."

Governor Paterson sat for his portrait, adding an important part to the collection: New York's first African American governor.

We rearranged the arbitrarily hung portraits in chronological order with each governor's name and the dates he was in office. I'm proud of the time line that runs beneath the portraits. It gives visitors a sense of what was happening in the world that surrounded state government—the building of the railroad, the Gilded Age, the Great Depression, civil rights, women's rights, Woodstock. I want schoolchildren to get something out of a mandatory visit to the capitol. I want them to *want* to return. We made the exhibit modern and interactive. Under each portrait is a hashtag that links you to more information about that governor.

Next we redesigned the Hall of New York into a gallery of landscape paintings, organized by region, lent to us by museums around the state.

The building today is spectacular, and I love to show it off. For better and for worse, it is our history, reflecting both our failings and our extraordinary potential. It celebrates the time when New York State was the indisputable center of great American advancements: the Erie Canal, modern government, and modern courts. And it acknowledges the years when we lost faith in that kind of progress and became inward looking and acquisitive, seeking quick fixes to problems that, in reality, would never go away without a systemic solution.

The restored capitol was a powerful message: Change and progress had arrived and triumphed. The once great New York State progressive, effective government was back—literally and figuratively.

CHAPTER 10

33

Marching with Michael Bloomberg, Christine Quinn,
and Sandy at New York's 2011 Heritage of Pride March,
which fell two days after the historic decision to
legalize same-sex marriage in New York.

I n my office at the state capitol, there is a door that opens
into the ornate and aptly named Red Room. To grasp the
cast-bronze doorknob decorated with the Great Seal of the
State of New York is to reach back into history.

I think about the governors who came before me and dared to aim high—the reform-minded men who guided the state in the late nineteenth and twentieth centuries. More than fifty years before the U.S. Supreme Court ruled segregation unconstitutional, Theodore Roosevelt forced New York public schools to integrate. Al Smith successfully fought for subsidized housing and a ninefold increase in the public education budget. After the 1929 stock market crash, Franklin Roosevelt gave thousands of newly unemployed New Yorkers jobs building roads and planting trees, as a precursor to the Civilian Conservation Corps he established as president. For each of his twelve years in office my father put his principles above politics and vetoed bills to restore capital punishment in New York.

New York State has traditionally been an early adopter. In 1775, a year and a half before the Declaration of Independence, the members of New York's provincial congress drafted and signed their own declaration, vowing "never to become slaves" to King George III. In 1848, the Finger Lakes town of Seneca Falls hosted the first women's rights convention, giving birth to the women's suffrage movement. The International Ladies' Garment Workers' Union, founded in 1900 in New York City, led the country in the push for better wages, working conditions, and hours. In 1965, activists in New York's Hudson Valley launched the modern environmental movement. Four years later, a riot in response to a police raid at a gay bar, the Stonewall Inn, in Manhattan's Greenwich Village, ignited a national crusade for gay rights. New Yorkers have always been the nation's progressive voice. I intended to help continue this legacy.

I believe the government is—and should be—the vehicle for social progress and collective reform. It has to be. As individuals, most of us are content with things the way they are. We're unlikely to stand up for a cause that doesn't affect us. But every necessary change, from emancipation to civil rights to women's rights, has come about because the government took action. Now, when we look back, most of us agree that these changes should have come far sooner.

Change was on my mind on March 9, 2011, when I walked into the Red Room. Originally the governor's private office, the Red Room lends itself to pomp, circumstance, and ceremonies. The ornate decor delivers the message that what happens between the wood-paneled wainscoting and gold-leaf-embossed walls is significant. That is why I chose it for this meeting.

I looked around the conference table. "I'm thinking about taking up marriage equality this session," I said. "I want your thoughts."

The people I'd invited were veterans in the struggle against LGBT discrimination: Christine Quinn, who was then speaker of the New York City Council; Richard Socarides, a friend since my days in the Clinton administration and founding president of the communications firm Equality Matters; Sean Eldridge of Freedom to Marry; Brian Ellner from the Human Rights Campaign; Ross Levi, then executive director of the Empire State Pride Agenda; Emily Giske. Mike Avella, the GOP lobbyist for the Log Cabin Republicans, was doing double duty, also representing the Gill Action Fund, a Colorado-based LGBT political group founded by software entrepreneur Tim Gill. Next to him was Kevin Finnegan, the political director at Service Employees International Union

(SEIU) Local 1199, who'd worked on my 2002 campaign. I'd invited Assemblyman Daniel O'Donnell and state senator Tom Duane, both of whom represented parts of Manhattan. Also included were key staffers: Steve Cohen, my top aide; Mylan Denerstein, my counsel; Alphonso David, deputy secretary for civil rights; Betsey Ball, legislative director; and a handful of young assistants.

I'd backed marriage equality when I was campaigning for attorney general in 2006. So I was surprised during my 2010 run for governor when the media questioned my commitment to same-sex marriage, predicting that it would fade if I got elected. *New York Times* reporter Michael Barbaro wrote that my relationship to gays and lesbians was "fraught." He quoted Libby Post, the founder of Empire State Pride Agenda, who said, "I don't think his heart is really there."

I guess people thought a straight Italian guy from Queens wouldn't make gay rights a priority. Their stereotype was not just unkind; it was unjustified. Living in Queens taught me to embrace people's differences. They also discounted the impact of my parents. From the cradle, my siblings and I were taught that we're all God's children. I'd built housing for homeless AIDS patients at HELP. At HUD I'd worked to stop housing discrimination against people with HIV. As attorney general, I'd gone after a retail chain that refused to hire transgendered people and an adoption agency that refused to deal with gay and lesbian couples.

By the time of the Red Room meeting the debate over marriage equality had been under way in courtrooms and living rooms for years. Our national thinking had advanced significantly since 1986, when the U.S. Supreme Court upheld laws against consensual sodomy in twenty-five states. Mike Bowers, the prosecutor, who was then Georgia's attorney general, had warned: "Once you do away with the sodomy laws, it's just a short step to debating same-sex marriages."

He was right. In April 1993, hundreds of thousands of activists, gay people, their families, and their supporters marched on Washington demanding equal rights.

A month later the state supreme court of Hawaii ruled that "marriage is a basic civil right." A giant step forward for gay rights, even though the case was sent back for review to a trial court, where it wasn't resolved until 2013.

Two steps forward, one unsteady step back. Bill Clinton sidestepped in July 1993 when he softened his firm campaign promise to allow openly gay people to serve in the military. His "Don't ask, don't tell" policy angered the gay community and inflamed the military. The compromise was far from ideal, but sometimes compromise is the only way to move ahead.

I was assistant secretary at HUD when, on September 21, 1996, at 12:50 A.M., President Clinton signed the Defense of Marriage Act (DOMA), giving states the right to decide if they wanted to legalize same-sex marriage. DOMA also specified that marriage was a contract between a man and a woman. Advocates of same-sex marriages were furious. Under DOMA married same-sex couples would not be entitled to the same federal spousal benefits as heterosexual couples, including Social Security and pension payments. Twenty-three states responded by amending their constitutions to ban same-sex marriage.

In 2000 Vermont became the first state to recognize same-sex civil unions. The next year, when I began my first guber-natorial run, only about 30 percent of the country favored marriage equality. Understanding that change is incremen-tal, and still evolving on the issue, I called for civil unions.

Some in the LGBT community didn't see civil unions as a solution: They said, "We don't want *almost* marriage. We want marriage."

The point was equality. Their love is not a lesser love. It's not a second-rate love. Their committed relationships have the same value as heterosexual relationships. In denying them equal rights, society is saying their relationships are inferior. They want to be treated equally, because they are equal.

What didn't go far enough for many in the gay commu-nity went too far for some heterosexuals. In 2002 Republi-cans introduced the Federal Marriage Amendment, often referred to by proponents as the Marriage Protection Act. It called for amending the U.S. Constitution to read: "Marriage in the United States shall consist solely of the union of a man and a woman."

I'm certain that everyone sitting with me in the Red Room had been relieved when the amendment failed to pass—and frustrated when it was reintroduced in 2003, 2004, 2005, 2006, and 2008 (and again in 2013). It never passed, and it wasted a lot of legislative time.

In 2004, Massachusetts became the first state where same-sex couples could legally marry. Connecticut; Iowa; Vermont; New Hampshire; and Washington, D.C., followed.

Suddenly change that had seemed a generation away was happening now.

Everyone in the Red Room meeting wanted to take advantage of this forward momentum. Our problem was that New York State had already tried and failed: three times. Once in 2007 and twice in 2009, Danny O'Donnell had introduced a same-sex marriage bill. It always passed in the Assembly, which was traditionally liberal because there are far more districts downstate in Democratic strongholds than upstate where the population tends to be more conservative. The opposite is true in the state Senate, where the first two bills were not taken up. When Senator Tom Duane finally introduced the third bill in December 2009, passage seemed a given. Wrong.

The bill lost by a lopsided 38 to 24 even though the Democrats controlled the Senate by a two-person majority, 32 to 30. Once again governmental "compassion without competence" fails.

The problem was actually worse. While the Democrats had the governor's office and controlled the Assembly and Senate, very few progressive pieces of legislation passed. I took note. It's not just enough having Democrats in the majority; it's having a functional body of reliable people with the same agenda. Even having legislators who would vote for legislation is not enough; there is no spontaneous combustion. Again, inaction is a legislative body's safest position. You, the executive, must initiate and maintain a well-coordinated effort with any difficult issue.

My theory is simple. Civics courses in high school were

wrong. Politicians often don't lead. Often the public leads and politicians follow. Create public sentiment and the politicians will follow. In 2009, pro-equality forces were not mobilized, and conservative groups, including New Yorkers for Constitutional Freedoms, lobbied hard against the legislation. Michael Long, the head of the Conservative Party of New York, made a threat that worked: anyone who voted for same-sex marriage would be taken off future party ballots. The conservatives demand discipline and have shown that they will penalize Republicans who disregard conservative dogma.

And so ended the 2009 marriage equality bill. Not one Republican approved the legislation, and eight Democrats voted no. Many did so not because they were rabidly against gay marriage, but because they strongly favored their own reelection. "Do the right thing" is a nice sentiment, but actually doing it can turn a viable candidate into an underdog, or worse. It's safer to follow the old Washington maxim "The legislator who does nothing, does nothing wrong." Whether legislators side with the ayes or the nays can become a real-time game of follow the leader, and a bill's probable passage can turn in midvote. A slightly negative tilt, with a few pebbles rolling down, can quickly become an avalanche.

Here we were in the Red Room fifteen months later weighing whether or not to try again. Everyone agreed that this would be our last shot with this set of legislators. Another loss could set the cause back by a decade. If we tried to pass the bill and it failed, we'd be telegraphing a terrible message to the world: the New York State Legislature considered Governor Cuomo's bill on whether or not to treat you equally— and decided against it.

Circumstances were tougher than in 2009. The ratio of Democrats to Republicans in the state Senate had flipped in 2010. Now the Republicans controlled it by a majority of thirty-two to thirty. If we tried a do-over bill and it fell short, we'd be handing state Republicans a potent issue to run on in the 2012 elections.

We could end up losing the battle and the war.

The timing wasn't ideal. We were still rookies. We'd been in office just sixty-eight days. We weren't fully staffed.

Still, everyone in the room wanted to take on the fight.

My daughters Mariah, Cara, and Michaela, then sixteen and fourteen, were eager to have the law changed. "I can't believe it's the twenty-first century, and we live in a state where marriage is still based on gender," one of the twins said. "It's not just stupid, it's outrageous!" Young people get it.

They wanted to show solidarity by walking in Manhattan's gay pride parade with me in 2010 when I was running for governor. Seeing my children living our family values—acceptance of all people and standing up for those without rights—filled me with parental pride.

It was a great experience, but my gubernatorial opponent, Carl Paladino, took public exception. "Young children should not be exposed to that at a young age, they don't understand it," Paladino told NBC's *Today* and other media. "Exposing them to homosexuality, especially at a gay pride parade. . . . They wear these little Speedos and they grind against each other, and it's just a terrible thing. Why would you bring your children to that?"

I took that criticism as a badge of honor.

As I met with the Red Room group, I recalled one of the

many conversations I'd had with Mariah, Cara, and Michaela over the years in which I tried to instill core beliefs. Most of these mini-lessons occurred when I was driving them to school. I heard myself telling my daughters, "Weigh every opportunity to do good. You can use it, or you can squander it. You can be the force for change, or you can leave the job for someone else. But before you let it go, remember the chance might not come around again."

After I'd dropped out of the 2002 race, questions that haunted me were: Had I made enough of my time at HUD? Could I have done more to fight discrimination through the Office of Fair Housing? Could we have helped U.S. mayors curtail gun violence? Could we have built more public housing?

I promised myself then that I would never again be left with similar doubts.

If I sat out this fight because I felt constrained by the institution of government or the culture of Albany—or the possibility of defeat—then I was bound to fail.

"We're going for it," I told the Red Room group. "And we're doing it my way. We're doing this as a professional, coordinated plan. We're running this out of my office on the Second Floor.

"But I'm not going to have another situation where three people have three conflicting notions about how to handle a senator," I said. "If the bill fails, I'll be blamed. I'm willing to take that risk. But in exchange, I'm going to call the plays.

"The first rule is: we must all focus on the goal and not our own politics. We're not moving legislation in either chamber unless we have a strong sense that it will pass in the Senate," I told them. "This time we're not going to give it to the Assembly until we know the Senate will take it up."

"How involved are you going to be, really?" Christine Quinn asked.

I said, "I am going to work for this as hard as I have ever worked for anything in my life."

So, how were we going to pull this off?

Getting any bill passed requires an inside strategy and an outside strategy, and the two are interlocking. The inside game is pure numbers. How many votes do we need? How many do we have? How many does the other side have? How can we change our opponents' minds?

The outside game involves a different set of numbers. How do we marshal public opinion? How do we get the money needed to reach millions of constituents?

The advocacy groups that had been with us in the Red Room meeting formed a coalition called New Yorkers United for Marriage, which launched a full-on campaign that included fund-raising, lobbying, and an extensive field operation to mobilize grassroots support. They were media masters who posted, blogged, and tweeted out the message: there's no question if, only when.

The Human Rights Campaign (HRC) introduced a PR blitz. Called New Yorkers for Marriage Equality (NYME), it created cutting-edge thirty-second spots using narrow-casting—a technique that sent tailored ads to specific constituents. This cost considerably less than the traditional generalized broadcast radio and TV ads. Delivered via taxicab TV and YouTube, the HRC ads featured everyday and iconic New Yorkers speaking up for same-sex marriage. A firefighter spoke about his gay son. An everyman (and woman and child) spot affirmed the belief that people are entitled to marry the one they love.

There were attention grabbers, like ice hockey bad boy Sean Avery, who played for the New York Rangers; then-mayor Michael Bloomberg; celebrity chef Mario Batali; actors Julianne Moore, Kevin Bacon, and Kyra Sedgwick; and former first daughter Barbara Bush. The often-married talk show host Larry King did a funny spot that made a great point. It started with him saying, "I know a thing or two about marriage—maybe three or four. Some of us can get married again and again and some of us not at all. I can't figure that out."

We needed thirty-two votes. We knew that one Democrat, Ruben Diaz, a senator from the Bronx, was a no-go. A Pentecostal minister, he could not be moved to change his mind. That meant we had to lock in the remaining twenty-nine Democrats and sway three Republicans. Difficult? Yes.

Some members of both parties were quietly rooting for the opposition. Some even said a few Democrats were hoping the Republicans wouldn't let the bill go to the floor. Why? They were receiving campaign contributions from groups supporting same-sex marriage. If marriage equality passed, the money would dry up: cynical but accurate.

Once again proving the adage that politics makes strange bedfellows, some Republican senators were quietly cheering us on. From marginal districts, they were losing more and more support to progressive candidates. They wanted to dispose of the issue before it disposed of them. While they couldn't vote in favor of marriage equality, they realized that passage would help them hold on to their seats because advocates would stop spending money to try to oust them. A short-term political loss for the New York Republican Party would be a long-term personal gain.

I looked for allies within my own party. Most Democrats were with me, but since New York legislators have to be reelected every two years, a few were worried about how this would affect their next race. In private meetings with these people, I'd talk about how my own views had evolved. Often their objections were based not on personal beliefs, but on being unable to predict the outcome. It's a rule of the game: if a controversial bill is likely to pass, jump onto the bandwagon. If it's likely to get scuttled or lose, maintain distance.

As a politician, I appreciated the bind they were in. "You're worried about a challenge from the right," I'd say. "You should be worried about the left. Go against the bill and you're rendering yourself vulnerable."

If they needed more nudging I'd say, "Look, it might happen in 2011, 2012, or 2014, but marriage equality is going to pass."

A good governor is like a good baseball pitcher; you need a number of different pitches in your arsenal. When soft pitches don't work, you sometimes need to throw one inside and tight. "If you want to call yourself a Democrat," I said, "you have to behave like one. This is the Democratic agenda. It's a definitional issue. A litmus test. Your colleagues are supporting this. You can't be a member in good standing if you vote against one of the main planks of the party platform."

Three Democrats were uncertain. Shirley Huntley was from Jamaica, Queens, a predominately African American district. Because her district did not support gay marriage, she was concerned that voting with us would drive away her base. Carl Kruger, from Brooklyn, was under indictment on bribery charges. He didn't want to cast a vote that many constituents would see as a second strike.

The third possibility was Joe Addabbo, who represented Howard Beach, Queens. Second in the state Senate's alphabetical roll call in 2009, he had voted no partly because he didn't know whether or not the bill would pass. This time around he was keeping a tally of calls and correspondence. If the constituents urged him to vote against it, he would. Or vice versa.

I invited the Republican senators to the mansion to make my case for marriage equality. "Here, in one move, we could open society's arms and embrace the people we have treated as outcasts," I said. "It would tell their fathers and mothers, sisters and brothers, cousins and bosses, 'We were wrong to be so judgmental. We are sorry.'"

I could see that they understood.

I was also meeting with Republicans one-on-one. Majority Leader Dean Skelos, to his credit, said publicly that he would let the individual members of his caucus vote their consciences. My job was to figure out which Republicans might be persuaded to vote with us.

The coalition had spent the previous year gathering every possible snippet of information about the senators, Democrats and Republicans, so we had a road map, of sorts. We knew how they and their families felt about the issue, if they had a gay relative, and if their church or synagogue had taken a stand.

I started with Tom Libous from Binghamton; Kenneth La-Valle of Port Jefferson, on Long Island; and Hugh Farley, who represented Schenectady, in the middle of the state. Betty Little, a smart, compassionate senator from the sparsely populated North Country, was also on our list. In these meetings the rationale for same-sex marriage always came first—it's as essential when you're trying to pass legislation as when you're running for office.

"For me, marriage equality is not about marriage, it's about equality," I told them. "It's one of the great civil rights issues of our day. The opposition says only a man and woman can marry. They argue that the institution is for childbearing. If that's so, then the law should say that the only people entitled to get married are fertile couples. But we don't have fertility tests before marriage. So what grounds do you have to discriminate against same-sex couples, besides their sexual orientation? You don't. There is no rational basis. It's discrimination."

I also spoke from my heart. "This country has stereotyped gay people since the beginning. They have been made to feel ashamed and inadequate," I said. "Parents have been pulled between a child they love and a culture that judges them as less worthy than the rest of us. Think of your fellow New Yorkers. Some have been closeted their entire life. Many have been bullied. Some have felt so isolated that they committed suicide.

"From a societal point of view, there is no single accomplishment that would affect millions of people more than legalizing gay marriage," I told them. "It is time to remove the taboo."

Then I asked if they'd be willing to vote for passage.

They all said no.

For the most part, many of them were kind and said, "Governor, I'm sympathetic, but I can't vote for same-sex marriage in my district."

I knew that how people felt about gay marriage was generational and geographic. Younger senators from moderate, urban districts, whether upstate or downstate, were our best shot. We thought we might persuade Kemp Hannon, a moderate from Nassau County; John Flanagan from Long Island; Andrew Lanza from Staten Island; Greg Ball, whose district included Westchester County; and Mark Grisanti from Buffalo.

Stephen Saland from Poughkeepsie, James Alesi from Rochester, and Roy McDonald from Troy, in eastern upstate New York, might also be gettable.

"We're going to be in this together," I said. "This legislation will pass, and it will be our great victory. It's a hard vote today, but in ten years you'll see it as easy."

Their political concern was a vindictive conservative party that could punish disobedience by pulling their support. A real threat. Another major concern for Republicans was that clergy who opposed gay marriage would be legally obligated to perform such unions. They, and we, were hearing from representatives from the Catholic Church and other religions. Saland, an observant Jew, was under immense public pressure from an Orthodox Jewish group, Agudath Israel. Having discovered that Saland was a descendant of a prominent late-nineteenth-century rabbi named Shmuel Salant, members of Agudath were said to be praying at Salant's grave in Jerusalem to influence Saland's vote.

The First Amendment protects religious freedom, so neither I nor my legal counsel, Mylan Denerstein, could imagine that the state could require religious organizations to go against their doctrine. "We're talking about civil law, not about redefining religious marriage ceremonies," I said. "But we'll add a religious exemption to the bill."

As a Roman Catholic I understood their feelings. I had the full Catholic education, starting at St. Gerard Majella in Queens so long ago that the nuns still wore black and-white habits. From there I went to the Marist Brothers at Archbishop Molloy High School and then to Fordham University with the Jesuits. I saw my father's torment when he was threatened with excommunication after he approved Medicaid funding for abortions. He, like me, has deep respect for people who are pro-life, and he felt pulled between his faith and his obligation as an elected official to uphold the law.

"The last time we spoke, you said you would listen to your constituents," I told Addabbo. "What are you hearing from them?"

"The phone calls and letters are running ten to one against," he said.

I knew an emotional appeal wouldn't move Addabbo.

Steve Cohen was constantly reminding the Red Room

group about what they were forbidden to do. "I do not want you protesting in front of senators' offices," he said. "I do not want you drowning them in mail. I do not want you making robo-calls. I do not want you to do anything until we understand what will push them in the right direction and what will push them away."

With Addabbo, we knew.

"We've got to change the numbers for Addabbo," Steve told Brian Ellner at the Human Rights Campaign.

"What can we do?" Brian asked. "Phone calls? Letters? E-mails?"

"Everything," Steve said. "We need to activate his constituents."

"Not a problem."

"OK," Steve said. "Turn on the faucet."

"We'll unleash a waterfall." Brian said.

Within an hour the HRC had e-mailed instructions to its members in Addabbo's district.

A few weeks later, I saw Addabbo.

"Senator," I said, "are you still keeping tabs on the will of your constituents?"

"I am," he said. "The tally has gone from seventy-three percent against to eighty percent in favor."

"Then I don't see that this is a hard vote for you," I said.

"Well, I'm up for reelection next year," he said.

"Joe," I said. "I'm from Queens. I'll be with you. I'll campaign with you. Queens is going to be for this legislation."

In my ongoing conversations with Republicans, I wouldn't say, "This is important for the State of New York." I'd say, "Let me explain what this means and how we can get this done together. I know there are risks, but your risk is my risk. I'm out there already. I need you. I'm going to be there for you. If we do this together, we're going to make history. I'm not going to forget what you did for me."

We worked nonstop to change minds, but lining up the votes wouldn't matter if we couldn't get the bill to the state Senate floor. In the New York capitol, the Assembly speaker and the Senate majority leader control the process. If they don't put the bill up for a vote, it's over before it's begun. Since that had happened in the Senate with two of the three previous marriage equality bills—and judging from the stalemate on legislation in both chambers—it seemed to be going the same way. I couldn't let that happen.

It would be nice if something as noble as ending discrimination could be a cozy Kumbaya moment. But that's rarely the way policy making works.

The good fight is still a fight.

In June, Majority Leader Skelos made a clever move that transferred all the pressure from his team to ours. A skillful tactician, he announced that he wouldn't let the bill go to the floor unless we had all the Democrats with us except Ruben Diaz, the Pentecostal minister who we both knew was unshakable.

Skelos wanted to make it clear that the Republicans weren't to blame—it was the Democrats who didn't support the bill. He was saying, "You don't have your own house in order. They haven't said publicly that they're for the bill. So how do we know?"

In forcing the three fence-sitting Democrats—Huntley, Kruger, and Addabbo—to declare their intentions, Skelos was gambling that they wouldn't go public. The three senators were saying: If it goes to the floor, I'll vote yes. But don't make me take a position needlessly and say so before a vote is actually happening. However, if we couldn't get them to come forward and stand with us now, the legislation was dead.

This was our dilemma, which some Democrats tried to use to undermine the effort. The story they were leaking to reporters was: "The governor doesn't even have Skelos's commitment to allow same-sex marriage to come to the floor."

Each party was using the other to provide cover. Our job was to expose both. We were not going to allow something so important to millions to be dashed by a few people.

I called Huntley, Kruger, and Addabbo individually. "You're in a box," I said to each. "We're in a box," I said. "It's yes or no time. We're going to say, 'We're all in favor.' If you don't come to the press conference that's fine but you will be saying you are against marriage equality."

I was very calm on the phone. I was laying out the situation for them. The legislative body thrives in the shadows and in anonymity. The body protects the body. Who killed the bill? Everybody killed the bill. It's murder on the Orient Express. My job is the opposite—to expose and reveal and make it so that people have to take a position. I let the facts and the situation do the work.

At the press conference, Addabbo went first. He leaned into the mike and said, "As of Friday, 6,015 people have weighed in on this issue. And in the end, 4,839 people wanted me to vote yes. So in the end, that is my vote. To represent the people of the Fifteenth District, which is what I said I would do when I raised my right hand and took that oath."

Huntley, who represented Jamaica, Queens, came next. She told reporters that, as in 2009, she had surveyed her constituents. "I can tell you that the numbers have changed: it [is] 60 [percent] to 40 [percent]," she said. ". . . That is the reason I decided to vote [yes]."

Kruger, from Brooklyn, said, "I believe today this is an evolutionary process. What we're about to do is redefine what the American family is, and that's a good thing." Kruger added, "Because as the world around us evolves and changes, so do we have to change with it."

After Kruger I took the podium. "I believe the votes will be there for marriage equality if the vote happens," I said. "I've had enough conversations with enough legislators. I believe the votes are there."

But I added this caveat: "Until you're over the goal line, you're nowhere."

That afternoon, Skelos told reporters, "I've said it again and again: I'll let it go."

By locking in the Democrats, we'd made it all about the Republicans. If the bill failed, they'd be blamed. Few wanted to be seen as antigay.

Later that day I asked Senator James Alesi of Rochester to drop by my office. I'd been trying to bring him along for months. Alesi had been telling people he was considering same-sex marriage as a matter of conscience. After we'd talked for about an hour, he said, "I'm open to voting for the bill."

Steve had been meeting with the advocates in the conference room next door. I said, "Let's go tell them." I sent a message to Steve to keep the advocates there. I didn't know that the meeting had just broken up and that he had to summon everyone back. "The governor wants to speak with you," Steve said. No one knew why.

I walked in ahead of Alesi. There were about twenty advocates in the room. I said, "I have a piece of news I want to share with you. I want to introduce you to your first Republican yes vote on marriage."

The advocates were so stunned and thrilled that a couple of people cried. Alesi went around the conference table and shook each person's hand.

Then Alesi held a press conference. "If the bill comes out in a way that does not force churches to do something that the churches don't want to do, then this becomes a matter of equality for people that are sons and daughters, brothers and sisters," he said. They "deserve the same freedom and same equality in this great country and in the state of New York that each and every one of us enjoys in our everyday life."

Once Alesi went public, he put a burden on every other Republican. The question was now fair. "Your colleague, Senator Alesi, is for it. Are you?" Exposure on a controversial issue is a legislators' nightmare. Hiding was no longer possible. It was the political equivalent of fight or flight: vote yes or vote no. As with the Democrats, the situation had created its own momentum.

Having a religious exemption made a huge difference to "our" Republicans' comfort level. But we couldn't take the language too far or we'd risk alienating the Democratic Assembly.

In politics it's not, How do I defeat my enemy? It's, How do I make my enemy an ally? Negotiation is about figuring out how to see a deal through other people's eyes and helping them win. That's what we were doing with the religious exemption.

Now Republicans had a new problem: the winning vote would be 32 to 30. It didn't matter that the roll call was alphabetical. After the vote was recorded, the only name people would remember was that of the crossover Republican who put us over the top: vote Number 32. That person would be seen as the decisive vote and he would be blamed. No one wants to be Number 32.

I realized that we needed an extra vote. That way, no one could blame one person for passage. I told the senators with whom I met, "There will be no thirty-second vote. We'll have two thirty-threes." It was like numbering the floors in a hotel twelve and fourteen, skipping the "unlucky" floor thirteen.

This way, every Republican could say, "I'm not the one who put the bill over the top. It would have happened with or without me."

On June 14, the day after Huntley, Addabbo, Kruger, and Alesi had signaled their intention to vote for same-sex marriage, we felt we were close enough in the state Senate to give Danny O'Donnell the go-ahead to move Bill A8354, the Marriage Equality Act, in the Assembly. With the end of the session, on June 20, less than a week away, the time had come for action. The New York State Legislature isn't like the U.S. Congress, where both the House and the Senate pass their own bills and then reconcile the two into a joint bill. In New York both chambers have to pass the identical bill.

The state constitution requires each bill to be printed and on the desks of all legislators for three days before a vote. But the governor can waive the wait by sending lawmakers a "message of necessity." That's what I did with the Marriage Equality Act. We needed resolution.

We knew the legislation would pass the Assembly as it did before, but we were still gratified when, at 9:15 P.M. on Wednesday, June 15, marriage equality won by a vote of 80 to 63.

Soon after the vote, Senator Roy McDonald, a Republican with a blue-collar background from the city of Troy, announced that he was backing marriage equality. "You get to the point where you evolve in your life where everything isn't black and white, good and bad, and you try to do the right thing," he told reporters.

He added: "You might not like that. You might be very cynical about that. Well, f— it, I don't care what you think. I'm trying to do the right thing."

This made him Number 31 and our good omen. But Dean Skelos still hadn't decided if there would be a vote. The indecision went on for days. There was no good answer for him. Skelos was worried that he suffered politically either way and that marriage equality could cost the Republicans their slim majority.

On Thursday, June 16, the vote was pushed to June 17, a

Friday. That morning, Dean told me he was postponing the vote until Monday, June 20, the last day of the session.

We had big hopes for Republican senator Stephen Saland, from Dutchess County in the Hudson Valley. According to the advocates' research, Saland regretted his vote against the 2009 bill. His rabbi and his wife were urging him to right his mistake this time. His wife had joined Saland and me at my office one afternoon in a long philosophical conversation about the meaning and purpose of public service.

That Friday, when we met again the Number 32 problem was weighing on Saland. "I'll make you a promise," I said. "If I don't lock in a senator willing to be the second Number Thirty-Three, you're free to vote however you'd like, and I'll always respect you."

"It's a deal," Saland said.

Besides Saland, I had secured one more Republican.

The second Number 33 was freshman senator Mark Grisanti from Buffalo. "Thank you," I said. "You are making this possible."

Now we had the votes. But there was, in my mind, always the fear that someone would renege and there would be nothing we could do about it. A handshake is nice but unenforceable. Unlike Alesi and McDonald, Saland and Grisanti kept their decisions private. In some ways it was helpful. When a controversial stand becomes public, unhappy constituents will dial up the pressure. As it was, supporters and critics had been arriving steadily and were camped out in the third-floor hall waving dueling signs every time a senator walked by.

But our danger zone was the weekend. When you're in Albany you're largely in a bubble. Over the weekend senators would be heavily lobbied in their districts. We felt good about Saland going back to his district, because we knew that his pro–marriage equality rabbi would reinforce his decision. But we didn't know about Grisanti. When the week wound down, no one in my office was thinking, "TGIF!" We were thinking, It's going to be a long weekend. "Stop," I told myself. "You're overreacting. They're not going to go back on their word at the eleventh hour."

Grisanti came to see me early Monday morning. "I know I said I'd be with you," he said, "but that position is very unpopular in Buffalo. I heard about it all weekend. I can't vote yes." This was a problem. I had told Saland he would not be 32. I needed Grisanti to make that possible. If I lost him I would probably lose Saland and still be one vote short.

"Mark," I said. "You looked me in the eye and shook my hand. Where I'm from, that means something. We're not trading marbles here. Other people are relying on your word. They said yes because you said yes, and now they have sustained significant political damage. We were explicit in our talks. You understood what you were doing. Going forward I will know that you can't be trusted. But if you don't believe this is going to affect our relationship then you don't know me. "This is no way for a public official to act," I said. "If you want to represent the people, you need integrity and credibility, and anyone who does this forfeits that. I will never forget it. I intend to tell the people of your district."

He stayed firm. It was the one interaction that truly got me

annoyed. I respect and support a principled stance in opposition, but going back on your word has no place at this level.

I asked Saland to come to my office—I had to tell him. He
never knew who the other Republican vote was, but I had
told him I had it. I had also told Grisanti that he wasn't the
deciding vote, but he never knew who the other vote was
either. Both men took my word and never told each other.
I said to Saland, "Right now we only have thirty-two votes,
and you may be *the* deciding vote. If you want to change your
mind, I understand. I'll release you from your promise. That
was our deal. If you bow out I will treat this as if it never
happened, no one will ever know. We will remain friends,
and I will respect you for your decision. You will always have
my support."

Saland asked for more time and left. I was sure he was
gone. He called me later and said, "I'm still in." What a
mensch, I thought to myself.

Saland was Number 32. We had what we needed for passage. We were ready and literally waiting.

That Monday, June 20, was a brass-tacks day. The legislature passed the ethics reform bill requiring assemblymen
and senators to disclose their outside earnings. But the
Senate was wrangling over how far the religious exemption
on the marriage bill should go. Some Republicans wanted to
include not just clergy but individuals and businesses that
provide wedding venues.

Every day that week was supposed to be the day of the
Senate vote. And each day, the finish line got moved back.

On Friday, June 24, the Senate held a nine-hour, closed-door debate. At the end, Skelos told me, "Some senators are afraid the bill will leave the Catholic Church and public vendors open to charges of discrimination if they refuse to perform same-sex marriages."

"We can resolve that," I said.

Five senators and I sat at my conference table and negotiated explicit language protecting churches and businesses. We went word by word for hours. We worked through complex, nuanced language until they were satisfied. Only then did Skelos announce that the marriage vote would go to the floor.

More than two thousand protesters had been in the capitol for so many days and nights that the building had started to smell bad. It was an eclectic crowd. Gilda Ward, a Tea Partyer from Norwich, New York, told the *Wall Street Journal* that as part of her protest, she had fasted for a day. "It's a way of petitioning God to let him know we're really serious."

As we waited for the vote to happen that evening we could hear both sides chanting down the stairs and through the walls, as they'd been doing all day. Bouncing off the stonework, the sound was deafening. The opposition was repeating, "God says no!" and singing "Victory Is Mine" and praying in small circles. Proponents of the legislation were chanting, "God is love!" and singing "God Bless America" and "This Little Light of Mine." There were also competing placards: CHRISTIAN CLERGY FOR EQUALITY, GOD'S MARRIAGE = ONE MAN + ONE WOMAN, and SAVE MARRIAGE. BIBLE BASHING DOES NOT DESERVE A VOTE versus MARRIAGE NOW.

At some point, we were in Steve Cohen's office, and I was staring out the window. "Come over here," I said. "You're not going to believe this." Grisanti was outside, pacing and chain-smoking, oblivious of the falling rain.

I asked Mark to come by one more time. We had a direct conversation. I told him about my father and the death penalty. Everyone disagreed with him but respected him for his honesty and integrity. That's what Mark would lose. And if you lose your integrity, you've lost everything. He was torn and noncommittal, but I could tell he got it and had a sense that he was a good guy in a tough spot.

At about 8:45 P.M., the Senate voted to pass other, long-stalled legislation.

Finally, the Marriage Equality Act was up.

I never take victory for granted. I'd spent the wait time worrying.

Republicans had asked for one concession. "We don't want long speeches," Skelos told us. They didn't want political rhetoric to inflame the already nervous senators. The Senate minority leader, a Democrat, John Sampson, who represented parts of Brooklyn, including Crown Heights and East Flatbush, assured us he would keep the Democrats' comments to a minimum. The plan was: Get the legislation on the floor. Do a rolling voice vote. Go home.

One way it could fall apart was if the Democrats reneged on the understanding and embarrassed the Republicans; that is, if too many Democrats spoke about the bill on record, saying, in effect, shame on all of you who said no.

If that happened, Skelos, who controlled whether the bill would go to a vote, would pull the legislation. I was worried about it. In the past, Skelos had reacted abruptly to the Democrats' tactics by ending the session. Sampson had previewed with both Skelos and Steve that the only speech from one of their members would be from Senator Diaz, the sole opponent on the Democrats side, who would speak for two minutes. Diaz, used to speaking from the pulpit, led with, "God, not Albany, has settled the definition of marriage, a long time ago." And he kept going. When Lieutenant Governor Bob Duffy cut him off, he said, "Senator, Senator, I know you want to go on but we have twenty-three people who want to speak on the bill."

Twenty-three people?

The proceedings ground to a halt as Diaz and his allies complained that he had been cut off, and the Republicans approached Steve and Mylan and warned that this is exactly what was *not* supposed to happen.

It was now clear that many of the Democratic senators saw this as their moment. Many saw themselves as future U.S. senators. The vote was being covered live on CNN. They wanted national exposure. And to some of these senators, if that put at risk the actual passage of the legislation, so be it.

Steve tracked down Sampson, who expressed a curiously lackadaisical attitude. "Hey, I can't control my members," he said. "They want to speak. This is how it works." More galling, Sampson claimed that he had never agreed with Skelos to limit the speeches. Alone with Mylan on the floor of the Senate, Steve feared that Sampson wanted this to unravel for his own political purposes, to preserve the issue for the next election, to embarrass the Republicans. And apparently, that's what he told Sampson, basically calling him out on the tactic and warning Sampson that it wouldn't work; that too many people were watching; and that the reporters and advocates would blame the Democrats if things unraveled now.

It was a sobering moment for Sampson. He was caught and relented.

The vote finally took place around 10 P.M. It was the last vote at the last minute on the last day of the Senate's legislative session.

We had a good opening act lined up. The roll call would start with Eric Adams, a Brooklyn Democrat. Republican James Alesi would be called on second. And he would be followed by Joe Addabbo. Three ayes. Every senator after Addabbo and before Grisanti voted nay. What would Grisanti do?

My stomach clenched. We thought we were in good shape. But we didn't underestimate how difficult this was for the men who were crossing party lines.

I was too nervous to sit down. I stood, riveted by the drama unfolding in real time on TV. Talk about a reality show! Grisanti's name was called. Which way would he go in this clutch moment? I heard Grisanti vote "Aye," followed a minute and a half later by Saland. Thirty-three votes, amen. Saland got the thirty-three votes even though he didn't require it. God is good. Grisanti did the right thing. There are men of conscience and courage. When the last vote was cast, a huge cheer went up in the Senate Chamber. In the hall, supporters and protesters were drowning one another out. Almost instantaneously, people started honking their car horns outside.

It was a surreal instant. I could hardly believe that such a monumental event had actually come to pass. My daughters leaped to their feet, and we bear-hugged.

I will forever remember that moment—standing with my girls in the office that once belonged to my father, their grandfather, celebrating a sweet, sweet victory together.

I had planned a press conference and bill signing for that night, but at 10:30, I called my press secretary, Josh Vlasto, and said, "A slight change in plans. I'm going up to the Senate Chamber to say thank you."

"I don't think that's a good idea, Governor," he said. "There are a lot of protesters up there."

"I'm going," I said.

We took the Senate staircase. The protesters were holding up placards. IF YOU VOTE YES WE WILL VOTE YOU OUT, one said. Fair enough, I thought. I'd campaigned for this bill using the same line. When we walked into the beautiful gilded Senate Chamber, Bob Duffy was standing on the dais.

Almost all of the Republicans and Ruben Diaz, who'd voted against marriage equality, were gone. But all of the pro–marriage equality Democratic senators, the advocates, and the press were still there. Bob Duffy pointed at me and said, "Ladies and gentlemen, the man who got it done!"

The chamber erupted into cheers. I flashed a thumbs-up. Everyone in the room was feeling the same mix of euphoria and disbelief.

The girls and I stayed forty-five minutes, shaking hands

and high-fiving. With the doors closed, the chamber was so loud it sounded like a roar. People in the balcony were crying and waving rainbow flags.

Finally we went downstairs to my office to get ready for the press conference. The Red Room was mobbed. Standing with Tom Duane and Danny O'Donnell on the podium, I said, "What this state said today brings the discussion of marriage equality to a new plane. . . . The other states look to New York for the progressive direction. And what we said today is, 'You look to New York once again.'"

Josh Vlasto told me later that in the middle of the press conference, a longtime openly gay political reporter answered his cell phone. His partner of fifteen years was calling to propose.

At ten minutes before midnight, I signed the Marriage Equality Act into law. As I scrawled the last "o" in "Cuomo," I was struck by something amazing. We had literally just created a civil right for gay people.

I do not mean we had enforced a civil right.

We had created one.

This is an accomplishment so rare we seldom hear the words spoken.

I'd been optimistic enough earlier in the day to ask the chefs and house staff to get ready for a party, and I invited everyone to come to the Executive Mansion that night.

Josh called at 2 A.M. "Everybody's reporting that people have poured into Sheridan Square, in the West Village, outside the Stonewall Inn. They're taking to the streets all over the world. There are celebrations in London and Paris. This is huge, Governor!"

I'd been inside the Albany bubble so long I had no inkling how far the reverberations of the Marriage Equality Act would carry.

But given the number of congratulatory and praising phone calls I received the day after the bill's passage—on a Saturday—I caught on.

Coincidentally, the next day, Sunday, June 26, the annual gay pride parade took place in Manhattan. It had started in 1970 to commemorate the Stonewall Inn riot. Now, forty-one years later, my girls, Sandy, and I; Mayor Mike Bloomberg; and City Council speaker Christine Quinn joined thousands of people who'd come to cheer New York's—and society's— resounding achievement.

As a child, I'd taken the train to Manhattan for the ticker tape parade to celebrate the Mets' improbable victory in the 1969 World Series. But the joy I felt from parade-goers now was far more intense.

You'd think that after the emotional outpouring on Friday night and Saturday, this level of elation wouldn't have surprised me. It did. The parade organizers put us at the front, just behind a sound truck that was blasting dance music. The staffer from Chris Quinn's office who was manning the PA system kept shouting: "Governor Cuomo! The man who passed marriage equality!"

For a few hours, I knew what it must feel like to be the Beatles and Elvis wrapped into one.

The crowd was ten deep on either side of Fifth Avenue. There were no spectators, only participants. Everyone was dancing. Hugging. Crying. Cheering. Thousands were waving blue-and-white placards that read THANK YOU, GOVERNOR CUOMO.

The parade was a cinematic moment foreshadowed by my gubernatorial opponent Carl Paladino's criticism. A year after I'd brought my daughters to the parade here I was with them again. I'd not only won the election but steered the passage of the Marriage Equality Act.

This was one of the high points in my life. I thought, If I were to die this moment, our accomplishment would still survive. I had vindicated my father's legacy as a man who governed by principle, not politics, and made sure that the Cuomo name I share with my daughters stands for progress and fairness. The dysfunctional New York State government just sent shock waves through the nation—positive ones.

At Thirty-Sixth Street and Fifth Avenue, where the parade starts, the avenue is five lanes wide. The parade route went from midtown to Greenwich Village. After we turned onto Eighth Street, the route narrowed. The crowd stood just five feet from us on either side. I felt as though I were walking through a tunnel of emotion. The crowd was electric. People felt liberated. Men and women were hanging from the fire escapes screaming, "We love you! Thank you! I'm getting married!"

A big, tough-looking man, maybe sixty years old, with a face wrinkled from years of weather, stepped out of the crowd and came over to me. He gripped my hand and forearm with his two hands. He was strong. Men, Queens men, often subtly compete through a show of strength on the handshake. I'm not so bad at it myself. But when this guy grabbed me, he had me. You can tell a lot about a man from his handshake and the lines in his face. He was a tradesman—a carpenter, steelworker, plumber. But what surprised me most was the tears in his eyes. "My son is gay," he said. "I didn't talk to him for twenty years, because I didn't think it was OK but I spoke with him today. I apologized. I was wrong. I shouldn't have needed you or anyone to tell me it was OK, but I did. Thank you, Governor."

Since that day I've run into countless people like him. A lot of people try to speak and start to cry. Many had been tormented for years, wondering, Did I cause this? Is it a good thing? Is it a bad thing? How do I deal with it? If I tell people, I'm ashamed; if I don't tell people, I'm ashamed.

Every so often someone suggests that I fought for marriage equality because it was good for my career. Let me be clear: I fought for marriage equality because it was the right thing to do.

In government service, as in life, all you have are the lasting effects of your actions. The speeches fade, but your significant accomplishments remain.

That's why I place the Republicans who crossed party lines in the marriage equality fight in my pantheon of political heroes. Like Tony Veteran, the eight-term town supervisor of Greenburgh who lost his seat after helping us fight for housing for the homeless, Stephen Saland, who took the right position for all the right reasons, Roy McDonald, James Alesi, and Mark Grisanti are profiles in courage. As Gregory Angelo, the chairman of the Log Cabin Republicans of New York State, told the *New York Times*: "The four G.O.P. senators who voted for marriage equality, they were ahead of their time."

I remain profoundly grateful to each of these men. After he voted aye, in June, Alesi had publicly affirmed his position, telling reporters, "I swore with my hand on the Bible to uphold the Constitution. . . . I didn't swear with my hand on the Constitution to uphold the Bible."

At election time, his district disagreed. Alesi dropped out of the 2012 race before the primary, telling the *Daily News* that his vote had cost him the support of the local Republican and Conservative leadership.

Having spent what the *New York Times* called a "Bloombergian outlay of $96.73 per vote" (Michael Bloomberg sank $268 million of his own money into his three successful mayoral campaigns), Roy McDonald still lost the Republican primary to Kathleen Marchione, the Saratoga County clerk. McDonald's name appeared on the Independent Party line in the general election, but he declined my offer to endorse him as a third-party candidate and sat out the race. Marchione, the conservative response to McDonald, bested her openly gay, newly married Democratic opponent, Robin Andrews, in the general election, to join the state Senate in 2013.

The extreme right made an example of Steve Saland, a New York State legislator for thirty-two years, by running a conservative candidate, Neil Di Carlo, against him. Di Carlo lost the primary but ran in the general election on the Conservative Party line, where he took thousands of votes from Saland. This ensured that the Democrat, Terry Gipson, won. The conservatives' message: we're willing to punish party members who aren't conservative enough, even if it means a Democrat wins.

This sort of punitive tactic petrifies moderate Republicans. Many people wonder why the Republican moderates don't tell off the conservatives. I can answer that question: they're afraid. They need not look past Steve Saland to know that the far right Republicans in New York and Washington, D.C., will do whatever it takes to kill them politically. In fact, of the four Republican senators who voted for marriage equality, only Mark Grisanti was able to keep his seat in the 2012 elections.

But ultimately the impact of this change transcends anyone's political career. And for New Yorkers, I believe the new law, which took effect on July 24, 2011, a month after I signed it, was the start of restoring our state's progressive luster. This change wasn't abstract. Even though New York was the sixth state to legalize same-sex marriage, it doubled the number of people in the LGBT community who could be married legally. Because New York City is the media center of the world, the message that the time had come to end discrimination against gay people rang out far beyond our state borders.

Interestingly, when our marriage efforts began, popular support for the proposition was about fifty-fifty. I read that to mean support was below 50 percent because I believe people "fib" on a poll on questions like this one and give the "proper" answer. In 2014, three years later, support is near

70 percent. We passed it and the world didn't explode. It still amazes me how quickly society can evolve. Once New York passed marriage equality, the issue became more legitimate and pressing elsewhere. Including in the White House.

After we passed marriage equality, Barack Obama told Robin Roberts of ABC News, "I asked myself—right after that New York vote took place, if I had been a state senator, which I was for a time—how would I have voted? And I had to admit to myself, 'You know what? I think that—I would have voted yes.'"

President Obama told Roberts: "I thought they did a good job in engaging the religious community. Making it absolutely clear that what we're talking about are civil marriages and civil laws. That they're respectful of religious liberty. . . . In this country we've always been about—fairness. And treatin' everybody—as equals. Or at least that's been our aspiration. And . . . that applies here, as well."

CHAPTER 11

Political Capital

A shot of the 2014 anti–SAFE Act
activists' rally in Albany, when pro-gun protesters
hanged my likeness in effigy.

Mid-December in New York City is magical. When I was a kid my mother would bundle us up and take us to Manhattan, where we'd join hundreds of other families on the slow parade past Macy's extraordinary Christmas windows. Being with my family, seeing the Salvation Army Santas, the tree at Rockefeller Center, the happy shoppers, the holiday show at Radio City Music Hall, made all seem right in the world. It still has that effect on me, so I was pleased when, on December 14, 2012, gubernatorial obligations had me working out of my New York City office. The early-morning drive from the house I share with Sandy and my daughters in Westchester had infused me with holiday spirit.

I was at my desk beginning to plan my State of the State speech for 2013 when Stephanie Benton, my office director, rushed in.

"There's been a shooting at an elementary school in Newtown, Connecticut," she said.

I looked at the clock. Nine-forty. Too early for lunch or recess. The kids were most likely in their classrooms.

I called Joseph D'Amico, New York state police superintendent. In less than a half hour we knew that twenty children— all six- and seven-year-olds—were dead.

The news hit me the way I imagine it hit all parents. I felt much as I had on 9/11. I was shocked—and angrier than I have ever been. And I was so very sad for the children and the parents who would forever live without them.

"What kind of monster does this?" I asked Larry Schwartz, who had become my top aide after Steve Cohen returned to his law practice in New York City.

I closed the door to my office and called Connecticut governor Dan Malloy. "How can I help you?" I asked. "Can I send you emergency resources? Do you need extra equipment?"

Next, I called Sandy, and then I texted "I love u" to each of my three girls. I knew my family was OK—Mount Kisco is miles away from Newtown—but I still wanted to hold them close.

By Saturday we were a nation in grief. I canceled all my official events and followed the story as it unfolded before us: the psychological history of the killer; which guns and ammo he'd used. We learned about the six heroic educators who died trying to protect their students. We were told that special education teacher Anne Marie Murphy was found dead, lying on top of the children she had unsuccessfully tried to shield with her own body. We heard that Principal Dawn Hochsprung left behind children, stepchildren, and a husband twenty years her senior, and a house in the Adirondacks, built for the years ahead when, they had no doubt, she would be a widow. And we found out something about one of the victims that she, herself, did not know. Rachel D'Avino, twenty-nine, died ten days before her boyfriend could make the Christmas Eve proposal he'd planned. Hardest to hear were the stories about the murdered children—Jack Pinto, who loved the New York Giants; Avielle Richman, who'd asked for an Easy Bake Oven for Christmas so she could make cookies for her mom. And James Mattioli, who gelled his hair into spikes and often asked when he'd be old enough to sing onstage.

Each of the slain first-graders, and their parents, had dreams that would never come to be. I had to do something for these children and the people who loved them.

The incident had grabbed the attention of the American people. The children made it different from the past procession of senseless gun killings. Even legislators, Democrats and Republicans, were calling me, saying, "Enough is enough. We have to do something." I called my staff together.

"You all know I'm not antigun," I said. "I believe that people who want to own a gun should own a gun. I'm one of them. I have a Remington shotgun. I keep it at home, unloaded, in a case with a child safety lock. This isn't about outlawing guns—it's about gun safety, public safety."

Larry said, "You know the gun issue is red-hot politically and there are a lot of Second Amendment types."

"No doubt," I said. "But lots of gun owners are like me. They want to have and use their guns, but they want the gun laws tightened because they never want another Newtown. They know we can protect gun rights and promote gun responsibilities."

"Governor, your approval rating is higher than it's ever been," Larry said. "Seventy-four percent of New Yorkers say you're doing a good job compared with thirteen percent who don't. Are you sure you want to mess with that?"

"If there's ever a good issue to spend political capital on, this is it," I said. "It doesn't do any good to have it if you don't use it."

One of the lessons I learned during my out-of-government years is that public service is a precious and fleeting opportunity to make lasting change. I said, "I don't understand politicians who try to ascend the political ladder but accomplish nothing. I get the political cost of dealing with controversy. I know you're more likely to rise politically if you steer away from anything remotely controversial. And you probably don't even need to accomplish anything to be seen as a successful politician. But politicians who do nothing affirm voters' cynicism and add to the dysfunction of the system. One of the Washington think tanks should do an 'accomplishments index' measuring what politicians actually get done. Not what they *said* they would do—or what they said *should* be done, or how many press releases they issued 'bringing attention' to a problem or 'promising action.' I'm talking about what they actually accomplished, completed, finished, resolved."

"I hear you, Governor," Larry said.

"Besides," I added, "the guns-don't-kill-people, people-kill-people argument doesn't hold up. No other legal weapon is as effective as a gun or can do so much damage in so little time."

On the same day that Adam Lanza shot the youngsters at Sandy Hook, a mentally ill man named Min Yingjunin attacked children at the Chenpeng Village Primary School in China. Armed with a stolen knife, he stabbed twenty-two children. Tragic, yes. But none of them died. "Every society has mentally ill citizens, some with paranoid, violent urges. Preventing them from having access to guns is essential for public safety."

New York State had a gun law and an assault weapon ban passed by George Pataki in 2000. But that law had more holes than Swiss cheese! It outlawed specific weapons, but manufacturers got around that by renaming them. It grandfathered in any assault weapon made before 1994. But you couldn't tell which weapons were pre-1994, because the legal magazines manufactured then didn't come with a date or a serial number.

"What are the key provisions?" Mylan Denerstein, my legal counsel, asked.

"I want to create background checks to screen for criminals and people with a history of mental illness, and ban dangerous assault weapons. The Assembly will have its own prerogative and want to ban guns and the Senate will come the exact opposite way and want to increase criminal penalties on illegal guns. We need a grand compromise," I said.

"OK," Larry said. "When do you want to do this, Governor?"

"Twelve years ago."

In 2000, when I was HUD secretary, I worked with the White House and the Department of the Treasury and we were to negotiate an agreement with Smith & Wesson, then the largest gun manufacturer in the United States. To its credit, Smith & Wesson was already working on "smart gun" technology that would enable the trigger to recognize the fingerprint of the purchaser. If the fingerprint on the trigger didn't match the fingerprint of the gun owner, the smart gun would not fire. In the hands of a child, a smart gun would not shoot; a suicidal person could not end his life with someone else's gun; and a gun owner could fire at a burglar, but if the burglar wrested the gun away it would turn useless in his hands. Had Adam Lanza's mother owned smart guns, he couldn't have shot his way inside Sandy Hook Elementary School.

Another huge advantage of the smart gun is that when

anyone was shot or killed with one, the police would know, instantly and irrefutably, the shooter's identity.

In 2000, Smith & Wesson had reached an agreement with the federal government that included a promise that, within three years, every gun it made would be a smart gun.

Why was Smith & Wesson willing to do this? Because the gun manufacturers were facing dozens of lawsuits any one of which could bankrupt the industry. There is an analogy here with tobacco: until 1994 the general belief was that the tobacco industry was immune to lawsuits. Then forty-six states filed suit against the four largest tobacco companies for overburdening the states' public health-care systems, and for selling a product the companies knew to be addictive and deadly. Four years later big tobacco settled. In exchange for being freed of class-action lawsuits, the companies agreed to pay $206 billion over twenty-five years for the long-term costs incurred in caring for people with smoking-related illnesses. They also agreed to stop marketing to teenagers.

Cities believed that, like big tobacco, gun manufacturers made a life-threatening product and could be vulnerable to lawsuits. Before the landmark tobacco settlement was finished, New Orleans became the first of twenty-nine American cities, which would include Baltimore, Atlanta, Chicago, and Los Angeles, to file a lawsuit against gun makers for negligence. Eliot Spitzer and Richard Blumenthal, the attorneys general of New York and Connecticut, were also considering legal action for their states. Dozens more cities were poised to sue.

In December 1998 the Matthews brothers, eleven and fourteen, were walking to the bus stop near their home in

St. Louis, on their way to see a movie. They watched as a passing car got caught in the cross fire of rival gangs. The Matthews brothers were wounded. The driver's son, three-year-old Kendrick Adams, was shot in the face and died in his car seat.

It's not uncommon for bystanders to get shot. But happening, as it did, during the slowest news week of the year, against the sentimental backdrop of the holiday season, the story played big.

In the spring of 1999, the city of St. Louis filed a suit against the arms industry, naming thirty firearms manufacturers, trade associations, and gun shops. As St. Louis mayor Clarence Harmon said, "The gun makers are aware that their products are used frequently in crime and accidental killings. Not only does the gun industry refuse to implement safety features and warnings that would drastically reduce gun violence . . . not only do they demonstrate their utter lack of concern about how their product is distributed by refusing to monitor their distributors, but they actively lobby against these [safety] precautions."

The cities challenging the gun manufacturers had three chief complaints. The first was that there was no federal limit on the number of guns a person could buy at one time. The unscrupulous could buy a dozen guns and resell them on the black market. The industry, the suits charged, was knowingly contributing to illegal gun trafficking.

The second issue was that the industry provided inventory to certain shops knowing they were selling to straw purchasers—people with clean records who buy firearms on behalf of those prohibited from owning a gun—felons,

domestic abusers, and people with a history of mental illness. Refusing to sell to shady dealers would help keep guns
out of dangerous hands and would affect few dealers. Most
federal firearm licensees (FFLs) are legitimate. The majority
of illegal guns are sold by a small number of bad actors—
small gun stores that purposely overlook a felon who brings
his girlfriend in to buy and then don't cooperate when police
need information on a gun recovered from a crime scene. A
2000 Bureau of Alcohol, Tobacco, Firearms, and Explosives
(ATF) study showed that nearly 60 percent of the guns found
at crime scenes were sold by 1 percent of FFLs.

The third problem was misleading marketing that encouraged people to buy guns for home security despite persuasive
information that gun ownership does not deter crime. When
the gun market hit a slump in the 1980s gun makers looked
for new customers. Moving away from the campaign traditionally featured in magazines like *American Handgunner*
and *Combat Handguns*, gun advertisements began targeting
women, and even kids. "Guns make excellent gifts for your
wife and children." A gun, these ads said, was like a fire ex-
tinguisher. "It may be better to have it and not need it, than
to need it and not have it."

Some advertising equated not owning a gun with bad
parenting. In the 1990s *Ladies' Home Journal* ran an ad that
showed a mom putting her child to bed. The window is open.
It's dark outside. Also shown are two semiautomatic handguns. The tagline: "Self-protection is more than your right.
It's your responsibility."

During the same time as the gun ads were appearing I
recall reading a story about fourteen-year-old Matilda Crab-

tree, a Louisiana girl who, as a prank when her parents came home late one night, jumped out of a closet shouting, "Boo!" Thinking he was facing a stranger her father shot. His daughter's last words were, "I love you, Daddy."

I have no doubt that Matilda's father was trying to be responsible.

The advertisements were controversial. Individuals and organizations petitioned the Federal Trade Commission to prohibit the ads on the grounds that they were deceptive: these petitioners said the gun makers' claim that a handgun in the home protected those who lived there was false. In 1997 the National Library of Medicine and National Institutes of Health weighed in, saying that "regulating the way guns are advertised may be a useful public health intervention."

Big tobacco could take a multibillion-dollar hit. Gun manufacturers could not. In 1997 tobacco sales hit $48 billion, but U.S. gun sales totaled $1.4 billion. One big loss and the industry would be wiped out.

The cities' lawsuits were gaining momentum, and President Clinton was eager to step in, and HUD provided the ideal vehicle. As HUD secretary, I asked mayors and public housing authorities from around the country, "What's the biggest problem you face?" Their invariable answer was: "Gun violence."

We knew we had to do more to shrink the gun count in areas with low-income housing. In 1998, sixty-six of the nation's hundred largest public housing authorities averaged nearly one gun-related homicide per day. We launched a buyback program, giving local police departments as much as $500,000, which they spent $50 at a time for each gun turned in. But the public housing authorities were spending $1 billion a year trying to keep their 3.25 million residents safe from gun violence. And the safety measures, which included twenty-four-hour security guards, weren't working.

In December 1999, with White House coordination, I publicly said that HUD was considering filing a class-action lawsuit against gun manufacturers on behalf of the nation's 3,191 public housing authorities. At his regular press briefing the next day, President Clinton told reporters that the proposed suit wasn't to get money from manufacturers but to pressure them to change "irresponsible marketing practices."

I believed in the strength of our legal case, but—just as important—it could be leverage to bring the gun manufacturers to the negotiating table. Having the federal government sue put us in a position where we could coordinate with all the other suits that had been filed nationwide. The gun lobby started calling President Clinton "gun snatcher in chief" after he signed the 1993 Brady Bill, requiring background checks and a mandatory waiting period (later replaced by the National Instant Criminal Background Check System) before a handgun sale could be finalized, and the 1994 assault weapons ban. The gun industry's hostility was administration-wide. Eliot Spitzer and the ATF had tried such talks and failed. But I thought there was a win-win. The gun manufacturers needed the lawsuits to end. Any suit could bankrupt the industry. We didn't want to outlaw guns; we wanted to get reforms in distribution and background checks. There could be a mutual resolution if we could get gun makers to agree to a code of conduct; we could create a safer environment and resolve all the lawsuits at once.

My HUD deputy general counsel, an intense, thorough guy named Max Stier, called five gun manufacturers. He heard back from none. We were disappointed but not surprised. But one day in January 2000, Max burst into my office, yelling, "He talked to me! He talked to me!" "He" was Ed Shultz, the chief executive of Smith & Wesson.

I immediately followed up with Shultz, a no-nonsense, fiftysomething Iowan, who unlike most gun executives hadn't grown up in the business. His previous job had been as president of a company that made office furniture.

From what I'd read about him, Shultz was straightforward and unconcerned with being politically correct. Interviewed in 1999, he'd told the *Boston Globe* that "unlike cigarettes, guns aren't addictive, and gun companies never sought to hide the deadliness of their products. We've always said that if you look down the barrel of a gun and pull the trigger, it's very likely to be the last thing you do."

He also told the *Globe* he wasn't bothered when gang members shot at one another. "I have almost no emotion on that issue. As a matter of fact, I just hope they're both good shots."

Shultz was unfazed by what people thought about him. "They use all those words that start with *C* to describe me . . . Cold, cruel, callous, condescending," he said.

Despite outspokenness that some found heartless, Shultz had been the first of the eight American gun manufacturers that voluntarily provided child safety locks and had attended

President Clinton's 1997 Rose Garden announcement. He had a reputation as a smart businessman. In the same *Globe* piece, Shultz admitted he "recoiled" every time he heard that one of his guns had hurt someone.

When I got him on the phone, I said, "Ed, we're in the real world here. We want to reduce gun violence, not hurt your bottom line. We're interested in two things: making guns safer and keeping them out of the wrong hands. We want to talk with you about changes that have been proved to make a difference. At the same time we can get you what you need. This is your best hope for protecting Smith & Wesson from all the lawsuits."

Savvy and experienced, he knew that prudent companies take reasonable measures to avoid courtrooms, legal bills, million-dollar settlements—and bad PR. The big tobacco lawsuits had scared him.

By the time we hung up, Shultz had agreed to talk further. His only condition: absolute secrecy. "I cannot be seen exchanging a single friendly word with you," he said.

"Ed's brave," I told Max.

I believe in meeting face-to-face. There's no substitute for shaking people's hands, looking them in the eye, and gauging their body language. But it would have been difficult for me to fly under the radar. Instead I sent Max Stier to Nashville. He and Ed would talk at the airport. Travelers would be on the lookout for country music stars. No one would recognize Ed or Max—or no one who did recognize either of them would care.

Since Alcohol, Tobacco, and Firearms was part of the Treasury Department, its general counsel, Neal Wolin, went with Max. Neal brought expertise on gun safety. Ed brought a friend with no knowledge about guns. "Since you brought someone," he told Max, "I brought someone." His friend's only qualification was keeping confidences.

Much of the first meeting, at an airport barbecue joint, was spent eating ribs, talking football, and taking each other's measure. Neal said, "We're willing to negotiate on anything." Then they delivered the administration's wish list. Besides safety locks, we wanted ballistic fingerprinting so guns recovered from crimes could be traced back to their source. It was a simple fix: Every firearm would be test-fired at the factory. A computer image of that casing, and the unique marks caused by firing, would be cataloged and available to every law enforcement agency. When a casing was found, the police would scan it and identify it as, for example, a Smith & Wesson 9-mm handgun, serial number XYZ123. They'd know the name of the retailer who sold the weapon.

This made it less likely that the manufacturer would risk selling to a dishonest retailer—and possible that a dishonest retailer might reform.

The good news is that out of the millions of guns manufactured and sold every year, all but a small percentage stay in the legal market. Ballistic fingerprinting was a threat only to the 0.5 percent of sellers who skirt the law.

Another priority was a limit of one gun per customer per month. This would substantially reduce gun trafficking.

When Stier and Wolin had laid out their demands, Shultz looked at Max and said, "How old are you?"

"Thirty-four," Stier said.

"If you live a long life you'll never see this agreement come to pass," Shultz said.

It sounded as though the door was being slammed, but Shultz didn't leave. And Max knew my philosophy: long shots are no shots unless you keep at them. Ed was taking a leap by being there, although none of us realized at the time how much he had at stake. By the time they walked back to their respective gates, both sides had tentatively decided to put skepticism aside and trust that they were all honorable people.

Shultz, Stier, and Wolin met at a number of airports around the country and at the U.S. Mint in Washington, D.C.

In February, Shultz brought Paul Jannuzzo, general counsel and vice president of Glock, into the discussions. Having another manufacturer present made Shultz more comfortable. But Jannuzzo and Shultz had different views about what would or wouldn't work. Shultz believed smart guns were technologically feasible. Jannuzzo did not.

Glock bowed out in early March, but we were making progress with Smith & Wesson. In between Max and Neal's meetings, Ed and I talked on the phone.

I had a confidential meeting with Shultz at the Sheraton Hotel near the Hartford Airport in Connecticut, close to the Smith & Wesson headquarters in Springfield, Massachusetts. I flew there on Wednesday, March 15, with Max Stier, Neal Wolin, and Stuart Eizenstat, who was the deputy treasury secretary and a legendary public official—I remember hearing my father talk about him during the Carter days when Eizenstat was domestic policy head.

By the time we sat down together Shultz and I had an easy

rapport. We both were clear about not letting the perfect be the enemy of the good. Our team had a well-considered rationale for wanting to impose restrictions, but we were careful not to say no just to flex our muscles. We didn't want to put Smith & Wesson—or any of the other gun makers that might sign on—out of business. But I had no idea whether or not I would leave the meeting with an agreement.

Ed was straightforward: "If I sign this, am I making a deal just with HUD, or will the cities drop Smith & Wesson from their lawsuits?"

"I can't make guarantees," I said, "But I will do everything I can to make that happen and I believe I can." That was the sole benefit for Shultz. But it was a big one.

It took us five hours to walk through the negotiation.

At the end, amazingly, we had a deal. We shook hands. I was impressed with Shultz. He had put his career in harm's way and taken a truly momentous step. He trusted me to do what I said: try to persuade the cities to grant Smith & Wesson immunity in their suits.

We quickly phoned Dennis Henigan from the Center to Prevent Gun Violence. He represented most of the cities in the lawsuits so we had to convince him that this was a deal worth taking. Henigan liked it enough to sign on, but he was unbending on one point: Smith & Wesson had to be willing to abide by any stricter terms that other gun manufacturers might agree to in the future. Shultz said yes to that, too.

Before I left for Washington, Ed gave me a Smith & Wesson pocketknife as a token of respect and friendship. He said, "I'll see you in Washington on Friday to announce the deal. I'll fly down that morning."

What was happening was so historic I could barely absorb it. I was on edge. I knew that anything could go wrong.

The end of any tough endeavor comes when you have to dig the deepest and stay the course. I told Max, "You have to stay in Hartford and fly down with Ed. Do not lose sight of that man."

The next day, we made call after call. Fifteen of the cities agreed to drop Smith & Wesson from their suits. Ed sounded pleased, and relieved, when I told him. The others were considering it or checking with higher-ups.

The deal was to be announced on March 17 at HUD in Washington with many officials present from cities and states that were dropping their suits, including Blumenthal and Spitzer. Overnight a blizzard had hit Massachusetts. Ed called me first thing that morning. "There's no way I'm getting on a plane," he said.

I'll never know whether he balked because of the storm or misgivings about the deal. Max hightailed it to the Smith & Wesson headquarters in Springfield. He later told me that when he walked in, the company's top executives were sitting around a conference table, looking shell-shocked.

During the noon announcement ceremony, covered live on CNN, Max put Shultz on speakerphone.

"Are you with us, Ed?" I asked.

"Yes, I guess I am," he answered with reluctance.

With that, Smith & Wesson agreed to install mandatory child-safety devices on all guns; and to spend 2 percent of its annual revenue on developing smart-gun technology that would be included in all newly designed handguns. It would bar gun sales—including sales at gun shows—without a background check of the buyer; stop marketing guns to appeal to children; and limit multiple handgun sales. A buyer could take home only one gun at the time of purchase and would have to wait two weeks to pick up additional guns. Within six months, new guns would be packaged with a warning on the risk of having a firearm in the home and suggestions for safe storage. Gun stores would have to implement a security plan, and guns and bullets would be kept locked and separated. Gun dealer employees would be required to complete annual training. Distributors would be allowed to sell only to other distributors or dealers that pledged to abide by the agreement. Smith & Wesson consented to work with the ATF to establish a ballistic ID system.

The pact respected gun owners, protected citizens, and preserved Smith & Wesson's profit margin.

I wished Ed were at the signing ceremony. I thought, He will never know how many lives he saved, but every year there will be more of them. Some—maybe most—of those people would be unaware that their lives had been saved by this agreement. Children who didn't get shot. Depressed teens who were unable to give in to the terrible, irreversible impulse to shoot themselves. When smart gun technology is perfected, there will be people walking on the streets who won't be accosted by thugs brandishing stolen guns that can't fire.

What we had done was lifesaving.

I leaned into the mike and said, "I can say without doubt that in my seven years in this department this is the most important announcement that we have made. We've all said that something must be done about unnecessary gun violence in this country. We've heard the statistics many times: 30,000 gun deaths every year; 100,000 injured by firearms every year; a rate of firearm deaths for children in this country twelve times higher than the other twenty-five leading industrial nations combined."

Shultz said: "We have reached an agreement today, which we believe will do two things: first, it will provide for the future viability of the business entity of Smith & Wesson by putting our efforts and our funds toward technology and to make our guns better and safer in the future [and] the ability for us to continue to produce products that can be sold to ordinary citizens in our country without threatening their Second Amendment rights."

Here was a manufacturer saying, We can do this and still be in the business of selling guns. People can go target shooting and hunting. In a few years, when the smart-gun technology is available, they'll be able to keep a firearm in their homes without risking the lives of their children.

President Clinton hailed the deal as "a major victory for America's families."

With Smith & Wesson's signature in hand, we expected the other manufacturers would soon follow.

Not so fast.

Ten days before the Smith & Wesson signing, on March 7, 2000—Super Tuesday—George Bush and Al Gore locked up their parties' presidential nominations. As Texas governor, George Bush had legalized concealed weapons and banned lawsuits by municipalities against the gun industry but was noncommittal about whether he would side with the gun manufacturers and back the congressional immunity legislation they were seeking. The Republican House of Representatives had already voted in favor of the Class-Action Fairness Act that would make it tougher, if not impossible, to bring a class-action suit against the tobacco and gun businesses. A campaign spokesman said that Bush declined to rule out the possibility, saying simply, "He has not addressed that at the federal level."

I saw Bush's silence as tacit approval of immunity. So did the gun manufacturers. "If Bush wins, we could be going in a whole new direction," Robert Delfay, president of the National Shooting Sports Foundation, the industry's trade organization, told the *New York Times*. A pro-Bush NRA videotape surfaced around the same time; in it, the gun group's first vice president, Kayne Robinson, told a Los Angeles audience, "If we win, we'll have a president where we work out of their office, unbelievably friendly relations."

On May 5, 2000, the Gore campaign called Bush out on gun immunity. "A real Texan would tell us where he stands," Gore 2000 press secretary Chris Lehane said sarcastically. "We know he's been in the hip holster of the NRA as governor of Texas. We recently found out that the NRA plans on having an office in the Bush White House. What the American people deserve to know is will George W. Bush carry the gun lobby's legislative ammo bag? So far he's tried to conceal his position. As president, Al Gore would veto any bill like the one Bush signed in Texas to shield gun manufacturers from lawsuits. We challenge Bush to make the same pledge. Will he veto any bill that lets gun manufacturers completely off the hook? Where do you stand, Governor? Will you support the gun industry or will you stand with local communities and families?"

I publicly pressed Bush to take a stand. "If gun manufacturers are saying they won't make guns safer until they hear from George Bush, then let Mr. Bush tell us what is his position," I said on a conference call with reporters. "Will he immunize these gun manufacturers or will he demand they act responsibly? Let us hear now; the American people have a right to know. No more secrecy on his position about guns. Let's resolve this matter one way or the other, let's end the violence and end the killing once and for all."

A few days later, I spoke out again. "It makes no sense to require safety locks on bottles of aspirin but not on guns. It makes no sense to say we can sue the manufacturers of everything except guns for producing an unsafe product. Right now we have the technology to make guns safer and we have the ability to do more to keep them away from children and criminals. Governor Bush should tell the American people and the gun makers where he stands on this life-and-death issue, and he should call on gun makers to resume negotiations to save lives."

"Let me save Andrew Cuomo some time," said Robert Delfay, head of the National Shooting Sports Foundation. "He doesn't have to wait for George Bush to state his position on legislation. This industry has absolutely no intention of meeting with Mr. Cuomo about anything."

The possibility that a Bush presidency would put an end to the cities' lawsuits stopped our negotiations with other gun makers. The manufacturers said, in essence, We can wait this out. If George W. Bush wins, we will have immunity, and the Smith & Wesson agreement will be moot.

And, with that, it was.

At the same time, the National Rifle Association (NRA), considered to be one of the three most influential lobbying groups in Washington, waged war against Smith & Wesson for cooperating with the Clinton administration's supposed infringement on the Second Amendment.

Thoughtful argument gave way to grandstanding. The loudest parts of both parties took to the evening news. The liberal fallback response was to demonize guns and demand they all be outlawed. Period. No sales.

The liberals pointed to the model passed in the UK in 1997, after an armed man entered the Dunblane Primary School in Scotland at 9:35 A.M. and killed fifteen children and their teacher—an eerie precursor to Sandy Hook.

In the UK, it is difficult to own a gun. Anyone who applies for a license is presumed to be up to no good. Only after massive paperwork and a thorough police investigation into applicants' background, character, and family life to prove that they're not a danger to society are they granted a five-year license, revocable at any point. All guns must be locked in boxes bolted to a floor or wall and are subject to random police inspection.

Second Amendment purists were just as vehement. They said: No regulation whatsoever. No waiting period! No limits! No background checks at gun shows! The NRA whipped its members into a frenzy, and they, worried that a government ban was imminent, bought more guns.

I believed that each side actually held a piece of the truth. I

thought that both the liberals and the conservatives could contribute to the debate—a real debate, not a rant. No shrill name-
calling. Just an honest look at what is best for our country.

The chance of that was zero.

The NRA punished Smith & Wesson with a boycott that
caused a 40 percent drop in its sales. Ed Shultz was fired.

Gun companies ran from the Clinton-Gore position. Al
Gore won the election but didn't become president. George
Bush did become president.

The new Bush administration interpreted the Smith &
Wesson agreement as a memorandum of understanding, not
a legally binding document, and facilitated a turnaround for
Smith & Wesson, awarding the company new government
contracts. In 2002, Smith & Wesson introduced a new line
of high-capacity pistols, which became top sellers for the
company. Three years later, President Bush signed the Class-
Action Fairness Act, transferring jurisdiction for most large
multistate suits against companies from state courts to the
backlogged federal judicial system. Later in 2005 he signed
the Protection of Lawful Commerce in Arms Act, relieving
gun makers and arms dealers of responsibility for crimes
committed with their weapons. The law, which mandated
safety locks on all handguns, passed only after an amendment renewing the 1994 assault weapons ban was barred
from inclusion. "Our laws should punish criminals who use
guns to commit crimes, not law-abiding manufacturers of
lawful products," Bush said. Thanking the president for signing the bill, the NRA called it "the most significant piece of
pro-gun legislation in twenty years."

We would now be living in a different world if the Smith &
Wesson agreement had stuck. I still second-guess myself.
What could I have done differently to get the gun manufac-
turers onboard sooner?

A few months would have made all the difference. If we'd
been able to bring more gun makers to sign on, we would
have reached a critical mass. No gun manufacturer would
have wanted to be the outlier. The timing was off. The political context changed everything. The Bush White House
could still have reversed the agreement, but by that time the
facts on the ground would have been different. Gun makers
would already be working on smart gun technology.

Today I keep my Smith & Wesson pocketknife on my desk
at the state capitol in Albany, not out of nostalgia but as a
daily, tangible reminder of how important our success or
failure can be. I believe if Smith & Wesson had played out,
and politics had not intervened, other manufacturers would
have signed on, the industry would have been protected from
suits, and reforms would have been implemented that might
have saved thousands of lives. There have been many nights
I've lain awake wondering what could have been. Every time
there is a mass shooting I feel a pang of guilt. And there have
been many: In 2006, a milk truck driver, Charles Roberts,
went into West Nickel Mines Amish School in Lancaster
County, Pennsylvania, and shot eleven girls with a 9-mm
handgun. They were all between six and thirteen. Five died.
Five were critically wounded. In 2007, a student at Virginia
Tech, in Blacksburg, Virginia, killed thirty-two people and
wounded seventeen more before committing suicide. He
fired at least 174 rounds in nine minutes. The massacre is still

the deadliest shooting incident by a single gunman in U.S. history. In 2011 U.S. Congresswoman Gabrielle Giffords and sixteen others were shot and severely wounded in front of a Tucson, Arizona, supermarket. The rampage killed six, including a nine-year-old girl. In July 2012 moviegoers who'd come to enjoy the midnight showing of *The Dark Knight*, in an Aurora, Colorado, Cineplex met with the unimaginable, when a twenty-four-year-old former graduate student opened fire on more than eighty people, leaving twelve dead.

After every tragedy since Smith & Wesson I have said to myself, This could have been averted.

Sandy Hook had galvanized the public. We needed to act.

I asked Larry Schwartz and Mylan Denerstein to take the lead in designing the new, tighter gun legislation. "One of my fundamental principles is to take advantage of existing knowledge," I said. "Don't reinvent the wheel. Talk to people. Find out what the best laws are. See what works and build on that. Then come back with a comprehensive package of ideas and proposals. Most of all, see what it will take to get the Senate and Assembly to pass it."

We studied every state. We spoke with authorities in California and New Jersey, district attorneys, members of the New York Police Department (NYPD), and Ray Kelly, the NYPD commissioner. We called criminal justice experts and advocacy organizations, including the Brady Center and New Yorkers Against Gun Violence (NYAGV). We realized again how important language is—and how fast the bad guys can spot a loophole. Under the existing statute, being caught with an unloaded gun was a misdemeanor, not a felony. So they'd enlist a fellow gang member or their girlfriend to hold the bullets while they held the empty gun. They'd put gun and bullets together when they were ready to pull the trigger.

At the same time as we started our research, we opened talks with the legislative leadership. Unlike the passage of our two on-time budgets and the same-sex marriage bill, where we had to persuade individual legislators to vote with us, these negotiations were mostly with Assembly Speaker Sheldon Silver and Senate Majority Leader Dean Skelos. Both told us there was near-unanimity among the legislators that *something* had to be done about gun safety. The question was what. The state Senate and the Assembly had different answers. The Senate wanted to crack down on illegal guns and impose tougher criminal penalties. The Assembly wanted more safety measures and a stronger assault weapons ban.

On December 22, the Gannett-owned *Journal News*, which covers the Lower Hudson Valley suburbs outside New York City, published the names and addresses of people who held gun permits in Westchester and Rockland Counties, complete with an online map. The paper had gotten the information legally from the county clerks' offices, through New York's Freedom of Information Law (FOIL). Thousands of people e-mailed and called in their complaints, suggesting that the information gave burglars a "shopping list" and endangered domestic violence victims under protective orders, who didn't want anyone to know that they had a weapon in the house. "We knew publication of the database would be controversial, but we felt sharing as much information as we could about gun ownership in our area was important in the aftermath of the Newtown shootings," said CynDee Royle, editor and vice president/news. "New York residents have the right to own guns with a permit and they also have a right to access public information," said Janet Hasson, president and publisher of the Journal News Media Group.

The Republicans in the New York Senate did what their party was doing in several states: they pushed to make information about permit holders less accessible. One of their negotiating points was an allowance for New York gun owners to maintain their privacy on request.

As public servants, New Yorkers, parents, and human beings, we were still reeling from Sandy Hook when we again saw how easy it can be for a mentally ill person to get a gun and how devastating it is for those in his path:

Around 5:30 A.M. on Christmas Eve, a sixty-two-year-old, William Spengler, set fire to a house and car in Webster, New York, outside Rochester, on Lake Ontario, in the western part of the state—a town where, ironically, the motto was "Where Life Is Worth Living." Mentally ill, Spengler had served nearly seventeen years in jail for killing his grandmother with a hammer. This time he got a Bushmaster AR-15 assault rifle, buying it illegally through a straw purchaser, his twenty-four-year-old former next-door neighbor. When volunteer first responders answered the fire alarm, Spengler took aim, killing Lieutenant Michael Chiapperini, a twenty-year veteran of the Webster Police Department; and Tomasz Kaczowka, a 911 dispatcher. He then turned the assault rifle on himself.

It was painful to see volunteers—people who routinely risked their lives to help others—killed while trying to do good. The Webster murders bolstered the tough-on-crime state Senate's motivation to pass gun safety legislation. Easy access to guns by criminals had to stop.

We worked through the holidays, and, as expected in politics, we had our obstacles.

The Assembly wanted significant restrictions that the Senate wouldn't impose, and vice versa. "Trigger locks on all guns," the Assembly said. The Senate responded, "Trigger locks? If someone's breaking into my home I want to take my gun out of my bureau and use it."

Individuals have their own political strategies. Negotiating is a chess game. We'd ask for more than we wanted in order to end up with what we needed. Sometimes we knew one chamber or the other would reject an idea, so we'd put it on the table as leverage. We'd push. They'd pull. Then we'd say, "If you agree to *this*, we'll drop *that*." If we hadn't put *that* on the table we would never get to the *this*. The talks went back and forth.

There are times when you make no progress. You keep coming back to the same points. You try to reason, and no one's being reasonable. It's stressful. It's frustrating. There's always pressure to close.

By January 9, when I delivered my 2013 State of the State Address at the Convention Center in Albany, we'd hammered out 95 percent of the agreement. We'd invited the families of the Webster firefighters, whom we presented with New York State flags. The Rochester police chief, James Sheppard, spoke.

I told the more than two thousand people gathered: "In the area of public safety, gun violence has been on a rampage—as we know firsthand, and we know painfully. We must stop the madness, my friends. . . . We need a gun policy in this state that is reasonable, that is balanced, that is measured."

I went on to outline a seven-point agenda:

No. 1: Enact the toughest assault weapon ban in the nation. Period.
No. 2: Close the private sale loophole by requiring federal background checks.
No. 3: Ban high-capacity magazines.
No. 4: Enact tougher penalties for illegal gun use, guns on school grounds, and violent gangs.
No. 5: Keep guns from people who are mentally ill.
No. 6: Ban direct Internet sales of ammunition in New York.
No. 7: Create a background check system.

I continued: "New York State led the way on guns once before. It was Sullivan's Law of 1911, which was the first gun control law in the nation—a model law that required a permit for possession of a handgun. New York was the first; it's still on the books. New York led the way then; let's pass safe and fair legislation and lead the way once again in saving lives."

The Sullivan Law of 1911 was relevant because there was opposition to registering existing assault weapons. The fear— unfounded as I believe it is—is based on the idea that if government officials had a record of gun ownership they could confiscate the guns to dominate a now defenseless society. The Sullivan Law mandated a record of handgun owners. If government was ever going to confiscate guns, why hasn't it happened in the hundred years that New York State has been keeping records? Why would I start now? Logic wins only when the issue is factual. The gun debate is much more emotional.

It might seem like a small, timing detail, but I believe it's always best for hard or controversial issues to be introduced at the start or end of the legislative session. It made sense to do gun legislation early, because we had such a narrow window of opportunity. We'd do it and get it out of the way. It would be tough, but then it would be over. We would put it behind us and move on to more operational pieces of legislation, such as our third on-time budget.

Both the Assembly's and the Senate's points of view were necessary to address our gun problems in New York. We had to crack down on gun crime and prevent guns from getting into the wrong hands. We were not only trying to get a deal done, but also to make a good law that would keep New Yorkers safer.

Our compromise package did both. We increased the penalties for illegal guns and put a tighter assault weapon ban and registration of ammunition sellers in place.

On the evening of January 14, five days after the State of the State Address, the Senate voted 43 to 18 to pass the Secure Ammunition and Firearms Enforcement Act, otherwise known as the New York SAFE Act. The next day, the Assembly passed it by a 61-vote margin, 104 to 43. It took us just a month and a day to design, negotiate, pass, and enact the law. In Washington, congressional hearings on the subject had not yet begun.

When I signed the SAFE Act into law in the Red Room on January 15, it was the first time since the Smith & Wesson agreement fell apart that I let go of that regret. The complaints started before the ink was dry.

State Senator Kathleen Marchione, the conservative Republican who replaced Roy McDonald, in retaliation for his marriage equality vote, wrote an inflammatory letter to her constituents saying she opposed the "restrictive new gun control," adding that it "was rushed through both houses of our state legislature without a single public hearing." She went on to say, "We must repeal and replace the restrictive parts of the enacted legislation. We should focus on increasing penalties for criminals who use firearms and addressing the issue of mental illness."

Within a few weeks, she had collected more than 100,000 signatures. Of course, she wanted to keep the parts of the bill she liked, but void the provisions she didn't like. Unfortunately, that's not how life or democracy works. It is always the same.

On Saturday, January 19, about two thousand protesters, many dressed in NRA baseball caps, held a rally in Albany and another thousand gathered in Buffalo. Chanting "Traitor, traitor" and "Impeach Cuomo," they held up handmade signs meant to incite anger and resistance: FROM MY COLD DEAD HANDS GOVENOR [sic]! WHEN GUNS ARE OUTLAWED I WILL BECOME AN OUTLAW! TO DISARM THE PEOPLE IS THE MOST EFFECTUAL WAY TO ENSLAVE THEM. BENEDICT CUOMO!!! I WOKE UP ON 1/15/13 TO DISCOVER THAT I HAD BEEN MADE A CRIMINAL BY CUOMO. One sign had a picture of my face with the word TYRANT written in bold red letters across the forehead.

Carl Paladino, my 2010 opponent, condemned the "gutless, cowardly legislators" who supported the bill. Another speaker in Buffalo said, "They are not going to come into our homes and steal our weapons, unless they want my ammo— one piece at a time."

We had expanded the definition of an assault weapon by including semiautomatic rifles that have a detachable magazine and one militaristic feature from a list that includes a folding or telescoping stock for improved conceal-ability, a muzzle compensator, and a pistol grip or thumbhole stock for better control during rapid firing. It's impossible to prevent every bad incident, but each of these features improves accuracy or makes a gun easier to conceal. Each meant that a shooter going into a crowded movie theater or shopping mall or school wouldn't have to be a marksman to hit his target. Less accuracy means more lives saved. We set similar requirements for semiautomatic pistols and semiautomatic shotguns. The SAFE Act made it a felony to be part of a straw purchase and imposed tougher penalties for illegal gun use. Private sales—a longtime loophole—must now run the same NICS check that stores do.

More than twenty years ago, Daniel Patrick Moynihan, the wise four-term U.S. senator from New York who died in 2003, said the best way to control gun violence was to control the bullets. The SAFE Act takes Senator Moynihan's prescient point into account, requiring background checks of both gun buyers and people buying ammunition. People may buy ammunition on the Internet but must pick it up from a dealer in person.

Now, under the SAFE Act, carrying an unlicensed, unloaded handgun is a felony, not a misdemeanor. This change has created a stronger deterrent, because anyone carrying a gun knows that if he gets stopped he's going to prison for three or four years. It has taken more guns off the streets.

Misinformation was everywhere. But the new law was not restrictive or outlandish. It was common sense. When you buy a used car from someone on Craigslist, the state requires that owner-transfer papers be filed. The idea that the state required no paperwork when someone bought a secondhand weapon in a private sale was ludicrous. New Yorkers have registered their handguns for more than a hundred years, so it made no sense that you didn't have to register an assault weapon.

Before the SAFE Act, every county handled handgun registration its own way. New York City and Westchester were stringent. But some counties required a onetime registration at the time of purchase. Others required reregistration every five years. If someone died, or moved, or sold or gave away his gun, there was usually no way of knowing what had happened to it. The old system was disorganized, and when a gun was found at a crime scene valuable time was spent tracking down its owner. Now there's a statewide electronic handgun registry. We created it in order to know who owns the gun, not to deny people the right to own the gun.

New York already had Kendra's Law, a 1999 state statute named after Kendra Webdale, a young woman killed when a mentally ill man receiving no medical treatment pushed her in front of a New York City subway train. We increased the outpatient treatment requirement for people who need supervision to live safely in their communities and added new stipulations. But new to the SAFE Act was a provision that when psychologists or psychiatrists believe any patients are an imminent threat to themselves or someone else, they are bound by law to contact the county mental health director. The next step: the patients' names are cross-checked to see if these individuals own guns so that their licenses could be revoked. The new provision also prevents such a person from obtaining a legal gun in the future without a judge's permission.

The law also includes a penalty for those who kill a first responder performing his or her duty. They will be sentenced to mandatory life without parole, period. The first responder—a police officer, a paramedic—is someone's father, brother, friend, sister, mother. We are obligated to keep him or her safe.

The biggest blowback came from the rule limiting magazines to seven rounds. Manufacturers said that ten-round magazines are the industry standard, and they refused to change their practices. In April, we amended the law to say that you could use ten-round magazines but you could load them with only seven bullets.

Two weeks after the SAFE Act became law, a lawyer from western New York challenged the requirement that anyone owning high-capacity magazines had to sell them outside the state, hand them over to the authorities, or retrofit them to hold a maximum of seven rounds. This lawyer argued that the requirement violated the Fifth Amendment's protection against the unlawful seizure of private property. Soon thereafter, the New York Rifle and Pistol Association filed notice of a suit claiming violations of the Second and Fourteenth Amendments, and Interstate Commerce Clause. It was as though gun purists were throwing any constitutional amendment they could at the SAFE Act to see what stuck.

The law survived largely intact, with one possible exception. On December 31, 2013, a federal judge in Buffalo struck down the seven-magazine limit, calling it "an arbitrary restriction."

(I said, "If you're going to throw seven rounds as arbitrary, then you're going to have to throw out all magazine limits as arbitrary.")

This part of the law is not being enforced while it is under appeal.

My strong belief is that placing the firing limit at seven rounds saves lives. Why? If you look at the rampages that have occurred, you find that many shooters had semiautomatic handguns, rifles, and dozens of magazines. That's why we eliminated high-capacity magazines and limited the number of rounds that could be placed in a magazine. If someone is shooting a gun at people, the only opportunity law enforcement has to step in comes when the gunman is changing the magazine. It may be only a matter of seconds to change the magazine, but that is the moment of opportunity for law enforcement. Some gun laws in the state are even stricter: New York City has a five-bullet limit. Most hunters and sportsmen have operated with a limit below seven as most hunting rifles can have only five rounds in the magazine and one in the chamber.

The U.S. Senate was not as successful. Five days after New-town, President Obama tapped his vice president, Joe Biden, to head an interagency task force on gun control. Barack Obama's message was clear: We will act. We will legislate guns. Nine in ten Americans favored broader background checks. But in April 2013, the U.S. Senate's 54-to-46 vote fell short of the 60 votes needed for passage, and the House of Representatives didn't take the legislation up. While sixteen states have tightened their gun laws since Newtown, seventeen have opted for looser restrictions.

The legal debate over what the Second Amendment allowed went on until the U.S. Supreme Court heard *Heller v. the District of Columbia* in 2008. In its landmark 5-to-4 decision, the Court said: "Like most rights, the Second Amendment right is not unlimited. It is not a right to keep and carry any weapon whatsoever in any manner whatsoever and for whatever purpose."

Overturning a handgun ban that was law in the District of Columbia, the Court also said that if you're a law-abiding citizen there should be a way for you to get a firearm that is not too onerous. The government can impose restrictions on the type of gun and the steps you need to take to approve a sale, but it cannot ban gun ownership outright.

As I said, I own a gun. I understand why the issue can be so intractable. We all agree that we need to keep guns out of the hands of criminals and the mentally ill. But we can't focus on those groups unless there's a system in place, and, by definition, legal gun owners are affected by the system. To ensure guns don't get into the hands of criminals or the mentally ill, all buyers must be checked. That is the fact and although it is a small intrusion on the legal owner—it is worth the price.

The problem is that we have lost our collective common sense and substituted its enemies: fear, extremism, fanaticism, and intolerance.

In 1934, Franklin Roosevelt outlawed machine guns. Why? Because they were too dangerous for society; because society said your right to have that gun extinguishes my right to be safe, and my right to be safe needs to be protected, too.

After a mass shooting in California, Joe Wurzelbacher, a Tea Party favorite known as Joe the plumber, wrote an open letter to the victims' parents saying, "[Y]our dead kids don't trump my constitutional rights." Actually, Joe, they do. Your constitutional rights do not outweigh their right to be safe.

The SAFE Act has been in place for more than a year, and it has proved itself. None of the horrors have come true. We now have facts to defeat the rhetoric and experience to dispel the fear. Between its passage and December 17, 2013, the SAFE Act resulted in 1,291 criminal charges—1,155 of which were for felony possession of an illegal firearm, a misdemeanor under the old laws. There are substantially fewer illegal guns on the streets these days. New York now has the fourth-lowest rate of gun deaths in the country.

There has been no slippery slope of government action. There has been no government confiscation of anything. None of the conspiracy theories have come true. No lawful, mentally stable person has been denied a gun, nor has there even been a complaint of a denial. There are also positives for the gun-owning community. The pistol permits are not subject to disclosure. Killers who murder first responders receive mandatory life sentences. Criminal penalties for illegal guns and "gang" guns have been increased.

The staunchest opponents of gun control and its most rabid proponents like certain aspects of the law and dislike others. Welcome to the controversial topic and government and democracy. It's called the art of compromise. The alternative is to do nothing. But my mantra is that doing nothing never accomplishes anything.

Nancy Lanza, the mother of the Newtown murderer, owned six guns. Two were high-capacity semiautomatic rifles; two were high-capacity semiautomatic handguns; and two were traditional bolt-action rifles, the kind that are used for hunting. One could accommodate a ten-bullet magazine. Adam Lanza used that one to shoot his sleeping mother.

When he went to the elementary school he took three semiautomatic weapons inside.

Had the bolt-action rifles been the only guns available to Lanza, Newtown would not have happened in the same way. Bolt-action rifles have a limited capacity and a slower rate of fire, meaning the number of times they can fire in one minute. With those rifles, Lanza would have been able to fire off a maximum of eleven shots before reloading. But the three guns he brought into the school had thirty-bullet magazines, giving Lanza ninety shots before he needed to reload. The rate of fire is as fast as you can pull the trigger.

The twenty children and six adults in Newtown had the right to be safe. That is common sense.

CHAPTER 12

———

All Things Possible

With Sandy in a Margaretville, New York, basement in 2011,
helping homeowners recover from the devastation of Hurricane
Irene as part of "Labor for Your Neighbor," a Labor Day
weekend service initiative.

At the end of the day the extreme arguments about government are just that—extremes. We can't "shut the government down," and big government is certainly not a panacea. We have tasks to perform that are indisputable and that only the collective can accomplish. That is the definition of government: public safety, education, defense, infrastructure, economic development, safety nets in housing and health care, and progressive social leadership.

The questions that fuel the debate are how those tasks should be performed, by whom, and whether we are still capable of completing them. Can we restore confidence that we have a collective competence? That was my first job as governor: restoring the state's credibility and competence—and, most important, belief in its own future. We couldn't lift the state out of its economic funk if New Yorkers didn't believe that it could be made strong again. When I was at HELP I saw that if people had faith in themselves they could change destructive behaviors. If they didn't think they could, they were doomed. At HUD I learned that if a community didn't believe in its future, its impending collapse would become reality.

Both HELP and HUD, and years of politics, had taught me that to inspire change I had to show, not tell. Speeches and rhetoric wouldn't change minds; what was needed was action and results. We wouldn't take the easy challenges; we would take the hard ones: the big, intractable long-term problems that defied government's ability. Our mission was clear. We know what we must be able to do.

We need to be able to build big things again. New York was all about building to excite the imagination: the Empire State Building, the Twin Towers, the Verrazano-Narrows Bridge, the subway system. Yet we now doubt our ability to begin any big projects, never mind to complete one on time.

We need to be able to help our struggling older manufacturing cities, like those in upstate New York, or Pennsylvania or Ohio or the Midwest. We need to be able to handle the new emergencies of extreme weather and terrorist threats. We must have the best public education system on the planet. Period. And we must come to terms with one of the greatest threats to our democracy, political extremism.

To begin my new administration I had a meeting with top construction and development people. I asked them what they thought were the overdue transformative projects: the languishing projects that we could take on and complete. What I learned was disappointing: Even the pros didn't believe government could accomplish big tasks!

"Anyone?" I asked. "Anything?"

Finally someone said, "Well, you could *say* you'll build a new Tappan Zee Bridge."

"What does that mean?" I asked.

"Saying that a new bridge was in the works would build enthusiasm," he said. "But we can't actually do it. It's too hard, too complex; there would be litigation and political opposition. It won't happen within your administration's lifetime."

A replacement for the Tappan Zee was two decades overdue. The Tappan Zee, a three-mile span over the Hudson River, connecting Westchester and Rockland counties, was completed in 1955. Built on the cheap, it was designed to last fifty years, half the time of most New York bridges. And with no emergency lane it was deficient from the start. A fender bender or a stalled vehicle stopped traffic as effectively as a wall. Some regular commuters traveled with survival kits—energy bars, water, and magazines—to take them through the long and frequent delays. The government had done one thing well: communicated the bridge's dangers to justify its replacement. Every year the bridge came closer to collapse, and the state threw away still more taxpayer money to patch the outdated structure.

Governor George Pataki had announced that he was going to replace the Tappan Zee in 1999. Since then the state has held 430 meetings, considered 150 design concepts, and spent $88 million in taxpayer money trying to come up with a plan for a new bridge.

"My belief is that if we could build it in 1955, it can be built again in 2011. If you think we can't do this," I said, "recuse yourself. I don't want you involved. I am not here to continue the state's culture of failure. I'm not interested in why things can't be done. I don't buy the same old, same old reasons for not trying. That thinking ends now."

After that first meeting with the doubters, I spent hours being tutored by experts on state-of-the-art bridge construction, great successes, and bad attempts. I learned early on that if you don't know the substantive facts, the bureaucracy will always beat you. There is no substitute for having the knowledge to make a discussion meaningful.

We worked through the contracts and approval process, talking with local officials and groups to understand their objections and reach the right decision.

The Hudson River is protected by aggressive environmental organizations. We knew the groups could sue, and often did, because the river gave them a cause to rally around and helped them raise funds. Any construction on a bridge would entail multiple environmental questions. "Protect the beautiful Hudson" was a chant waiting to be called forth, and who could disagree? To allay the environmentalists' fears, we agreed to use fish-protecting bubble curtains and noise-reduction devices during construction. Some of the stipulations struck me as overkill, but to avoid incurring a lawsuit and risking years of delay, the extra precautions seemed worth it.

We redesigned the way government goes about large-scale construction projects. The old way required government architects to provide the blueprint and private contractors to handle the construction, an arrangement that lent itself to a high-level blame game. In December 2011, we passed design-build legislation that allowed us to contract out the entire project for a guaranteed lump sum and an agreed-to timetable, with penalties for delays and incentives for beating the deadline.

The ultimate decision to go forward wasn't entirely in our control. A regional transportation group made up of eight local politicians had to sign off—unanimously. Any member could object, and the project would be—well, dead in the water. This council had Democrats and Republicans. Lining up the votes required micro-level politicking. I reverted to the Cuomo Rule: move the people, and the politicians will follow. Raise public awareness of the project and make it a popular cause so that politicians oppose it at their peril. But to convince people that government could efficiently build a bridge was no easy task! Public cynicism is justified.

Watching the local news one night I had a lightbulb

moment. Anchorman Brian Conybeare had broadcast on the local TV station, Channel 12 News, for years—the Walter Cronkite of Westchester. I called Conybeare. "Brian," I said, "do you want to make the world better and do something that your children can show your grandchildren? How about making news rather than reporting it?"

Conybeare agreed to join the state to help explain to citizens why it was a good idea to undertake a multibillion-dollar government project with a history of chaos. Between the two counties involved—Rockland and Westchester—we held more than one hundred meetings, in schools, church basements, public libraries, and people's kitchens. People trusted him not to say anything he didn't believe in. They were right.

The politicians on the commission threatened to sink us. But by then the project had about a 70 percent favorable rating among constituents. Leaders knew that if they opposed the bridge the voters would crush them.

Meanwhile, every step of the process created opportunities and raised questions. It is as if the bureaucracy sees progress or decision making as the enemy! Every step takes energy and diligence. We met at least weekly, often several times a week, constantly questioning and pushing. Luckily I know bureaucratic inertia and I know construction and I fully believe that one must create tremendous positive energy to deflect bureaucratic negativity. After hundreds of hours of meetings—in small conference rooms with teams of officials—we got to "yes." Larry Schwartz was the main manager who just refused to let us fail. It worked. Matt Wing coordinated the outreach. They were a great team.

In August 2012 we had a bill-signing ceremony on the Rockland County side. After putting out bids to private sector companies around the globe, our evaluation team chose Tappan Zee Constructors, a consortium of internationally renowned bridge builders. The contract reduced our projected cost from roughly $5 billion to about $3.9 billion, and shaved nearly a year off our estimated construction schedule.

The last wrinkle: the project had to be approved by the Army Corps of Engineers and a phalanx of federal regulatory agencies. President Obama had just announced a fast-track initiative in Washington for nationally significant states' projects requiring federal approval. We applied for this federal initiative and were designated a priority.

Despite that, I was skeptical about the federal government's ability to complete the contracts and approvals to meet our timetable. But in September 2012, the feds signed off on the documents; this meant that we had gone from announcement to approval in less than a year. The feds delivered. New York State was awarded $1.6 billion, the largest loan in the fifteen-year history of the Transportation Infrastructure Finance and Innovation Act. We have forty years to pay back the money, which we will do through toll collection.

Now the new Tappan Zee Bridge is under construction. It will have two spans, with four lanes on either side, plus emergency lanes and a pedestrian and bike path. It will be mass-transit-ready. One side will be completed by November 2016 and the other in 2018.

In May 2014 President Obama made a trip to Tarrytown, in Westchester County, to celebrate the bridge's successful start, pointing out that it is a powerful example of this country's capacity to rebuild. "Businesses are going to come where there's good infrastructure," the president said.

"This is a bridge that symbolizes what was and what can be," I said. "This is a bridge from gridlock to bipartisanship. This is a bridge from paralysis to progress. And this is a bridge from yesterday to tomorrow."

During my 2010 campaign one promise I'd made to myself and the people of New York was to rebuild Buffalo. The city, once a thriving manufacturing hub, now communicated resounding defeat and was suffering the most of all cities in upstate New York. That area is New York's biggest economic challenge, and Buffalo was the most significant example.

While at HUD I spent a lot of time working with mayors in medium-size Rust Belt cities—Scranton and Pittsburgh, Pennsylvania; Akron, Ohio; East St. Louis, Illinois. Part of the agency's mission was to help redevelop the country's left-behind places.

For one hundred years Buffalo was a thriving part of New York's manufacturing beltway along the Erie Canal, which included Albany, Utica, Syracuse, and Rochester. When the manufacturing jobs dried up so did Buffalo.

I had a conversation about the economy with a longtime resident. "Buffalo," he said, "has had a bad fifty years."

He wasn't kidding. In fact he was short by a decade. Buffalo has struggled since the 1950s. Three generations had moved away. Now the city was struggling to develop business that would be relevant in the new economy.

The first order was to make Buffalo believe in its own future. In life you have to believe in yourself. That applies to the collective also. Working at HUD on economic development projects all across the country I learned something important: a city's attitude about itself determines its survival. Visitors judge places—often unconsciously—by what the locals project. If their waitress carries a sense of hopelessness and their cab driver grumbles about business, that attitude resonates. If the newspaper is filled with gloom and doom, it is a powerful negative. In short, no one moves into a town that radiates defeat.

We had to make Buffalo's residents believe that a renaissance was possible. Compounding matters, Buffalo had already heard it all, politician after politician promising a "new plan" for a "new Buffalo." I needed something dramatically different. In my 2012 State of the State Address I announced the "Buffalo Billion," a huge economic package designed to shock the downtrodden city and communicate that this time would be different. "We have big problems," I said, "but we are confronting them with big solutions." We asked economic development consultants from the Brookings Institution, an influential nonpartisan Washington think tank, to join with the University of Buffalo Regional Institute and the Buffalo Niagara Enterprise research department to identify Western New York's competitive advantages and recommend possible investment options for its windfall.

We set up a Regional Economic Development Council, with top business people, academics, and politicians all on one task force to design one strategy—cooperation, not competition. The group was led by two cochairs: Howard Zemsky, a superior businessman and attractive personality who was the spark plug for the effort; and Satish K. Tripathi, the brilliant head of the University of Buffalo, which is part of the State University of New York (SUNY) system. The group set priorities: develop clean-energy manufacturing and medical genomics research, increase tourism, launch a $5 million new business plan competition, and create a partnership to align workers' education and training with employers' needs to counter the city's above-average number of residents near retirement and above-average unemployment rate. Business executives expect certain services and cultural amenities— good schools, restaurants, theater, and art. We had to make it attractive and worthwhile for cutting-edge businesses to set up shop in Buffalo.

We have invested. It's worked. Every month more local workers got jobs with the new companies. "The list of [construction] projects is breathtaking for Buffalonians unused to development," reads a January 2013 *Buffalo News* editorial. "Look around. This is no longer the City That Couldn't. It's the City That Does."

Since the Buffalo Billion was announced, more than ten thousand jobs have been created in Erie County. The tipping point for Buffalo came in late 2013, when we announced the state's $225 million investment in RiverBend, a ninety-acre "clean energy" research campus, which will be anchored by two solar energy manufacturers. The former home of the Republic Steel plant, which shut down in 1984, has been transformed from a brownfield—the "grave site" of old Buffalo—to a symbol of the future.

To add more rpm to upstate New York's economic engine,

in June 2013 we passed legislation to create sixty-eight state and local tax-free zones called START-UP New York. This initiative encourages businesses to launch, relocate, or expand on state-owned property—mostly SUNY campuses. The program extends the ten-year tax benefits to employees. Already in Western New York, twelve biotechnology, biopharmaceutical, and software development companies have come onboard, investing $50 million.

The simple fact is that we will not build a successful future if we ignore our children's failing education system.

This is one of the rare instances when liberals and conservatives agree. Our current education system is failing. In terms of our gross domestic product (GDP) the United States is the wealthiest country in the world. But our children's proficiency in reading, math, and science is not proportional. A 2012 assessment of education systems in fifty countries by the Economic Intelligence Unit ranked the United States seventeenth, behind front-runners South Korea, Finland, and Canada but also below Estonia, Poland, and Iceland. Clearly that means we must spend more on education, right? Not necessarily.

In New York, we spend an average of $19,522 per pupil annually—$8,914 more than the national average. New York spends more per pupil than any other state. But our students are ranked number thirty-two in the country in graduation rates.

I am not pining for a nonexistent golden past: I'm certain that our education system has improved since St. Gerard

Majella, my Catholic elementary school in Queens, stuffed forty-three kids into a classroom. We know more about how children learn. We no longer ask, "Why can't Johnny read?" because we know how to recognize and compensate for learning disabilities. We know a great many things. We don't always implement the lessons. But it's time to use every tool in the box. Technology makes it possible to customize a child's education. Early intervention should be used at all levels. Pre-K must be standard. If a first-grader is struggling with phonics or a ninth-grader with algebra, it makes sense to bring in resource teachers for intense tutoring as soon as a problem becomes apparent, before so much time has passed that catching up is nearly impossible. Early action saves students' self-esteem and taxpayers' dollars. It is much less expensive to provide help at the start than to pay for summer school or to have a student repeat the year.

This is not a rant against public school. I believe in public education. My older daughters, Cara and Mariah, attended public school through tenth grade. Michaela, my youngest, will graduate from a public high school. All three of them had outstanding teachers who took the time to mentor them. But all of them attended public school in a wealthy suburban district—and that is the key.

I am acutely aware that their experience isn't every child's.

Schools in advantaged communities can afford to focus only on the learning that takes place inside classrooms. A school in a poor district has to be educator, nutritionist, after-school center, mentor, tutor, family therapy center, surrogate parent, coach, and homework helper. We need to be honest about the challenges of single parenthood and dysfunctional communities and provide social services outside the classroom that make teaching in the classroom effective—what I call "community schools" that offer one-stop "shopping" for families. If this sounds too expensive, look ahead to money saved. Children who feel safe, valued, and supported are more likely to finish high school. They are less likely to turn to using or selling drugs. They are less likely to go to prison at a cost of $30,000 per year. They are less likely to become pregnant as teenagers. Putting aside moral concerns and looking at this only from an economic point of view, investing in the expert—and, admittedly, sometimes costly—help and emotional support that allow students to learn and graduate produces future taxpayers.

It's not that school systems haven't tried to right the ship but the fixes are usually the same thing that didn't work the year before and the year before that. As Albert Einstein said, "Insanity is doing the same thing over and over again and expecting a different result."

We need to try a radically different tack. We have to change the bureaucracy from a 1950s public monopoly to a performance- and outcome-driven system. This means evaluating the individual performances of teachers and schools and providing incentives and sanctions.

In New York we introduced teacher evaluations that measure classroom performance using several yardsticks, including observation, peer review, and student achievement as evidenced by progress on statewide tests. Our plan is to let the evaluations, not the number of years in the classroom, determine who deserves raises and promotions. This also helps us identify underperforming teachers who need more training. It is a big shift and I respect the union leaders who are working to ensure that the evaluation process is fair and accurate. It also has to be expeditious and meaningful.

We must also reward and continually train teachers who want to progress. That's one reason we introduced the Master Teacher Program, which debuted in 2013 and 2014 by selecting, from all the applicants, the first 319 teachers statewide— experts in science, technology, engineering, or math, subjects collectively known by the acronym STEM. Each educator will be paid an additional $60,000 over four years to share his or her knowledge and experience with colleagues, work with early-career STEM teachers, and attend and lead professional development sessions. Proven techniques for firing up students will be brought to classrooms around the state. The ultimate goal of the Master Teacher Program is to help improve college readiness for young New Yorkers.

I also support trying new, unconventional, well-thought-out teaching methods. Some experiments will work; some may not. Some may make the difference we need. Remember that ideas that were first seen as avant-garde are now mainstream. When educators tested the concept of bilingual schools we learned that children pick up a second language more quickly than most adults. Dedicated math and science schools have become incubators for Westinghouse prizewinners. And New York's High School of Music & Art, founded in 1936 by Fiorello La Guardia during his time as mayor of New York City, has repeatedly shown why the public school system must value all talents. If you measure the success of the school by the success of its students, it must be seen as an investment that paid off a hundredfold. Listing the well-known singers, composers, dancers, directors, and actors who received their training there would take another chapter, but as governor I can brag that the graduates include graphic artist Milton Glaser; painter Wolf Kahn; designer Isaac Mizrahi; actors Ellen Barkin, Robert De Niro, Vanessa Williams, Adrien Brody, and Liza Minnelli; and hundreds of other composers, dancers, producers, directors, architects, and writers.

I'm in favor of government-funded public charter schools. About 5 percent of our public schools are charter schools, so they are not on a scale that can ever substitute for a public education system, but they do offer comparison and competition. The best will raise the bar for all schools.

I am committed to giving all students an education that will serve them throughout their working life. But that cannot happen without radical change. It won't be easy. Change of the status quo brings controversy and the teachers union is a formidable advocate. But failure is not an option.

An absolutely essential function for government is how we respond during emergencies. We must train our first responders to handle all the emergencies we hope will never happen, because when the worst occurs there is no time to ponder or debate. Reactions must be uniform and automatic. How fast and well you work determines how much is lost. Prepared, we will save lives. If we're unprepared, people will die. It's that clear-cut. There are no do-overs.

Emergency situations bring home the fact that government has a *function*. Life-or-death crises make the political arguments disappear. No one asks if you are liberal or conservative. No one accuses the government of being over-involved. People never refuse a rescue because they don't believe in big government.

There are far too many examples of government *incompetence*. Hurricane Katrina was a top-to-bottom federal failure that cost more than 1,800 lives and $108 billion. The failure was set in place years before, when government officials approved the building of levees they knew couldn't withstand a Category 5 hurricane. It was made worse by a woefully unprepared Federal Emergency Management Agency (FEMA).

The 2005 hurricane was on my mind on August 27, 2011, as Hurricane Irene approached landfall. Sophisticated weather tracking systems calculated that the storm, a Category 1, would pummel New York City. Scientists at the National Weather Service issued the first hurricane warning for the city in twenty-six years. They expected wind damage and life-threatening flash floods in the low-lying areas of Manhattan, Brooklyn, and Staten Island and a storm surge of four to eight feet on Long Island.

This was my first major experience with a natural disaster since I'd been elected governor. My office kicked into high gear, managing the response teams. From the capitol in Albany, I dispatched my staff to command centers in the areas expected to be clobbered. Declaring a state of emergency in the days before the storm, we deployed all of our state resources to help New York City, sending trucks in from as far away as Buffalo to wait on the outskirts of the city, prepared to go to work as soon as the storm passed. In Lower Manhattan, subways, buses, and commuter trains were shut down.

Broadway theaters went dark. Joe Percoco and Josh Vlasto were driving to Ground Zero. Storm trackers expected the site of the twin towers lost on 9/11 to be the storm's center. Josh and Joe were my on-the-scene "road crew." Faster than storm chasers, they got there *before* the hurricane.

I needed be in New York City when the storm hit. Not me, Andrew Cuomo, but me, the governor of the State of New York. When situations are chaotic people need to see that their government is handling the situation. Being there, showing competence—projecting calm—is critical to public trust. It sends the message that people will be safe.

Waiting for a hurricane is not sleep-inducing. On the morning of August 27, I got up in Albany with the intention of driving down to the city after a stop at the Blenheim-Gilboa Dam. Forty miles southwest of Albany, it provides power and fresh water to New York City. Less than a week before, an earthquake in Virginia had rocked more than a dozen states, including New York. Two days before Irene, a second quake registered near the dam. A compromised dam is a big problem. I inspected it with the head of the power authority.

The dam was fine. Grateful for that, I resumed my trip in a state police SUV with the head of the state police detail, Major Steve Nevins; Howard Glaser, my director of state operations; and another state trooper, Investigator Keith Ryan. We started out in a light rain that soon turned into pounding sheets of water.

"Luckily, the road is fine," I said, as we careened down the winding roads of the Catskill Mountains on our way to the city.

"Look at the water pouring off the mountain ridges," Steve said. "And there's no cell phone reception," he added. "The GPS can't pick up a signal."

We knew the Delaware River was off to our left somewhere, but we couldn't tell where, exactly, because it had overrun its banks.

As we followed Route 30 into the village of Margaretville, a small Catskills hamlet with a population under six hundred, the water continued to rise around our vehicle.

"Is this a good idea, boss?" Howard asked as the vehicle began to fill with water.

"Yeah, let's keep going," I said. "We really can't go back at this point."

From inside the car we could see household stuff floating down the middle of the street. The houses were flooded. Steve Nevins got out to assess our situation and began walking in front of the SUV to make sure there were no submerged branches or other tire poppers in our path. He jumped back into the car when the water rose up nearly to his waist. Within seconds, the water was starting to lap over the hood of the SUV. We were amazed that any vehicle could get through that much water. Unable to contact other state police or highway crews, even a governor is at the mercy of nature.

"The water's running faster," Steve said.

Miraculously, Keith Ryan powered through flooded Main Street to a relatively dry stretch in the middle of the town. A group of local first responders on the side of the road surrounded our SUV, demanding to know why we were out driving. I rolled down my window. When they saw it was me, they were astonished that we'd made it through what turned out to be the heart of Hurricane Irene's impact in New York State. "I've always heard that you shouldn't try to drive if there are more than two inches of water in the road," one of the men said.

I thought, If it's this bad here, New York City must be underwater. The forecasters were still focused downstate. "I need to get to Manhattan," I said.

With the routes south impassable and portions of the Thruway closed by state police, we turned north and east, planning to pick up the Taconic Parkway, another road that runs south toward the city. The Taconic proved no better. As we approached a section called Wilbur Flats, the road was closed off, blocked by an empty Department of Transportation truck parked sideways. The driver, presumably, had left for higher ground.

I was still determined to review the situation in the city, as well as upstate. When we picked up a cell signal, we learned that a window in the weather had cleared enough that we could fly the state plane down toward the city. We lucked into an open stretch of the Taconic that was under only a couple of inches of water, and we headed for the airport in Albany. Keith Ryan was driving relatively fast. We proceeded down a hill, and when we got to the bottom where the road started uphill again a small lake appeared that covered the road. It was perfectly flat and nearly invisible—until we hit it. Suddenly it sounded as if we'd hit a wall, as the SUV hydroplaned across the flooded pavement and stopped short. Water was everywhere and everyone was thrown forward. I was dazed.

And then I heard a woman's voice—disorienting, as there

were only men in the car. In an angelic tone it asked, "Are you OK? Do you need help?" Still disoriented, I didn't respond, nor did anyone else. "Is there anything I can do to help?" she repeated. "Is everyone OK?"

"Yes, everything is OK," I answered, "but who are you? And where are you?"

The mysterious voice responded, "I am the OnStar lady."

"Who?" I asked.

"The OnStar lady."

"What star?"

"OnStar," she said.

"What's that?" I asked.

"Your vehicle is equipped with OnStar, and we want to know if you need help," she said.

I had no idea there was such a system in the vehicle. But I was glad I wasn't at the pearly gates. We continued to Albany to get to the plane.

Steve Nevins got a call telling him that the meteorologists had been way off the mark. Irene, by then downgraded to a tropical storm, had all but bypassed New York City. The storm had let Nassau and Suffolk counties on Long Island off lightly compared with what we had experienced in the Catskills. Several major roads and communities were flooded, and heavy winds knocked out power in more than 350,000 homes and businesses. But it had slammed upstate like a wrecking ball. We were in the right place at a terrible time. The damage was all around us. But personnel and equipment were downstate, ready to clean up a city that was expected to get the brunt of the storm. We immediately redeployed our resources to the hard-hit areas upstate.

Later we learned that some towns were under as much as eight feet of water. Raw sewage had spilled into Hudson Valley water supplies, putting residents and rescuers at risk of tetanus and hepatitis. Farther north, flooding along the Schoharie Creek wiped out the historic Old Blenheim Bridge and destroyed nearly a third of the region's properties. Over-all, there were ten deaths in the state, most due to drowning.

Landslides threatened areas throughout the Adirondack Mountains.

For days, our local sheriffs and firefighters, teams from the Department of Environmental Conservation (DEC), and the state police used boats to rescue people from the roofs of their homes. Initially cleaning up was almost impossible. Floods are much nastier than they appear on TV.

The great misconception is that floodwater comes from rain or rivers. Some of it does but it's mostly a mixture of mud, sewage, chemicals, and debris—a toxic brew that poisons everything it touches and doesn't drain off for days.

The devastation was gut-wrenching. The small towns didn't have the resources to deal with the extreme damage. The homeowners—good, honest, hardworking people—were struggling; few had insurance or bank accounts big enough to handle such a catastrophe.

A week later, when the hopeful were starting to think that they could recover, Tropical Storm Lee deluged the area all over again.

As the storms receded and cleanup began, I witnessed the remarkable spirit of New Yorkers. Neighbors shared food, clothing, and shelter. Grocers threw open their doors and gave away all their food. Customers came out to scrub local businesses clean and return them to operation. So many New Yorkers wanted to help that we organized a series of cleanup events, "Labor for Your Neighbor." On Labor Day weekend, thousands of New Yorkers from all over the state descended on devastated communities and helped salvage belongings, scrape mud, and remove rubble from residences and businesses. It was inspiring. New Yorkers are great! I returned to Margaretville with Sandy, to help with the cleanup there. We joined hundreds of New Yorkers, sweeping dried mud off Main Street and hauling mildew-covered trash out of homes. An elderly woman told me that her hope returned when a stranger offered to get the mud out of her basement. The outpouring provided new proof of what I have long believed about New Yorkers: it's in our darkest hours when we shine the brightest.

But Irene and Lee did not bring out the best in everyone.

In the private sector it's understood that it's all about performance. Do a good job; you're hired again. Don't; you're soon out of business. But in government procrastination, half-baked excuses, and overly burdensome regulations are the norm. Even under extreme circumstances, the bureaucracy often fails to respond. Government is about the process. The process becomes the product. That's the natural bureaucratic inclination, and it's dangerous.

In my office our management culture is different. It's not about process. We don't give points for effort. We evaluate people on whether or not they accomplished the task. Period.

Irene and Lee washed out a hundred-yard stretch of Route 73, which runs from the North Way to Lake Placid and Saranac in New York's North Country—the main access point for tourists visiting some of the state's prime destinations. The detour added an extra sixty miles to the drive.

The damage was substantial, and I asked our State Department of Transportation (DOT) to move heaven and earth (pardon the pun) to get the roadwork completed ASAP. A day and a half later, when I called for a progress report, I learned that there had been none. A roomful of top-level bureaucrats told me, "Even if we move as fast as we possibly can, the repair work will take approximately three months."

"Come back with a better deadline," I said.

At our next meeting they'd whittled the deadline to two months.

Still not OK.

The list of obstacles they gave me was long. So I turned to one of the most old-fashioned tools of all: I picked up the phone. When I called the DOT I found that the requirements for an environmental assessment and the design and approval process for rebuilding a road weren't much different from those for building a new road. That didn't make sense.

The bureaucrats blamed a private contractor who said he couldn't get the men and equipment any sooner. I called the contractor, who explained that he was bogged down by DOT regulations. The DOT required certain work hours, equipment, and procedures that made a condensed time frame impossible.

Twenty phone calls and a lot of cajoling later we set a new timetable: three weeks. I used my emergency powers as governor to suspend normal permit rules and contracting rules. And in the end the road crew finished the job in less than two weeks.

Ultimately, Hurricane Irene and Tropical Storm Lee resulted in more than 390,000 ordered evacuations; 1,065,000 power outages; and significant damage to water systems and critical infrastructure, including scores of bridges and roads in New York State. As Irene moved through the Caribbean and along the East Coast during its life cycle between August 20 and 29, it caused at least fifty-six deaths and was among the ten costliest catastrophes in U.S. history. A year later those numbers were dwarfed by Superstorm Sandy.

There's debate over global warming, but surely we must all agree that extreme weather patterns have developed. And most scientists believe these will accelerate in the coming years. During my time as governor I have had nine federally declared disasters: on average one every four or five months—more than any other governor in the history of the state. Besides the floods we've had earthquakes, tornadoes, hailstorms, and snowstorms. These were all freak events defying any precedent. People whose families had lived in their homes for a hundred years without a single flood saw their houses torn from the foundations by wind. It alarms me to ponder what's coming.

The destruction can be made worse by local first responders who were trained to handle infrequent, low-level natural disruptions. In the past that worked pretty well, but the scale and complexity of the recent storms overwhelmed our current infrastructure and competence level. In truth, we were lucky that more people haven't died and more property hasn't been lost. That is due to heroic first responders who went beyond the call of duty. We must resolve to provide the tools and top-notch training they need to be thoroughly prepared.

In October 2012, Superstorm Sandy, the largest natural disaster in New York history, arrived. We spent the previous days reviewing preparations, including the locking down of the World Trade Center site. Much of the infrastructure was underground. The critical infrastructure that lay beneath the surface of New York City led me to a controversial decision. Days before the storm was projected to hit, I ordered all subway service shut down so that thousands of subway cars could be moved from low-lying yards and out of tunnels to more protected ground. Underground New York was designed to accommodate millions of people, not millions of gallons of water. The transit system is the lifeblood that keeps the city moving. We could not afford to expose it to the flooding that Sandy might bring.

As Sandy began to wash over the region, I visited the Long Island shore with Nassau County Executive Ed Mangano, an able manager and a good guy, a Republican with whom I had developed an effective working relationship. Even though it was hours before the storm surge, seawater was higher than the boardwalk at Long Beach and pouring into the streets. We held a wind-whipped briefing on the boardwalk. We would be among the last visitors to stand on that boardwalk—by morning it would be washed into the sea.

I returned to the city office at Third Avenue and East Forty-First Street to monitor Sandy's path.

One of the lessons I learned from my federal disaster work is that communication with the public is key. "Stay indoors."

"Stay off the roads." Spoken and unspoken: Don't panic. Panic is the enemy because panic brings chaos. Good communication provides comfort. My head of communications was Allison Gollust, a corporate professional from NBC. She knew the business and the right tone. It worked well. People responded and were at relative ease.

Around 8 P.M., near the height of the storm surge, I asked Howard Glaser to drive downtown to the World Trade Center site with me so we could see how our preparations were holding up. I wanted to make sure this powerful symbol for New Yorkers came through the storm. As we approached East Twenty-Third Street, overflow from the East River had reached Second Avenue. A few blocks later, the lights in Lower Manhattan were out. Our drive was circuitous, slow, and dark, with streets increasingly blocked by rising water. By the time we got down to Wall Street ten minutes later, the East River was jumping its banks and the Hudson River was coming from the west. They met in the middle, submerging Lower Manhattan. Much of the island's southern tip is landfill. We had to ditch the state police vehicle and continue by foot. Nothing can make you feel as powerless as Mother Nature enraged.

When we arrived at the 9/11 Ground Zero site, it looked like a scene from an apocalypse. The site was dark. Water was pouring into the uncompleted foundations with a deafening roar.

I thought I had seen the worst when I was involved in disaster relief and reconstruction during my HUD years. I'd worked with the Federal Emergency Management Agency (FEMA) in the aftermath of the Mississippi floods in Minnesota and Iowa; the Northridge, California, earthquakes; Hurricane Andrew in Florida; and Hurricane Georges in Puerto Rico, the Dominican Republic, and Ecuador. But those situations were a fait accompli when I arrived. Sandy came in with a record-breaking tidal surge. I was near enough to see it roll in. It was terrifying.

One of the few people still onsite at Ground Zero was the longtime chief of construction, Steve Plate. Using a flashlight we'd taken from our vehicle's emergency kit, we surveyed the rubble-strewn area. Plate aimed the flashlight into a humongous concrete tub, filled with about twenty feet of water. Water from the Hudson River was cascading into deep pits being dug for the foundations of the new buildings.

"It's filling so fast I'm not sure whether it's all coming over the top of the foundation or some is coming up from the bottom," he said. "It could be that the retaining wall has cracked." Wow!

The foundations of the former Twin Towers are the retaining wall for the Hudson River. "We'd better take a look," he said.

We went down flights of stairs into the foundations, past the basement and subbasements. Unable to see more than a foot ahead, we descended into the vast man-made caverns. We couldn't hear each other over the sound of rushing water. Eventually we came to the slurry wall, a massive structure hundreds of feet wide and high. It was wet top to bottom.

"We're going to need a bigger flashlight," I said and instantly thought of a line from *Jaws*, when Roy Scheider says, "You're going to need a bigger boat." But we had to go with the small flashlights we had.

We scanned strips at a time. Plate didn't see any obvious cracks. To the extent there was any relief during the evening, this was it.

We climbed up to ground level, and I peeled off, walking toward the tip of Manhattan, a few blocks away. As I got close, I could see that water from the Hudson was rushing into the mouth of the Hugh L. Carey Tunnel (formerly the Brooklyn-Battery Tunnel) as if the world's largest fire hydrant had been opened. It was moving so fast it created white water. The tunnel, which connects Lower Manhattan and Brooklyn, is like a C-shaped hose buried underground. I spotted Joe Lhota, head of the Metropolitan Transportation Authority (MTA), which oversees the tunnel. I'd appointed Joe to the position. Now I stood with him on the pedestrian footbridge, a governor and the head of the MTA, with thousands of people and billions of dollars under our control, now powerless. We'd have to wait for the tide to crest to assess the damage.

Mother Nature wins.

One of the great engineering marvels of New York City is not how high we've built the city, but how deep—sometimes as far as fifteen stories underground. The subways, water conduits, and electrical systems form an underground labyrinth. The large buildings are designed to have the major services in the basement: the boilers, electrical systems, backup generators, and fuel tanks.

No one anticipated these floods or designed an emergency system to remove the water or repair the damage that happens when salt water meets electrical equipment. The buildings would be unusable for months.

Something else we hadn't counted on: the emergency power system at NYU Langone Medical Center at East Thirty-Fourth Street and the East River failed, making it necessary to evacuate all 215 patients in heavy winds, during the blackout. Transporting critical care patients, expectant and new mothers from labor and delivery, and infants from the neonatal intensive care unit was a real feat.

New York City and the southern part of the state were developed because of their proximity to water. But on that day our greatest asset became our worst liability. Parts of Queens, Brooklyn, Staten Island, and Nassau and Suffolk counties on Long Island were devastated. The damage extended up the Hudson, to Westchester and Rockland counties.

The first action in these situations is safeguarding life and property. The second is stabilizing the population for short-term recovery.

After Sandy hit, my team and I worked twenty-hour days, assessing damage and directing recovery operations. It was the most extensive response effort I'd ever been involved with. At 8 P.M. on Day Five, there was still one thing I wanted to do. "Let's get out to the Rockaways," I said. It was a tough sell for my exhausted staff, but I went, anyway.

The Rockaway Peninsula in Queens, an area whose residents had been hit hard by 9/11, looked like a war zone. A fifteen-foot storm surge flooded houses and buildings, and electrical fires had destroyed entire neighborhoods, including 126 homes in Breezy Point. Nine people had died. More than half of the Rockaway Beach boardwalk was swept away. Thousands of homes were without heat, power, or running water. With 20 percent of the area's population living below the poverty line, already struggling families were left in the cold. The Long Island Power Authority (LIPA) was supposed to be working 24/7 to restore electricity.

But when I got there, the area was completely dark and LIPA was nowhere to be seen. Residents, some of whom had made small bonfires with storm debris to try to keep warm, were panicked. As I walked along in the blackness, I ran into then NYPD Commissioner Ray Kelly. He was on a similar errand, checking up on the National Guard. We both had the same thought: No power means no heat and no food. It's easy for looting and mayhem to fill the vacuum.

The next morning I went to my office and gave the head of LIPA hell: How could you not be there? You work for the people. You said you'd be there! Where were you? I want to know right now. We established a commission to investigate why LIPA was so unresponsive. When I read its report I made an announcement: "The aftermath of Superstorm Sandy made it undeniably clear that the LIPA status quo was unacceptable," I said. We ultimately transformed LIPA and brought in a new electricity provider.

I am critical of government when I feel criticism is deserved. On the flip side, when government does what it's supposed to do. I will be the head cheerleader. The government response to Sandy was among the most effective ever. Federal, state, and local forces were coordinated and their work was expedited. I worked with my colleagues in neighboring states, especially Governor Chris Christie of New Jersey, forming a bipartisan coalition for a supplemental appropriation by the U.S. Congress of more than $60 billion to rebuild our states. Between Governor Christie's outreach to Republicans and mine to Democrats we were successful. Without the supplemental appropriation, some communities would have stayed vacant for years. Christie was very effective and collegial. It reminded me of the cooperation my father had with Governor Keane; government first, politics second. This is the way government should work.

The third step in coming back from Sandy was long-term reconstruction. The destruction was unprecedented. Never before had New Yorkers' homes and businesses suffered so much damage. Insurance companies were overwhelmed with tens of thousands of claims. Billions of dollars in commercial real estate needed to be vacated and remained empty for months. New York prides itself on its resilience, but Sandy tested our limits.

It also taught us to prepare for the future. Just as 9/11 made Americans aware of the constant threat of terrorism, Sandy was the moment when many New Yorkers realized that extreme weather is permanent. We now have hundred-year floods every three years. Soon we will just call it weather. As I told my staff, "That's why we are taking this moment to redesign our infrastructure and prepare for the next storm— and the one after that. To deny reality is foolhardy."

Our emergency services demand a level of precision and proficiency unlike any existing government operation except the military. The logistical challenges are similar. We took a multipronged approach, looking at all the ways things can go wrong and brainstorming about the most effective ways to handle a crisis. Part One was to develop exercises and protocols so the federal, state, and local responses would be seamless. That's why in New York we propose to build and operate the first college in the country for first responders. Part Two is creating the Citizen First Responder Corps to give free emergency response training to New Yorkers. Our goal is to train 100,000 citizens around the state.

In emergency situations, panic is the enemy. Try to imagine 8 million people in New York City trying to evacuate at once. Traffic would halt. People would be running for the bridges and tunnels with their belongings. I have seen people trying to reach their loved ones at home. Law, order, and civility evaporate. We need emergency alerts and communications systems that operate in power outages.

We are preparing for the next Sandy by challenging ourselves to come up with ways to prevent the level of destruction the superstorm caused. We have questions to answer: Where do we rebuild? How do we seal New York City's vast underground infrastructure and subway tunnels? Can we redesign commercial buildings so that vital services are placed on upper floors? Fortunately, my longtime friend and former HUD colleague Bill de Blasio is now mayor of New York, and being able to work cooperatively will be a major asset.

Society is already adapting to the new reality, designing seawalls and restoring natural habitats. Many Americans dream of owning a house at the shore. But we must stop trying to browbeat Mother Nature into cooperating with our building plans and instead respect and rebuild the natural barriers, dunes, and buffers we once thought unnecessary.

Trying to make sure New York is prepared for weather catastrophes takes up so much of my brain that I sometimes find myself rehashing past emergencies. About a year after Superstorm Sandy, I fell asleep on the couch watching TV. Around midnight Michaela woke me up, and I went upstairs to bed. At breakfast the next morning, she said, "When I woke you up, you asked me, 'Was there a flood?'"

That incident took me back to 1983, when my father was governor. We had worked without a day off throughout the months leading up to the primary, the general election, the transition, and my father's State of the State Address.

Eleven days into his first term, he called me. "We're going to take tonight off," he said.

"Tonight" was a Saturday, and it was already close to seven. We went to a Spanish restaurant—just my father and me—on Second Avenue in Manhattan. While we were enjoying our appetizers, a state trooper came to our table. "No, no, we're off tonight," my father said. The trooper walked away, but a few minutes later, he came back. "Excuse me, sir," he said. "I'm sorry to bother you, but they say it's really important. It's Thomas Coughlin"—the state correctional services commissioner. "He says there's been an uprising at Sing Sing."

Sing Sing is the nickname for the state correctional facility at Ossining. Prisoners had taken corrections officers hostage.

That began a three-day around-the-clock crisis. We drove to the command center at the World Trade Center, where, for the next fifty-three hours, my father, Tim Russert, others in my father's inner circle, and I monitored the dicey situation. The ringleaders had divided up the hostages among the different inmate cliques, determined by race. Through Tom Coughlin, my father had to negotiate with each group separately to get it to release the guards. As with any disaster response, dozens of small decisions had to be made on the fly. Do you turn out the lights to quiet things down or keep them on to make the situation safer? Do you give the prisoners food or not? Every decision is from the gut. And any one of them can be wrong.

From then on, the specter of another uprising traumatized my father. If I woke him suddenly, his instinctive response was, "Something happened at Sing Sing?"

When you are governor and the worst happens it's your job to show up. People elected you to lead. So lead. Don't overthink it. Don't calculate it. Show up.

On the Sunday morning after Thanksgiving in 2013, I was sitting in my bathrobe at home in Mount Kisco, sipping my first cup of coffee and looking at the newspapers, when my cell phone pinged. A text message read: "Metro-North train derailed north of Spuyten Duyvil Station at 7:20 A.M. Passengers evicted." My blood went cold. I knew the spot, at the confluence of the Harlem and Hudson rivers on the southern tip of the Bronx, about thirty miles from our house.

"I have to go," I told Sandy and Michaela.

I texted Josh Vlasto, then my chief of staff: "I'm going to the train accident. Meet me there." I dressed and left.

By the time I arrived, a swarm of first responders had already freed passengers aboard the 5:54 A.M. from Poughkeepsie to Grand Central from the wreckage. Four people died and sixty-three were injured. I thanked God it wasn't a rush-hour train. It would have been carrying 800 people instead of 115.

The scene before me was frozen, final, absolute. The train's seven cars—steel hulks—looked as though they had been flung off the tracks. One car had flipped and landed on the embankment about a foot from the water. Shattered glass and twisted metal were strewn everywhere.

Inside one car the seats had all been uprooted from the floor. A body lay nearby. A young girl. Someone's daughter or wife or mother, gone. How terrifying it must have been for those on the train.

Josh and I stayed a few hours, walking around, looking at the cars, talking to transportation officials, trying to understand how this happened. The official cause of the derailment was not immediately known, but surveying the destruction we could see that the train hadn't made it around a sharp curve—the cars were still facing south when they should already have made the westward turn.

"What we do know is that four people lost their lives today, right after Thanksgiving, in the holiday season," I announced at a press conference. ". . . Let's all say a prayer and remember those people who we lost this morning and their families."

Although Metro-North had suffered two other incidents within the past few months, this was the first fatal accident in the railroad's thirty-year history.

We also considered the next steps. How were we going to get the cars hauled away and the track repaired so that commuters needing to come into New York City the next day could get to work? Later that day we met with investigators from the National Transportation Safety Board (NTSB), who opened a federal investigation into the accident.

The NTSB report noted that the train was equipped with fail-safe brakes. But later investigators found that when it jumped the tracks it was traveling at eighty-two miles per hour, nearly three times the speed limit. The engineer admitted that he had gone into "a daze" moments before the accident, probably as a result of the sleep apnea he would later be diagnosed with. He had attempted to deploy the brakes too late.

That evening I held a second press conference at the crash site. "Safety is job one," I said. "We want to see the trains perform and perform on time, but safety is job one.

"If there is a lesson to be learned from this tragedy," I added, "we want to learn it."

But sometimes tragedy strikes and there is no lesson in it— only heartbreak. Talking to the family and young children after a trooper dies in the line of duty is the saddest, most difficult part of being governor. You ache for their loss, and you can do nothing about it.

The funerals are also hard: being in a church or temple with a thousand law enforcement officers who are all thinking that they could have been the victim. Seeing the fathers and mothers who lost a son or daughter, I know there is nothing I can say that will ease the pain of the most difficult loss. Hugging the young wife who is wondering how she will manage the children and the mortgage alone. Kneeling down so I am at eye level with the children. I know that they will always remember this black day—the troopers in uniform, the processions, the guns, the coffin. They know I am governor. Surely I must have answers. From the youngest: "Can you make him come back?" From the older sibling: "Who is going to take care of us?" From the oldest: "I miss him so much, when will the pain stop?"

One night I was in a hospital, having been briefed on a trooper hit by a truck while doing a traffic stop. The doctors were attending to the trooper and the family members were crammed into a small waiting room. Father, mother, wife, kids, sisters, brothers were praying, hoping, looking into my eyes searching for answers: Will he make it? How bad is it?

A doctor entered and, with the clinical coolness doctors must develop as an antidote to human pain, said, "He will not recover due to severe trauma to the brain." What does that mean? The mind couldn't comprehend it. Then all at once the small room erupted into howls and tears, why, why, why?

I was in charge, and I was powerless.

The state police agency offers elaborate family services and financial aid, but these are little comfort in the face of such devastation.

We face challenges from outside and within. A united America triumphs, of that I am confident. But the internal stresses are formidable and getting worse.

Americans are people with great expectations. We acclaim capitalism, and throughout our nation's history the promise of making a fortune has motivated many immigrants, including my grandparents, to move to the United States. Sound reasoning. There are hundreds of billionaires and millions of millionaires in the United States, more than in any other country. In 2014 the number of American households with a net worth of at least $1 million, not including the value of their home, reached an all-time high of 9.63 million.

But income inequality and the polarization of wealth and opportunity are serious and growing problems in our society—the Pew Research Center reports that by one measure the schism between rich and poor is at its widest since 1928. Research by Emmanuel Saez, a University of California-Berkeley economist, shows that in 2012 the top 1 percent of the country held 22.5 percent of all pretax income, compared with 10.8 percent in 1982. The share of the bottom 90 percent dropped from 64.7 percent to 49.6 percent in the same thirty-year period. Saez's data also show that between 2009 and 2012, income for the top 1 percent jumped 31 percent, after adjustment for inflation, but it rose an average of only 0.4 percent for the lower 99 percent. It's no wonder that resentment among the poor and middle class has become palpable. The United States has experienced plenty of downward cycles before, but they have normally been characterized by a rapid drop and a fast rebound. This time a recession or semi-recession has lasted since around 2007, and it has ratcheted up the low-level but constant anger of hardworking Americans.

The number one asset for most American families is equity in their homes. A discouraging, and often financially debilitating, fact for many homeowners is that their property is worth less today than seven years ago. Home equity is a security blanket, retirement fund, first business loan, child's wedding, nest egg, and health fund. People count on this bonanza, and seeing it disappear has been maddening.

Improving the economy will take time. But meanwhile, the political challenge is to keep people's fear and anxiety from getting the best of us as a society. This is not just a "poor" person's issue. It is the working poor and middle class who still suffer from economic anxiety—and have been suffering for about seven years. That's a lot of suffering and resentment. It has already become a divisive force in our political system.

The most glaring consequence of the downturn is the so-called Tea Party conservatives, who have challenged the moderates of the Republican Party, yanking it to the extreme right with several high-profile political victories.

I get the economic anger. The supporters of the Tea Party are financially strapped, and they believe their taxes are being wasted on inefficient, misguided projects. I don't agree, but I can understand their point of view. They are a major political force on the right.

People often say, "I don't understand why the Republican moderates don't tell off the ultraconservatives." The reason is that they're afraid. In New York, moderate Republicans remember the plight of Stephen Saland, one of the Republicans in the New York State Senate who voted for marriage equality. The Tea Party ran a conservative candidate who took thousands of votes from Saland, guaranteeing victory for his Democratic opposition. The conservatives' message: We're willing to punish members who aren't conservative enough, even at the expense of the Republican Party.

In New York, Carl Paladino, my opponent in the 2010 race for the governorship, was a rabid conservative who bested the Republican moderates. This was unheard of in New York. If it is happening in New York I can imagine what is going on in the rest of the country. Indeed, this year the moderate Republicans capitulated to the conservatives, giving them the candidate and positions they wanted.

There is a similar but less dramatic movement on the extreme left of the Democratic Party. Those in the movement speak of punitively raising taxes on the rich and transferring the money to the poor. Once again, I understand their view. When I was attorney general and realized that Merrill Lynch and AIG had handed out bonuses using taxpayers' money, we wasted no time in calling for its return. But the purpose of taxation is not to penalize those who have earned money; it's to pay for necessary services for the collective good and measures that can improve society. The answer to me is not to pull down the rich but to lift up the poor.

Both extremes, left and right, are fueled by emotion and truly outraged at the unfairness of the system. Their power is compounded by media outlets, which have become pitchmen for ideologies, creating their own echo chamber where information bounces from blogs to radio to social media to cable TV and reverberates. The combination is basically a large-scale chat room for those with similar political positions. Part of the fallout has been the pass-along factor.

And there are always lots of people willing to believe what they see on the Internet. Just ask Steven Spielberg. Recently an old photo of him sitting in front of a prop dinosaur on the *Jurassic Park* set made the rounds on Facebook. A funny guy

488]   ANDREW M. CUOMO

named Jay Branscomb added a caption: "Disgraceful photo of recreational hunter happily posing next to a Triceratops he just slaughtered. Please share so the world can name and shame this despicable man." Within a few days it had been shared forty thousand times, generating hundreds of serious responses chastising Spielberg for being an "inhumane trophy hunter."

The timeframe for dissemination of information is truly amazing. Within minutes, a tweet becomes a blog becomes viral hysteria. There is almost no time to verify. The competition places a premium on speed, not accuracy. This is reinforced by the ideology of many of the media outlets wanting a particular perspective to reinforce their viewpoint. One must look long and hard to find honest, objective, thoughtful dialogue. One of the reasons the "moderates" are uninspired and unmotivated is that much of the energy is through opinionated outlets.

I have learned firsthand about these distortions. On one occasion, I made a statement during a radio interview that the conservatives chose to interpret as my saying they have no place in the State of New York. It didn't matter that I had not said it, or that I issued clarifying statements. They would not be dissuaded with facts.

It is clear that I was talking about extremist candidates and politicians, not ordinary citizens, and that my point was there is little political statewide support for politicians with extreme conservative positions, as New York is overall a moderate state. By the way, since New York is a moderate state, there is no statewide support for an extreme-left candidate, either. This is indisputable. But the critics claimed I said people who are pro-gun or antiabortion should physically leave the state. Ridiculous. I said no such thing. I am a gun owner and a lifelong Catholic! I respect New York State as a place of tolerance of all views. That is what we were founded upon and that's what makes us special. But however irresponsible their characterization, it fueled the conservative media machine.

My astute communications guru Melissa DeRosa had it right. There is nothing I could say because the issue wasn't really about what I had said; it was about what they wanted to say to fuel the dialogue.

There is also an extreme movement on the Democratic far left capable of incendiary, divisive rhetoric designed to mobilize people and garner attention. Some seek to essentially demonize those who are very wealthy. Wall Street itself became a target. The legitimate issue is income inequality and tax policy, but the rhetoric was overblown. Occupy Wall Street took over a park in New York City and refused to leave. Eventually Mayor Michael Bloomberg evicted them.

The good news is that the political extremes are just that—extremes. They represent a small minority—albeit increasingly vocal and powerful in primary elections. But extremism is not a new phenomenon: there were extremists in Forest Hills who protested in front of my family's house, secessionists in Greenburgh during my HELP years, and the Ku Klux Klan and racists whom we battled at HUD. Many politicians and political movements use this negative energy to whip people up, leading to polarization and gridlock. But the extremes win only by default. The overwhelming majority of voters have reasonable viewpoints. The challenge is to harness the positive energy of the majority, to come together and build for our shared future. Our political system must be better at mobilizing moderate citizens and building centrist coalitions. We have done that in New York with success. Moderate Democrats and Republicans are reasonable and believe that people can disagree and still find common ground. Our budget successes, marriage equality, and gun-control legislation passed with a coalition of centrist Democrats and Republicans reacting to a mobilized majority in support. We must do this more and better. That is the lesson of our founding fathers: Focus on finding and forging commonalities rather than highlighting differences. Realize that the centrist majority must be proactively organized. It takes energy and commitment. The extremists have a natural energy that must be created for the overlooked majority.

I am now in the midst of my reelection campaign. I announced my plan at the state convention in Suffolk County with an introductory video by Bill Clinton, my father standing next to me onstage, and my daughters looking on with pride. "New York State government has been transformed into an engine of action"—former President Clinton said—"standing in stark contrast to the gridlock that plagues Washington, D.C."

Wow, what a glowing statement—and something that really makes me proud. We brought people together who had remained at odds for many years. We forged agreement among Democrats and Republicans and then we made the machinery of government function. We proved it could work.

I am running for reelection because I want to continue and increase our progress. I know how tenuous the system is and I don't want to see New York go back to the old days of gridlock. Our current culture of compromise and good faith can quickly give way to extremism and zealotry. Our political balance is predicated on the philosophy I crafted: a state that is fiscally moderate and socially progressive. That is who we are as a people and a state. We had a deep hole to dig out of four years ago. We are now stable and can do even more ambitious work. And we must, because while we have made more progress than I thought we could have made in the first four years, there is so much more to do.

Public education is at the top of the list. The system must be transformed into one that measures and rewards performance and results. The higher-wealth districts are doing well, but the poorer districts need a different model of comprehensive, coordinated service, which is the Community Schools model. It's not an education challenge alone in those districts. All needs must be addressed. We must also install technology in classrooms to a far greater degree than we are doing now. It can customize education to make a system that works best for each child. Taking on the bureaucracy will be a fight, but it must happen.

Another priority in education is statewide kindergarten and pre-kindergarten. It is expensive and difficult, but the best single investment we can make in our children.

The upstate economy is moving forward better than it has in decades, but it has been abandoned for so long that much needs to be done. I am excited about our progress in Buffalo. This progress can be accelerated and the model exported to other upstate cities. Rochester, Syracuse, Utica, Watertown, and others merit their own version of the Buffalo model. Buffalo showed that the approach works—in the most difficult application. These intensive economic models take tremendous time, energy, and expertise, and my administration is committed to them.

The ramifications of extreme weather are the most daunting challenge. We need a wholly redesigned emergency management response, a designated series of equipped shelters, and seamless coordination between emergency teams.

We must give Mother Nature back some of our waterfront property and move homes to safe locations. Manhattan is a difficult challenge in the new world because it is an island, susceptible to flooding, and the way it was designed and built is very hard to protect. Skyscrapers have all their operating systems—electrical, climate-control—in basements often below grade. Manhattan also extends ten to fifteen stories underground. Water conduits and subways are all located there. Sealing Manhattan's surface is an awesome engineering feat.

New York State taxes have gone down in my administration. State income taxes are down to 1953 levels, corporate taxes down to 1968 levels, and manufacturing taxes down to 1917 levels. The property taxes, which are imposed by local governments, are still too high. Some 10,500 local governments operate with little efficiency or coordination. Property taxes are New York State's true tax problem.

I have worked hard to clean up Albany and corruption in the government. I have done more than ever before with new disclosure and transparency laws and new tools for prosecutors to bring bribery cases. But more needs to be done. I think that the best path forward is through public finance, which doesn't limit the money in politics but does help those with less money run for office. I am also reconsidering my position on term limits, which while imperfect limit the institutionalization of money and power. There is a cost, that we lose good talent and knowledge from the system, but it may be worth it in the long run. It is worth studying further.

It is important that New York remain the nation's capital of social progress. I want to pass the Women's Equality Act, which would codify in New York a woman's "right to choose" as protected in *Roe v. Wade*. Believe it or not, the conservatives oppose it. There is a disturbing national trend to chip away at a woman's right to choose. I want to pass a Dream Act that helps New York–born children afford higher education. They are New Yorkers and they are not going anywhere, and we want them fully educated to help grow our state.

Our environmental and energy activity is innovative and leading the nation to a balanced, environmentally-friendly, and sustainable energy system.

We are moving forward with programs to end the insanity of our incarceration system, which still spends more money per year on a prison cell than on a year of college. Combined with a 50 percent recidivism rate, this expenditure is nonsensical, unintelligent, and inhumane.

I want to increase the minimum wage to reward work— staying true to the American dream.

Our SUNY system, combined with our new tax-free START-UP New York ten-year zones, has great potential. I believe we could make New York into a new Silicon Valley.

Our airports are New York's front doors. They are important, and will be more so in the future. Right now La Guardia is rated one of the worst airports in the country, and Kennedy is not much better. Tourism is a key growth market, and I want to redesign the airports from the ground up. The same must also be done to our mass transit system. It is the only feasible long-term transportation system that is sustainable. New York also needs a state-of-the-art convention center because right now we are not competitive with the largest shows.

We, as a state, have learned much over the past four years and I want to capitalize on that knowledge, goodwill, and progress. If we complete this agenda, the New York we leave our children will be stronger, sweeter, safer, and richer than the New York our parents left us. To me, that is the goal of every parent and citizen: to leave this place better than we found it. It is the essence of the Judeo-Christian tradition. In Judaism, it's *tikkun olam*, to repair the world. Christians follow Matthew 25, dictating compassion and generosity for the least fortunate of us.

The Native Americans have another way of saying it: "We didn't inherit the land from our parents. We are borrowing it from our children." New York State's motto is "Excelsior," or "Ever upward." We will not just rebuild New York; we will build it to be better than ever before.

I truly believe all of these things are possible.

Why are all things possible?

Because four years ago Buffalo was a city with a glorious past but no future, and Western New York was the most depressed region in the state. Today polls show that it's New York's most optimistic region: literally tied with Manhattan! As the *Buffalo News* wrote in 2013: "All one really need do is to engage in conversation with virtually any Buffalonian at a local pub to gauge the positive shift in perspective. . . . Buffalo has become . . . cool."

Because New York State government was the epitome of dysfunction. The one activity the state had to perform, the annual budget passage, had become gridlocked between the liberal urban population from downstate and the more white, conservative, suburban, and rural Republicans. The result was that the budget had been habitually late and riddled with scams, and no one believed it could be changed.

In thirty years, the budget was late twenty-three times, by an average of about two months. Today we celebrate passing four budgets in a row on time, with a bipartisan legislature, a new norm of collegiality and compromise. In spring 2014 the state's credit rating was increased, bearing the triple distinction of earning the best Moody's rating in fifty years, the highest Fitch rating ever for New York, and the first upgrade ever from Standard & Poor's.

Because after my candidacy for the governorship in 2002 ended in disaster and every pundit wrote my political obituary, returning to elected office seemed impossible. I had alienated the entire Democratic establishment. Everyone, including me, thought I was finished. But we can learn from our mistakes, loss can be a great teacher, people are kind, and second chances are real. Why are all things possible? Because, for me, I am the fifty-sixth governor of New York State.

Because when I took office three governors and fifteen years had come and gone since the first announcement that the Tappan Zee Bridge would be replaced. Voters were justified in thinking that the government had a competence deficit and was incapable of executing large projects efficiently. Today the Tappan Zee is under construction—one year from the date of the announcement.

Because in 2002 I went through a heart-wrenching divorce that shattered my family and I thought it would be hurt my girls and that the comfort and joy of a family were gone for me. Today my girls are all amazing, successful, healthy young women whom I couldn't be more proud of; and Sandy, my girls, and I are the family I always hoped for and more.

Because Americans are welcoming and generous and because my father, Mario Cuomo, who was born to immigrant parents with no money and no education, became governor of New York State.

It was proved again when the voters of this country elected

an African American named Barack Hussein Obama to be president of the United States.

Today, in the early years of a new millennium, I believe many of our limits are self-imposed. Somewhere along the way we stopped believing in ourselves; as individuals and as a society. And we were wrong.

Americans are a magnificent collection of the most daring, strong, entrepreneurial people on the planet. They are the rare souls and offspring of people who were brave enough to get into small boats to cross great oceans to come to a faraway land. They built the greatest nation on earth, defended it through two world wars, and continue to be the global force for freedom. Pioneer and immigrant blood is in the veins of this country. That is the resilient, resourceful, supportive character of this nation.

This is what makes all things possible.

Acknowledgments

This book was much more difficult to complete than I ever imagined. It is a reality only because of the talented professionals who helped birth it:

Linda Kulman assisted me in crafting the book and wove a tapestry from personal stories and government tedium. She is a gifted analyst and communicator—a powerful combination.

Claire Wachtel, my editor, is as patient as she is persistent, and as wise as she is witty.

Jon Cowan, who was my chief of staff at HUD and is one of the greatest policy minds I have ever worked with, is a dear and generous friend who spent countless hours on this venture.

Robert Barnett, my lawyer and adviser, has an incredible reputation—and he actually deserves it.

The team at HarperCollins Publishers, including President and CEO Brian Murray, President and Publisher Michael Morrison, SVP and Publisher Jonathan Burnham, SVP and Associate Publisher Kathy Schneider, SVP of Publicity Tina Andreadis, Associate Editor Hannah Wood, and everyone else who worked behind the scenes.

The content of this book is generated by two spheres in my life: family and professional.

My rise, fall, and rise was possible because of the love and support of my family:

Cara, Mariah, and Michaela (listed in birth order, with no other significance) and Sandy—they became the center of my universe and showed me what is really important in life.

My mother and father, who showed tremendous love—and were right when they said that children never really do leave the house! They just come back with *their* kids and their problems.

My siblings—Margaret, Howard, Maria, Ken, Madeline, Brian, Chris, and Cristina. I list my in-laws as siblings because that is how I feel about them. And a special thank-you to my brother, Chris, who has great advice and laughs for his older brother, and who showed me that there is at least one reporter whom I can trust.

"Friends" are the safety net and support structure, and should be measured in quality and not quantity. Andrew Farkas, Jeff Sachs, and a small handful of real friends lifted me from the depths.

The second sphere in this book is my work and passion, which is politics and government. My main contribution was having the wisdom and luck to attract the most dedicated, talented, honorable people to public service. Some of the people in my current team and my advisers have been with me for twenty years. Some have been with me for two years. Interestingly, the team culture is dominant and is the unifying ethic. They are great at what they do, and they do it for all the right reasons.

Larry Schwartz runs the ship. I have known him for thirty years, and he is as skilled a government and management professional as I have seen.

Joe Percoco worked for my father first and then with me at HUD, and he knows New York politics and government as well as anyone in the state.

Mylan Denerstein is a lawyer's lawyer and a woman who maintains her sweetness in the sourness of Albany.

Stephanie Benton is my right-hand woman and the emotional and informational switchboard of the operation. She is as smart as she is kind.

Linda Lacewell was our secret weapon in the AG's office; a former federal prosecutor, she was key to our best cases, did the work, and let others take the limelight.

Bob Duffy, my great lieutenant governor, is always going above and beyond the call of duty.

And my extended team, my second family: Marc Altheim, Irene Baker, Andrew Ball, Jennifer Bayer, Ellen Biben, Tonio Burgos, Steve Cohen, Jacquie Lawing Ebert, Gary Eisenman, George Haggerty, Karen Hinton, John Howard, Howard Glaser, Ben Lawsky, John Maggiore, John Marino, Bob Megna, Joe Rabito, Richard Sirota, Josh Vlasto, and Drew Zambelli.

Special thanks to the men and women who actually allow me to do my job by getting me to where I need to go, through hurricanes, snow, or protesters; by plane, truck, or Humvee— whatever it takes—the New York State Police Protective Services Unit, headed by a great leader, Major Steve Nevins: Bob Leary, Ken Cano, Vincent Straface, Pete Cirigliano, Andrew Werner, Bernie Keller, and Fabricio Plaskocinski.

Index